Revisiting Multiculturalism

MW01536203

TRANSNATIONAL MIGRATION AND EDUCATION

Volume 1

Scope:

Migration has been adopted by many countries as a strategy to compete for the most talented, skillful, and resourceful and to ameliorate aging populations and labour shortages. The past few decades have witnessed both an expansion and transformation of international migration flows. The resulting demographic, social and cultural changes have reconfigured the landscapes of education in the receiving societies.

Transnational Migration and Education aims to bring together international scholars with contributions from new and established scholars to explore the changing landscapes of education in the age of transnational migration. The Series includes authored and edited collections offering multidisciplinary perspectives with a wide range of topics including:

- global and comparative analyses of migration
- the impact of migration on education and society
- processes of exclusion and inclusion in migration and education
- tensions between mobility, knowledge, and recognition
- intersections of race, class, gender, sexual orientation and education
- transnationalism, diaspora, and identity
- transnational migration and youth
- race and ethnic relations
- ethnicity, diversity and education

Revisiting Multiculturalism in Canada

Theories, Policies and Debates

Edited by

Shibao Guo
University of Calgary, Canada

and

Lloyd Wong
University of Calgary, Canada

SENSE PUBLISHERS
ROTTERDAM / BOSTON / TAIPEI

A C.I.P. record for this book is available from the Library of Congress.

ISBN 978-94-6300-206-6 (paperback)
ISBN 978-94-6300-207-3 (hardback)
ISBN 978-94-6300-208-0 (e-book)

Published by: Sense Publishers,
P.O. Box 21858,
3001 AW Rotterdam,
The Netherlands
https://www.sensepublishers.com/

All chapters in this book have undergone peer review.

Printed on acid-free paper

TABLE OF CONTENTS

TABLE OF CONTENTS

LLOYD WONG AND SHIBAO GUO

REVISITING MULTICULTURALISM IN CANADA

An Introduction

BRIEF HISTORY AND GENEALOGY OF MULTICULTURALISM IN CANADA

Multiculturalism existed demographically in Canada at the time of confederation when the country was formed in 1867. While the situation in 1867 was one of inequalitarian pluralism, with the British being dominant, much of the current historical literature refers to the colonial and confederation periods as having three founding ethnic groups, Aboriginal peoples, French, and British. However, the latter two groups are considered to have been the charter groups due to their dominance in the pre-confederation period from the early 1600s to 1867 beginning first with the French regime and then followed by the British. Shortly after confederation, from the late 1800s to the early 1900s, ethnic diversity increased with the arrival of many European groups and also some non-European groups such as the Chinese (railway workers), Japanese (agricultural workers) and Blacks (underground railway) to name a few. In the 1901 Census Canada was overwhelmingly British and French (88%) however there were twenty-five different ethnic origins listed (Basavarajappa & Ram, 1999, Table A125-163). Over one hundred years later in the 2001 Census the British and French were still the majority but less so as they comprised only 63%[1] of Canada's population and there were now over 200 different ethnic origins listed. Much of the increase in the number and proportions of non-European ethnic origins occurred after the liberalization of immigration policy in Canada in the late 1960s. Since the 1980s with an increasing number of immigrants coming from Asia, Africa, and South and Central America Canada's ethno-cultural diversity over the past three decades has become increasingly racialized with the increase of non-white ethnic groups. In 1981, when the Canadian Census first started counting Canada's "visible minority" population, racialized persons in Canada constituted 4.7% of the population. This proportion increased to 9.4% in 1991, to 13.4% in 2001 and to 19.1% in 2011 (Statistics Canada, 2008, 2013). Thus currently approximately one in five people in Canada are racialized persons with the proportions much higher in the larger cities of Toronto (47%), Vancouver (45.2%), and Calgary (28.1%) (Statistics Canada, 2013). While Canada began demographically as a multicultural nation the breadth and intensity of this cultural and racial diversity has increased over time. However multiculturalism, as public and state policy, has only existed since the 1970s.

In 1963 Prime Minister Lester B. Pearson established the Royal Commission on Bilingualism and Biculturalism in Canada (B and B Commission), also known as

S. Guo & L. Wong (eds.), Revisiting Multiculturalism in Canada, 1–14.

the Laurendeau-Dunton Commission, in response to growing political discontent and unrest amongst the French in Quebec against assimilationist policies of Anglo-conformity. While the Quiet Revolution in Quebec had just begun in the early 1960s, with the election of the Liberal Party of Quebec under Premier Jean Lesage, not so quiet militant and violent actions began in early 1963 after the founding of the Front de Liberation du Quebec (FLQ) as one revolutionary organization of a growing independence movement in Quebec. The FLQ started a campaign of bombings in Montreal that included among other places, military barracks, federal government buildings, railways, and residential mailboxes. Thus the B and B Commission set out to investigate Quebec's role and place in Canada and the relationship between the English and French in Canada. The B and B Commission's tenure was from 1963 to 1969 and its most significant impact on Canada was the recommendation of the 1969 Official Languages Act. However, during the B and B Commission's hearings across Canada, they heard from many non-British and non-French who refuted the notion that Canada was "bicultural" and who argued that Canada was more than just the two cultures of French and English. The B and B Commission acknowledged this argument, investigated further, and this resulted in one of the six volumes of their final report, entitled *The Cultural Contribution of the Other Ethnic Groups* published in 1969 as Book IV. Shortly thereafter, in 1971, Prime Minister Pierre Trudeau created Canada's multiculturalism policy, within a bilingual framework. This meant that Canada was the first nation in the world with an official multiculturalism policy and thus was the first in terms of establishing corporate pluralism where state policy protected the cultural differences amongst groups and provided institutional means to encourage ethnically proportionate distribution of power and privilege (Marger, 2015). Subsequently, Canada's official multiculturalism policy was written into Canada's constitution in 1983 and then in 1988 when Canada's first Multiculturalism Act was passed in parliament led by then Prime Minister Brian Mulroney. The provinces followed suit with some form of multiculturalism policy or enacted legislation. Saskatchewan was the first in 1974, followed by Ontario in 1977, then Alberta, Manitoba, Quebec, New Brunswick, Nova Scotia, and P.E.I. in the 1980s, B.C. in 1993 and finally Newfoundland in 2008.

At the federal state level the chronology and genealogy of multiculturalism as public policy has been succinctly summarized by Dewing (2013) as evolving through three developmental stages: 1) incipient stage (pre-1971); 2) formative stage (1971-1981); and 3) institutionalization state (1982-present).

In incipient stage (pre-1971) the stage was set for multiculturalism policy in the post-WW II period with the large wave of European immigrants and refugees from the Baltic states, the Netherlands, Italy, and Hungary mostly through Pier 21. These immigrants supplemented the previous generation of Europeans (Germans, Americans, Swedes, Ukrainians, Dutch, Icelanders, Norwegians, and Russians) who came to Canada in the early mass migration period during the early 1900s through the recruitment of Clifford Sifton, minister of the Interior, and author of Canada's first immigration act in 1896. Also, in 1947 the Canadian Citizenship Act was passed and Canadians were no longer deemed as British subjects thus facilitating the questioning among many Canadians the legitimacy of British cultural hegemony. Thus the social and political events of the 1960s in Quebec and the establishment and report of the B and B Commission (mentioned above) meant the official end of assimilationist public policy with the introduction of multiculturalism as public policy.

The following formative stage (1971-1981) began with the adoption of Multiculturalism Policy in 1971 under Prime Minister Trudeau and this policy had identified programs including ones for Multicultural Grants, Culture Development, Ethnic Histories, Canadian Ethnic Studies, Teaching of Official Languages, and Federal Cultural Agencies, as well as fourteen specific recommendations (e.g., the teaching of languages other than English and French and cultural programs in public elementary schools). Overall, the key objectives of the policy were: 1) to assist cultural groups to retain and foster their identity; 2) to assist cultural groups to overcome barriers to their full participation in Canadian society; 3) to promote exchanges amongst cultural groups; and 4) to assist immigrants to learn an official language (Dewing, 2013). Thus in this formative stage federal funds of approximately $200 million, over ten years, were allocated to implement multiculturalism policy objectives and this saw, among other things, the establishment of a Multicultural Directorate (within the Department of Secretary of State) and then a Minister and Ministry of Multiculturalism to facilitate the programs and recommendations of the policy which also included liaising ethno-cultural organizations.

In the institutionalization stage (1982-present), which has been the past three decades or so, multiculturalism policy became formalized and codified as official legislation with the passing of the Canadian Multiculturalism Act in 1988. However, even prior to 1988 institutionalization of multiculturalism policy was occurring that was enhancing a corporate pluralism model in Canada. While there are debates about the effectiveness of this policy, some of which will be addressed in this volume, it can be argued that institutionalization has continued over the past three decades. One of the many examples of institutionalization beyond the Act itself include the recognition in the 1982 Canadian Charter of Rights and Freedoms of Canada's multicultural heritage and the inclusion of ethnic origin along with race, colour, religion, sex, age, and mental and physical disability under equality rights in Section 15 (1). Other examples were the passing of the Employment Equity Act in 1986 and the establishment of the Canadian Race Relations Foundation in 1996 as part of the redress to Japanese Canadian in 1988. More recent examples of continued institutionalization of multiculturalism include the establishment of Canadian Multiculturalism Day (June 27) in 2002, Asian Heritage Month (May), Canada's Action Plan Against Racism in 2005, and in 2010 new objectives for Canada's Multiculturalism Program were implemented (Dewing, 2013).

Another approach to chronicling the genealogy of multiculturalism, as public and state policy, is to focus on its evolution with respect to its policy objectives over the past four decades. Kunz and Sykes (2007), building on the analysis of Fleras and Kunz (2001), summarize the changing focus, reference point and mandate of Canadian multiculturalism policy for each of the decades of the 1970s, 1980s, 1990s, and 2000s. While their summary must be considered fairly crude and superficial, given that there were no abrupt policy shifts at the end of each of these decades, overall their analysis is insightful. For the decade of the 1970s multiculturalism policy was one of *ethnicity* multiculturalism with the focus on "celebrating differences," the reference point being "culture" and the mandate of "ethnicity." For the decade of the 1980s multiculturalism policy was one of *equity* multiculturalism with the focus on "managing diversity", the reference point being "structure" and the mandate of "race relations." For the 1990s it was *civic* multiculturalism, "constructive engagement," "society building" and "citizenship." And in the 2000s multiculturalism policy was one of *integrative* multiculturalism with the focus on "inclusive citizenship", the reference point being "Canadian identity" and the mandate of "integration". Using more colloquial terminology Canada's multiculturalism policy has evolved from *song and dance* in the 1970s, to *anti-racism* in the 1980s, to *civic participation* in the 1990s, and to *fitting in* in the 2000s.

DIMENSIONS OF MULTICULTURALISM

Multiculturalism as a concept has many different layers or dimensions. These dimensions or conceptualizations are usually clarified, defined or elaborated by scholars in the beginning of their writings. For example, Garcea (2008) distinguishes between "multicultural public philosophy (ideology) and "multicultural public policy" (official state policy) in his analysis of the fragmentary effects of multiculturalism in Canada and Fleras and Elliott (2002) distinguish between official multiculturalism (policy) and critical multiculturalism (discourse). Furthermore, approaches to multiculturalism can be differentiated by disciplinary perspectives and this point will be addressed briefly in a latter section to follow.

In Fleras and Elliott's comprehensive book on multiculturalism in Canada (2002) the distinctions are made regarding the dimensions of multiculturalism as: 1) an empirical fact; 2) ideology; 3) practice; 4) critique; and 5) state policy. Multiculturalism as an empirical fact and state policy have been discussed earlier and refers to demographic diversity and corporate pluralism. Multiculturalism as ideology (or public philosophy) reflects upon the ideal of multiculturalism or what ought to be. Multiculturalism as practice reflects on what actually happens on the ground in terms of the commodification of diversity as a "resource" and the political, commercial, and minority interests in its utilization. Multiculturalism as critique involves challenging traditional authority and may involve the case where minority interests challenge multiculturalism as official policy that disguises as assimilationist or monoculturalism policy (see discussion below) or the case where official policy is absent.

The distinction between multiculturalism as official state policy and multiculturalism as practiced on the ground or street has been termed multiculturalism "from above" vs. "from below." Multiculturalism "from below"

4

pertains to multiculturalism as a discourse with political dimensions played out in local communities and as distinct "from above" where the state engineers multiculturalism through policy (Werbner, 2012) and engages in the management of diversity. In this sense multiculturalism "from below" is the everyday multiculturalism pertaining to the daily life experiences and political struggles of ethno-cultural and racialized peoples.

CRITIQUES OF MULTICULTURALISM

Since there are many dimensions of multiculturalism the critiques of multiculturalism are equally varied. Over the past several decades multiculturalism, as ideology and as public policy, has been critiqued by scholars both from the left and the right. More recently with the increase in terrorism, particularly "home-grown" terrorism over the past decade or so, a backlash against multiculturalism has emerged particularly in Europe. Arguably, after the terrorism attacks of 9/11 in the United States, the critique of multiculturalism has grown. In Europe anti-multiculturalism, both academically and in public discourse, has been driven by terrorist attacks in the Union with major events such as the Madrid train bombings in 2004, the London bombings in the summer of 2005, and more recently in France the firebombing of the Paris offices of Charlie Hebdo in 2012 and the shootings in the Charlie Hebdo offices in early 2015. By 2011, a decade after 9/11, the three major political leaders in Europe, David Cameron (United Kingdom), Nicolas Sarkozy (France) and Angela Merkel (Germany) were making public speeches about the failure of multiculturalism and condemning it as a social and public policy. David Cameron went so far as to blame multiculturalism for fostering Islamic extremism. Academic work critiquing multiculturalism in Europe has been fairly prolific from both the right and the left. As early as 2004 Joppke (2004) was writing about the retreat of multiculturalism in the liberal state and more recently Vertovec and Wessendorf (2010) have analyzed the public discourse, policies, and practices, associated with the European backlash against multiculturalism. This discourse has produced the term "post-multiculturalism" or "end of multiculturalism" that has been used by scholars to suggest the need to move beyond current policies and practices of multiculturalism and to find different approaches to the processes of immigrant and ethnic integration. The term itself "post-multiculturalism" has been particularly popularized in Europe by Vertovec (2010) who meant it to be a call for alternatives to multiculturalism that includes a search for new models that foster social cohesion and promote assimilation and a common identity. Not surprisingly then in Europe the dominant discourse, both academically and publically, views multiculturalism as a failed project.

In contrast to Europe's dominant anti-multiculturalism discourse Canada's dominant discourse favours multiculturalism. Recent public opinion polling by the Environics Institute (2015) suggests: "An increasing majority of Canadians identify multiculturalism as one of the most important symbols of the country's national identity" (p. 2). Thus, not surprisingly, mainstream politicians in Canada are either silent on multiculturalism or are vocally in favour of it.

It is not within the scope of this introduction to the book to engage in a detailed description of the various critiques by scholars of multiculturalism (either as public philosophy or public policy), nor to engage in a description of the counter arguments in the literature to these critiques. Moreover, the purpose of this volume is precisely to provide a venue for the furthering of the appraisals, critiques and debates about multiculturalism. The authors in this volume have been central to many of the debates and criticisms of multiculturalism in Canada.

Augie Fleras and Jean Elliott (2002) provide an informative ideal typical summation of the various critiques of Canadian multiculturalism as official public policy. He contends that there are five distinct but related types of critiques (and costs) of multiculturalism and they are as follows:

1. Multiculturalism is *divisive*: it undermines Canadian society (identity and coherence) by promoting cultural diversity at the expense of national unity
2. Multiculturalism is *marginalizing*: it ghettoizes minorities, their aspirations, and commodifies culture by invoking cultural solutions to structural problems
3. Multiculturalism is *essentializing*: it fossilizes differences and envisions Canada as a collection of autonomous ethnic groups that are self-contained, determining, and controlling
4. Multiculturalism is a *hoax*: it does not address the root cause of inequality as it is a symbol without substance that promises much but delivers little except to delude, conceal, evade, or distort
5. Multiculturalism is *hegemonic*: it does not empower minorities but rather contains them as it is an instrument of control that achieves consensus by manipulating people's consent without their awareness. (Fleras & Elliott, 2002)

To each of these critiques Fleras and Elliott also summarize the opposing beneficial position where multiculturalism is praised as 1) unifying; 2) inclusive; 3) hybridizing; 4) catalyst; and 5) counter-hegemony (Fleras & Elliott, 2002). Multiculturalism in Canada and elsewhere continues to be heavily debated. Scholars in this volume are central to some of these debates in the literature. By way of an example Kymlicka (2014) challenges the essentialism critique (#3 above) by questioning whether multiculturalism is to blame and turns the argument on its head around by suggesting that liberal multiculturalism may be a remedy to essentialism.

ANTHOLOGIES ON MULTICULTURALISM IN CANADA

It is surprising how few anthologies exist on the topic of multiculturalism in Canada given the controversies and heavily debated nature of the topic in the academic literature. The first academic anthology on multiculturalism was published in 1989, one year after multiculturalism in Canada became an official piece of legislation with the passing of the Canadian Multiculturalism Act (1988), and was entitled *Multiculturalism and Intergroup Relations* and edited by James Frideres (1989). This volume had leading scholars in ethnic studies at the time including Jean Burnet, who was a research associate for the B and B Commission in the late 1960s and Raymond Breton. The chapters in Frideres' volume grappled with the fundamental theoretical and empirical issues of individual rights vs. group rights as it pertains to ethnic maintenance, retention, and relations and the involvement of the state in such matters. It is interesting to note that the issue of individual and collective (group) rights remain contentious in Canada today over a quarter-century later.

In 2007 a multi-authored book, entitled *Uneasy Partners* (Stein et al., 2007), provided not only scholarly but also personal reflections of multiculturalism in Canada. The authors are a group of distinguished scholars and journalists with the scholars being Janice Stein, David Cameron, John Meisel, Will Kymlicka, and the journalists being John Ibbitson, Haroon Siddiqui, Michael Valpy and the introduction was written by the Hon. Fran Iacobucci. The central focus of this book was on the conflict between the Charter of Rights and Freedoms' equality rights and multiculturalism as both policy and practice. In this book, where each author wrote one chapter, there was consensus on the meaning of multiculturalism and an acknowledgment of the positive consequences of a multicultural approach. However, there was disagreement with respect to some substantive and specific issues such as the role of religious freedom in multiculturalism (equality rights) and immigration and its conflict with social policy or lack thereof (Iacobucci 2007, p. xi). Overall this book provides practically based commentaries on multiculturalism rather than a more narrow academic focus that is historical, theoretical, philosophical, etc.

Chazan, Helps, Stanley and Thakkar (2011a) edited a recent anthology that is entitled *Home and Native Land: Unsettling Multiculturalism in Canada* which, as they acknowledge, has the objective to unsettle multiculturalism by having authors track its manifestations in contradictory discourses such as having little to say about diversity and integration (Chazan et al., 2011b). As well another aspect of multiculturalism being unsettled is the fact that different groups and interests have taken advantage of the fluidity of multiculturalism to make a variety of claims that aim to settle identities and arrangements while contestation remains. Suffice to say that this volume does not prove a coherent critique or analysis of multiculturalism policy in Canada but many of the authors provide a coherent critique of multiculturalism from the Left and these include scholars such as Rinaldo Walcott, Himani Bannerji, Nandita Sharma, and Grace-Edward Galabuzi to name a few.

In 2012 Wright, Singh and Race (2012a) edited an anthology pertaining to the viability of multicultural education. The terrain that this book covers is not only Canadian but includes the United States, Australia, and Britain as the genesis of the volume stems from a double session entitled "International Perspectives on the End(s) of Multicultural Education" at the *American Association for the Advancement of Curriculum Studies Conference* at the University of British

Columbia in 2009. The volume begins with a generalized overview that contextualizes multiculturalism and multicultural education and then addresses specific issues that include topics such as critical pedagogy, critical ethnography, youth identity, teacher education, interculturalism, multicultural literacy, and education and multicultural backlash, to name just a few. The lead editor of the volume, Handel Wright, argues that the volume appears at a "... moment of danger for multiculturalism and less immediately apparent, for multicultural education" (Wright, Singh, & Race, 2012b, p. 3; Wright, 2012). The authors include a wide range from new graduate student scholars to established and distinguished scholars in the field such as Peter McLaren, Michael Singh, Shirley Steinberg and Handel Wright.

Most recently Jack Jedwab (2014a) edited a volume entitled *The Multicultural Question: Debating Identity in 21st-Century Canada*. This volume brings together many distinguished scholars on Canadian ethnic pluralism and multiculturalism to reflect on "policy, ideology and message" and to capture the contours of the various debates (p. 5). While the term "identity" is in the title of the anthology this is a misnomer as the chapters cover a broad area of topics and do not focus particularly or specifically on the concept of identity in a social-psychological sense with perhaps the exceptions of Elke Winter's and John Berry's chapters. Overall this volume covers an extremely broad range of topics (e.g., Canada's multiculturalism program, Canadian national identity, liberal multiculturalism, nationalism, interculturalism, language, immigrant integration, residential concentration) of which some pertain to the five distinct but related criticisms and debates mentioned above. An example of the latter is Randall Hansen's chapter which argues that Canada's multiculturalism policy is a hoax (#4 above) because it conceals the real objective of being an integration policy hence the title "Assimilation by Stealth". Jedwab (2014b) avers in his introduction that "... the essays in this volume aim to help Canadians better understand the essence of a debate that is likely to remain with us for the foreseeable future" (p. 5). This is certainly the case as the chapters here in this volume continue to the effort to understand the various debates by revisiting and re-examining multiculturalism in Canada in terms of theory, policy, and empirical findings on specific cases.

This volume brings together many distinguished Canadian researchers from a breadth of disciplines to continue the debates on multiculturalism. What is unique about this anthology, compared to the recent ones mentioned above, is that the body of work goes beyond commentaries, discourses, and reflections on multiculturalism. Similar to the most recent anthology *The Multicultural Question: Debating Identity in 21st-Century Canada* this volume's scholars cover a broad range of theoretical issues and debates with critical analysis of multiculturalism. Moreover three scholars, Elke Winter, John Berry, and Will Kymlicka have written chapters for both volumes. However, what is unique about this volume is that it also presents specific case studies that are organized around thematic topics related to multiculturalism. In this sense this anthology is very much a reader, akin to *Home and Native Land: Unsettling Multiculturalism in Canada* (Chazan et al., 2011a) but going beyond discourse and narrative analysis. This volume, somewhat similar to *Precarious International Multicultural Education* (Wright et al., 2012a), provides some very concrete empirical research studies to show how multiculturalism is practiced or, in other words, how it is played out on the ground or street. For example there are chapters that examine Canadian Jews, Sri Lankan Tamils, Lebanese, Chinese, and Blacks as well as a section on multicultural education in Canada. These substantive case studies explore how the integral relationships and contestations of multiculturalism with loyalty, belonging, integration, identity, youth, religion, and education among others.

OUTLINE OF THE VOLUME

This volume is organized into five sections: Section I focuses on the various debates and theorizing on multiculturalism in Canada. Then in the next three sections, Sections II, III and IV, some of the debates and issues discussed in Section I are carried forward into areas and case studies in Canada. Section II contains specific case studies on multiculturalism and aspects of ethnicity and belonging. Section III relates to specific case studies on youth, identity, and racialization and Section IV examines multicultural education in the Canadian context. The volume ends with Section V, entitled *Future of Multiculturalism*, which entails a chapter that engages the reader to think about governance models beyond current conceptualizations of multiculturalism in a postnational society.

In Chapter 1 Will Kymlicka leads off the volume and Section I by arguing that the longevity of multiculturalism policy in Canada, since 1971, is due to its evolutionary nature. He delineates the evolving shifts in multicultural policy from emphasis on ethnicity to race, and then from ethnicity and race to religion, over the past four-plus decades. His chapter is one of optimism for the continued adaptability of multiculturalism policy in Canada in the foreseeable future. John Berry follows in Chapter 2 by focusing on the social psychological dimensions of multiculturalism and extant intercultural relations in plural societies like Canada. His analysis includes an examination of three core interrelated hypotheses on intercultural relations: 1) multiculturalism hypothesis; 2) integration hypothesis; and 3) contact hypothesis. By examining these hypotheses he argues that researchers are now in a position to provide evidence-based recommendations for policymakers for long-term interests. Elke Winter, in Chapter 3, continues Kymlicka's analysis of the longevity and resilience of multiculturalism by analyzing the changing relationship between multiculturalism in Canada and Québécois nationalism with respect to the construction of national identity. Her thesis is that English-French conflict best explains the consolidation of multicultural national identity as the dominant discourse in the 1990s. She then points out that by the 2000s, with Québécois nationalism at an ebb, there was a revival of nationalist discourse and a shallow redefinition of multiculturalism more in individualistic terms. In Chapter 4 Lloyd Wong focuses on the critiques and discourse of multiculturalism (mentioned above) that claims it is divisive and marginalizing. This is essentially the fragmentation thesis and he examines it comparatively with other models such as assimilation, cosmopolitanism and interactive pluralism. Then he looks at the works of popular sociologists in Canada and in Europe who have subscribed to the fragmentation thesis by using a sociology of knowledge approach to help explain their positions. He concludes by advocating an interactive pluralism approach to multiculturalism policy. Sourayan Mookerjea's Chapter 5 assesses the current state of multiculturalism by deconstructing the Hérouxville affair and the reasonable accommodation debate in Quebec of 2006. His assessment of multiculturalism in Canada is that it is a weak policy and he critiques it utilizing the perspectives of historical sociology, transnational feminism and cultural studies and argues that multiculturalism and racism are connected. The 6th and last chapter in this section is by Ho Hon Leung who, akin to Kymlicka and Winter, demonstrates that multiculturalism is constantly evolving. He asserts that the discourse of 21st century Canadian multiculturalism is integrally related to other Canadian values and culture, identity, and nation-building. Leung ends his chapter on an optimistic note suggesting that while multiculturalism in Canada has been successful there are still many challenges and so it can be a better policy.

Shibao Guo and Yan Guo open Section II in Chapter 7 with two study studies exploring the tensions between immigration, ethnicity, and minority rights. Through the examination of the role of ethno-cultural organizations in responding to the changing needs of the Chinese communities in Calgary and Edmonton, the chapter addresses the question of how multiculturalism facilitates or hinders the development of ethnic community organization in Canada. The findings reveal the salience of ethnicity as both an important resource utilized by the state as a way to mobilize ethnic political support to serve an ethno-specific community, and a liability for the state to legitimize its political agenda in multiculturizing ethno-specific organizations with an ultimate goal of assimilation. In Chapter 8 Morton Weinfeld shifts the focus from Chinese communities and draws upon the (in)famous "Tebbit cricket test" to discuss the dual and divided loyalties of Canadian Jews. Norman Tebbit, a conservative British politician in 1990, questioned the loyalties of Asian immigrants to the United Kingdom by asking which side they would cheer for in a cricket match between England and their Asian home country. After suggesting that divided loyalties is not a new phenomenon in Canada Weinfeld then looks at the Jewish case where he applies the Tebbit test in preliminary conversations with Canadian Jewish leaders when beginning interviews. While the results for the Tebbit test were mixed, with the majority refusing to pick a position, Weinfeld goes on to suggest that while Canadian Jews are seemingly "successful poster children" for multiculturalism in Canada the issue of dual loyalties potentially can become more serious one of divided loyalties. Furthering the case study of Canadian Jewry and multiculturalism in Chapter 9 Rebecca Margolis examines the relationship of language (Yiddish) to the practice of multiculturalism in Canada. She maps out how the use of Yiddish, as a communicative language, was impacted by multiculturalism policy as it evolved over the past several decades. Beyond a language Margolis points out that Yiddish is also an expression of symbolic ethnicity and Jewish identity. She concludes that Canadian multiculturalism policy has been a mixed blessing for Yiddish. Kalyani Thurairajah concludes this section in Chapter 10 by bringing attention back to the issue of dual and divided loyalties with a case study of the Sri Lankan Tamil diaspora in Canada because of their homeland politics and the existence of the Tamil Tigers. She examines, using in-depth interview data with second-generation Tamils, their extent of political engagement, reaction to the labelling of the Tamil Tigers as a terrorist organization and their overall Tamil identity. Thurairajah goes on to assess how multi-culturalism plays out in Canada with respect to suspect minorities and the boundaries of support within the community.

Section III presents concrete empirical research studies demonstrating how multiculturalism is practiced on the ground in relation to youth, identity and racialization. In Chapter 11 Evangelia Tastsoglou and Sandy Petrinioti explore the question of whether and how multiculturalism has become part of the lived experience of second-generation Canadian youth of Lebanese descent in Halifax. The authors shed light on multiculturalism as collective identity and a normative framework for national identity building in relation to individual identity negotiation and formation. They confirm the idea that ethnic identity and Canadian identity are not a zero sum game, but the two co-exist and inform each other. Dan Cui in Chapter 12 continues the examination of the lived experience of multiculturalism. Cui's study on second-generation Chinese-Canadian youth in Alberta contextualizes two major debates of multiculturalism as a politics of recognition and as a divisive force. Her study examines racial discrimination and stereotypes in school, biased media representation, and the relationship between ethnic language maintenance, sense of belonging and multicultural policy within a bilingual framework. Cui points out that multiculturalism, as an integration policy offering symbolic recognition of different cultures, is far from adequate to address racial and ethnic relations in an increasingly diverse society. As such, she underscores the importance of racialization as an important concept and research topic in contemporary multicultural society. The 13th and last chapter of this section by Carl James and Selom Chapman-Nyaho take up some of the themes discussed by Cui. Informed by the concepts of racialization, governance, and interest-convergence, their study examines a summer employment program for racialized minority youth from Toronto's marginalized communities. The program is designed to help them gain meaningful work experience with the Toronto Police Services and was found instrumental in helping reduce the social distance between police and racialized youth, but also worked to advance the institutional interests of policing. The authors raise important questions about how programs designed for 'at-risk' youth are caught up in racialized assumptions and anxieties.

Multicultural education is the focus of Section IV presenting more empirical studies examining how multiculturalism is practiced in schools and classrooms. Anna Kirova opens the section in Chapter 14 with an analysis of critical and emerging discourses in the academic literature on multicultural education. In this chapter Kirova highlights a number of critiques of multicultural education and discusses implications for change in the context of post-multiculturalism. This discussion provides a useful mindmap in helping us rethink and reconceptualize multicultural education theory and practice. Next is Yan Guo's Chapter 15 on multiculturalism and minority religion in public schools. As Canada's population is becoming increasingly ethno-culturally diverse, Guo argues, it becomes imperative for schools to make necessary changes to embrace cultural and religious diversity in schools. Despite the fact that religious freedom is enshrined in Canada's Charter of Rights and Freedoms Guo's study highlights the tensions and contradictions between multiculturalism and minority religion when Muslim immigrant parents came to negotiate religious practices within public schools. Chapter 16 by Johanne Jean-Pierre and Fernando Nunes is a historical-comparative analysis which traces the effects of multiculturalism on policies and practices of regional school boards. By comparing the written records of the meetings of Toronto Board of Education prior to, and after, the announcement and implementation of the Policy of Multiculturalism, the authors found a paradigm shift in the Board's approach to diversity from an integrationist approach throughout the 1960's to an empowerment model of multicultural education. They conclude that policies adopted at the federal level can have direct impacts on the philosophies and practices at local levels of policy and administration. In Chapter 17, Mariusz Galczynski, Vilelmini Tsagkaraki, and Ratna Ghosh unpack multiculturalism in the classroom. Through the discussion of current events in the media, the authors help to bridge the gap between theory and practice by demonstrating how to bring multiculturalism into the classroom. Their analysis also contributes to a broadened understanding of multicultural education that goes beyond students' ethnicity and race to recognize a range of societal differences, such as gender, class, religion, sexual orientation, and (dis)ability.

Augie Fleras concludes the volume with a conceptually challenging and provocative chapter that complements, as well as contrasts with, Will Kymlicka's opening chapter. He argues that with increasing transmigration, transnationalism, fluid boundaries, deterritorialization, dual/multiple statuses (identities, and loyalties), and hyperdiversity the nation-state will no longer be the source of legitimacy (postnational) but rather the transnational community. As such Fleras anticipates that current multiculturalism policy, as a governance model, will suffer a crisis of legitimacy and lose its saliency as Canada becomes increasingly a postnational society. He begins the chapter by examining three models of diversity governance: monoculturalism, multiculturalism, and postmulticulturalism and then he advocates the latter. For Fleras the notion of postmulticulturalism is different from how the term is used earlier in this Introduction and does not mean a rejection or retreat from multiculturalism. He views postmulticulturalism governance as building upon, as well as transcending, multicultural governance hence he also refers to it as multiculturalism 2.0. He feels this latter governance model of postmulticulturalism, which is postethnic, will be necessary for managing the extremely complex mobilities, diversities, multiplicities, and identities in a postnational society that Canada is becoming.

NOTE

[1] This figure is complicated by the fact that "Canadian" was introduced as an ethnic origin category in the 1996 Census.

REFERENCES

Basavarajappa, K., & Ram, B. (1999). *Section A: Population and migration*. Table A125-163. Retrieved from http://www.statcan.gc.ca/pub/11-516-x/pdf/5500092-eng.pdf

Chazan, M., Helps, L., Stanley, A., & Thakkar, S. (Eds.). (2011a). *Home and native land: Unsettling multiculturalism in Canada*. Toronto: Between the Lines.

Chazan, M., Helps, L., Stanley, A., & Thakkar, S. (2011b). Introduction: Labours, lands, bodies. In M. Chazan, L. Helps, A. Stanley, & S. Thakker (Eds.), *Home and native land. Unsettling multiculturalism in Canada* (pp. 1-14). Toronto: Between the Lines.

Environics Institute. (2015). *Focus Canada-Spring 2015 – Canadian public opinion about immigration and multiculturalism*. Retrieved from http://www.environicsinstitute.org

Frideres, J. (Ed.). (1989) *Multiculturalism and intergroup relations*. Westport, CT: Greenwood Press.

Dewing, M. (2013). *Canadian multiculturalism (Background paper)*. Ottawa: Library of Parliament.

Fleras, A. (2002). Multiculturalism as critical discourse: Contesting modernity. *Canadian Issues*, February, 9-11.

Fleras, A., & Elliott, J. (2002). *Engaging diversity: Multiculturalism in Canada* (2nd ed.). Toronto: Nelson.

Fleras, A., & Kunz, J. (2001). *Media and minorities: Representing diversity in a multicultural Canada*. Toronto: Thompson Education Publishing.

Garcea, J. (2008). Postulations on the fragmentary effects of multiculturalism in Canada. *Canadian Ethnic Studies, 40*(1), 141-160.

Iacobucci, F. (2007). Introduction. In J. Stein, D. Cameron, J. Ibbitson, W. Kymlicka, J. Meisel, H. Siddiqui, & M. Valpy (Eds.), *Uneasy partners: Multiculturalism and rights in Canada* (pp. vii-xiii). Waterloo: Wilfred Laurier Press.

Jedwab, J. (Ed.) (2014a). *The multiculturalism question: Debating identity in 21st-century Canada*. Montreal & Kingston: McGill-Queen's University Press.

Jedwab, J. (2014b). Introduction. In J. Jedwab (Ed.), *The multiculturalism question. Debating identity in 21st-century Canada* (pp. 1-9). Montreal & Kingston: McGill-Queen's University Press.

Joppke, C. (2004). The retreat of multiculturalism in the liberal state: Theory and policy. *The British Journal of Sociology, 55*(2), 237-257.

Kunz, J. L., & Sykes, S. (2007). *From mosaic to harmony: Multicultural Canada in the 21st century*. Ottawa: Policy Research Initiative.

Kymlicka, W. (2014). *The essentialist critique of multiculturalism: Theories, policies, ethos (EUI Working Papers)*. Badia Fiesolana: European University Institute.

Marger, M. (2015). *Race & ethnic relations: American and global perspectives* (10th ed.). Stamford, CT: Cengage Learning.

Statistics Canada. (2008). 2006 Census: Ethnic origin, visible minorities, place of work and mode of transportation. *The Daily*, Wednesday, April 2, 2008. Retrieved from http://www.statcan.gc.ca/daily-quotidien/080402/dq080402a-eng.htm

Statistics Canada. (2013). *Immigration and ethnocultural diversity in Canada*: National Household Survey, 2011. Catalogue no. 99-010-X2011001. Ottawa: Minister of Industry. Retrieved from http://www12.statcan.gc.ca/nhs-enm/2011/as-sa/99-010-x/99-010-x2011001-eng.pdf

Stein, J., Cameron, D., Ibbitson, J., Kymlicka, W., Meisel, J., Siddiqui, H., & Valpy, M. (2007). *Uneasy partners: Multiculturalism and rights in Canada*. Waterloo: Wilfred Laurier Press.

Vertovec, S. (2010). Towards post-multiculturalism? Changing communities, conditions and contexts of diversity. *International Social Science Journal, 199*(61), 83-95.

13

Vertovec, S., & Wessendorf, S. (2010). *The multiculturalism backlash: European discourses, policies and practices*. London: Routledge.

Werbner, P. (2012). Multiculturalism from above and below: Analysing a political discourse. *Journal of Intercultural Studies, 33*(2), 197-209.

Wright, H. (2012). Between global demise and national complacent hegemony: Multiculturalism and multicultural education in a moment of danger. In. H. Wright, M. Singh, & R. Race (Eds.), *Precarious international multicultural education: Hegemony, dissent and rising alternatives* (pp. 103-114). Rotterdam: Sense Publishers.

Wright, H., Singh, M. & Race, R. (Eds.). (2012a). *Precarious international multicultural education: Hegemony, dissent and rising alternatives*. Rotterdam: Sense Publishers.

Wright, H., Singh, M. & Race, R. (2012b). Multiculturalism and multicultural education: Precarious hegemonic status quo and alternatives. In. H. Wright, M. Singh, & R. Race (Eds.), *Precarious international multicultural education: Hegemony, dissent and rising alternatives* (pp. 3-13). Rotterdam: Sense Publishers.

Lloyd Wong
Department of Sociology
University of Calgary

Shibao Guo
Werklund School of Education
University of Calgary

SECTION I

THEORIZING AND DEBATING MULTICULTURALISM

WILL KYMLICKA

1. THE THREE LIVES OF MULTICULTURALISM

INTRODUCTION

Canada today faces challenges that were not foreseen when the Multiculturalism policy was first adopted in 1971, and serious doubts have been raised about whether the policy can be adapted or updated to deal with these new realities. Even those who supported multiculturalism in the past have wondered whether it is time now to move to a 'post-multicultural' approach, and to give multiculturalism "a dignified burial."[1]

In this chapter, I will argue that multiculturalism has some life left in it, and that the original goals and tools of multiculturalism still provide a strong foundation for addressing issues of diversity and inclusion in Canada. To be sure, like all public policies, multiculturalism needs to continually adapt, but it has done so successfully in the past, and I believe it can do so again.

To foreshadow my main argument, I will distinguish three stages in the unfolding saga of Canadian multiculturalism. In its original incarnation, multiculturalism was based on a logic of ethnicity – that is, the policy encouraged the self-organization, representation and participation of ethnic groups defined on the basis of their country of origin. In the 1970s and 1980s, this logic of ethnicity was supplemented by programs intended to deal with processes of racialization and racial discrimination. And, more recently, we have seen yet another basis for self-organization emerge, as groups defined by religion seek a seat at the multicultural table. As a result, we have three distinct dimensions of diversity at work in the multiculturalism policy – ethnicity, race, and religion.

At first glance, it may appear that this multiplication of forms of diversity has undermined any coherence to the multiculturalism policy. Many commentators have argued that we need to pull these issues apart, and that we are likely to mismanage issues of race and religion if we address them using a policy framework initially designed for issues of ethnicity.

The evolution of multiculturalism has indeed taken place in an unplanned and ad hoc way, and Canada's approach therefore lacks the conceptual clarity or ideological purity that we can see in some other Western democracies. I will argue, however, that this is in fact a virtue of Canada's approach. The contingencies by which the logics of ethnicity, race and religion have evolved and interacted over time in Canada have created, largely by accident, a framework that retains powerful potential to help build more inclusive models of democratic citizenship in Canada. Or so I will argue in this chapter.

S. Guo & L. Wong (eds.), Revisiting Multiculturalism in Canada, 17–35.

My main concern is with the current and future potential of multiculturalism, but in order to assess this, we need to start by examining its history. So I will begin with the origins of multiculturalism, and attempt to identify its initial goals. I will then examine how it has evolved over time, and suggest how this evolving framework can help address the new challenges we face.

I should note that my focus will be on the *federal* policy of multiculturalism, not on the panoply of multicultural initiatives adopted at the provincial or municipal levels across Canada, or on the many experiments in multicultural accommodations adopted within private businesses, churches or other civil society organizations. The spread of multiculturalism throughout different levels and spheres of Canadian society is testament to its powerful impact – its "long march through the institutions." But the federal level provides the overarching legal and constitutional framework within which these more local initiatives take place, and we can most easily trace the evolution of multiculturalism by focusing on this larger framework.

THE ORIGINS OF MULTICULTURALISM

What then were the original goals of the federal multiculturalism policy when it was adopted in 1971? What was it intended to achieve? I would argue there were two main goals. In this first instance, multiculturalism was part of a larger political bargain designed to deal with the national unity crisis in Canada raised by the rise of Quebec nationalism. The 1960s witnessed the dramatic (re)-emergence of Quebecois nationalism, including the first manifestations of a significant secessionist movement. The federal government needed to do something to blunt this growth in separatist sentiment. It therefore undertook a series of reforms to make Quebecers feel more at home in Canada, including enhancing the status of the French language, so as to make the federal government genuinely bilingual, and to increase the representation of francophones in the civil service. More generally, the federal government sought to re-emphasize Canada's "duality" – i.e., to re-emphasize the equality of British and French as the "founding nations."

One component of this strategy was the establishment of the Royal Commission on Bilingualism and Biculturalism in 1963, with the mandate to explore ways of strengthening equality between the British and French. As soon as the mandate of this Commission was released, however, leaders of various "ethnic groups" expressed concern, particularly long-settled groups such as the Ukrainians, Italians, and Poles. All of the talk about "duality," "two founding nations," and "bilingualism and biculturalism" seemed to render these ethnic groups invisible, and ignored the role they had played in building the country.[2] They worried that government funds and civil service positions would be parcelled out between British and French, leaving immigrant/ethnic groups on the margins. This fear generated some of the first serious attempts at ethnic group political mobilization in Canada, at least at the federal level. Indeed, many commentators argue that the establishment of this Royal Commission was the spur that precipitated the political mobilization of "ethnic groups" as a "third force" in Canadian politics. These groups insisted that the accommodation of Quebec not be done at their expense, and that any strengthening of linguistic duality therefore be accompanied by recognition of ethnic diversity.

The federal government was nervous about this unexpected hostility amongst ethnic groups to the work of the Royal Commission. The government believed that if ethnic groups strongly opposed the idea of duality, including the idea of strengthening official bilingualism, they could undermine the delicate process of accommodating Québécois nationalism. In order to defuse this problem, the Royal Commission was instructed to consider ways of recognizing the contribution of ethnic groups to Canadian society. This resulted in a series of recommendations, released by the Commission in 1969, which became the basis for the multiculturalism policy in 1971.

In other words, the whole idea of multiculturalism arose as an "afterthought" (Jaworsky, 1979, p. 48), tacked on to a series of government reforms intended primarily to accommodate Québécois nationalism. And the goal of these multiculturalism reforms was primarily to gain ethnic group support for (or at least neutralize ethnic group opposition to) what the government perceived as the real issue: namely, defusing Quebec separatism. The idea of "multiculturalism within a bilingual framework" was, in effect, a slogan hastily devised to name a political bargain: in return for not opposing efforts to accommodate Quebec nationalism, ethnic groups would be given a measure of official recognition of their own, and modest financial support to maintain their identities.

This may sound rather crass, but it has in fact been a very stable and successful bargain. Indeed, I would argue that something like 'multiculturalism within a bilingual framework' is the only possible basis for Canada to survive as a country. The only way to keep Quebec in the country is to re-affirm duality in the form of official bilingualism. But the only form of duality that can be politically sustained is one that does not come at the expense of ethnic groups, excluding them from public space and state resources. I see no other viable formula for keeping the country together.[3]

So the initial impetus for multiculturalism was a political bargain to help address the national unity crisis. But it wasn't just a crude bargain. There were also important values and principles that inspired and guided the policy. Indeed, we could say that the bargain was only possible because it reflected the progressive and reformist spirit of the age. In particular, multiculturalism was seen as a natural and logical extension of the civil rights revolution that was sweeping Canada at the time, which was itself part of a larger post-war human rights revolution.

It's important to remember that the adoption of multiculturalism in 1971 occurred during the most concentrated period of social and political liberalization that Canada has ever witnessed. The decade between 1965 and 1975 witnessed liberalizing reforms across virtually the entire range of social policy – liberalizing abortion laws, access to contraception, and divorce laws, abolishing the death penalty, prohibiting gender and religious discrimination, decriminalizing homosexuality, amongst many other such reforms. This era is often characterized as reflecting a "human rights revolution" in Canada, and indeed it witnessed the establishment of human rights commissions in virtually every province, and at the federal level in 1977. Others have characterized it as the triumph of a "rights-based liberalism," or a "civil rights liberalism," in Canada.

The adoption of multiculturalism is part of this general dynamic of liberalization. Like these other reforms, it was seen as contesting inherited prejudices and constraints that inhibited the freedom and equality of citizens. This link is not always sufficiently appreciated, in part because many commentators have assumed that multiculturalism by definition must be a conservative and collectivist doctrine, committed to the preservation of group traditions, rather than a liberal doctrine committed to individual freedom. But in fact multiculturalism, from the start, has been understood in Canada as a policy of reducing the barriers and stigmas that limit the ability of individuals to freely explore and express their ethnic identities. It insists that individuals should be free to express their ethnic identity, in public and private, and should not be subject to stigmatization, discrimination, prejudice or undue burdens for doing so. Like reforms in the sphere of gender and gay rights, multiculturalism was conceptualized as a way of expanding the scope of individual autonomy, by tackling the relations of hierarchy, stigmatization and oppression that had precluded or penalized particular life choices.

This liberal impulse is reflected in the way the multiculturalism policy has been legally drafted and judicially enforced. Multiculturalism is tightly and explicitly connected to broader norms of human rights and liberal constitutionalism, both conceptually and institutionally. Consider the preamble to the Multiculturalism Act. It begins by saying that *because* the government of Canada is committed to civil liberties, particularly the freedom of individuals "to make the life that the individual is able and wishes to have," and because it is committed to equality, particularly racial equality and gender equality, and because of its international human rights obligations, particularly the international convention against racial discrimination, *therefore* it is adopting a policy of multiculturalism. It goes on, in the main text, to reiterate human rights norms as part of the substance of the multiculturalism policy. You could hardly ask for a clearer statement that multiculturalism is to be understood as an integral part of the human rights revolution, and as an extension of, not brake on, civil rights liberalism. There is not a whiff of cultural conservatism or cultural preservationism in this statement.

In fact, this point had already been made explicit in the original 1971 parliamentary statement on multiculturalism, which stated that "a policy of multiculturalism within a bilingual framework is basically the conscious support of individual freedom of choice. We are free to be ourselves" (Trudeau, 1971, p. 8546).[4]

These formulations are obviously intended as an instruction to the relevant political actors, from ethnic activists to bureaucrats, that multiculturalism must be understood as a policy inspired by liberal norms. Nor was this left to chance, or to the good will of political actors. The Multiculturalism Act is located squarely within the larger institutional framework of liberal-democratic constitutionalism, and hence is legally subject to the same constitutional constraints as any other federal policy. Any federal action done in the name of multiculturalism must respect the requirements of the Charter, as interpreted and enforced by judicial bodies such as the Canadian Human Rights Commission and the Supreme Court.

So the way in which multiculturalism in Canada has been legally defined makes clear that it does not exist outside the framework of liberal-democratic constitutionalism and human rights jurisprudence, or as an exception to it, or deviation from it. Rather, it is firmly embedded within that framework. It is defined as flowing from human rights norms, as embodying those norms, and as enforceable through judicial institutions whose mandate is to uphold those norms.[5]

In short, the second goal or function of multiculturalism was to reinterpret the role of ethnicity in light of the broader human rights revolution. And here again, I think this aspect of the original multiculturalism policy remains as relevant today as ever. While we face new challenges of diversity, the only morally acceptable and politically viable framework for addressing them is that of liberal-democratic constitutionalism and global human rights principles.

AN EVOLVING POLICY: FROM ETHNICITY TO RACE

So national unity and civil rights liberalism were the two key goals of the original multiculturalism policy, underpinning its adoption in 1971, and both remain relevant. Very soon thereafter, however, multiculturalism had to confront unexpected challenges. Indeed, the core constituency for multiculturalism dramatically changed. As I noted earlier, the initial push for multiculturalism came primarily from long-settled and well-established European ethnic groups – the Ukrainians, Poles, Italians etc. – the so-called "white ethnics."[6] Non-European ethnic groups – the "visible minorities" – played a peripheral role in this original debate. It was only in the late-1960s that the immigration rules were changed to admit non-European immigrants on a non-discriminatory basis, and it took several years for these new immigrant groups to settle and become politically engaged.

By the mid-1970s, however, these newer immigrant groups were becoming more active. And it quickly became clear that they faced serious challenges and risks of exclusion that were not faced by, say, 2nd or 3rd-generation Ukrainian-Canadians. For one thing, as new immigrants, they had needs relating to settlement, integration and naturalization that were not addressed in the initial multiculturalism policy, designed for long-settled groups. Moreover, and perhaps more importantly, as visible minorities, they faced barriers of racism. While Poles, Italians, and Ukrainians certainly suffered from ethnic prejudices and stereotypes when they arrived in Canada – and the original multiculturalism was designed in part to address these prejudices – they nonetheless joined the British and French on the same side of the global colour line. Throughout the 19th and early 20th-centuries, the world order had been restructured by ideologies of European racial supremacy, and in relation to that global ideology, southern and eastern Europeans shared in the white racial privilege. Newer visible minority immigrants, by contrast, suffered from the enduring effects of these long-standing ideologies and

21

practices of white/European supremacism, and this called for new policy responses.

At first, it was unclear whether multiculturalism could adapt to these new challenges. Indeed, some commentators write about multiculturalism as if the policy never did adapt, as if support for Ukrainian cultural activities are still the main focus of the policy (e.g., Gwyn, 1995). However, the policy did shift focus to incorporate policies of anti-racism and immigrant integration. Indeed, it shifted to such an extent that by the early 1980s, some white ethnics were saying that the policy which they had fought for had been "hijacked" by newer non-European immigrants. This two-fold shift – towards anti-racism and immigrant integration – characterized what I am calling the second stage of the multiculturalism saga.

However, this shift was neither quick nor easy. Indeed, it raised profound questions about the very organizing logic of the policy. The original policy, as I noted earlier, was founded on the logic of ethnicity – that is, it encouraged immigrants to create organizations defined by their country of origin, such as the Ukrainian Canadian Congress, and created forums and mechanisms for such organizations to participate in the social and political life of the country. But this logic of ethnicity does not work well when dealing with issues of racial discrimination. Immigrants from the Caribbean are not discriminated against on the basis of their country of origin – most white Canadians probably cannot distinguish a Jamaican from a Trinidadian. Rather, they are discriminated against as blacks, on the basis of their race, with skin colour as the main marker. Similarly, immigrants from East Asia are not discriminated against primarily on the basis of their national origin as Vietnamese or Korean – many white Canadians have difficulty distinguishing these national groups – but rather are discriminated against as "Asians" or "Orientals" on the basis of their race and skin colour. Processes of racialization involve a different logic than those of ethnicity, national origin or mother-tongue, and must be tackled using different tools (Commission on Systematic Racism, 1995; Henry, 1994).

The federal government recognized this fact, and so adopted new programs that encouraged self-organization and participation along racial lines, such as the Urban Alliance on Race Relations, and the National Organization of Immigrant and Visible Minority Women. However, and this is a key point, it added this new logic of anti-racism *on top of*, rather than in place of, the earlier logic of ethnicity. It continues to support organizations defined by ethnicity and national origin – such as the older UCC, or newer organizations such as the National Council of Trinidad and Tobago Organizations, and the National Federation of Pakistani Canadians – as well as organizations whose mandate focuses on anti-racism and race relations.

Some say that this approach of supplementing ethnicity with race obscures or minimizes the problem of racism, and that it would have been better to base public policy solely on racial groups, and encourage newcomers to self-organize and engage politically as discriminated racial groups rather than as ethnic groups. This is essentially the strategy taken by the US, the UK, and (in a different way) by France. They all espouse a commitment to fight racial discrimination, but provide little or no public support to organizations defined on ethnocultural lines, often on the grounds that while racism is a profound evil that the state has a duty to tackle, there is no comparable moral justification for state support of ethnocultural diversity as such. Some critics go so far as to argue that the ongoing support for ethnically-defined groups in Canada is a deliberate attempt to weaken anti-racist alliances – a kind of modern 'divide and conquer' strategy to keep non-white groups focused internally on their ethnic differences, rather than cooperating together to fight their shared subordination.

It is indeed true that more emphasis and resources are needed to fight racism in Canada. Yet I would argue that the decision to maintain ethnicity along with race as an organizing principle of multiculturalism was the right one, at least for Canada. There is no evidence that abandoning support for ethnic organizations is needed to combat racism, or that anti-racism measures in the US, UK or France have been more effective than in Canada. On the contrary, there is anecdotal evidence that the Canadian model of combining ethnic accommodation with anti-racism is preferred by immigrants themselves. For example, a recent study interviewed Vietnamese immigrants in both Canada and the United States, and the results suggest that while the immigrants in both countries are indeed deeply concerned about being subjected to anti-Asian racism, they also care about their ethnic identity. After all, the Vietnamese have their own language, history and culture, different from that of other Asian immigrants, and they want to be able to participate in public life as Vietnamese-Canadians or Vietnamese-Americans, and not just as 'Asians.'[7] Vietnamese immigrants in the US resent the fact that they are always pigeon-holed into racial categories for the purposes of public debate and public policy, while their co-ethnics to Canada appreciate the fact that the government accords legitimacy to their ethnic identity (Bloemraad, 2006). We see similar anecdotal results from studies comparing immigrants from the Indian subcontinent to Canada and Britain. In Britain, immigrants often resent that the state views them solely through the prism of race relations rather than as bearers of distinct and valuable ethnic identities and cultures (Berns-McGown, 1999; Modood, 2003).

To be sure, there is an omnipresent danger that the recognition and celebration of ethnic diversity will become a pretext for ignoring structural racism (Bannerjee, 2000). But the solution to this, I believe, is not to subordinate ethnicity to race, but precisely to highlight the role that both can play in building more inclusive models of democratic citizenship.

The second distinctive challenge raised by the post-1965 influx of immigrants concerns the relationship between multiculturalism and immigrant integration. As I mentioned earlier, the policy was originally demanded by long-settled groups, and the policy as originally drafted implicitly assumed that its beneficiaries were already Canadian citizens.[8] Indeed, multiculturalism was formulated as an attribute of Canadian citizenship: it was a new way of understanding Canadian citizenship, a new way of understanding one's Canadian-ness, not an alternative to being (or becoming) a Canadian. The policy said that one appropriate and honourable way of being a Canadian is to be a proud Ukrainian-Canadian; that one worthy and constructive way of participating as a citizen in Canadian democracy is to participate as an Italian-Canadian.

In this sense, multiculturalism in Canada is very different from Germany, for example, where (a form of) multiculturalism was adopted as a policy for "foreigners" or "aliens" who were not able or encouraged to become citizens. Multiculturalism in Germany was a consolation prize to make non-citizenship bearable (and to facilitate migrants' return to their countries of origin). In Canada, by contrast, multiculturalism was adopted as a policy for citizens, as a way of reformulating the role of ethnic identities and ethnic organizations within the theory and practice of Canadian citizenship.

This initial focus on long-settled and already-naturalized citizens, however, became a problem when dealing with newer immigrant groups, many of whose members were not yet settled, integrated or naturalized. As a result, multiculturalism programs have had to intervene earlier in the integration process, to help people in the first stages of their landing, settlement and integration. Since the 1980s, therefore, multiculturalism has increasingly been seen in the public's eye as tied to processes of the integration of newcomers, and to nuts and bolts issues of social service provision, settlement services, language training, job training, and so on.

But here again, this shift was a matter of supplementing, not replacing, the original emphasis on legitimizing and facilitating the role of ethnic identities and ethnic organizations in Canadian civic life generally, for long-settled groups as well as newcomers. Indeed, even as multiculturalism programs adapted to serve the needs and interests of newcomers who may not yet be citizens, it remained primarily conceptualized as a policy about what it means to be a Canadian citizen.[9] Multiculturalism has never been seen in Canada as an alternative to citizenship, or as a transitional phase that immigrants pass through on the road to becoming "real" Canadians who no longer need multiculturalism. Multiculturalism is a right in Canada, but it is seen as a right that one possesses *as a Canadian:* it is about how we conceptualize the role of ethnic identities and ethnic organizations in our ongoing civic and political lives, and not just about techniques of newcomer integration.

So even as multiculturalism expanded and adapted to deal with newcomer integration, it maintained its original focus on legitimizing and acknowledging ethnicity as a component of Canadian identity. Some critics worry that it was a mistake to maintain this original focus. They worry that while celebrating ethnic identities and ethnic heritages may have mattered for well-integrated Ukrainian-Canadians, it is a luxury and distraction for newcomers, who have more urgent and prosaic needs relating to housing, jobs, and social services. On this view, the very visible public support for multiculturalism as a celebration of ethnic heritage has masked our policy failures with respect to newcomer settlement and integration.[10]

I think this is indeed a danger. The vocal support for multiculturalism by both the Mulroney and Chretien governments masked some devastating cuts to immigrant integration programs (Abu-Laban & Gabriel, 2002). And yet I would argue that it would have been a mistake to reduce multiculturalism to (or replace it with) a policy exclusively focused on newcomer integration. Multicultural integration works best when it is tied to ideas of multicultural citizenship. Where multiculturalism is seen entirely as a transitional strategy, relevant only to the initial stages of settlement and integration, it provides no basis for challenging exclusionary ideas of Canadian national identity, Canadian citizenship, or Canadian patriotism. On the contrary, a transitional model of multiculturalism creates the suspicion that if immigrants continue to cling to ethnic identities and ethnic organizations after the first few years of settlement, they are failing to integrate, and failing to become real or true Canadians. This is precisely the dynamic we see in Europe today, where the persistence of ethnic identities is taken as evidence for the failed integration of immigrants, and where multiculturalism is blamed for this failure. We can only avoid this poisonous dynamic by articulating models of multicultural *citizenship* – by showing that one way of being a proud and active Canadian citizen is by being a proud and active Vietnamese-Canadian. That, of course, is precisely what the original multiculturalism policy set out to show, and in my view, it remains an essential component of the multiculturalism policy.

So if we examine the evolution of the policy from the 1970s to the 1980s, we see an interesting development. On the one hand, the policy was dramatically transformed almost beyond recognition, from a policy initially focused on acknowledging the contributions of long-settled European ethnic groups to a policy focused on facilitating the integration of newly-arriving non-European immigrants. And yet, in another sense, there were also strong continuities in the policy, as new programs were built on top of, rather than in place of, the original foundations. By the late 1980s, these first two stages of the multiculturalism saga had resulted in a policy that involved a complicated and inter-connected set of goals and tools. I've focused on four of these inter-connections. In the first stage, the recognition and accommodation of ethnic diversity was linked to (a) French-English linguistic duality; and (b) liberalization and human rights. In the second stage, those two initial links were preserved, but in addition, it was linked to (c) anti-racism; and (d) Canadian citizenship. In my view, all four of these links remain essential components of a successful multiculturalism policy,[11] and it would be a mistake to move to a "post-multiculturalism" approach if this means abandoning or weakening any of them. In fact, much of the fragility of multiculturalism in other countries derives precisely from the fact that it isn't tightly connected to national unity, human rights, anti-racism and citizenship.

The existence of these links in the Canadian case is, to a large extent, a matter of contingency and good luck, rather than far-sighted planning. But the result, I believe, was that Canada developed by the late 1980s a distinctly creative and progressive framework for thinking about inclusive citizenship. Indeed, we can see this as an impressive example of policy adaptation and social learning, meeting new challenges while building on old strengths. Critics often bemoan the inability of public policies to adapt to changing circumstances and new challenges. But here we have an example of policy evolution that was, in broad strokes, reasonably successful. As I mentioned earlier, there are certainly shortcomings in our response to racism and in our integration policies, which the celebratory rhetoric of multiculturalism sometimes masks. But at least when compared to other Western democracies, there is considerable evidence that this policy framework has made a positive contribution, whether measured by levels of immigrant naturalization and political participation rates, levels of inter-ethnic trust and friendship, comfort with ethnic diversity, or low levels of support for far-right, anti-minority political parties and movements. On all these measures, Canada consistently outscores other Western democracies, and while multiculturalism is not the only factor at work here, it almost certainly is one of the sources.[12]

This relative success is also attested by the growth of international interest in the "Canadian model." The first stage of multiculturalism was widely ignored by other countries as the outcome of a uniquely and parochially Canadian concern – namely, how to make sure white ethnics were not squeezed out by the accommodation of Quebecois nationalism. The second stage, however, has been intensively studied by other countries, since it addresses what are endemic issues facing all Western democracies – namely, how to integrate non-European immigrants in a way that combines and links cultural accommodation, anti-racism, human rights, and citizenship-promotion. And it has been widely acknowledged by both academic commentators and international organizations that no country has met this challenge better than Canada, even if there are doubts about whether the Canadian model can be adopted elsewhere.[13]

THE THIRD STAGE: FROM ETHNICITY AND RACE TO RELIGION

So by the late 1980s, the second stage of multiculturalism had become more or less consolidated, reflected in the all-party endorsement of the 1988 Multiculturalism Act, which reaffirmed all of the linkages I have been discussing. However, almost immediately after the passage of this Act, a new set of challenges started to appear, challenges that were not foreseen by either the original 1971 policy or the 1988 Act.

In particular, Canada started to witness the emergence of religion as a basis for multicultural claims, alongside earlier claims based on ethnicity and race. Consider the Somali community in Canada, which started to arrive in large numbers in the 1980s, and started to become organized and politically active by the end of that decade. Like previous immigrant groups, they have organized and participated on the basis of their ethnicity and national origin, by establishing ethnic organizations, like the Canadian Somali Congress. They have also participated in anti-racist organizations of Black Canadians, alongside other Canadians of African descent. But many Somalis also want to participate in Canadian life as *Muslims*, alongside other Canadian Muslims from different ethnic and racial backgrounds. And this has raised a problem for the multiculturalism policy. It was designed to allow and indeed encourage the participation of immigrants along lines of ethnicity and race – as Somalis and Blacks – but it was not set up to deal with representation and claims-making based on religion.

There are a number of reasons for the increased prominence of religion as a basis for political participation and claims-making. In part, it reflects a global trend towards the (re)-politicization of religion, as believers of various faiths mobilize politically, and contest the attempt to exclude religion from politics and the public square. We see similar dynamics amongst conservative Protestants in the US, Hindus in India, Jews in Israel, Muslims in Egypt, and Buddhists in Sri Lanka. But it also reflects a trend towards the "ethnicization" of Muslim identities, particularly amongst secularized younger Muslim immigrants in the West. Whereas their parents may have been primarily interested in participation in organizations based on national origin – as Turks, Algerians or Somalis – the children increasingly seem more interested in participating in organizations based on religious identity, even when they themselves are not particularly devout. "Muslim," for many in the younger generation, is not a faith, but a quasi-ethnic identity, and one which matters more to them than national origin or mother-tongue. So even secular or atheist Muslims may prefer to participate in Muslim-Canadian student organizations than in, say, Pakistani-Canadian student organizations. One reason for this, of course, is that Islamophobia affects all Muslims, no matter what their country of origin, and no matter whether they are devout or not.

So there are "bottom-up" reasons why Somali immigrants have become more likely to mobilize and participate as Muslims, and not just as Somalis or Blacks. But there are also top-down reasons. The reality is that governments today, particularly after 9/11, are desperately concerned to find out what "the Muslims" think and feel, and whether they are becoming radicalized or not. They want to find interlocutors who can speak for "Muslims," and not just interlocutors who can speak for Somalis or Blacks. They want to find Muslim organizations with whom they can enter into negotiations and partnerships to help reduce alienation, monitor radicalism, and promote cooperation with state officials. And so governments have their own reasons for creating new mechanisms for encouraging the self-organization and participation of groups defined along lines of religious affiliation.

For a mixture of reasons, therefore, multiculturalism is now under pressure to add a third track of religion, alongside ethnicity and race. This, indeed, is the third stage of multiculturalism, and its evolution is still very much a work in progress. There remains much uncertainty about the role of religion within the multiculturalism policy, and about the sorts of religious organizations and faith-based claims that should be supported by the policy. For example, should multiculturalism support the funding of faith-based schools, or faith-based family law arbitration? These issues are increasingly coming to the fore, but there is no consensus even amongst the traditional defenders of multiculturalism about how to address them. While there are guidelines and principles for how multiculturalism deals with issues of ethnicity and race, there are no comparable guidelines for how to deal with religious groups or faith-based claims.

Can multiculturalism adapt to this new challenge? Can it expand to deal with religion, in the same way that it earlier expanded from ethnicity to race? This is perhaps the key question for multiculturalism in Canada at the start of the 21st century. We are still at the first stages of this debate, and it is too early to tell where it will lead. As I said, the rise of politicized religion is a global issue that all Western countries are struggling with, and it is clear that there are no magic formulas. But I am cautiously optimistic that multiculturalism will be up to the task. I believe that we can and should take advantage of our existing multiculturalism policy, and build upon it. The basic goal of multiculturalism – namely, enabling the expression and accommodation of diversity within a larger framework of linguistic duality, human rights, anti-racism, and citizenship-promotion – is a sound one for Canada, and I think it applies as much to religion as to race and ethnicity. As with ethnic and racial minorities, religious minorities have historically suffered from various forms of discrimination, disadvantage and stigmatization in Canada – some official and state-sponsored, others informal – which have inhibited their ability to exercise full and equal citizenship, and to lead the lives they choose. And as with ethnic and racial minorities, the basic norms and strategies of multiculturalism – strategies of self-organization, participation and accommodation – can provide an effective vehicle for addressing these obstacles. So far as I can tell, all of the arguments for adopting multiculturalism as a way of tackling the legacies of ethnic and racial hierarchies apply to religion as well.

To be sure, there are obvious difficulties and pitfalls. For example, how should governments decide which religiously-defined organizations to speak to? How do we ensure that the full diversity of voices within religious groups are heard, including those of women and youth, and not just the voices of conservative and patriarchal elites, or of self-declared spokesmen? How do we determine whether self-declared leaders really represent the people they claim to represent?

These are critically important questions, but notice that similar questions arose during the first two stages of multiculturalism, in relation to groups based on ethnicity and race (e.g., das Gupta, 1999). As a result, we have built up a wealth of experience about how to address these issues – about how to encourage forms of organization, representation and participation that are inclusive, and that promote the policy's objectives of freedom, gender equality, and human rights.[14] This is precisely what I mean by building on our strengths: the evolution of multiculturalism has been an exercise in social learning, and we need to draw upon those lessons. Just as the second stage of multiculturalism built on the strengths of the first stage, so too we should build on the second in addressing the third stage.

However, there are other deeper worries about extending multiculturalism to deal with religion. Many people worry that religious claims, more so than those based on ethnicity or race, are likely to violate the liberal ethos of multiculturalism. As I've emphasized, multiculturalism was originally conceived as part of the post-war human rights revolution, and as one component of a larger process of social liberalization, including gay rights and gender equality. But many people worry that faith-based claims, more so than ethnic or racial claims, are likely to be repressive of individual freedom. Conservative religious groups may seek to use the ideology and institutions of multiculturalism to defend practices that are oppressive rather than emancipatory – for example, practices of forced arranged marriages, honour killings, female genital cutting, or the preaching and teaching of hatred against homosexuals or apostates. Multiculturalism, in short, can be invoked not to contest inherited hierarchies and inequalities between minorities and the mainstream society, but rather to defend religiously-sanctioned hierarchies *within* the minority community. How do we ensure that the participation of religious groups and the accommodation of religious claims lead to the enhancement of individual freedom – the freedom of all Canadians "to make the life that the individual is able and wishes to have" – rather than to the suppression of individual freedom in the name of religious orthodoxy?

This is indeed an important challenge, but we shouldn't overstate it. Insofar as religious groups have attempted to make multiculturalist claims, they have rarely contested the basic liberal values of the policy. For example, there have been no attempts in Canada to defend female genital mutilation or coerced marriages.[15] And even if such claims were raised, there is no chance they would be accepted by the state, or by the general public. The multiculturalism policy is framed as part of a larger human rights agenda, and principles of gender equality and human rights are clearly articulated within the policy. From a legal point of view, therefore, there is no possibility that multiculturalism can be invoked to justify abridging the rights of women or children within minority communities.

However, determining the precise "limits of tolerance" remains a difficult and unresolved issue, in Canada as in all Western democracies. For example, under what conditions would the funding of faith-based schools be a threat to liberal values? There has recently been a trend for religious conservatives, from various faiths, to invoke multiculturalism to demand public funding of religious schools. This claim is understandable, particularly in provinces (like Ontario) where public funds are already provided to Catholic schools. This seems like a paradigmatic example of multiculturalism, extending to new groups a right or benefit historically granted to a dominant group.

Yet we know that some of these faith-based schools would teach illiberal doctrines. Indeed, part of the motivation for demanding such schools is precisely the desire to shield their children from exposure to ideas of gay rights, feminism and indeed multiculturalism itself. Conservative Protestants, for example, initially fought tooth and nail against the introduction of multiculturalism into the public schools in Ontario, fearing it would undermine the privileged position of Christianity, and expose their children to other faiths. Having lost that battle, these groups now (paradoxically) invoke multiculturalism to demand publicly-funded religious schools in which they can again avoid having to teach multiculturalism (Davies, 1999).

Some people worry that we can only ensure that children receive a liberal and tolerant education if we reject all public funding of religious schools. But others argue that since a liberal state cannot prohibit privately-funded religious schools, the better solution is to ensure that all schools, public or private, teach the essentials of democratic citizenship, including human rights, gender equality and multicultural tolerance. And if these essentials are taught, then perhaps there is no reason to rule out public funding of faith-based schools, particularly where other types of private schools or charter schools receive public funding. Indeed, public funding can be used as an incentive to ensure that these core requirements are fulfilled.

This issue of religious schooling remains deeply contested and unresolved in several Western democracies. Another controversial example involves attempts to invoke multiculturalism to defend faith-based arbitration of family law disputes. Here again, there is no obvious answer about which models of private arbitration best fulfil the emancipatory aims of the multiculturalism policy. There is ample evidence that allowing for alternative dispute resolution can provide parties with valuable options that are not available through the normal family law courts, which are notoriously slow, expensive, adversarial and often insensitive to the needs of immigrants and minorities. Yet there is equally ample evidence that the enhanced flexibility provided by private arbitration can increase the vulnerability of weaker parties, who lack the procedural safeguards provided by the regular legal system. Any liberal conception of multiculturalism has to balance these competing considerations. Banning all private arbitration, like banning all private schools, would be a radical solution, difficult to reconcile with a liberal constitutional order. Yet we are far from having a consensus on what kind of private arbitration, subject to what kinds of safeguards and monitoring, is appropriate.[16]

As I said, we are at the first stages of these debates, and I do not intend to resolve them here. In my view, we need to look at these issues case-by-case. Some claims for religious accommodation promote individual freedom and equal citizenship, others threaten it. So too with faith-based education or faith-based arbitration. Some versions of these proposals are consistent with a liberal-democratic human rights framework of multiculturalism, others are not. We need to take our time, and do the due diligence. We need to create better mechanisms of consultation with all the affected parties, consider the experiences of other countries, examine the full range of alternatives, and assess their likely impacts in light of the broader goals of the policy. There is no shortcut here.

Unfortunately, all too often, commentators have tried to take a short-cut, by ruling out all faith-based claims in principle, on the grounds that they violate the principle of secularism. According to this view, the problem with extending multiculturalism to deal with religion is not just the logistics of determining which religious groups to invite to participate, nor the danger that certain religious claims will be oppressive of individual freedom. The deeper problem is with the very idea that the state should be involved with religion. According to some commentators, extending multiculturalism from ethnicity and race to religion violates a fundamental principle of liberal democracy – namely, the separation of state and church, or secularism. On this view, while the evolution from ethnicity to race can be seen as extending the liberal logic of multiculturalism, extending it further to religion violates that logic. For example, many of the groups that mobilized against the proposal for faith-based family-law arbitration in Ontario did so, not on the grounds that it jeopardized the rights or interests of vulnerable individuals, but on the grounds that it violated "secularism."

In my view, this is a serious misunderstanding which impedes our ability to think through the issues. For one thing, these appeals to secularism often smack of double-standards, if not hypocrisy. After all, Canadian governments have a long history of making special accommodations for Christians and Jews, of funding Catholic and Protestant schools, and of invoking Christian symbols and language in state symbols and rituals. It often appears that secularism is only invoked when it is Muslims who ask for accommodation and recognition.

But in any event, this is a misinterpretation of the principle of secularism, and of the role it plays in liberal-democratic theory. A secular state is one that does not affiliate itself with any particular religion – the state is not an instrument for promoting one religion over others, or for promoting faith over non-belief. But by itself, this does not resolve the question of whether or how such a secular state should accommodate religious beliefs, fund religious institutions, or deliver services through faith-based organizations. A secular state can provide tax breaks to religious institutions, as indeed virtually Western democracies do; it can exempt religious believers from certain laws, such as animal slaughter laws or dress codes, as most Western democracies do; it can provide funding to faith-based schools, or deliver health care or other social services through faith-based organizations, as many Western democracies do. So long as these policies are adopted in an even-handed way, rather than privileging some religions over others, then there is no violation of secularism.

So very few, if any, of the religious-based claims being raised in Canada today threaten the principle of secularism. No one is seriously proposing to replace the secular state with a religious state, or to privilege one faith over others in tax codes or service delivery. The real issue, I believe, is not secularism, but human rights, and in particular norms of individual freedom and equal citizenship. The task for the third stage of multiculturalism is to determine which claims for religious accommodation enhance the freedom of individuals to lead the kinds of lives they choose, strengthen their ability to participate as democratic citizens in our collective life, and remedy the inherited stigmas and burdens that minorities have faced. As I said, this can only be done on a case-by-case basis: there is no magic formula, such as 'secularism,' that can solve all these issues at once. And we can only address these case-by-case issues if we create new mechanisms of consultation, participation and deliberation that enable the expression of the full range of voices within religious communities.

This will require a major rethinking of our existing models and mechanisms of multiculturalism in Canada. Many people who have grown comfortable with the first two stages of multiculturalism feel a deep anxiety about this emerging third stage, and understandably so. But as I have tried to emphasize throughout this chapter, we are not starting from scratch. We have developed a framework for thinking about diversity that has proven its strengths and its adaptability, and if we take advantage of that strong foundation, I'm cautiously optimistic that we can convert the challenges of religious accommodation into an opportunity for building an even more inclusive model of Canadian citizenship.

KYMLICKA

NOTES

[1] The quote is from Trevor Phillips, head of Britain's Commission for Racial Equality. For discussion of the new 'post-multiculturalism' literature, and its difference from the older 'anti-multiculturalism' literature, see Alibhai-Brown (2000, 2004), Ley (2005), Vertovec (2005), and Wong, Garcea and Kirova (2005).

[2] It also, of course, rendered invisible the Aboriginal peoples of Canada. However, Aboriginals did not view the B&B Commission as a direct threat to their rights and status, which had a separate legal basis that fell outside the B&B's mandate, and so did not mobilize strongly against it. They mobilized much more strongly a few years later, in response to the 1969 White Paper on Indian policy, which did directly threaten their treaty rights and status. Since then, these two struggles – by ethnic groups for multiculturalism and by Aboriginal peoples for Aboriginal rights – have moved on legal and political separate tracks. Each is a response to the potential exclusion of the original "two nations" picture, but they have responded in different ways, with different claims. I explore the relationship between these two tracks in Kymlicka (2007a).

[3] The role of multiculturalism as a constituent of national unity was reaffirmed in the 1995 referendum in Quebec, when the immigrant vote tipped the balance in favour of federalism over secession. It was the commitment of immigrants to the model of a bilingual and multicultural Canada that prevented the country from breaking up.

[4] Cf. "Multiculturalism appeals to the common understanding of freedom as choice" (Forbes, 1994, p. 94).

[5] This liberal impulse is confirmed by the nature of the political coalitions and public opinion that generated and supported Multiculturalism. Multiculturalism has always been supported primarily by the socially liberal segment of the Canadian populace – the same segment that supports gender equality and gay rights – who view this set of reforms as expressions of a single logic of civil rights liberalism (Adams, 2000; Dasko, 2005; Howard-Hassman, 2003). The liberal character of multiculturalism was often just taken for granted. After all, the groups who initially demanded multiculturalism – such as the Ukrainians – were widely seen as falling well inside the mainstream liberal-democratic consensus. Many of them had fought loyally in World War II, were staunchly anti-communist in the Cold War, and were well-integrated into the Canadian democratic process. The thought that these groups might attempt to use multiculturalism to challenge liberal-democratic values did not occur to anyone. That the Ukrainian-Canadian activists viewed their struggle as part of civil rights liberalism is made clear in Manoly Lupul's memoirs about the mobilization for multiculturalism (Lupul, 2005).

[6] For the role of white ethnic groups in the process, see Blanshay (2001), Jaworsky (1979), and Lupul (2005).

[7] Indeed, since one of the standard tropes of white racism is to deny that non-European peoples are capable of producing admirable or worthy forms of culture, multiculturalist policies that accord public recognition to ethnic cultures can themselves be seen as anti-racist.

[8] This connection between multiculturalism and citizenship is implicit in multiculturalism's two original functions: both the national unity and liberal human rights motivations for multiculturalism presuppose that members of ethnic groups are citizens.

[9] This link between multiculturalism and citizenship is clear from public discourse. If members of an immigrant group said that they wanted multiculturalism but didn't want to become Canadian citizens, the response from the general public (and indeed from policy-makers) would almost certainly be hostility and resentment. Multiculturalism is conceived of as a way of belonging to Canada, not as a way of avoiding a commitment to the country.

[10] This criticism parallels those who argue that preserving ethnic-based multiculturalism distracts from the more urgent issues of anti-racism.

[11] These linkages are sometimes described as involving a "delicate balance" between multiculturalism and, say, bilingualism, human rights, or citizenship. But this is misleading. Talk of a "balance" implies that there is an inherent opposition between (say) multiculturalism and human rights (or

32

bilingualism, or citizenship), and that our aim is to split the difference between these opposing values, as if more of one automatically entailed less of another. In fact, these linkages are mutually supportive: we can have more of both. Indeed since the 1960s, Canada the strengthening of multiculturalism has gone hand in hand with the strengthening of bilingualism, human rights protection, anti-racism and citizenship-promotion.

[12] For relevant evidence, see Adams (2007), Bloemraad (2006), Kymlicka (1998, 2012), and Parkin and Mendelsohn (2003).

[13] On the international diffusion of multiculturalism, see Kymlicka (2007b).

[14] For example, while many critics argue that claims for sharia-based family law arbitration in Ontario are an example of 'multiculturalism run amok,' it's important to remember that many of the Muslim women's groups that contested this proposal were themselves funded by the multiculturalism program, precisely to ensure that the interests and voices of Muslim women were heard. If multiculturalism created the political space for the voicing of claims for faith-based arbitration, it also supported the organizations and forums through which Muslims and others challenged the representativeness of the original claimants, and contested their claims in the name of the broader human rights principles of the policy. This is how multiculturalism is supposed to work: it is an ongoing process of claims-making, contestation, and deliberation and policy-making guided by the overarching values of the policy.

[15] There were disagreements within various groups about how best to end these illiberal practices, but not over whether they should be ended. On the case of female genital mutilation, for example, see Government of Canada (1995), Levine (1999), and OHRC (1995).

[16] I discuss the sharia tribunal debate and its relationship to multiculturalism in Kymlicka (2005). On the tendency to deny religious accommodations to newly-settled groups that were historically granted to Christian or Jewish groups, and the genuine dilemmas this raises for multiculturalism, see Kymlicka (2009).

REFERENCES

Abu-Laban, Y., & Gabriel, C. (2002). *Selling diversity: Immigration, multiculturalism, employment equity and globalization*. Peterborough: Broadview.

Adams, M. (2000). *Better happy than rich?* Toronto, Ontario: Penguin.

Adams, M. (2007). *Unlikely utopia: The surprising triumph of Canadian pluralism*. Toronto, Ontario: Viking.

Alibhai-Brown, Y. (2000). *After multiculturalism*. London. Foreign Policy Centre.

Alibhai-Brown, Y. (2004). Beyond multiculturalism. *Canadian Diversity/Diversité Canadienne, 3*(2), 51-54.

Bannerji, H. (2000). *The dark side of the nation: Essays on multiculturalism, nationalism and gender*. Toronto: Canadian Scholars' Press.

Berns-McGown, R. (1999). *Muslims in the diaspora: The Somali communities of London and Toronto*. Toronto: University of Toronto Press.

Blanshay, L. (2001). *The Nationalisation of ethnicity: A study of the proliferation of national mono-ethnocultural umbrella organisations in Canada*. Glasgow, Scotland: Department of Sociology, University of Glasgow.

Bloemraad, I. (2006). *Becoming a citizen: Incorporating immigrants and refugees in the United States and Canada*. Berkeley, CA: University of California Press, Berkeley.

Commission on Systemic Racism in the Ontario Criminal Justice System. (1995). *Racism behind bars: The treatment of Black and other racial minority prisoners in Ontario prison*. Toronto: Interim Report.

Das Gupta, T. (1999). The politics of multiculturalism: 'Immigrant women' and the Canadian state. In E. Dua & A. Robertson (Eds.), *Scratching the surface: Canadian anti-racist feminist thought* (pp. 187-205). Toronto, Ontario: Women's Press.

Dasko, D. (2005). Public attitudes towards multiculturalism and bilingualism in Canada. In M. Adsett, C. Mallandain, & S. Stettner (Eds.), *Canadian and French perspectives on diversity: Conference proceedings* (pp. 119-125). Ottawa: Department of Canadian Heritage.

Davies, S. (1999). From moral duty to cultural rights: A case study of political framing in education. *Sociology of Education, 72*(1), 1-21.

Forbes, D. (1994). Canada: From bilingualism to multiculturalism. In L. Diamond & M. Plattner (Eds.), *Nationalism, ethnic conflict and democracy* (pp. 86-101). Baltimore: Johns Hopkins University Press.

Government of Canada. (1995). *Female genital mutilation: Report on consultations held in Ottawa and Montreal* (Research, Statistics and Evaluation Directorate, WD1995-8e). Ottawa: Department of Justice.

Gywn, R. (1995). *Nationalism without walls: The unbearable lightness of being Canadian.* Toronto: McClelland and Stewart.

Henry, F. (1994). *The Caribbean diaspora in Toronto: Learning to live with racism.* Toronto: University of Toronto Press.

Howard-Hassmann, R. (2003). *Compassionate Canadians: Civic leaders discuss human rights.* Toronto: University of Toronto Press.

Jaworsky, J. (1979). *A case study of the Canadian Federal Government's multiculturalism policy.* Carleton: MA Thesis, Dept. of Political Science, Carleton University.

Kymlicka, W. (1998). *Finding our way: Rethinking ethnocultural relations in Canada.* Toronto: Oxford University Press.

Kymlicka, W. (2005). Testing the bounds of liberal multiculturalism? Presented at the conference on *Muslim Women's Equality Rights in the Justice System: Gender, Religion and Pluralism.* Canadian Council of Muslim Women, April 2005. Translated into French as "Tester les limites de multiculturalisme libéral? Le cas des tribunaux en droit familial," *Éthique publique, 9*(1) (2007), pp. 27-39.

Kymlicka, W. (2007a). Ethnocultural diversity in a liberal state: Making sense of the Canadian model(s). In K. Banting, T. Courchene, & L. Seidle (Eds), *Belonging? Diversity, recognition and shared citizenship in Canada* (pp. 39-86). Montreal: Institute for Research on Public Policy.

Kymlicka, W. (2007b). *Multicultural Odysseys: Navigating the new international politics of diversity.* Oxford: Oxford University Press.

Kymlicka, W. (2009). The governance of religious diversity: The old and the new. In P. Bramadat & M. Koenig (Eds), *International migration and the governance of religious diversity* (pp. 323-334). Montreal: McGill-Queen's University Press.

Kymlicka, W. (2012) Multiculturalism: Success, failure, and the future. In Migration Policy Institute (Ed.), *Rethinking national identity in the age of migration* (pp. 33-78). Berlin: Verlag Bertelsmann Stiftung.

Levine, A. (1999). Female genital operations: Canadian realities, concerns and policy recommendations. In H. Troper & M. Weinfeld (Eds.), *Ethnicity, politics and public policy* (pp. 26-53). Toronto: University of Toronto Press).

Ley, D. (2005) *Post-multiculturalism?* Working Paper Series No. 05-18. Research on Immigration and Integration in the Metropolis, Vancouver Centre of Excellence.

Lupul, M. (2005). *The politics of multiculturalism: A Ukrainian-Canadian memoir.* Edmonton: Canadian Institute of Ukrainian Studies Press.

McAndrew, M., Helly, D., & Tessier, C. (2005). Pour un débat éclairé sur la politique Canadienne du multiculturalisme: Une analyse de la nature des organismes et des projets Subventionnés (1983-2002). *Politiques et Sociétes, 24*(1), 49-71.

Modood, T. (2003). Muslims and the politics of difference. In S. Spencer (Ed.), *The politics of migration: Managing opportunity, conflict and change.* Oxford: The Political Quarterly, Blackwell.

OHRC – Ontario Human Rights Commission. (1996). *Policy on female genital mutilation.* Toronto: Ontario Human Rights Commission.

Parkin, A., & Mendelsohn, M. (2003). *A new Canada: An identity shaped by diversity.* CRIC paper #11, October. Montreal: Centre for Research and Information on Canada.

Trudeau, P. (1971). *Statement to the House of Commons on Multiculturalism.* House of Commons, Official Report of Debates, 28th Parliament, 3rd Session, 8 October 1971, pp. 8545-46.

Vertovec, S. (2005). *Pre-, high-, anti- and post-multiculturalism.* Oxford: ESRC Centre on Migration, Policy and Society, University of Oxford.

Wong, L., Garcea, J., & Kirova, A. (2005). *An analysis of the "anti- and post-multiculturalism" discourses: The fragmentation position.* Edmonton, Alberta: Prairie Centre for Excellence in Research on Immigration and Integration.

Will Kymlicka
Department of Philosophy
Queen's University

JOHN W. BERRY

2. INTERCULTURAL RELATIONS IN PLURAL SOCIETIES

Research Derived from Canadian Multiculturalism Policy

INTRODUCTION

One result of the intake and settlement of migrants is the formation of culturally plural societies. In the contemporary world, all societies are now culturally plural, with many ethnocultural groups living in daily interaction. A second result is that intercultural relations become a focus of public and private concern, as the newcomers interact with established populations (both indigenous and earlier migrants). How, and how well, these intercultural interactions work out is one of the main contemporary issues to be addressed by researchers, policy-makers, institutions, communities, families and individuals.

This existing cultural diversity will become more and more so over the coming years. With research, it may be possible to discern some basic cultural, social and psychological principles that underpin the processes and outcomes of intercultural relations in these plural societies. Much of this research has been carried out within the fields of cross-cultural psychology (Berry, Poortinga, Breugelsman, Chasiotis, & Sam, 2011) and acculturation psychology (Sam & Berry, 2006).

THE MULTICULTURAL VISION

There are two contrasting, usually implicit, models of intercultural relations and acculturation in plural societies and institutions. In one (the *melting pot* model), the view is that there is (or should be) one dominant (or *mainstream*) society, on the margins of which are various non-dominant (or *minority*) groups. These non-dominant groups typically remain there, unless they are incorporated as indistinguishable components into the mainstream. Many societies have this implicit model, including France (where the image is of the "unité de l hexagon," that is, of one people with one language and one shared identity, within the borders of the country; see Sabatier & Boutry, 2006), and the USA (where the motto is "*e pluribus unum*" or "out of many, one": see Nguyen, 2006).

In the other (the *multicultural* model), there is a national social framework of institutions (called the *larger society*) that accommodates the interests and needs of the numerous cultural groups, and which are fully incorporated as *ethnocultural groups* (rather than minorities) into this national framework. The concept of the *larger society* refers to the civic arrangement in a plural society, within which all

S. Guo & L. Wong (eds.), Revisiting Multiculturalism in Canada, 37–49.

ethnocultural groups (dominant and non-dominant, indigenous and immigrant) attempt to carry out their lives together. It is constantly changing, through negotiation, compromise and mutual accommodations. It surely does not represent the way of life of the "mainstream," which is typically that preferred by the dominant group, and which became established in the public institutions that they created. All groups in such a conception of a larger society are ethnocultural groups (rather than "minorities"), who possess cultures and who have equal cultural and other rights, regardless of their size or power. In such complex plural societies, there is no assumption that some groups should assimilate or become absorbed into another group. Hence intercultural relations and change are not viewed as unidirectional, but as mutual and reciprocal. This is the conception that has informed the multicultural vision in Canada (1971), and more recently, in the European Union (2005).

Both implicit models refer to possible arrangements in plural societies: the mainstream-minority view is that cultural pluralism is a problem and should be reduced, even eliminated; the multicultural view is that cultural pluralism is a resource, and inclusiveness should be nurtured with supportive policies and programmes.

The first Multiculturalism Policy was advanced by the Government of Canada (1971):

> A policy of multiculturalism within a bilingual framework ... (is) the most suitable means of assuring the cultural freedom of all Canadians. Such a policy should help to break down discriminatory attitudes and cultural jealousies. National unity, if it is to mean anything in the deeply personal sense, must be founded on confidence on one's own individual identity; out of this can grow respect for that of others, and a willingness to share ideas, attitudes and assumptions ... The Government will support and encourage the various cultural and ethnic groups that give structure and vitality to our society. They will be encouraged to share their cultural expression and values with other Canadians and so contribute to a richer life for all. (Government of Canada, 1971, p. 1121)

There are three main components to this policy. The first component was the goal "to break down discriminatory attitudes and cultural jealousies." That is, to *enhance mutual acceptance* among all cultural groups in order to improve intercultural relations. This goal is to be approached through two main program components. One is the *cultural* component, which is to be achieved by providing support and encouragement for cultural maintenance and development among all cultural groups. The other is the *social* (or *intercultural*) component, which promotes the sharing of cultural expressions among ethnocultural groups by providing opportunities for intergroup contact, and the removal of barriers to full and equitable participation in the daily life of the larger society. A third component acknowledged the importance of learning a common language(s) in order to permit intercultural participation among all groups.

Most recently (2011), the Canadian Federal Government has asserted that:

Integration is a two-way process, requiring adjustment on the part of both newcomers and host communities ... the successful integration of permanent residents into Canada involves mutual obligations for new immigrants and Canadian society. Ultimately, the goal is to support newcomers to become fully engaged in the social, economic, political, and cultural life of Canada. (p. 2)

Together, and by balancing these components, it should be possible to achieve the core goal of the policy: the improvement of intercultural relations in Canada, where all groups and individuals have a place, both within their own heritage environment and within the larger society. In this sense, multiculturalism is for everyone, not only for non-dominant groups. This aspect emphasizes that all groups and individuals are engaged in a process of cultural and psychological change. Research on the acceptance of this policy, and its various programmes, shows a high level of support in Canada (Berry, 2013; Berry, Kalin, & Taylor, 1977; Berry & Kalin, 2000; see also Adams, 2007, and Kymlicka, 2007).

The European Union adopted a set of "Common Basic Principles for Immigrant Integration" in 2005. The first of these principles is:

Integration is a dynamic, two-way process of mutual accommodation by all immigrants and residents of Member States. Integration is a dynamic, long-term, and continuous two-way process of mutual accommodation, not a static outcome. It demands the participation not only of immigrants and their descendants but of every resident. The integration process involves adaptation by immigrants, both men and women, who all have rights and responsibilities in relation to their new country of residence. It also involves the receiving society, which should create the opportunities for the immigrants' full economic, social, cultural, and political participation. Accordingly, Member States are encouraged to consider and involve both immigrants and national citizens in integration policy, and to communicate clearly their mutual rights and responsibilities. (p. 6)

While little-known and even less well-accepted, this EU statement contains the three cornerstones of multiculturalism: the right of all peoples to maintain their cultures; the right to participate fully in the life of the larger society; and the obligation for all groups (both the dominant and non-dominant) to engage in a process of mutual change. Research on the acceptance of this policy in Europe has only just begun. However, there is some indication (e.g., van de Vijver et al., 2008) that Europeans make a clear distinction between the right of immigrants to maintain their cultures in *private* (i.e., in their families and communities), and the right to expect changes to the *public* culture of the society of settlement. In much of this research, it was found that it is acceptable to express one's heritage culture in the family and in the community, but that it should not be expressed in the public domains, such as in educational or work institutions. This view is opposed to the basic principles outlined by the European Union, where the process is identified as one of mutual accommodation.

However, in much of Europe, there is a common misunderstanding that multiculturalism means only the presence of many non-dominant cultural communities in a society (i.e., only the cultural maintenance component), without their equitable participation and incorporation into a larger society. It is this erroneous view that has led some in Europe to declare that "Multiculturalism has failed" (Berry & Sam, 2013). However, from the perspective of the Canadian Multiculturalism policy, it has not failed because it has not even been tried!

I have been involved in the examination and evaluation of the Canadian Multiculturalism Policy on two previous occasions. The first evaluation (Berry, 1984) was ten years after the policy was first announced. In that evaluation, I proposed that a number of core policy elements (and linkages among elements) formed a coherent set of social psychological concepts, principles and hypotheses. Ten years later (Berry & Laponce, 1994), I co-edited a volume that included essays that examined a number of facets of the policy.

From the original policy statement, I discerned a number of ideas that were ripe for social psychological examination; Figure 1 portrays some of these (from Berry, 1984). The clear and fundamental goal of the policy is to enhance mutual acceptance and to improve intercultural relations among all ethnocultural groups (upper right). This goal is to be approached through three programme components. On the upper left is the *cultural* component of the policy, which is to be achieved by providing support and encouragement for cultural maintenance and development among all ethnocultural groups. The second component is the *social* (or *intercultural*) component (lower left), which seeks to support the sharing of cultural expressions, by providing opportunities for intergroup contact, and the removal of barriers to full and equitable participation in the daily life of the larger society. The last feature is the *intercultural communication* component, in the lower right corner of Figure 1. This represents the bilingual reality of the larger society of Canada, and promotes the learning of one or both Official Languages (English and French) as a means for all ethnocultural groups to interact with each other, and to participate in national life.

In addition to these four components, there are links among them. The first, termed the *multiculturalism hypothesis,* is expressed in the policy statement as the belief that confidence in one's identity will lead to sharing, to respect for others, and to the reduction of discriminatory attitudes. Berry, Kalin and Taylor (1977) identified this belief as an assumption with psychological roots, and as being amenable to empirical evaluation.

A second link in Figure 1 is the hypothesis that when individuals and groups are "doubly engaged" (in both their heritage cultures and in the larger society), they will be more successful in their lives. This is essentially a higher level of wellbeing, in both psychological and social domains. This is the *integration hypothesis,* in which involvement with, and competence in both cultural communities provides the social capital to succeed in intercultural living in plural societies.

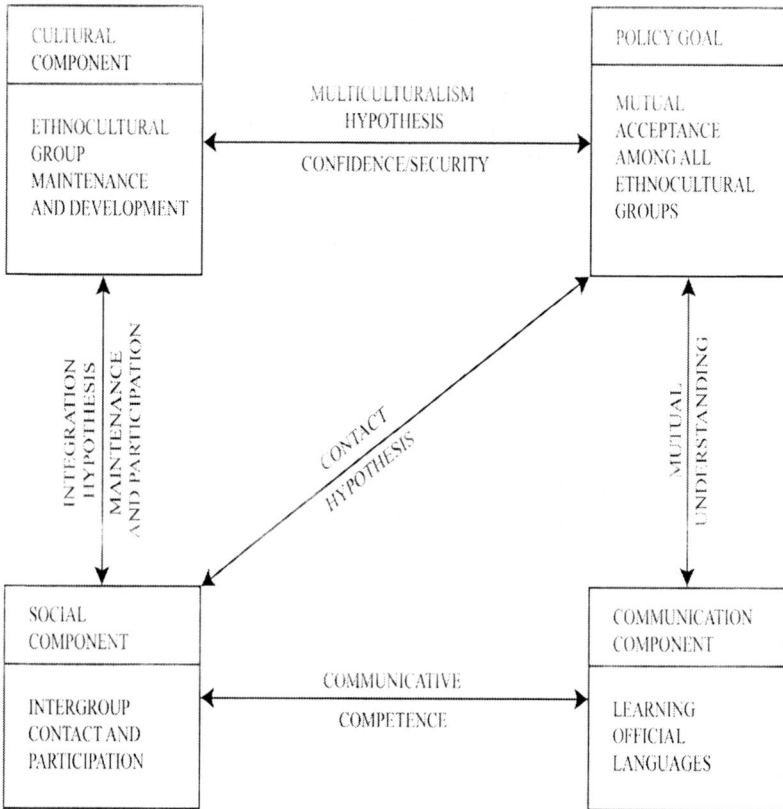

Figure 1. Components and linkages in the Canadian Multiculturalism Policy (from Berry 1984).

A third link portrayed in Figure 1 is the *contact hypothesis*, by which contact and sharing is considered to promote mutual acceptance under certain conditions, including especially that of equality and voluntariness of contact.

All three hypotheses are now being examined in over 20 plural societies around the world (such as Australia, Brazil, Canada, China, Germany, India, Indonesia, and Russia). The project is called Mutual Intercultural Relations in Plural Societies (http://www.victoria.ac.nz/cacr/research/mirips). Guided by these hypotheses, the purpose of this research is to discover whether there are any regularities in how individuals and groups engage each other interculturally. And if there are, can some general principles be discerned that will assist plural societies to develop and implement policies and programmes that will improve their intercultural relations.

INTERCULTURAL STRATEGIES

The question of *how* groups and individuals engage in their intercultural relations has come to be examined with the concept of *intercultural strategies*. Four ways of engaging in intercultural relations have been derived from two basic issues facing all peoples in culturally plural societies. These issues are based on the distinction between orientations towards one's own group, and those towards other groups (Berry, 1974; 1980). This distinction is rendered as a relative preference for (1) maintaining one's heritage culture and identity, and (2) a relative preference for having contact with and participating in the larger society along with other ethnocultural groups. These are the same two issues that underlie the multiculturalism policies outlined above (i.e., the "cultural" and the "social" components).

These two issues can be responded to on attitudinal dimensions, ranging from generally positive or negative orientations to these issues; their intersection defines four strategies, portrayed in Figure 2. On the left are the orientations from the point of view of ethnocultural peoples (of both groups and individuals); on the right are the views held by the larger society (such as public policies and public attitudes).

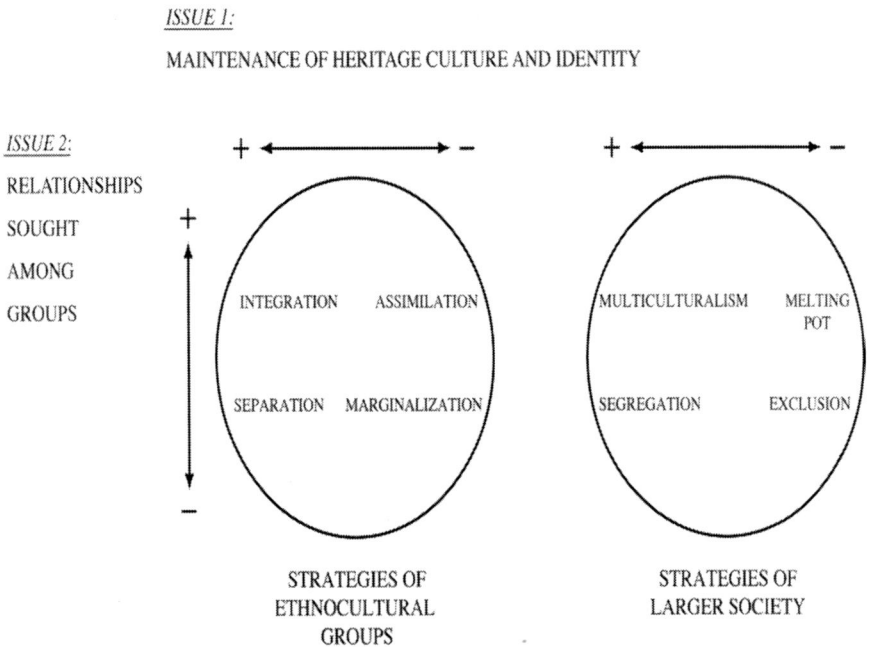

Figure 2. Varieties of intercultural strategies in ethnocultural groups and in the larger society.

42

Among ethnocultural groups, when they do not wish to maintain their cultural identity and seek daily interaction with other cultures, the Assimilation strategy is defined. In contrast, when individuals place a value on holding on to their original culture, and at the same time wish to avoid interaction with others, then the Separation alternative is defined. When there is an interest in both maintaining ones original culture, while in daily interactions with other groups, Integration is the option. In this case, there is some degree of cultural *integrity* maintained, while at the same time seeking, as a member of an ethnocultural group, to participate as an *integral* part of the larger social network. Finally, when there is little possibility or interest in cultural maintenance (often for reasons of forced cultural loss), and little engagement with the larger society (often for reasons of exclusion or discrimination), then Marginalization is defined.

These two basic issues were initially approached from the point of view of the non-dominant ethnocultural groups. However, there is a powerful role played by the dominant group in influencing the way in which ethnocultural individuals' groups would relate (Berry, 1974). The addition of the views of the larger society produces the right side of Figure 2. From the point of view of the larger society, Assimilation when sought by the dominant group is termed the Melting Pot. When Separation is forced by the dominant group, it is called Segregation. Marginalisation, when imposed by the dominant group, is termed Exclusion. Finally, when both diversity maintenance and equitable participation are widely-accepted features of the society as a whole, Integration is called Multiculturalism.

It is important to emphasize that within this framework, the concept of *integration* involves engagement with *both* cultures. It is not a euphemism for assimilation, which involves engagement with only the larger society; that is, cultural maintenance is a core part of the concept of integration. And the concept of *multiculturalism* does not refer to engagement only within their own ethnocultural groups (i.e., separation); members of these communities also engage with, and become constituents of, the larger society.

These intercultural strategies are related to a number of psychological and social factors. The most important is the discrimination experienced by an individual; less discrimination is usually reported by those opting for integration and assimilation, while more is experienced by those opting for separation or marginalization (see Berry, Phinney, Sam, & Vedder, 2006). This is an example of the reciprocity of intercultural attitudes found in the literature (Berry, 2006); if persons (such as immigrants or members of ethnocultural groups) feel rejected by others in the larger society, they reciprocate this rejection by choosing a strategy that avoids contact with others outside their own group.

We now examine three hypotheses that lie at the core of intercultural relations research: the *multiculturalism hypothesis,* the *integration hypothesis,* and the *contact hypothesis.* As we shall see, they are very much inter-related, each one influencing the conditions under which the others may be supported by empirical evidence.

MULTICULTURALISM HYPOTHESIS

The multicultural vision enunciated in Canada in 1971 had a key section with implications for research on intercultural relations. Berry et al. (1977) developed the *multiculturalism hypothesis*, based on the assertion in the policy that freedom from discrimination "must be founded on confidence in one's own individual identity" (Government of Canada, 1971, p. 1121). The basic notion is that only when people are secure in their identities will they be in a position to accept those who differ from them; conversely, when people feel threatened, they will develop prejudice and engage in discrimination (see also Stephan et al. 2005). The *multiculturalism hypothesis* is thus: only when people are secure in their own identity will they be in a position to accept those who differ from them (ie. when there is no threat to their culture and identity).

There is now substantial evidence to support this hypothesis. For example, in two national surveys in Canada (Berry et al., 1977; Berry & Kalin, 2000), measures of cultural security/threat and economic security/threat were created with respect to extant diversity and the continuing flow of immigration. These two security scores were correlated positively with each other and with various intercultural attitudes. Cultural security was negatively correlated with ethnocentrism, and positively with multicultural ideology and with perceived consequences of multiculturalism. Economic security had a similar pattern of correlations with these variables. In New Zealand, using a structural model, Ward and Masgoret (2008) found that security was positively related to multicultural ideology and with attitudes towards immigrants. In Russia, Lebedeva and Tatarko (2012) studied migrants from the Cacausus to Moscow and resident Muscovites. They found that cultural security predicted tolerance, integration and social equality in both groups, but to a lesser extent among Muscovites. Most recently, a representative sample of Russian speakers in Estonia was asked about their intercultural strategies, their ethnic self-esteem, their experience of discrimination, and their level of cultural threat, civic engagement and economic and political satisfaction (Kruusvall, Vetik, & Berry, 2009). The four usual intercultural strategies were found. Groups following the separation and marginalization strategies had the highest levels of threat and lowest levels of self-esteem and civic engagement. In contrast, the integration and assimilation groups had the lowest threat and discrimination, and highest civic engagement and satisfaction. Public policy attempts in Estonia (which are largely assimilationist) seek to make the Russian-speaking population "more Estonian," while placing barriers to achieving this. Such a policy appears to have led to the development of a "reactive identity" among Russian-speakers, and their turning away from the country of Estonia.

From this sampling of empirical studies, it is possible to conclude that security in one's own identity underlies the possibility of accepting "others." This acceptance includes being tolerant, accepting cultural diversity in society, and accepting immigrants to, and ethnocultural groups in, that society. In contrast, threatening an individual's or a group's identity and place in a plural society is likely to lead to hostility.

INTEGRATION HYPOTHESIS

In much research on intercultural relations, the integration strategy has often been found to be the strategy that leads to better adaptation than other strategies (Berry, 1997). A possible explanation is that those who are "doubly engaged" with both cultures receive support and resources from both, and are competent in dealing with both cultures. The social capital afforded by these multiple social and cultural engagements may well offer the route to success in plural societies. The evidence for integration being associated with better adaptation has been reviewed (Berry, 2011). More recently, Nguyen and Benet-Martínez (2013) carried out a meta-analysis across 83 studies and over 20,000 participants. They found that integration ("biculturalism" in their terms) was found to have a significant and positive relationship with both psychological adaptation (e.g., life satisfaction, positive affect, self-esteem) and sociocultural adaptation (e.g., academic achievement, career success, social skills, lack of behavioral problems).

These general relationships have been further examined in some specific contrasts between societies that have different immigration and settlement policies. In one, second- generation immigrant youth in Canada and France were compared (Berry & Sabatier, 2010). The national public policy and attitude context was found to influence the young immigrants' acculturation strategies and the relationship with their adaptation. In France, there was more discrimination, less orientation to their heritage culture (identity, behaviour), and poorer adaptation (lower self-esteem and higher deviance). Within both samples, integration was found to be associated with better adaptation, and marginalisation with poorer adaptation. However, the magnitude of this relationship was less pronounced in France than in Canada. This difference was interpreted as a result of it being more psychologically costly to express one's ethnicity in France than in Canada, and to be related to differences in national policy and practices.

Overall, it is now clear that when individuals are engaged in both their heritage cultures and (are accepted in) the larger society, there are higher levels of both psychological and sociocultural wellbeing. The integration hypothesis is now well supported in comparative research.

CONTACT HYPOTHESIS

The *contact hypothesis* asserts that "Prejudice ... may be reduced by equal status contact between majority and minority groups in the pursuit of common goals" (Allport, 1954, p.12). However, Allport proposed that the hypothesis is more likely to be supported when certain conditions are present in the intercultural encounter. The effect of contact is predicted to be stronger when: there is contact between groups of roughly equal social and economic status; when the contact is voluntary (sought by both groups, rather than imposed); and when supported by society through norms and laws promoting contact and prohibiting discrimination. A good deal of research has been carried out to test this hypothesis. In a massive comparative examination, Pettigrew and Tropp (2011) conducted a meta-analysis of hundreds of studies of the contact hypothesis, which came from many countries and many diverse settings (schools, work, experiments). Their findings provide general support for the contact hypothesis: intergroup contact does generally relate negatively to prejudice in both dominant and non-dominant samples: overall, the results from the meta-analysis reveal that greater levels of intergroup contact are typically associated with lower level of prejudice. This effect was stronger where there were structured programs that incorporated the conditions outlined by Allport than when these conditions were not present.

One remaining issue is whether the association between intercultural contact and positive attitudes is due to situations where those individuals with positive attitudes seek more intercultural contact, or whether more such contact leads to more positive attitudes. In the national surveys in Canada, we found substantial support for this relationship, especially when status is controlled. For example, Kalin and Berry (1982), using data from a national survey in Canada, examined the ethnic attitudes of members of particular ethnocultural groups towards members of other ethnocultural groups. Their attitude data were aggregated by census tracts (essentially neighbourhoods), in which the proportion of particular ethnocultural groups was also known from the Census. They found that the higher the proportion of members of a particular group in a neighbourhood, the more positive were the attitudes of non-members towards that group. This kind of ecological analysis permits the suggestion that contact actually leads to more positive intercultural attitudes. The alternative possibility is that individuals actually move to particular neighbourhoods where already-liked ethnocultural groups are residing. More such research is needed, and in other intercultural settings, before firm conclusions can be drawn.

Longitudinal studies are very important to the disentangling of the direction of the relationship between intercultural contact and attitudes. One study (Binder et al., 2009) has shown an interactive effect of contact and intercultural attitudes. They conducted a longitudinal field survey in Germany, Belgium, and England with school student samples of members of both ethnic minorities and ethnic majorities. They assessed both intercultural contact and attitudes at two points in time. Contact was assessed by both the quality and quantity of contact. Attitudes were assessed by social distance and negative feelings. The pattern of intercorrelations, at both times, supported the positive relationship between contact and attitudes. Beyond this correlational analysis, path analyses yielded evidence for the relationship working in both directions: contact reduced prejudice, but prejudice also reduced contact. Thus, in this study, support for the contact hypothesis is partial: contact can lead to more positive attitudes, but initial positive attitudes can lead people into contact with each other.

A key element in the contact hypothesis is the set of conditions that may be necessary in order for contact to lead to more positive intercultural relations. The three hypotheses are linked because the first two hypotheses speak to some of these conditions under which contact can have positive outcomes. First, for the multiculturalism hypothesis, we saw that when the cultural identities of individuals and groups are threatened, and their place in the plural society is questioned, more negative attitudes are likely to characterize their relationships. This consequence applies to all ethnocultural groups, both dominant and non-dominant. For example, when members of the larger society feel threatened by immigration, and when members of particular groups have their rights to maintain their heritage cultures and/or to participate in the larger society questioned or denied, a mutual hostility is likely to ensue. Under these conditions, increased contact is not likely to lead to more positive intercultural attitudes.

Second, for the integration hypothesis, we saw that "double engagement" (that is, maintaining contact with, and participating in both the heritage culture and the larger society) is associated with better wellbeing, including greater self-esteem and life satisfaction. When psychological and social wellbeing are low (that is, when confidence in one's identity is low) there can be little basis for engaging in intercultural contact. And when contact does occur, as we saw for the multiculturalism hypothesis, it is likely to lead to more hostile mutual attitudes.

The evidence is now widespread across cultures that greater intercultural contact is associated with more positive intercultural attitudes, and lower levels of prejudice. This generalisation has to be qualified by two cautions. First, the appropriate conditions need to be present in order for contact to lead to positive intercultural attitudes. And second, there exists many examples of the opposite effect, where increased contact is associated with greater conflict. The conditions (cultural, political, economic) under which these opposite outcomes arise are in urgent need of examination.

CONCLUSION

Intercultural relations research has been guided by a number of concepts, and has resulted in a number of findings. First, we always need to understand the cultural underpinnings of individual human behaviour; no person develops or acts in a cultural vacuum. Second, in addition to examining these hypotheses in Canada, we need to carry out research comparatively; research findings from one cultural or social setting alone are never a valid basis for understanding intercultural behaviour in another setting. Comparative research is also required if we are to achieve an understanding of some general principles that underpin intercultural behaviour. Third, policies and programs for improving intercultural relations take many forms. Some have been shown to threaten individuals and groups, and provide the conditions that generate mutual hostility. Conversely, there are policies and programs (termed integration and multicultural in this paper) that appear to provide the cultural and psychological bases for enhancing positive intercultural relations.

Plural societies now have the possibility to use concepts, hypotheses and findings from research to guide the development and implementation of policies and programmes that will improve intercultural relations. This way forward stands in sharp contrast to using preconceptions and prejudices that are currently often the basis for intercultural policies. In my experience, policymakers would usually prefer to make informed decisions which are more likely to achieve their goals in the long run, than are decisions based on short-term interests. As researchers, we now have the opportunity to provide the information required for such effective policy decisions, and in a form that can be used.

REFERENCES

Adams, M. (2007). *Unlikely utopia: The surprising triumph of Canadian pluralism.* Toronto: Viking.

Allport, G. W. (1954). *The nature of prejudice.* Reading, MA: Addison-Wesley.

Berry, J. W. (1974). Psychological aspects of cultural pluralism: Unity and identity reconsidered. *Topics in Culture Learning, 2*(1), 17-22.

Berry, J. W. (1980). Acculturation as varieties of adaptation. In A. Padilla (Ed.), *Acculturation: Theory, models and some new findings* (pp. 9-25). Boulder, CO: Westview.

Berry, J. W. (1984). Multicultural policy in Canada: A social psychological analysis. *Canadian Journal of Behavioural Science, 16*(4), 353-370.

Berry, J. W. (1997). Immigration, acculturation and adaptation. *Applied Psychology: An International Review, 46*(1), 5-68.

Berry, J. W. (2006). Attitudes towards immigrants and ethnocultural groups in Canada. *International Journal of Intercultural Relations, 30*(6), 719-734.

Berry, J. W. (2011). Immigrant acculturation: Psychological and social adaptations. In A. Assaad (Ed.), *Identity and political participation* (pp. 279-295). London: Wiley.

Berry, J. W. (2013). Research on multiculturalism in Canada. *International Journal of Intercultural Relations, 37*(6), 663–675.

Berry, J. W., & Kalin, R. (2000). Multicultural policy and social psychology: The Canadian experience. In S. Renshon & Duckitt, J. (Eds.), *Political psychology in cross-cultural perspective* (pp. 263-284). New York: MacMillan.

Berry, J. W., & Laponce, J. A. (Eds.) (1994). *Ethnicity and culture in Canada: The research landscape.* Toronto: University of Toronto Press.

Berry, J. W., & Sabatier, C. (2010). Acculturation, discrimination, and adaptation among second generation immigrant youth in Montreal and Paris. *International Journal of Intercultural Relation, 34*(3), 191-207.

Berry, J. W., & Sam, D. L. (2013). Accommodating cultural diversity and achieving equity: An introduction to psychological dimensions of multiculturalism. *European Psychologist, 18*(3), 151-157.

Berry, J. W., Kalin, R., & Taylor, D. (1977). *Multiculturalism and ethnic attitudes in Canada.* Ottawa: Ministry of Supply and Services.

Berry, J. W., Phinney, J. S., Sam, D., & Vedder, P. (Eds.) (2006). *Immigrant youth in cultural transitions: Acculturation, identity, and adaptation across national contexts.* Mahwah, NJ: Erlbaum.

Berry, J. W., Poortinga, Y. H., Brugelmans, S., Chasiotis, A., & Sam, D. L. (2011). *Cross-cultural psychology: Research and applications.* Cambridge: Cambridge University Press.

Binder, J., Zagefka, H., Brown, R., Funke, F., Kessler, T., Mummendey, A., Maquil, A., Demoulin, S., & Leyens, J. (2009). Does contact reduce prejudice or does prejudice reduce contact? A longitudinal test of the contact hypothesis among majority and minority groups in three European countries. *Journal of Personality and Social Psychology, 96*(4), 843-856.

European Union. (2005). *Common basic principles for immigrant integration policy in the EU.* Brussels: Author. Retrieved from: www.iccsi.ie/resources/EU%20Basic%20Principles.

Government of Canada. (1971). *Multicultural policy: Statement to House of Commons.* Ottawa: Canada

Government of Canada, Citizenship and Immigration (2011). *Statement on integration.* Ottawa: Canada

Kalin, R., & Berry, J.W. (1982). Social ecology of ethnic attitudes in Canada. *Canadian Journal of Behavioural Science, 14*(1), 97-109.

Kruusvall, J., Vetik, R., & Berry, J.W. (2009) The strategies of inter-ethnic adaptation of Estonian – Russians. *Studies of Transition States and Societies, 1*(1), 3-24.

Kymlicka, W. (2007). *Multicultural Odysseys: Navigating the new international politics of diversity.* Oxford: Oxford University Press.

Lebedeva, N., & Tatarko, A. (2012). Immigration and intercultural interaction strategies in post-Soviet Russia. In E. Tartakovsky (Ed.), *Immigration: Policies, Challenges and impacts* (pp. 179-192). New York: Nova Science Publishers.

Nguyen, H. (2006). Acculturation in the United States. In D. L. Sam & J. W. Berry (Eds.), *Cambridge handbook of acculturation psychology* (pp. 311-330). Cambridge: Cambridge University Press.

Nguyen, H., & Benet-Martinez, V. (2013). Biculturalism and wellbeing: A meta-analysis. *Journal of Cross-Cultural Psychology, 44*(1), 122-159.

Pettigrew, T., & Tropp, L. (2011). *When groups meet.* London: Psychology Press.

Sabatier, C., & Boutry, V. (2006). Acculturation in francophone European countries. In D. L. Sam & J. W. Berry (Eds.), *Cambridge handbook of acculturation psychology* (pp. 349-367). Cambridge: Cambridge University Press.

Sam, D. L., & Berry, J.W. (Eds.). (2006). *Handbook of acculturation psychology.* Cambridge: Cambridge University Press.

Stephan, W., Renfro, C. L., Esses, V., Stephan, C., & Martin, T. (2005). The effects of feeling threatened on attitudes toward immigrants. *International Journal of Intercultural Relations, 29*(1), 1-19.

van de Vijver, F. J. R., Breugelmans, S. M., & Schalk-Soekar, S. (2008). Multiculturalism: Construct validity and stability. *International Journal of Intercultural Relations, 32*(2), 93-104.

Ward, C., & Masgoret, A-M. (2008). Attitudes toward immigrants, immigration, and multiculturalism in New Zealand: A social psychological analysis. *International Migration Review, 42*(1), 222-243.

John W. Berry
Queen's University, Kingston, Canada, and
National Research University, Moscow, Russia

49

ELKE WINTER

3. A CANADIAN ANOMALY?

The Social Construction of Multicultural National Identity

INTRODUCTION[1]

In many countries, it has become increasingly popular to blame multiculturalism for all sorts of societal ailments (Vertovec & Wessendorf, 2009). Fears have been growing about "home-grown terrorism" and the "lack of integration" of immigrants and their children. Canada, by contrast, is one of the few countries that still subscribes to multiculturalism as a normative framework of immigrant integration. First enacted in 1971, Canada's policy of multiculturalism came into full force with the Multiculturalism Act of 1988. Legal support for multiculturalism was further enshrined in Canada's Constitution, signed in 1982. Designed to protect individual and collective rights, Section 27 requires that Canada's Charter of Rights and Freedoms "be interpreted in a manner consistent with the preservation of and enhancement of the multicultural heritage of Canadians" (Canada, 1982).

Admittedly, even in Canada, the success of multiculturalism is not undisputed. Social inequalities along ethnocultural lines persist (Galabuzi, 2006) and some commentators view multiculturalism as a strategy of cementing White supremacy and domination (Bannerji, 2000). Nevertheless, it must be underlined that, as a social fact, multiculturalism has become a reality in Canada. At present, 20% of the Canadian population – namely 6.2 million people are foreign-born. They have come from over 200 countries and speak 94 different languages (Statistics Canada, 2006). At the policy level, multiculturalism has been enshrined in law and even in the Constitution. Finally, as an ethos or normative framework for constructing society and national identity, multiculturalism's success in the Canadian context is perhaps most strongly demonstrated by the utter lack of any anti-immigrant right-wing parties. Although, as I will argue below, the current Conservative government is reintroducing a more nationalist understanding of Canadian citizenship and immigrant integration, it has been careful not to pursue these goals overtly (Abu-Laban, 2014).

In this chapter, I will scrutinize the much-touted relationship between Québécois nationalism and multiculturalism and the ways in which representations of this relationship have evolved over the past two decades. I will argue that the component that best explains the consolidation of multiculturalism as dominant discourse of national identity in the 1990s was the conflict between the country's two linguistically defined "founding nations." I will then show that the revival of

S. Guo & L. Wong (eds.), Revisiting Multiculturalism in Canada. 51–68.

nationalist discourse and the redefinition of multiculturalism in fairly shallow individualist terms in the early 2000s are accompanied by a relative absence of Québécois nationalism. In the next section, I will briefly locate my theoretical approach. I will then examine multiculturalist discourses in the 1990s. Next, I will discuss the new language of groups and Community, which has lost much of its earlier sympathy for ethnocultural diversity among minority groups.

HOW TO EXPLAIN MULTICULTURALISM'S RESILIENCE IN THE CANADIAN CONTEXT?

Some scholars have argued that the solidification of multiculturalism as a national identity discourse during the 1990s can be explained by "changing times:" increasing ethno-racial diversity within the Canadian population, successful demands for and enshrining of minority rights, and changing values over generations (Harell, 2009). Canada's geographic location, historical immigration patterns, and the specific categories of immigrants attracted to the country have also been suggested as causal factors for the initial rise of multiculturalism, in the Canadian context (Kymlicka, 2004). Furthermore, it has been pointed out that, in Canada, immigrants are quickly given permanent residence, citizenship status and voting rights (Bloemraad, 2006).

Other scholars credit the tumultuous but gradual accommodation and coexistence of three distinct minority groups over time with forging a national identity and notion of citizenship founded on multiculturalism. In this equation, demands for recognition of nationhood and distinctness asserted by Aboriginal peoples and Francophones (specifically those living in the province of Quebec) amount to the construction of a multi-national society (Kymlicka, 1995), while the policy of multiculturalism is deployed to incorporate ethnic groups of immigrant origin. David Cameron, for example, argues that "the experience of a country with a profound ethnocultural division [...] equipped Canadians with the capacity to accommodate the [factual] multiculturalism that is the product of postwar immigration" (Cameron, 2007, p. 80). Multiculturalism is here viewed as being a part of a wider set of pluralist arrangements within Canadian society. Similarly, the theoretical framework adopted here states that different types of diversity – although analytically distinct – are highly interdependent in practice. Being incorporated as traditions within the organization of the nation-state, historic group relations define the cognitive and moral horizon for reinventions of a "multicultural we."

In addition, as I have shown with respect to the Netherlands and Germany (Winter, 2010), a contemporary component of limited conflict between dominant groups is necessary to explain ongoing support for multiculturalism: be it tensions among nationalist groups, minority rights movements or other demands for recognition. On the condition that struggles between the established groups are peaceful and democratic, such movements can successfully challenge notions of cultural homogeneity on the national level and help paving the ground for the multicultural integration of immigrant communities. By contrast, when the nature of the agreement between the established groups changes – even tips over in enmity or moves to stronger agreement – the horizon of normatively accepted possibilities for newcomer accommodation – such as multiculturalism – is also altered. A caveat: obviously reality is never shaped by a single cause, but within the scope of this paper, I only have space for one line of argument.

THE CONSOLIDATION OF MULTICULTURALISM IN DOMINANT DISCOURSES

If we look at polling numbers for the past 30 years, we can see that support for multiculturalism among the Canadian public was at its lowest point during the 1990s (see Figure 1).[2] These dropping numbers gave cause for a review of the multiculturalism program that was commissioned in 1995 by Jean Chretien's Liberal government. In 1997-1998 a new multiculturalism program was announced in response to what has become known as the Brighton Report. This new program reduced the multiculturalism budget from its peak during the early 1990s at $27 million down to $18.7 million, restricted funding for minority groups, and subsumed the expression of ethnocultural diversity under the notion of shared Canadian identity (Abu-Laban & Gabriel, 2002, p. 15).

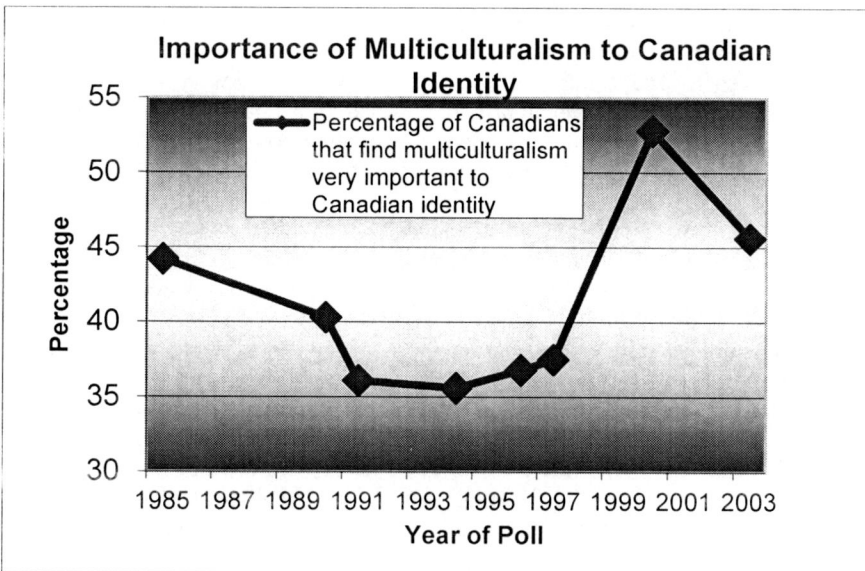

Figure 1. Importance of multiculturalism to Canadian identity (1985–2003).

At the same time, however, public support for immigration, ethnic and racial diversity, and multiculturalism had been growing steadily over the 1990s (Harell, 2009). Whereas criticism of multiculturalism effectively derailed programs in Australia and the Netherlands at the start of the decade, only a short-lived downturn in public support was seen in Canada (see Figure 1), which was then followed by a rise to historic heights in 2002-2003 (Kymlicka, 2004, p. 843). Support levels continued to be above their pre-1990s levels in 2006-2007. Karim summarizes the paradoxical leanings concisely: "as the bureaucratic target for anti-multiculturalism attacks has shrunk, Canada is increasingly described as a multicultural country in current dominant discourses" (2002, p. 454).

This bears the question: what happened in Canada in the mid-1990s? In fact, this was the moment when the country was paralyzed with mounting tensions between Canada's so-called founding nations, the predominantly French-speaking Quebec population and the overwhelmingly English-speaking population in the remaining provinces. It is certainly no mere "coincidence" that the Quebec referendum on independence of 1995 occurred at the same time as the public endorsement of multiculturalism as the dominant discourse on national identity (Karim, 2002). The 1995 referendum was the second such attempt to find a definitive resolution to festering tensions between the Québécois and the rest of Canada. Held fifteen years after the first plebiscite, the 1995 vote for sovereignty was defeated by less than 1%, with 50.6% of voters casting a "No" ballot against 49.4% who voted "Yes."

Although the conflict between nationalists in Quebec and English Canada might have caused another wave of criticism against multiculturalism, the opposite was the case: support for multiculturalism, lowest in 1995, rebounded quickly in the following years. The latter half of the 1990s even saw a resurrection of multiculturalism in governmental discourse, albeit with a dubious new dimension – as a means of enhancement for Canada's economic competitiveness and global prominence as a leader in diversity management (Abu-Laban & Gabriel, 2002, p. 117).

Let's take a closer look at what happened to multiculturalism as a national identity discourse in the 1990s. Traditionally, Quebec tended to be represented as a national minority that is at the heart of Canadian identity and that needs to be accommodated by "typically Canadian" pluralist compromise and concessions. Both were said to distinguish the "Canadian" way of dealing with ethnic diversity from the "American" one. With respect to multiculturalism, Quebec was then overwhelmingly represented as a predecessor of diversity proliferation with contradictory normative connotations: For commentators closer to the political right, all group rights, whether relating to Francophones or immigrants – such as "official bilingualism and its fraternal twin, official multiculturalism" (Thorsell, 1992) – were suspect, as they are seen as being at the heart of centrifugal powers undermining social cohesion. The image evoked was that of a deadly spiral towards fragmentation/identity politics and the destruction of society.

By contrast, commentators located closer to the political centre and left argued that the historical compromises reached to accommodate Quebec's cultural and linguistic difference have helped to prepare the rest of Canada to deal with the challenges of newer sources of ethnocultural diversity, particularly those that are produced through immigration at a time of globalization (i.e. the "cultural distance" and variety of sending countries (see Cameron, 2007).

In the years leading up to the 1995 referendum, Québécois separatist nationalism – as opposed to the simple notion of "the French fact'"– came to be regarded more and more as the enfant terrible of Canadian multiculturalism. References to Quebec started to serve not only to point out the "root cause" for social disintegration, but also operate as an "awful example" of what multiculturalism as a normative framework for dealing with ethnocultural diversity may lead to (Gwyn, 1993a). In the Canadian English-language media, francophone Quebec was identified as an inferior "Other," its difference was naturalized, and its population seemed vulnerable to the conspiracy and irrational appeals of political agitators (Potvin, 2000). English Canadians, by contrast, were portrayed as having superior (rational and universalist) institutions and as having created "the best country in the world" (Lacombe, 1998, p. 278).

The rejection of "ethnic nationalism" gained particular salience against the backdrop of international events, such as the rise of nationalisms in the former Soviet Union after the fall of the Berlin Wall in 1989, the 1994 Rwandan genocide, and ethnic cleansing during the 1996–99 Kosovo war. At the same time, from the perspective of many European countries, finally accepting the fact that refugees and former guest workers were there to stay, Canada gained a reputation as "the place where multiculturalism actually worked." These external factors contributed to rendering the expression of nostalgia for Anglo-conformity within representations of Canadian identity increasingly unpopular.

On the domestic front, the potential scenario of a separating Quebec and the growing number of immigrants from a variety of source countries produced a situation where English Canadians were in desperate need of rethinking their national identity beyond expressions of mono-culturalism (Resnick, 1994). In this context, the notion of a "multicultural Canada" gained new appeal. On the one hand, a seemingly ethnoculturally oppressive Quebec is no longer viewed as the (positively or negatively connoted) predecessor of multiculturalism, but rather constructed as the mirror image of the nation that English Canada wants to be and/or stands for. On the other hand, compared with a hostile, French-speaking, and potentially separating Quebec, the claims for cultural maintenance and non-discrimination by English-speaking (-learning) immigrants did appear harmless and "integrative."

In the period that followed the referendum, English Canadian attitudes vis-à-vis Quebec hardened (Lacombe, 1998; Potvin, 2000). The referendum's narrow defeat sent a shock wave through the rest of Canada. The "Parizeau gaffe" – Quebec's premier blaming "money and the ethnic vote" for the loss of the referendum – reinforced the image of a fundamental difference between Quebec and the rest of Canada. At a time of political adversary, the long-standing images of a Québécois *Gemeinschaft* (community) and a Canadian English-speaking *Gesellschaft* (society) – to paraphrase a well-respected Canadian political scientist (Meisel, 1999, p. 113) – became exacerbated. While Quebec was increasingly described as a narrow-minded "ethnic nation" (Globe and Mail, 1995), the rest of Canada was portrayed as an open, tolerant "multi-ethnic World Nation" (Gwyn, 1993b).

The publication of Will Kymlicka's influential *Multicultural Citizenship* in 1995 gave academic authority to the widely shared impression that the multicultural rights demanded by immigrant groups and ethnic associations were indeed fundamentally different from the "self-government rights" claimed by the Franco-Québécois and, in a less threatening way, by Canada's First Nations. The paradigm change within the academy was echoed in public discourse and also made its way into mainstream media representations of Canadian diversity. In academia, Kymlicka's theory has been criticized for privileging minority nations. In Canadian public discourse, however, his distinction was increasingly used to distance ethnic groups of immigrant origin from the potentially secessionist intentions of minority nations – and thus to liberate them from the stigma of causing "social fragmentation" (Winter, 2011a, chapter 8).

In addition, Kymlicka's scholarly distinction was forcefully underlined by Canadians' experience with the so-called "ethnic vote" in the 1995 Quebec referendum on sovereignty. While Quebec's premier had to resign over his ill-suited comments in the referendum night, 95% of Quebec's non-francophone population voted indeed against separation (as opposed to 60% of Franco-Québécois). The voting pattern in the 1995 referendum was a powerful example of both the "destructive" potential of a self-government demanding minority nation, on the one hand, and the "unifying" pan-Canadianism expressed by Canadians of immigrant origin, on the other. The symbolic importance of this widely recognized demonstration of loyalty to Canada should not be underestimated. It fed into a new political assertiveness of "ethnic Canadians" of immigrant origin, primarily in Canada's major cities. Underlining the many contributions that immigrants – new Canadians as well as those who are not (yet) Canadian citizens – make to Canadian society, in the city of Toronto, for example, initiatives are currently under way to provide non-citizens with local voting rights.

Elsewhere I suggest that this change in public discourse is highlighted in two ways (Winter, 2011a, chapter 9). First, in Canada's largest local newspaper, the *Toronto Star*, a new strand of discourse emerges which interprets issues of national identity and ethnic diversity from a non-French-, non-English-Canadian perspective and promotes a national self-understanding that embraces liberal multiculturalism. Second, within mainstream newspaper discourses, the idea of a multicultural Canada becomes accepted, and this even by critics that previously rejected all types of "groupism" and drew parallels between Franco-Québécois and ethnic groups. Not surprisingly, mainstream newspaper discourses continue to expose different views as to who is unconditionally included within the "Canadian we" and which groups should be "grateful" for being accommodated. Nevertheless, these views converge in their rejection of ethnically motivated nationalism and separatism (rightly or wrongly) imputed upon Quebec.

As a consequence, over the course of the 1990s, a vaguely defined multiculturalism emerges as the "smallest common denominator" of otherwise diverging perspectives on Canadian nationhood (Winter, 2014b). On the one hand, the conflict between Canada's so-called founding nations has helped to render immigrant multiculturalism socially acceptable by underlining its liberalism and inclusiveness. On the other hand, identifying multiculturalism as a "smallest common denominator" of otherwise diverging interpretations of nationhood cautions us to be careful with interpreting public support for multiculturalism in opinion polls, newspapers, and government speeches as a wholehearted and unambiguous expression of deep-seated cultural tolerance and a readiness to grant far-reaching concessions to minorities. Although official representations of Canadian values and national identity would like to have it this way, the consolidation of multiculturalism as a part of Canadian identity is better characterized as a lukewarm compromise, which, while not purely accidental, owes much of its existence to a series of lucky, unintended circumstances.

Can we nevertheless speak of a "consolidation" of multiculturalism in dominant discourses in the 1990s? I answer this question in the affirmative, bearing in mind that there are two important qualifications to my claim that the idea of a "multicultural Canada" became consolidated in dominant discourses during the second half of the 1990s. These two qualifications pertain to the containment of Quebec separatism and the decommunitarization of multiculturalism.

THE CONTAINMENT OF QUÉBÉCOIS SEPARATISM

The Canadian government put in place several political measures in the years following the 1995 referendum on Quebec sovereignty. One key step was to ask for clarification from the Supreme Court of Canada on the legality of a future unilateral declaration of independence by Quebec. In August 1998, the Court was unanimous in its finding that, according to both the Canadian Constitution and international law, Quebec did not have legal standing to secede unilaterally from the rest of Canada. However, the Court urged Quebec and the Canadian government to explore creative and democratic means of preserving both the very country and the ethno-cultural pluralism that Canada has come to represent. According to James Tully, the Court stressed that constitutional democracy in Canada is not static, but consists of "a 'global system of rules and principles' for 'the reconciliation of diversity with unity' by means of 'continuous processes' of democratic discussion, negotiation and change" (2000, p. 4).

In June 2000 Parliament responded to the Supreme Court's decision by adopting the Clarity Act, which laid out the rules for any future Quebec referendum on sovereignty or secession. The Act requires that any future referendum be based upon both a "clear" question and majority of votes. Predictably, interpretation of the Clarity Act has largely been determined by political positions along nationalist lines: for some, "debate is ended and democracy, even as the court defined it, is stifled" (Rocher & Verrelli, 2003, p. 233). For others, the Act ensures Canada's viability as a united nation-state (Ryan, 2000).

The legal strategy to contain Québécois separatism was accompanied by a large-scale campaign to boost the government's public presence and perception, particularly within Quebec. This effort consisted largely of unprecedented financial support for Canada Day celebrations, distribution of Canadian flags, and self-promotion of federal services (Turp, 2000). While the sponsorship program (1996-

2004) was touted as a means of fostering national unity and boosting the federal image among Francophone Canadians, critics of the campaign accused the federal government of attempting to undermine Québécois nationalism by promoting itself as the sole legitimate national body (Labelle & Rocher, 2004). It was later revealed that federal efforts to promote national unity had exceeded the boundaries of the law. In what became known as the "sponsorship scandal," widespread corruption was uncovered in the program's operations.

Quebecois nationalism resurfaced on the political stage in 2006 when Prime Minister Stephen Harper surprised many observers by tabling a pan-Canadian motion in the House of Commons affirming that "the Québécois form a nation within a united Canada." The motion was passed by 226 votes in favour to 16 against on November 27, 2006. Once again, response to this government action was split. On one side of the political divide the motion was viewed as federal acquiescence to pressure from Québécois separatists, while other commentators read the move as a political silencing of the very same group. They underline the final clause of the motion ("within a united Canada") and the identification of "Quebecois" as "a people," rather than a territorial and institutional body (i.e. Quebec).[3] The media widely debated the use of "Québécois" (as opposed to Quebeckers) in the motion, as the word – when used in English – was seen as referring to "*pur laine* Québécois, those residents of Quebec who can trace their roots back to New France'"(Winnipeg Free Press, 2006: A11). One minister even resigned on the grounds that he could not support a resolution that he described as a vindication of ethnic nationalism.

In the coming years, the independence movement in Québec receded. Between 2003 and 2012, the (non-separatist) Liberal Party was in power in Quebec. Between 2012 and 2014, the Parti Québécois governed the province as a minority government, but failed to be re-elected on 7 April 2014, when the Quebec Liberal Party won a landslide majority of 70 seats. In the federal election of 2011, the Bloc Québécois was reduced to four seats.

THE DECOMMUNITARIZATION OF MULTICULTURALISM

Although official multiculturalism in Canada recognizes the importance of cultural communities, observers have been adamant that the policy's legal framework should not be seen as discounting the individual in lieu of the group (Kymlicka, 1995). It should be noted, however, that the policy was written in a way to address ethnocultural communities throughout its first twenty years. For example: the Royal Commission on Bilingualism and Biculturalism recommends in the fourth volume of its report that "the contributions of other ethnic groups" be taken into account (Royal Commission on Bilingualism and Biculturalism, 1969, vol. 4). As famously said by Prime Minister Pierre Trudeau while announcing his multiculturalism policy to Parliament in 1971, "there is no official culture, nor does any ethnic group take precedence over any other" (House of Commons, 1971). A more robust legislative version of Trudeau's initial policy, the Multiculturalism Act of 1988 declares it to be Government of Canada policy "to recognize the existence of communities whose members share a common origin and their historic contribution to Canadian society, and enhance their development" (Government of Canada, 1988).

In response to pointed criticism of multiculturalism, the Liberal government separated itself from the language of communities in the mid-1990s, when it emphasized multiculturalism's mandate to ensure that "people of all background feel a sense of belonging and attachment to Canada" (Canadian Heritage, 1998, p. 2). Describing such policy changes as a "movement away from the [Multiculturalism] Act," the Canadian Ethnocultural Council insisted that the revised program "dilutes multiculturalism in Canada and diminishes the role and ability of Canada's ethnocultural communities to contribute to the national enterprise" (Kordan, 1997, p. 138).

McAndrew and her colleagues (2005) came to a similar conclusion after examining the multiculturalism program between 1983 and 2002 to determine which projects and associations were granted funding. For the years 2001-2002, projects that aimed to transform institutions and public opinion to align Canadian society more with increasing "racial" and ethnocultural diversity received over 80% of allotted funding. Mono-ethnic associations (representing a single ethnic group) received less than 10% of funding granted by the multiculturalism program in 2001-2002, while multiethnic organizations (serving a coalition of ethnocultural groups) received more than 65% of the allotted funds. It is up to the reader to determine whether such a distribution should be seen as promoting greater inclusiveness in society and strengthening individual equality or, alternatively, as reducing institutional pluralism and thereby weakening the level of substantive diversity.

Indisputable is that the recent policy changes have left ethnic groups and "visible minorities" – which have largely replaced the traditional mono-ethnic organizations representing communities of European origins – without financial support to cover operational costs of their organizations. Ethnic associations are increasingly losing their institutional completeness. The more they depend upon ad hoc projects funded by the government, the less likely they are able to take on radical positions and assume their role as interest groups (2005, p. 70). To put it with McAndrew and her colleagues: "one wonders whether, during the year 2000, the [federal] government is not slowly putting the policy to sleep, ready to be forgotten, without that any official announcement was made in this respect" (2005, p. 68, my translation).

Therefore, the consensus in dominant discourses during the 1990s on the central role of multiculturalism in Canadian national identity is also a result of its increasing de-communitarianization. Multiculturalism as a means of integration became attractive in direct relation to the demands for self-government rights by Quebec and Aboriginal peoples. If the policy was once characterized by both, the fostering of cultural integration of immigrants *and* the active promotion of institutionally supported diversity alongside group identities (Berry, 2013), the current interpretation of multiculturalism is veering further and further away from the original definition of the term.

In sum, until the mid-1990s, Canadian multiculturalism largely followed the logic that immigrants deserved the same – or at least similar – cultural recognition and rights as members of the French Canadian minority. In the wake of the 1995 Quebec referendum on sovereignty, by contrast, the proponents of multiculturalism insisted (rightly or wrongly) upon a fundamental difference between integrative liberal multiculturalism, on the one hand, and separatist nationalism, on the other (Kymlicka, 1995). Constituted in opposition to – rather than in extension of – French/English "dualism" and its allegedly outdated communitarian understanding, multiculturalism became consolidated as a descriptive element of Canadian national identity. For example, immigrants, who had formerly claimed equal rights in comparison to French Canadians and Franco-Québécois were, in the second half of the 1990s, mostly concerned with underlining the liberal attitudes of immigrant organizations and their members, their rejection of ethnocentrism, and their desire for integration into (rather than separation from) a non-assimilative multicultural Canada (Winter, 2011a, chapter 9). Ironically, the new discourse that emerged from the opinion pages of Toronto-based newspapers in the late 1990s very much reflected the framing of multiculturalism in liberal, individualist, and entrepreneurial terms that had then been promoted by the Liberal government for over a decade (Abu-Laban & Gabriel, 2002). Indeed, in a social climate increasingly characterized by super-diversity (Vertovec, 2007), claiming group rights seemed no longer a priority for members of immigrant minorities.

In the next section, I will argue that having abandoned the language of groups, multiculturalism was unprepared to creatively react to the claims for religious accommodation, which became more and more prominent in the new century. In the Canadian context, the debates about "Sharia tribunals" in Ontario and "reasonable accommodation" in Quebec have shown this. Within these debates, the language of groups and Community has made its way back into the political arena, albeit with altered connotations and two very different constituencies.

THE NEW LANGUAGE OF GROUPS AND COMMUNITY

When, in reaction to the terrorist attacks in Washington and New York on 11 September 2001, well-known columnists of Canada's two "national" newspapers – the *Globe and Mail* (Wente, 2001) and the *National Post* (Coyne, 2001) – declared that "We are all Americans now" they not only symbolically erased Canada's cherished difference from their neighbours to the South. They also expressed a fundamental belief in the moral superiority of the "civic nation" over other forms of social relations and governance. In principle, the civic nation is said to be artificial, universalist, and individualist. It stands for equality without relevance of social determinations such as ethnicity, gender, class, descent, or status. It also stands for democracy as the outcome of rational deliberations among free individuals. After the horrors of Nazi fascism and the Holocaust, which discredited all romanticist nostalgia for the idea of nations based on shared language and ethnocultural roots, the ideal-type of the civic nation has become the beacon of the West, where it is usually associated with the idea of a secular state governed by elected representatives. Multiculturalism as an ethos and normative principle challenges some assumptions of civic nationhood, specifically those related to a strictly neutral state and a citizenry that is unmarked by differentiations of gender, culture, race or religion. It aims to de-ethnicize the nation, normalize ethnic diversity and act as a modest remedy for nationalist exclusion by granting a certain amount of rights and recognition to minority groups.

As mentioned in the introduction to this paper, the beginning of the new century, specifically in the aftermath of the events of 11 September 2001 – instilling a climate of islamophobia and fear of terrorism – was characterized by a growing sense in Western immigrant-receiving countries that "multiculturalism has gone too far." Astute observers notice a "retreat" from multiculturalism (Joppke, 2004) and the "return of assimilation" (Brubaker, 2001). While Canada – for reasons explained in this paper – is a latecomer to this trend, it does not seem to be an exception. In the Canadian context, a new language of groups and community emerged in the political arena in two stages. While in the first stage the civic nation is contrasted with its "groupist Others," in the second stage, the language of groups evolves into a language of Community (with a capital C) that no longer refers to minority groups but circumscribes the pivotal Canadian community: the pan-Canadian nation.

First, the new language of groups is best exemplified through the debates about the so-called Sharia tribunals in Ontario and about the "reasonable accommodation" of religious groups (including both Muslims and Orthodox Jews) in Quebec.

In October 2003, a non-governmental organisation, the Islamic Institute of Civil Justice, announced that it planned to apply Islamic principles of family and inheritance law to resolve disputes on these matters within the Muslim community in Ontario. All "good Muslims" would be expected, as part of their faith, to have family matters resolved in this forum as opposed to the secular courts of Canada. In the heated Ontario "Sharia debate" that followed these announcements, multiculturalism was repeatedly blamed for facilitating pre-modern and mysogenic practices within Canada: "Sharia, the 'law' that in its extreme form mandates amputating the hands of thieves and stoning adulterers to death, may soon be a fact of life in Canada. It is the country's latest adventure in multiculturalism" (Adams, 2004). Furthermore, the debate mobilized frameworks that "installed a secular/religious divide [...] marking the difference between the white, modern, enlightened West" (Razack, 2007, p. 6) on the one hand, and, on the other, oppressed "imperilled Muslim women" (Razack, 2007, p. 9) who were said to be under the dominance of culturally/religiously backward-oriented men. Under intense national and international pressure, the government of Ontario ended all family arbitration based on religious principles. Not only would there be no "Sharia law" in Ontario, there would no longer be any religious arbitration of any kind, but only "one law for all Ontarians" (CTV, 2005).

The debate on reasonable accommodation in the province of Quebec started in March 2006 with the "Kirpan affair" – the question whether a Sikh student could wear his ceremonial dagger at school or whether it was to be banned as a weapon –

and included a number of incidents involving clashes, controversies, and accommodations between members of religious minority groups (mostly Sikhs, Muslims and Jews), and the members of the Quebec's Francophone society, which had overthrown much of its conservative Catholic culture during the "Quiet Revolution" of the 1960s. In one notorious incident a municipal council (in Hérouxville) developed a "code of conduct" instructing prospective immigrants that they would not tolerate certain practices such as "the stoning of women." Realizing the volatility of the issue, the Liberal Quebec government created the "Consultation Commission on Accommodation Practices Related to Cultural Differences," with the vast mandate to conduct an extensive public consultation on this topic. When, in May 2008, the commission released its final report, it recommended, among other things, that the government strengthens Quebec's secularism ("laïcité ouverte"), promotes interculturalism (the integration of newcomers into a French-speaking majority society) and encourages the dejudicializing of the handling of accommodation requests. The government's responses to these recommendations have been lukewarm at best (Leroux, 2010).

Remarkably, in both cases, the constructed oppositions involve, on the one hand, religious groups that are attributed pre-modern, anti-egalitarian and anti-liberal cultural characteristics and, on the other hand, a liberal, secular, culturally neutral mainstream society that is, at most, guided by some vaguely defined shared values or legal principles. The Declaration of the common values of Quebec society, for example, is a direct political outcome of the "reasonable accommodation" debate. This declaration, which was integrated into Quebec's Application Selection Certificate form in January 2009, must now be signed by prospective immigrants as part of their application procedure. It describes Quebec's values as follows: "Quebec is a free and democratic society. Political and religious powers are separate in Quebec. Quebec is a pluralist society. Quebec society is based on the rule of law. Women and men have the same rights. The exercise of human rights and freedoms must respect the rights and freedoms of others and the general well-being. Quebec society is also governed by the Charter of the French language, which makes French the official language of Quebec" (Gouvernement du Québec, 2014, p. 7). Most readers will agree that there is nothing particularly cultural or Québécois about this declaration. Apart from the emphasis on French language, the society described could be that of English Canada. Indeed, few Western countries would not feel represented by these values, although some may be reluctant to use the term "pluralist."

Second, yet another trend can be observed in federal government discourses and policies. This trend leads away from the pretence of cultural neutrality and moves towards a more culturally circumscribed meaning of Canadianness. In January 2006, after twelve years of Liberal federal government, the newly created Conservative Party (since 2003) was elected to power, winning two minority governments (2006 and 2008) and a majority in 2011. Under the Liberal government, changes to Canada's citizenship legislation had been planned, but were never implemented due − in part − to concerns over national unity (Winter, 2013). The situation had fundamentally changed when the Conservatives came to power. A number of changes to the citizenship rules were implemented within only eight years.

On 17 April, 2009, for example, an amendment to the 1977 Citizenship Act came into effect. In an attempt to "protect [Canadian citizenship's] value by ensuring that citizens have a real connection to this country" (former Immigration and Citizenship Minister Finley cited in Foot, 2008), it grants Canadian citizenship retroactively to individuals (of de facto, predominantly white European background) who became Canadian citizens under the first Citizenship Act in 1947 and who subsequently either lost Canadian citizenship (e.g. in the case of acquiring a new citizenship) or never acquired it (e.g. being born out of wedlock or falsely registered at birth). In addition, the new amendment limits citizenship by descent to one generation born outside Canada (and is thereby more likely to hurt recent immigrants – dominantly from non-European countries – with transnational lives and businesses). Elsewhere (Winter, 2014a), I examine the ways in which this new law re-culturalizes – and, to a certain extent, re-ethnicizes – the pan-Canadian nation.

In November of the same year, a new, more comprehensive citizenship study guide was released, which engages in what some commentators have called a Conservative "re-branding" of what it means to be Canadian (Ibbitson, 2009). It depicts "Canadian values" as being synonymous of unabashed patriotism, pride in the armed forces (rather than in peacekeeping), individual responsibility for one's economic wellbeing (rather than on the welfare state), as well as support for the rule of law and the monarchy. As in Quebec's *Declaration of common values*, the new federal citizenship guide turns gender equality into a central theme, although words it more drastically: "Canada's openness and generosity do not extend to barbaric cultural practices that tolerate spousal abuse, 'honour killings,' female genital mutilation or other gender-based violence" (Citizenship and Immigration Canada, 2009, p. 9).

In March 2010, a new citizenship test was introduced and revised a year later to recalibrate the high failure rate. In June 2010, standardized language tests become mandatory for skilled immigrant applicants including native English and French speakers (Winter, 2014c). Furthermore, the number of initiatives taken to emphasize the importance of the British monarchy in the Canadian national identity is accelerating: in July 2011, modern artworks by Quebec painter Alfred Pellan were removed from the lobby of the Department of Foreign Affairs and replaced with a portrait of Elizabeth II. A month later, the Conservative government under Stephen Harper restored the word "royal" in the front of the names of Canada's navy and air force, reviving designations that had been discarded in the 1960s. In September, all Canadian embassies and missions abroad were ordered to display a portrait of the Queen.

A number of commentators have raised concerns about this type of symbolic politics that "harkens back to a time, a generation or more ago, when [the] monarchy occupied a more prominent position in the public affairs and political identity of this country" (Paris cited in Horgan, 2011). Let's be clear: there is nothing wrong as such with rendering history relevant. This being said, "retrofit[ting] Canada for the 1950s" (Simpson, 2011) obtains a bad aftertaste if we recall that this was also the time of Anglo-conformity and "speak white" ideology, and that the 1947-77 age-group of "lost Canadians" was given retroactive citizenship privileges while, under the new law, (grand-)parenthood has become more complicated for contemporary cohorts of transnational citizens.

In sum, the entity that is at stake here is not "immigrant groups" or "minorities"; rather, it is the national Community (with a capital C) that – although keeping its civic legal frame – is no longer pretended to be culturally neutral. On the contrary, with the threat of Québécois nationalism largely gone, even one of Canada's most important newspapers argues that Canadians should "strike multiculturalism from the national vocabulary" (Globe and Mail, 2010). Hence, observations made in the European context also seem to hold true for Canada: "good citizens are now not only those who support themselves economically and have no criminal record, but they must also prove that they speak the national language" (Faist, 2009, p. 178), and – we may add – be prepared to give birth on Canadian soil, defend the country, swear allegiance to the Queen, fly the Canadian flag and, since 2011, call the citizenship fraud tipline to report on suspected mischief by their fellow countrymen.

CONCLUSION

In the late 1990s, Will Kymlicka predicted that "liberal culturalism" was becoming an emerging consensus among scholars and policy makers in the field of immigration and citizenship (2001, chapter 2, originally published in 1998). Indeed, this paper has shown that, in the case of Canada, support for multiculturalism rose steadily since the mid-1990s, and this even into the early years of the new century. At a time when multiculturalism was already under heavy attack in other countries, the international admiration for the "Canadian way" of dealing with immigration and ethnic diversity, the threat of and shared opposition against Québécois allegedly ethnic nationalism and separatism, and the increasing redefinition of multiculturalism in liberal, individualist and integrative terms rendered the multicultural transformation of pan-Canadian identity acceptable, even to many of the most outspoken critics. Canada was represented – and represented itself – as an open, tolerant "multi-ethnic world nation."

While we can therefore indeed speak about a consolidation of multiculturalism in dominant representations of Canadian nationhood and citizenship in the late 1990s and early 2000s, an interpretation of the past eight years suggests that this development must not necessarily be linear. Several years into the new century, Kymlicka withdrew from his position and admitted that he might have been too optimistic (2005). Despite his disappointment with the backlash against multiculturalism in many countries, we may say that Kymlicka's earlier prediction still holds true. Liberal-culturalism has become a widely accepted paradigm in public opinion and politics – however, over the course of the first decade of the 21st century, the signs seem to have been turned around. Today, even in Canada, it is no longer (different types of) ethnic groups whose accommodations attract intuitive sympathy and political efforts. Rather, with Québécois nationalism banned out of the picture, the pivotal community to "strengthen and protect" seems to have become the pan-Canadian nation whose cultural boundaries are being redrawn to correspond to cherished ideals of national identity that existed long before the implementation of multiculturalism.

NOTES

1 This chapter draws upon research originally published in Winter (2011a, 2011b). The author gladly acknowledges funding received from the Social Sciences and Humanities Research Council of Canada. Many thanks to Shawn Jackson for excellent research assistance.

2 Figure 1 (source: Winter, 2011a) uses data from Environics Focus Canada surveys, which are based on samples of 2,000 Canadians. The data were accessed through the Canadian Opinion Research Archive (CORA) based at Queen's University (http://www.queensu.ca/cora). The graphic shows that support for multiculturalism policy was at its lowest in 1994 (35.6%); it then rebound quickly to 45.3% in 2003.

3 In French, the word Québécois is commonly understood to be inclusive of the increasingly diverse population of the province. Cutting Quebeckers off from the non-ethnic "civic" dimensions of their social existence reduces them to a group characterized by cultural and linguistic particularities. In other words, they are first ethnicized and then charged with practising "ethnic nationalism."

REFERENCES

Abu-Laban, Y. (2014). Reform by stealth: The Harper conservatives and Canadian multiculturalism. In J. Jedwab (Ed.), *The multiculturalism question: Debating identity in 21st century Canada* (pp. 149-172). Montreal: McGill-Queen's University Press.

Abu-Laban, Y., & Gabriel, C. (2002). *Selling diversity: Immigration, multiculturalism, employment equity, and globalization.* Peterborough: Broadview Press.

Adams, C. (2004, June 6). Canada is giving sharia law a trial run; Koranic judgments subject to appeal, but repression is feared. *South China Morning Post.*

Bannerji, H. (2000). *The dark side of the nation: Essays on multiculturalism, nationalism and gender.* Toronto: Canadian Scholars' Press.

Berry, J. W. (2013). Research on multiculturalism in Canada. *International Journal of Intercultural Relations, 37*(6), 663-675.

Bloemraad, I. (2006). *Becoming a citizen: Incorporating immigrants and refugees in the United States and Canada.* Berkeley/Los Angeles, CA: University of California Press

Brubaker, R. (2001). The return of assimilation? Changing perspectives on immigration and its sequels in France, Germany and the United States. *Ethnic and Racial Studies, 24*(4), 531-548.

Cameron, D. R. (2007). An evolutionary story. In J. G. Stein, D. R. Cameron, W. Kymlicka, J. Meisel, H. Siddiqui, & M. Valpy (Eds.), *Uneasy partners: Multiculturalism and rights in Canada* (pp. 71-94). Waterloo: Wilfrid Laurier University Press.

Citizenship and Immigration Canada. (2009). *Discover Canada: The rights and responsibilities of citizenship.* Ottawa: Minister of Public Works and Government Services Canada. Retreived from http://www.cic.gc.ca/english/pdf/pub/discover.pdf (accessed 5 December 2009).

Canadian Heritage. (1998). *1996-1997: 9th Annual Report on the Operation of the Canadian Multiculturalism Act.* Ottawa, Minister of Public Works and Government Services Canada.

Coyne, A. (2001, October 3). We are all Americans now. *National Post*, p. A7.

CTV. (2005, September 12). *McGuinty rules out use of Sharia law in Ontario.* Retreived from: http://www.ctv.ca/servlet/ArticleNews/story/CTVNews/1126472943217_26/?hub=TopStories (accessed 20 December 2005).

Faist, T. (2009). Diversity – A new mode of incorporation? *Ethnic and Racial Studies, 32*(1), 171-190.

Foot, R. (2008, April 11). Critics denounce citizenship bill. Would deny status to children born outside country whose parents' births were abroad. *The Gazette (Canada)*. Retrieved from: http://www.canada.com/montrealgazette/news/story.html?id=a9f580dc-cc39-4aaf-945c-b306a47cce10 (accessed 8 January 2015).

Galabuzi, G. (2006). *Canada's economic apartheid: The social exclusion of racialized groups in the new century*. Toronto: Canadian Scholars' Press.

Globe and Mail. (1995, November 1). Mr. Parizeau resigns. P. A18.

Globe and Mail. (2010, October 8). Strike multiculturalism from the national vocabulary. Retrieved from: http://www.theglobeandmail.com/news/national/time-to-lead/multiculturalism/part-6-editorial-strike-multiculturalism-from-the-national-vocabulary/article1748958/ (accessed 8 January 2015).

Gouvernement du Québec. (2014 [2009]). *Immigration and communautés culturelles, Application for Selection Certificate, (A-5020-AA)*. Retrieved from: http://www.immigration-quebec.gouv.qc.ca/publications/en/dcs/Application-selection-certificate-dyn.pdf (accessed 8 January 2015).

Government of Canada. (1982). *Constitution Act*. Retrieved from: http://laws.justice.gc.ca/en/charter/ (accessed 8 January 2015).

Government of Canada. (1988). *Canadian Multiculturalism Act, Chapter 24, an Act for the Preservation and Enhancement of Multiculturalism in Canada*. Ottawa: Queen's Printer.

Gwyn, R. (1993a, February 8). Is multiculturalism becoming multinationalism? *Toronto Star*, p. B3.

Gwyn, R. (1993b, January 31). Quebec, rest of Canada march to different beats. *Toronto Star*, p. B3.

Harell, A. (2009). *Minority-majority relations in Canada: The rights regime and the adoption of multicultural values*. Paper presented at Canadian Political Science Association Annual Meeting, Carleton University, Ottawa, 27-29 May.

Horgan, C. (2011, August 16). Canada's armed forces are royal again. *iPolitics*. Retrieved from: http://ipolitics.ca/2011/08/16/canadas-armed-forces-are-royal-again-it-has-legal-constitutional-and-governing-implications/ (accessed 11 September, 2011).

House of Commons. (1971, October 8). *Debates*. Ottawa, Queen's Printer.

Ibbitson, J. (2009, November 13). The tory guide to a blue Canada. *National Post*, p. A1.

Joppke, C. (2004). The retreat of multiculturalism in the liberal state: Theory and policy. *British Journal of Sociology*, *55*(2), 237-257.

Karim, K. H. (2002). The multiculturalism debate in Canadian newspapers: The harbinger of a political storm? *Journal for International Migration and Integration (RIMI)*, *3*(3-4), 439-455.

Kordan, B. S. (1997). Multiculturalism, citizenship and the Canadian nation: A critique of the proposed design for program renewal. *Canadian Ethnic Studies*, *29*(2), 136-143.

Kymlicka, W. (1995). *Multicultural citizenship: A liberal theory of minority rights*. Oxford: Oxford University Press.

Kymlicka, W. (2001). *Politics in the vernacular: Nationalism, multiculturalism, and citizenship*. New York: Oxford University Press.

Kymlicka, W. (2004). Marketing Canadian pluralism in the international arena. *International Journal*, *59*(4), 829-852.

Kymlicka, W. (2005). The uncertain futures of multiculturalism. *Canadian Diversity/Diversité canadienne*, *4*(1), 82-85.

Labelle, M. & Rocher, F. (2004). Debating citizenship in Canada: The collide of two nation-building projects. In P. Boyer, L. Cardinal, & D. Headon (Eds.), *From subjects to citizens: A hundred years of citizenship in Australia and Canada* (pp. 263-286). Ottawa: University of Ottawa Press.

Lacombe, S. (1998). 'Le couteau sous la gorge.' Ou la perception du souverainisme québécois dans la presse canadienne-anglaise. *Recherches Sociographiques*, *39*(2-3), 271-290.

Leroux, D. (2010). Québec nationalism and the production of difference: The Bouchard-Taylor commission, the Hérouxville code of conduct, and Québec's immigrant integration policy. *Québec Studies Journal*, *49*(10), 107-126.

McAndrew, M., Helly, D., & Tessier, C. (2005). Pour un débat éclairé sur la politique canadienne du multiculturalisme: Une analyse de la nature des organismes et des projets subventionnés (1983-2002). *Politique et Sociétés, 24*(1), 49-71.

Meisel, J. (1999). The Making of the Welfare State. In J. Meisel, G. Rocher & A. Silver (Eds.), *As I recall. Si je me souviens bien. Historical perspectives* (pp. 109-113). Montreal: The Institute for Research on Public Policy.

Potvin, M. (2000). Les dérapages racistes à l'égard du Québec au Canada anglais depuis 1995. *Politique et Sociétés, 18*(2), 101-132.

Razack, S. (2007). The 'sharia law debate' in Ontario: The modernity/premodernity distinction in legal efforts to protect women from culture. *Feminist Legal Studies, 15*(1), 3-32.

Resnick, P. (1994). *Thinking English Canada.* Toronto: Stoddart.

Rocher, F. & Verrelli, N. (2003). Questioning constitutional democracy in Canada: From the Canadian supreme court reference on Quebec secession to the clarity act. In A-G. Gagnon, M. Guibernau, & F. Rocher (Eds.), *The conditions of diversity in multinational democracies* (pp. 209-237). Montreal: The Institute for Research on Public Policy.

Royal Commission on Bilingualism and Biculturalism. (1969). *Report of the Royal Commission on Bilingualism and Biculturalism.* Ottawa, Supply and Services Canada.

Ryan, C. (2000). *Consequences of the Quebec secession reference: The Clarity Bill and beyond.* Toronto, C.D. Howe Institute Company, Section 139, April.

Simpson, J. (2011, September 9). Here's a royal suggestion. *Globe and Mail,* A15.

Statistics Canada (2006). *Analysis of immigration.* Ottawa: Statistics Canada.

Thorsell, W. (1992, Janurary 11). Getty's bilingualism stand reflects english Canada's growing nationalism. *Globe and Mail,* D6.

Tully, J. (2000). The unattained yet attainable democracy: Canada and Quebec face the new century. Paper presented at *Les Grandes Conférence Desjardins,* Montreal: 23 March. Retrieved from: http://francais.mcgill.ca/qcst/publications/desjardins/ (accessed 4 February 2006).

Turp, D. (2000). *La nation bâillonnée: Le plan B ou l'offensive d'Ottawa contre le Québec,* Montreal: VLB Éditeur.

Vertovec, S. (2007). Super-diversity and its implications. *Ethnic and Racial Studies, 30*(6), 1024-1054.

Vertovec, S., & Wessendorf, S. (Eds.). (2009). *The multiculturalism backlash: European discourses, policies and practices.* London/New York: Routledge.

Wente, M. (2001, September 13). We're all Americans now. *Globe and Mail,* N3.

Winnipeg Free Press. (2006, November 30). *Qui sont les Québécois?* Editorial. P. A11.

Winter, E. (2010). Trajectories of multiculturalism in Germany, the Netherlands, and Canada: In search of common patterns. *Government and Opposition, 45*(2), 166-186.

Winter, E. (2011a). *Us, them and others: Pluralism and national identity in diverse societies.* Toronto: University of Toronto Press.

Winter, E. (2011b). L'identité multiculturelle au Canada depuis les années 1990: De la consolidation à la mise en question? *Canadian Ethnic Studies/Études ethniques au Canada, 43-44*(3-1), 35-57.

Winter, E. (2013). Descent, territory, and common values: Redefining citizenship in Canada. In D. Kiwan (Ed.), *Naturalization policies, education and citizenship: Multicultural and multi-nation societies in international perspective* (pp. 95-122). London/New York: Palgrave Macmillan.

Winter, E. (2014a). (Im)possible citizens: Canada's 'citizenship bonanza' and its boundaries. *Citizenship Studies, 18*(1), 46-62.

Winter, E. (2014b). Multiculturalism in the 1990s: The smallest common denominator in defining Canadian national identity. In J. Jedwab (Ed.), *The multiculturalism question: Debating identity in 21st century Canada* (pp. 53-72). Montreal, Kingston: McGill-Queen's University Press.

Winter, E. (2014c). Becoming Canadian – Making sense of recent changes to citizenship rules. *IRPP Study*, *44*, 1-28. Retrieved from: http://www.irpp.org/en/research/diversity-immigration-and-integration/becoming-canadian/ (accessed 8 January 2015).

Elke Winter
School of Sociological and Anthropological Studies
University of Ottawa

LLOYD WONG

4. MULTICULTURALISM AND ETHNIC PLURALISM IN SOCIOLOGY

An Analysis of the Fragmentation Position Discourse

INTRODUCTION

Over the past several decades Canadian sociologists generally have been supportive of cultural and ethnic pluralism in Canada and supportive of official multiculturalism policy, as have the general Canadian population. Public opinion polling since the 1990s has consistently found that the majority of Canadians approve of, or support, multiculturalism in Canada. For example, a recent public opinion poll indicates that 55% of Canadians think multiculturalism has been "very good" or "good" for Canada while only 30% think it has been "bad" or "very bad" (Angus Reid Public Opinion, 2010). However, this 30% may be a growing minority. Thus, one would also expect to find that in the academic sociological literature, in Canada and elsewhere, that there would be a clear critique of ethnic pluralism or multiculturalism.[1]

Sociological literature that is anti-multiculturalism has also increased over the past decade or so. In one vein this literature includes the term "post-multiculturalism" that suggests the need to move beyond current policies of multiculturalism to different approaches to the processes of immigrant and ethnic integration. The term "post – multiculturalism" was recently popularized in Europe by Vertovec (2010) referring to alternatives to multiculturalism that include a search for new models that foster social cohesion and promote assimilation and a common identity. While there has been a recent and noticeable rise of "post-multiculturalism" discourses some of this discourse had been articulated already in the 1990s. This discourse was rooted in the view that multiculturalism was "everywhere" and that there was "too much" of it. This view was particularly evident in the "anti-multiculturalism" and "anti-immigration" movements in Europe at that time. A central aspect of "post-multiculturalism" discourse is based on the perception and claim that multiculturalism is not working, or perhaps has not worked, and is segregating (rather than integrating) diverse 'racial,' ethnic, and religious groups. In other words, the perception and claim is that multiculturalism policy, and the reality of cultural pluralism, contributes to a fragmentation of society and makes social cohesion difficult if not impossible despite the fact that empirical research does not univocally confirm this (Levrau & Loobuyck, 2013).

S. Guo & L. Wong (eds.), Revisiting Multiculturalism in Canada, 69–90.
© *2015 Sense Publishers. All rights reserved.*

This chapter will provide an overview and analysis of some of this sociological discourse that views multiculturalism as a force of societal fragmentation. More specifically, it will begin with a contextualization of multiculturalism in terms of sociological theory. This will allow for different conceptualizations of multiculturalism vis-à-vis the bases of social cohesion. Then a brief description of the sociological literature search methodology follows along with the findings of what the sub-themes are of the fragmentation perspective. This is then followed by a highlighting of some of the major sociologists in Canada and Europe over the past four to five decades who have adopted some form of the fragmentation perspective on multiculturalism. These sociologists include John Porter, Reginald Bibbly, Michel Wieviorka, Bruno Latour, and Tahir Abbas and for each of them there is not only a description of their fragmentation position on multiculturalism but also a brief application of a "sociology of knowledge" approach to provide a social context to their work. Finally this chapter ends with a discussion and conclusion that considers what the implications of this discourse might be.

ETHNIC PLURALISM AND SOCIOLOGICAL THEORY

The sociological literature on the meaning of ethnic and cultural pluralism is muddled and is often situated or framed within national perspectives. Recently Hartmann and Gerteis' work has provided a lucid approach to mapping multiculturalism sociologically in terms of social cohesion (2005). Their model is adopted here to provide a framework in which to position the sociological critiques of multiculturalism that focus on fragmentation. Hartmann and Gerteis suggest that there are two approaches to conceptualizing multiculturalism. The first approach is a one-dimensional conceptualization that is a narrow and binary approach to social order where the two extremes encompass notions of unity and fragmentation (see Figure 1).

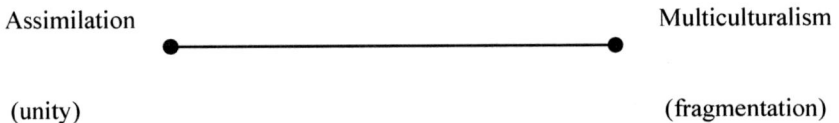

Assimilation   Multiculturalism

(unity)   (fragmentation)

Figure 1. A one-dimensional framework (Source: adapted and modified from Hartmann & Gerteis, 2005, p. 220, figure 1).

In order to move beyond the problematic one-dimensional framework Hartmann and Gerteis conceptualize a framework for some visions of pluralism in American culture by providing a theoretical grid that has two dimensions and encompasses what they term as their "visions of difference" (2005, p. 222). One dimension specifies two different cultural bases for social cohesion that include 1) substantive moral bonds and 2) procedural norms (see Figure 2). The former emphasizes shared substantive moral bonds and practices and is deemed as a "thick" form of social cohesion. The latter emphasizes that adherence to common norms and legal codes (rule of law) is all that is required and this is deemed as a "thin" form of social cohesion. The second dimension relates to the basis for association and is segmented into the centrality of 1) individual interaction and 2) mediating groups. By combining these two dimensions they create a two-by-two table with four cells of which three cells portray their distinct "visions of difference" or what can be considered as three forms of multiculturalism: cosmopolitanism, interactive pluralism, and fragmented pluralism.

Dimension 2	Dimension 1	
	Basis for Social Cohesion	
Basis for Association	Substantive Moral Bonds	Procedural Norms
Individual in Society	Assimilationism	Cosmopolitanism
Mediating Groups	Interactive Pluralism	Fragmented Pluralism

Figure 2. A two-dimensional framework (Source: adapted and modified from Hartmann and Gerteis, 2005, p. 224, figure 2).

This two-dimensional framework can be further elaborated diagrammatically to illustrate the nature and strength of internal or sub-national group boundaries where the salient boundaries would normally be ethnic, cultural, and religious (see Figure 3). Fragmented pluralism is the direct opposite of assimilationism and social homogeneity and some political projects (particularly on the right) fear what they deem as the disuniting and moral relativism of this vision (Hartmann & Gerteis, 2005, p. 230). It is precisely the fragmented pluralism vision that is the focus of this analysis as this is the heart of where the sociological critiques of multiculturalism lie in the English language literature. After this analysis there will be a brief discussion of interactive pluralism in the discussion at the end of this chapter.

Dimension 2	Dimension 1	
	Basis for Social Cohesion	
Basis for Association	Substantive Moral Bonds	Procedural Norms
Individual in Society	Assimilationism	Cosmopolitanism
Mediating Groups	Interactive Pluralism	Fragmented Pluralism

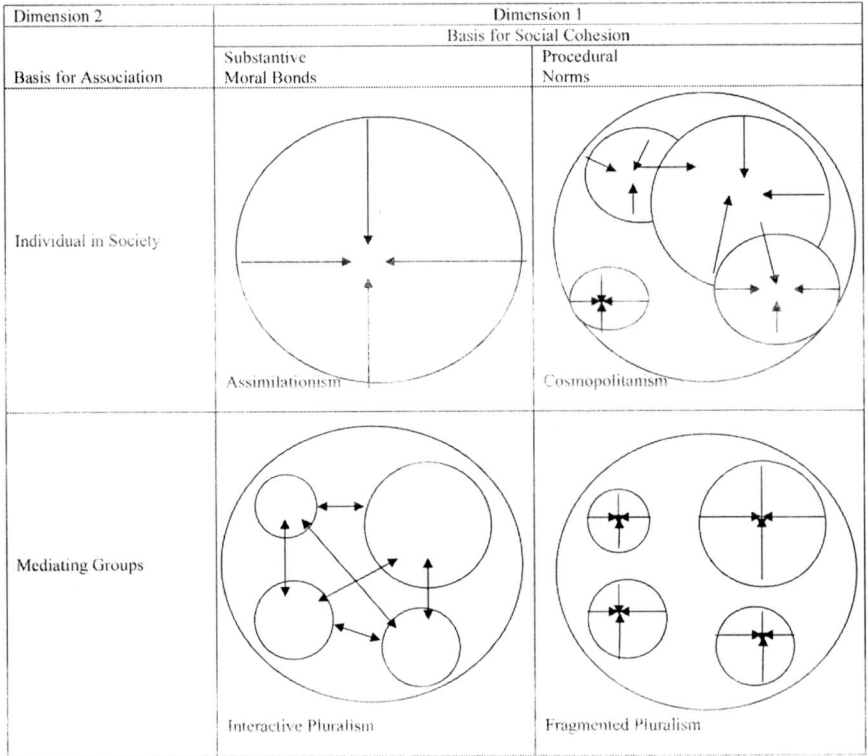

Figure 3. Structural images of social order (Source: Adapted and modified from Hartmann & Gerteis, 2005, pp. 224, 225, figures 2 & 3).

METHODOLOGY AND THEMATIC FINDINGS

In the fall of 2006 an extensive search of the sociological literature in English was conducted looking for direct or indirect critiques of multiculturalism because of its alleged fragmentary characteristic. This literature search yielded 46 articles and books[2]. What is revealing is that most of these articles and books, 35 of them, were published in the 2000s or in what may be called the post 9/11 era. There was only one work in the 1960s, none in the 1970s and 1980s, and 10 works in the 1990s. A follow-up sociological literature search[3] from 2007 to 2013 found only three more substantial articles on fragmentation and that overall the recent literature is more focussed on discussing whether there is a retreat, decline, or failure of multiculturalism (Banting & Kymlicka, 2013; Gozdecka, Ercan, & Kmak, 2014; Kymlicka, 2010; Uberoi & Modood, 2013). Nevertheless, the fragmentation thesis has now become more specified where some scholars argue that religious fundamentalism (and more specifically Islam/non-Islam) constitute multiculturalism's new fault lines (Singh & Cowden, 2011). As such the topic of multiculturalism and religion has generated much debate and critique in the last few years (Lentin & Titley, 2012; Modood, 2013).

Thus one can conclude that the post-multiculturalism trajectory in the sociological discourse utilized the fragmentation critique well into early 2000s. From a reading of summaries of these works it is possible to identify some sub-dimensions or sub-themes of the overall fragmented pluralism theme. This covers the nature of the fragmentation itself and in some cases, where applicable, its implication for Canada. These sub-themes of fragmented pluralism include:

1. Multiculturalism leads to ethnic marginalization and ethnic stratification particularly when there is unequal distribution of power.

2. Multiculturalism emphasizes differences, hence it is divisive and subverts social cohesion and the development of a national identity.

3. Multiculturalism's emphasis on cultural relativism potentially leads to clash of cultures. The notion of clash of culture is best exemplified by the notion of "clash of civilizations" (Huntington, 1993, 1996).

These three sub-themes overlap with several of those found by Prins and Slijper (2002) in their summary of the themes in the public debates on multiculturalism and the third sub-theme can also be characterized as a "domestic clash of civilizations." Within these three sub-themes numerous criticisms are articulated either explicitly or implicitly in the extant literature. The primary focus here is on a few scholars and their work in this literature mostly revolving around sub-themes 2 and 3. In this analysis, as mentioned earlier, a sociology of knowledge approach is also utilized to contextualize the works of these scholars.[4] In assessing these works it is important to situate their work in terms of their social setting, background, and theoretical position.

JOHN PORTER: ETHNIC PLURALISM POTENTIALLY KEEPS THE MOSAIC VERTICAL

In the 1960s and 1970s John Porter was the first sociological voice critiquing multiculturalism as a form of fragmented pluralism. His 1965 watershed classic *The Vertical Mosaic*, on class, ethnicity and social inequality in Canada, covered this position briefly at the end of the work. Subsequently, this position was repeated in several journal articles written in the 1970s after multiculturalism had became official Canadian state policy. Porter concluded *The Vertical Mosaic* by stating:

It seems inescapable that the strong emphasis on ethnic differentiation can result only in those continuing dual loyalties which prevent the emergence of any clear Canadian identity.

> From the point of view of this study of social class and power, it is likely that the historical pattern of class and ethnicity will be perpetuated as long as ethnic differentiation is so highly valued. (Porter, 1965, p. 558)

The first part of the quote illustrates second sub-theme of fragmented pluralism mentioned earlier where multiculturalism's emphasis on differences is seen to be divisive, subverts social cohesion, and hence is a barrier to the development of a unified Canadian identity. The second part of the quote above also illustrates the first sub-theme that suggests that multiculturalism, when practiced in inequalitarian societies, leads to ethnic marginalization and ethnic stratification. Thus Porter argued that multiculturalism has the potential to keep the mosaic vertical and thus ensuring an ethnic stratification system.

In his 1972 article "Dilemmas and Contradictions of a Multi-Ethnic Society" published in the *Transactions of the Royal Society of Canada* Porter forecasted the decade of the 1970s in Canada as the decade of organized minorities. This was contrasted to the 1960s as the decade of concern with poverty and the 1950s for its naïve belief in the affluent society. As such he reaffirmed the argument he made in the *The Vertical Mosaic* that the cost of multiculturalism would be the perpetuation of an ethnic stratification system. It should be noted that Porter did not deny the value of cultural diversity as he stated: "No academic would seriously dispute the desirability and responsibility of preserving culture ...," nevertheless, he felt that diversity should not be promoted via institutionalized and permanent ethnic communities (1972, pp. 199, 201). Porter's self-described position was a "liberal assimilationist" where he clearly supported assimilationism as a better choice than an ethnic stratification system resulting from ethnic pluralism. Further, Porter pointed out that multicultural practices were contradictory to the upcoming post-industrial era: "There is much confusion in the current discussion of multi-ethnicity and multiculturalism.... I am not able fully to understand how biculturalism and multiculturalism have any meaning in the post-industrial world into which we are moving." (1972, p. 198). With this assimilationist position Porter also critiqued the ethnicity question in the Canadian Census at that time suggesting that it creates a statistical artifact and that it also poses a dilemma for liberal social scientists.

Porter's next essay that discussed multiculturalism was entitled "Ethnic Pluralism in Canadian Perspective" published in 1975. This work appeared initially in Glazer and Moynihan's cross-national comparative entitled *Ethnicity: Theory and Experience*, where he was asked to write about Canada (Porter, 1975), and then subsequently re-printed in his *Measure of Canadian Society* (Porter, 1979a). This work continued to articulate the theme of the dilemmas and contradictions of ethnic pluralism and that cultural differences were not only divisive but highly risked the development of a socially stratified society along ethnic lines. He stated: "My own view is that ethnic saliency or differentiation in social structure always creates a high risk of ethnic stratification" (Porter, 1975, p. 289; 1979a, p. 122). Moreover, he predicted in 1975 that with the coming of a post-industrial society the next twenty-five years would see rapid social change and possibly the end of cultural differentiation (Porter, 1975, pp. 303-304).

Porter's liberal assimilationist position was reiterated shortly before his passing in his 1979 essay shortly entitled "Melting Pot or Mosaic: Revolution or Reversion?" that compared historically the developments of ethnicity and ethnicization between the United States and Canada. Here Porter (1979b) firmly arrives at a conclusion that the "melting pot" is more revolutionary than the "mosaic." He stated: "A melting pot course towards the development of a universalistic modern character and culture emphasizing common human qualities and the unity of mankind and shedding the particularisms of history continues as the revolutionary option" (Porter, 1979b, p. 160).

When Porter was critiquing multiculturalism in the mid-1960s and early 1970s Canada was experiencing a time of strained English-French relations, Quebec nationalism, and political violence. The FLQ, a group of ultra Quebec nationalists, conducted bombings of mailboxes and public monuments during this time period which culminated in the October Crisis of 1970 and their kidnapping of James Cross and the kidnapping and murder of Pierre Laporte. At the same time the Royal Commission on Bilingualism and Biculturalism was not only inquiring about the state of the "deux nations" in Canada but also responding to the voices of the "third force" of non-English and non-French in Canada and facilitating the creation of official multiculturalism. As Winter (2011) has recently demonstrated, the view that multiculturalism and binationalism are integrally related forces, rather than opposing forces, dates back to the B' and B' Commission.

In this time period that Porter's lens was focused on a fragile Canada, the ethnic population consisted of approximately 75% who were either English or French and another 23% who were other Europeans. This was the social context that undoubtedly influenced Porter's concern for a singular Canadian identity and a Canadian unity that might not be possible if there is an emphasis on ethnic differentiation that would contribute to divided and dual loyalties. Porter, a strong Canadian nationalist, was a researcher, teacher, and senior administrator at Carleton University in Canada's capital city for three decades. His Canadian nationalist background led some observers, such as Buchignani to note: "Crudely put, it seems that Canadian nationalists like Porter have long argued that ethnic culture is intrinsically divisive and destructive of a unified Canadian identity: so, the argument goes, its perpetuation inevitably leads to less than full socioeconomic participation for minority groups members" (1982, p. 28). Kallen (1982, p. 54) also noted Porter's critique of multicultural social policy as being divisive and fragmentary. She states:

> One line of argument put forward by scholars who oppose this policy objective (notably, the late John Porter, 1975, 1979) is that encouragement of ethnic diversity and cultural distinctiveness fosters (implicitly, if not explicitly) ethnic separation, enclavement and retention of traditional values. Ethnic particularism, in turn, perpetuates the vertical (ethnic) mosaic by creating barriers to upward mobility in post-industrial society which is predicated on universalistic norms. In this view, government encouragement of ethnic diversity legitimates the proliferation of particularistic value

differences among Canadians and thus impedes the development of national unity.

It should be remembered that when Porter was writing, sociological research in Canada tended to reflect majority group views on ethnicity and also had methodological and theoretical constraints on what was considered an appropriate lines of social science inquiry (Buchignani, 1982, p. 16).

REGINALD BIBBY: EXCESSIVE RELATIVISM LEADS TO MOSAIC MADNESS

In the 1980s there were virtually no critical academic works on multiculturalism but in the 1990s this changed dramatically. Reginald Bibby's (1990) popular book *Mosaic Madness: Pluralism Without a Cause* utilized sociological language to critique official pluralism in the form of multiculturalism policy[5]. A few years later Neil Bisoondath (1994) wrote *Selling Illusions: The Cult of Multiculturalism*, which utilized a more personal and individualistic account to suggest that multiculturalism is subscribed to by unthinking individuals and creates ethnic segregation and ghettoization. Although both books are interesting and insightful, for purposes of this article only Bibby's work will be summarized here as it is more directly sociological. Before doing so, however, it should be noted that in addition to these two books and a few other academic critiques (approximately ten articles were found in the literature search for the 1990s), there was also strong criticism of official multiculturalism by the Reform Party of Canada in the 1990s. In the 1991 policy manual of the Reform Party there is explicit stated opposition to the "...current concept of multiculturalism and hyphenated Canadianism pursued by the Government of Canada. We would end funding of the multiculturalism program and support the abolition of the Department of Multiculturalism" (as quoted in Kirkham, 1998, p. 257). Coincidentally there was a withering away and hollowing of the Department of Multiculturalism under Chretien's Liberal Government in the 1990s.

Bibby's critique touches on sub-themes 2 and 3 of the fragmented pluralism position noted earlier. He sees multiculturalism as entailing an over emphasis on cultural relativism and difference that is divisive, prevents moral consensus, and creates individual mosaic fragments. To him, cultural relativism and pluralism go hand-in-hand and he uses a baseball analogy to illustrate his point:

In Canada, pluralism articulates the pathway to group and individual freedom. But relativism plays the important role of providing the rationale for freedom of thought and behavior. If pluralism is the pitcher, relativism is the center-fielder. Relativism pronounces that it is appropriate and ideal that a culture encourages a wide variety of views and lifestyles. Pluralism establishes choices; relativism declares the choices valid. (1990, pp. 9-10)

However, he feels that cultural relativism and pluralism, while desired virtues in Canada, lack overarching societal expectations regarding the preferred outcomes of such virtues. In other words the overarching expectation of social cohesion. Consequently, one of the unintended consequences is strain between ethnic groups.

The result is having "too much of a good thing" and that it would be naive to assume that it will lead to social cohesion. Bibby states:

> ... our expectation has been that fragments of the mosaic will somehow add up to a healthy and cohesive society. It is not at all clear why we should expect such an outcome. To encourage individual mosaic fragments may well result in the production of individual mosaic fragments and not much more. (1990, p. 10)

So, according to Bibby, "relativism has slain moral consensus" as it has "stripped us of our ethical and moral guidelines, leaving us with no authoritative instruments with which to measure social life" (Bibby, 1990, p. 14). What we are left then, he argues, are just the standards of our local cultural and religious domains and not anything more, which is tantamount to ethnocentrism without a common culture. He felt multiculturalism creates ethnic separation and ethnic solidarity that takes away from broader social participation. His critique of relativism continues as a theme throughout his work and he has various sections in the book with sub-titles such as" Excessive Relativism" and "Open-Minded Mindlessness." He also discusses "visionless coexistence" in Canada where he suggests that the outcome of multiculturalism policy is coexistence – no more, no less. However, the danger he feels is there is no subsequent vision, nor national goal, nor common purpose. Hence he states "Pluralism ceases to have a cause. The result: mosaic madness" (1990, p. 104).

Was it "mosaic madness" in the late 1980s and early 1990s when Bibby was reflecting on multiculturalism policy and practice and writing his book? Certainly, as the now trite expression indicates, the "changing face of Canada" had been dramatic from the time John Porter was writing a decade or two earlier. In 1965 approximately 14% of immigrants to Canada came from non-European and non-U.S. regions of the world but by 1985 almost 70% of immigrants were now coming from these regions of the world. Consequently Canada became much more diverse in the decade or so between Porter and Bibby's critiques. The visible minority population in Canada doubled from approximately 5% of the population in 1981 to almost 10% of the Canadian population in 1991. Correspondingly, for Canada's larger metropolitan areas, where most visible minorities are located, their population also doubled so that by 1991, for example, approximately 26% of people in Toronto and 24% people in of Vancouver were visible minorities. Bibby's critique of multiculturalism policy in Canada was the first in the 1990s and others followed from various other perspectives, such a Bisoondath mentioned earlier, and most were non-sociological. In the 1980s, when Bibby was writing *Mosaic Madness*, Canada was a relatively tranquil country in terms of ethnic and racial conflict. While the decade began with the first Quebec Referendum of 1980, the rest of the decade was void of overt ethnic and racial tensions. Multicultural policy, however, was "under siege" as there was considerable opposition in popular discourse and the platforms of the Reform Party and the Conservative Party (Abu-Laban & Stasiulis, 1992). In terms of the implementation of multiculturalism as state policy this decade has been referred to as "equity" multiculturalism as distinct from "ethnicity" and "song and dance" multiculturalism of the 1970s. Equity multiculturalism meant that the focus of the policy was to manage diversity or ethnic and race relations by addressing the problem of systemic discrimination with solutions of employment equity and equality of opportunity (Fleras & Elliott, 2002, p. 69; Kunz, 2007). For Bibby it was important at this time to be looking for a more macro-level purpose of Canadian life in the sense of a "Canadianess" where diverse peoples would engage in a national conversation. He felt that this was not happening and people in Canada did not have any moral bonds or moral consensus (see Figures 2 and 3) and what existed was fragmented pluralism or individual mosaic fragments. For Bibby moral consensus was necessary for civil society.

In 2008 he reflected on his 1990 book and his thesis of mosaic madness. This was a topic of a lecture he had given in Japan. He states:

> My presentations [in Japan] involved my revisiting the "mosaic madness" of the 1990 period. I was intrigued to realize that much of the madness that characterized Canada then and was anticipated to continue and perhaps become even worse has largely dissipated. In 2008 we find Canada characterized by a remarkable calm. My data and that of others such as Michael Adams document what most of us know experientially – that Canada today seems quite sane, complete with highly positive interpersonal life, an extremely positive economic environment, and highly content individuals. In the title of my first presentation, one might well ask, "Whatever Happened to Mosaic Madness?" (Bibby, 2008)

At the time of writing Mosaic Madness Reginald Bibby was a professor of sociology at the University of Lethbridge, and currently he holds the Board of Govenors Research Chair, where his main area of research interest is social trends in Canada and the sociology of religion.

By the late 1990s, particularly in Europe the number of critiques of multiculturalism were increasing and by the time of the post 9/11 era the numbers increased dramatically. In the extensive literature search of the fragmentation critique of multiculturalism in sociology nine articles in the Canadian and European literature were published between 1990 and 1999. The next section examines one of these works from the European literature.

MICHEL WIEVIORKA: MULTICULTURALISM IS NOT THE SOLUTION

Of the European critiques of multiculturalism Wieviorka's 1998 work tops the list in terms of a clear theoretical explanation and dissection of the fragmentation critique. He covers not only a sociological approach but also a political philosophy approach and a political science approach. Wieviorka argues that a sociological approach is interested in the social processes of multicultural societies and the nature of social differentiation and cultural differences. Moreover this sociological approach suggests it is multiculturalism itself that is problematic:

A sociological approach, *stricto sensu*, will primarily be interested in the working of the society in which multiculturism is found, in the way in which the cultural differences within it are produced, received or reproduced: and in the questions and tensions which this generates. This approach will describe multiculturalism as the problem rather than the response. (Wieviorka, 1998, p. 883)

As he argues in this quote, ethnic pluralism and cultural differences are not only reproduced, but they are also in the constant process of being produced which means that fragmentation and recomposition are a permanent probability. He argues that the tendency for cultural fragmentation is much greater than the tendency and trend toward homogenization because of the impact of the globalization of the economy and/or the internationalization of mass culture under American hegemony (Wieviorka, 1998, p. 891).

In the beginning of his article *Is Multiculturalism the Solution?* he provides a history of the concept of multiculturalism and then discusses multiculturalism in practice. He discusses Canada, along with Australia and Sweden, as an example of a relatively "integrated multiculturalism" (1998, p. 884), while the U.S. is discussed as an example of a "disintegrated multiculturalism" (1998, p. 886). He then discusses the tensions inherent with cultural differences that are produced by multicultural societies even when some societies are able to demonstrate tensions that may be at equilibrium. In other cases disequilibrium is considerable with tensions reaching a breaking point:

The tensions reach breaking point and the logic of fragmentation gains the upper hand, with all that this implies – some people assimilating into the society as a whole, others possibly opting for radicalization and living in a closed community. (Wieviorka, 1998, p. 892)

In his conclusion Wieviorka cautiously answers the question embodied in the title of his article and suggests that multiculturalism is not the solution. He feels that multiculturalism is "more of a risk than a satisfactory response" and multiculturalist policies and approaches are dated and that we now need to go further than multiculturalism or, in other words, toward "post-multiculturalism." In the mid 1990s, when Wieviorka wrote this piece, France was experiencing a re-emergence of racism and increasing ethnic and immigrant unrest. For example, the controversial issue of Islamic veils and head scarfs worn by Muslim women and girls in French public school system emerged at this time and stirred heated debate. France was also coming to terms with the tension resulting from the realization of the economic necessity of immigrants and immigrant communities and the growing visibility in, and occupation of, French social spaces by immigrants. Thus, issues of assimilation, ethnic pluralism, and racial and ethnic fragmentation came to the forefront of French public, policy, and academic discourses.

In the early- and mid-1990s the "clash of civilization" or "cultural contestation" thesis and discourse had also emerged (Lewis, 1990; Huntington, 1993, 1996) with the main premise of a fundamental conflict between the Islamic world and the

West. Huntington had suggested that that the fundamental source of conflict in global politics would no longer be primarily ideological or economic. He stated:

> The great divisions among humankind and the dominating source of conflict will be cultural. Nation states will remain the most powerful actors in world affairs, but the principal conflicts of global politics will occur between nations and groups of different civilizations. The clash of civilizations will dominate global politics. The fault lines between civilizations will be the battle lines of the future. (Huntington, 1993, p. 22)

Thus, the critique of multiculturalism over-emphasizing cultural relativism and potentially leading to clashes of cultures, could by extension, be conceptualized also as a domestic clash of civilizations. The clash of civilization thesis, fraught with overtones of Orientalism, was considered by many scholars in the mid- to late-1990s as simplistic and racist. Nevertheless, Silverman (1992) pointed out the headscarves affair in France was symptomatic of a wider national or nation-state crises in contemporary France related to immigration, race, ethnicity. It was at that time, and arguably still is today, a crisis of the l'étranger and citizenship in France and also other parts of Europe. Wieviorka has been a professor at The School of the High Studies in Social Sciences (EHESS) in Paris since 1989 and the director of the Centre for Sociological Analysis and Intervention from 1993 to 2009. Since the mid 1990s his research has focused on cultural difference, multiculturalism, and more recently on violence in the European context. More recently, from 2006 to 2010, Wieviorka was president of the International Sociological Association which currently has a membership of 5,000 sociologists from 167 countries. At the recent 2014 World Congress of Sociology held in Yokohama Japan he presented at a session entitled *Facets of Multiculturalism and Transnationalism* where he discussed the topic of "The End of Multiculturalism?" and visited very briefly the topic of fragmented multiculturalism (Wieviorka, 2014).

From the years 2000 to 2013 the literature search for the fragmentation critique of multiculturalism in sociology produced thirty-eight works. As noted earlier, relative to earlier times, this is a vast and growing literature and the next two sections will briefly examine the work of Latour in 2002 and Abbas in 2005 as two prominent examples of this current period.

BRUNO LATOUR: WAR OF THE WORLDS

The events of 9/11 and subsequent terrorist bombings contribute to the angst that some European sociologists now have about multiculturalism. Moreover, soon after 9/11, the work of Lewis and Huntington and the "clash of civilizations" thesis soared in popularity and became more widely accepted.

Latour's focus is the "war of the worlds." He argues that it has been in existence all along in the so-called "modern age" (2002, pp. 3-4). He feels that 9/11 served as a reminder that peace and unity has to be made through diplomatic efforts. He further argues that modernists made the notion of culture sacred and that this gave rise to multiculturalism of which he is highly critical of: "In this combination of respect and complete indifference, we may recognize the hypocritical condescension of cultural relativism ..." (2002, p. 15). Latour is highly critical of multiculturalism and he states that multiculturalism is a form of condescension of ethnocentrism. In the height of modernization, according to Latour (2002, p. 16), the West says that "the one world is ours, the many worlds are yours; and if your disputes arc too noisy, may the world of harsh reality come in to pacify your disputes" and that this is "a peculiar offer of peace, one which had never recognized the existence of a war in the first place!" Latour looks at the rise of both "globalization" and "fragmentation" and points to a paradox:

> ... we identify precisely the deep transformation that took us out of modernism and the convenient solution it offered to the problems of unity and multiplicity. Fragmentation shatters mononaturalism; globalization destroys multiculturalism. On both sides, whether the aim is to create multiplicity or unity, opponents, fronts and violent contradictions are finally starting to appear. (2002, p. 24)

Latour's general message is that humanity might be able work its way out of the "war of the worlds" given the awareness that the West can no longer view minority groups as the "other" and that honest dialogue is essential.

Writing in the immediate year after 9/11 era, Latour is critical of the West regarding its practice of using cultural relativism in a condescending way to "others" in the world and thus causing fragmentation at a global level and this analysis moves downward toward a critique of multiculturalism at the national level. Arguably ethnic tensions and hatreds have increased not just in the post 9/11 era but over the past couple of decades of neo-liberalism. As Chua (2003) points out in her book *World on Fire*, the movement and exportation of free markets and democracy has not diminished ethnic and ethno-religious conflict as it was supposed to do. Rather the dynamic of globalization and free market democracy has led to heightened situations where some ethnic groups dominate markets and contribute to ethnic tensions. This dynamic, she argues, explains the rise of anti-Americanism in recent decades. Thus the global context of Latour's work was not just 9/11 as a watershed event but rather a global movement that has been occurring for decades. Latour's affiliation at the time he wrote *War of the Worlds* was at Centre for Sociology of Innovation in Paris where he studied the anthropology and sociology of science. At the time of writing he is professor at Sciences Po Paris and Centennial professor at the London School of Economics.

TAHIR ABBAS: THE RETREAT OF MULTICULTURAL THEORY, POLICY AND PRACTICE

Since 9/11 Europe has seen a retreat in multiculturalism at the level of theory and policy for many liberal states. This backing away from multiculturalism is due to a perception by policy makers and many academics that cultural recognition does not contribute to minority and immigrant integration. Abbas' work reflects this retreat as he critiques, using the case of British Muslims, liberal multicultural political philosophy and British multiculturalism policy. He argues that the management of diversity, via British multicultural policy, has been ineffective and he goes so far as to support the argument made by others for a return to assimilation (Abbas, 2005). His critique, however, is from the left and is congruent with sub-theme 1 mentioned earlier. He believes that multiculturalism leads to further ethnic segregation and stratification under already existing economic and political inequality. He states that a multicultural society:

> ... is seemingly where 'African immigrants clean toilets,' and the 'upper-middle-class English gents are lawyers, pilots, surgeons and bankers.' The word multicultural no longer carries with it any connotation of equality or respect – if it ever did. Worse, it implies that all 'moral obligations' have been met when a society is 'multicultural.' (Abbas, 2005, p. 156)

Abbas' argument is that in an already ethnically stratified society, multiculturalism reinforces the existing fragmentation by not addressing social inequality. He also argues that multiculturalism oppresses migrants culturally in that they are obliged to rejoin the culture of their ancestral origin and that cultures in multiculturalism are thought to narrowly correspond to existing nation-states so you have a cultural nationalism (Abbas, 2005, p. 156). Consequently, he argues that policy needs to move toward emphasizing "shared citizenship" and areas of "sameness." For Abbas the political climate of the time will determine the future of multiculturalism. He asserts that in Britain the development of multiculturalism policy is closely tied to what happens with British Muslims because in the post 9/11 era they have become the test case and the gaze of the "other" (Abbas, 2005, p. 164).

It must be remembered that official multiculturalism policy is relatively new in Britain, having been implemented in the late 1990s and, like multiculturalism policy in the Netherlands, quickly became a target due in part to specific situations of ethnic and religious antagonism and terrorist events in Europe in the mid 2000s. These include, among others, the 2004 murder of Dutch filmmaker Theo Van Gogh in Amsterdam, the Danish cartoons issue in 2005, the previously mentioned Madrid and London train bombings of 2004 and 2005, and the 'urban riots' in France in 2005. The practice of multiculturalism was increasingly associated with forms of "unhealthy" political transnationalism that made it potentially divisive and fragmentary. Thus, the context of Abbas' work is a continuation of these current times that began when Latour was writing with a narrower focus on Europe "being on fire" rather than the world "being on fire" (Chua, 2003). Much of this discourse utilizes terms such as "the death of multiculturalism" (Kundnani, 2002); "farewell to multiculturalism?" (Bauböck, 2002); "retreat of multiculturalism" (Joppke, 2004); "Too Diverse" (Goodhart, 2004); "re-inventing multiculturalism" (Uitermark, Rossi, & Van Houtum, 2005); all of which fall into the purview of the post-multiculturalism genre where multiculturalism itself is viewed as being problematic. Currently Tahir Abbas is professor of sociology at Fatih University, in Istanbul Turkey and works on multiculturalism, extremism, Islamism and radicalisation.

DISCUSSION AND CONCLUSION

This last section begins with a discussion of some of the sociological literature and discourse mentioned above, that critiques multiculturalism as a form of "fragmented pluralism," in light of multiculturalism as a form of "interactive pluralism."[7] Then this is followed by a brief discussion of the policy implications that this discourse has for Canada, while at the same time being cognizant that academic research in Canada by sociologists has limited impact and influence on immigration related policies and programs (Richmond, 2000).

The Sociological Literature on "Multiculturalism as Fragmentation"

The work of the five scholars in the previous section illustrate aspects of the fragmentation critique of multiculturalism in the sociological literature over the past several decades and the three sub-themes of the fragmentation thesis found in the literature review regarding social divisiveness, clash of cultures, and ethnic marginalization and stratification. Of these Porter and Bibby's work represent Canadian sociological critiques of multiculturalism that touch upon these three sub-themes. These critiques, along with many non-sociological critics such as Bisoondath (1994) may have led to the Canadian government commissioned reviews of it's multiculturalism program in the mid-1990s that included the Spicer Commission and the Brighton Report with the latter including recommendations that grappled with the fragmentation critique of multiculturalism (Abu-Laban and Gabriel, 2002, p. 113). Not surprisingly, many popular non-sociological critiques utilizing the fragmentation perspective continue in popular journalistic form such as Allan Gregg's article in *The Walrus* (2006) and Stein et al.'s book entitled *Uneasy Partners* (2007) as two cases in point. On the other side non-sociological adherents of multiculturalism include the scholarly work of Banting and Kymlicka (2010) and Kymlicka (2012) in political philosophy.

What all five of these scholars' works have in common is a lack of a clear meaning or definition of what constitutes societal "fragmentation." These works point to social divergence, conflict and tension, and examples thereof, as illustrative of fragmentation. In many respects these works take a one-dimensional and binary approach to multiculturalism (see Figure 1). For example Bibby (1990, p. 14) argues that cultural relativism erases agreement on the norms that are essential to social life. Antecedent to this is Bibby's assumption that multiculturalism inevitably leads to relativism. As Satzewich and Liodakis (2007, p. 134) recently illustrate, using examples from Canadian law, this is not necessarily the case. Further, in response to Bibby's argument one could also ask why agreement on procedural norms, such as rule of law and democracy, is not sufficient and does not meet the essence of social life? If it is sufficient, then social cohesion is not at risk and the "fragmentation" is simply at the level of differential values. One can then ask the question of whether it is necessary for Canadians to have a set of common values as the evidence is clear that Canadians diverge on many social issues and values[6] but in a democracy this is certainly deemed

83

acceptable. Regardless, what was assumed here is that these five works fall under the fragmented pluralism vision noted earlier where multiculturalism is viewed as disuniting and problematic. If this fragmented pluralism is really problematic then the alternative visions are: assimilationism, cosmopolitanism, or interactive pluralism.

According to Jedwab (2005, p. 96) recent polling shows that more Canadians agree that multiculturalism helps rather than hinders integration, yet only one-half of Canadians believe that multicultural policy helps people with various backgrounds and religions to fully integrate into Canadian society. If fragmented pluralism is problematic then how does a society move toward an interactive pluralism that involves some substantive moral bonds as the basis for social cohesion and integration? Fragmented pluralism represents a "thin" citizenship while interactive pluralism represents a "thick" citizenship. What are the conditions necessary for interactive pluralism to exist? It would require a context where particularism and universalism are recognized simultaneously. This would be a new strategic approach to multiculturalism requiring a new political logic that makes it possible to "effect a new and radical reconfiguration of the particular and the universal, of liberty and equality with difference" (Hall, 2000, p. 236). For example, in reference to Britain Modood (2005) argues for an extension and strengthening of multicultural policy so that there is a "politics of equal respect" that is inclusive of British Muslims into a shared multicultural Britishness. A new approach also entails the backing away from culturally essentializing ethnic and immigrant communities and recognizing that communities and their cultures are not static but instead are undergoing cultural translation. Li (1999, pp. 165-166) succinctly points out that one cannot assume: 1) that ethnicity and race as essentially primordial in nature; 2) that ethnic culture primarily determines how ethnic groups relate to each other; and 3) that ethnic groups are distinct and culturally homogeneous. Moreover, drawing upon the work of Bhabba, Hall points out that cultures revise their own systems of reference, norms and values in negotiations (2000, p. 226). This new strategic approach also entails recognizing that diversity and difference does not mean fragmentation and lack of social cohesion. Here Hall draws upon Derrida's work on *différance* to argue that:

> This is *not* the binary form of difference, between what is absolutely the same, and what is absolutely 'Other.' It is a 'weave' of similarities and differences that refuse to separate into fixed binary oppositions. (2000, p. 216)

Moreover he points out that *différance* does not prevent any system or society from stabilizing or reaching social cohesion or as he puts it as a "a fully sutured totality" (2000, p. 216). The current state of most multiculturalism policies, such as those in Canada and elsewhere, is a situation of what Hall describes as "pluralist multiculturalism" that entails enfranchising the differences between groups along cultural lines and also according different group-rights to different communities within a communitarian political order (Hall, 2000, p. 210). This is the kind of multiculturalism that the critics have called fragmented pluralism. To move to the interactive pluralism vision there needs to be a civic component to pluralist multiculturalism.

Soutphommasane (2005, p. 412) describes civic pluralist multiculturalism as a form of multicultural citizenship which is grounded in a shared civic culture but that this civic culture is constantly exposed to critical collective reflection and re-examination. A move in this direction of interactive and civic pluralism was advocated by Bibby (1991) back in the early 1990s when he advocated the necessity of making "... it possible for Canadians of diverse backgrounds to interact with each other in order to speak openly about their differences and concerns, to reflect on their values and dreams, to evaluate the merits of their respective ideas and lifestyles." By interacting with each other the national or Canadian conversation, as advocated by Kymlicka (1998, p. 175), might emerge over time and this could lead to a shared identity.

Policy Implications for Canada

It is easy to say that interaction and conversation needs to occur and that when it occurs then there is interactive pluralism. However for it to actually occur there are certain ground rules and presuppositions that would need to be affirmed and accepted by everyone. Although it should not be thought of as a contested political battlefield, there is an element of negotiation and contestation that would be involved. With the waning of assimilationism there were increasing numbers of immigrants who demanded that the "reigning formula" be adapted in order to accommodate them, as opposed to the other way around (Taylor, 2001, p. 187). This has contributed to a debate about the nature of integration in many multicultural countries. The former Metropolis Project in Canada had summed up this debate succinctly by referring to two major approaches to frame integration. These two approaches are referred to as 1) immutable core and 2) dynamic nucleus with the former being basically the assimilationism position and the latter being interactive pluralism. With an immutable core there is conformity to common values, language and culture while with the dynamic nucleus there is constant negotiation about what constitutes the core so that there is a social compact that sees the core as dynamic and evolving over time[8] (Metropolis, 2003). Metropolis had outlined these two approaches as a way of framing the debate and posed it as a question in terms of which one of these approaches is preferable? The expectation of conformity is based on the belief that many cultural differences are unbridgeable and irreconcilable with the core values of democracy and liberalism thus many academics adopt the principle of conformity to an immutable core as the benchmark of integration and do not interrogate the relationship between diversity and integration (Li, 2003, p. 328).

In conclusion I would argue that the immutable core approach represents the "old reigning formula" referred to by Taylor and that the viability of multiculturalism as social and public policy requires a vision of interactive pluralism. This can only occur under a dynamic nucleus approach where there is ongoing discussion, negotiation, critical collective reflection and re-examination of what Canada is in terms of identity and how it works in terms of social processes. This then would allow movement away from a fragmented pluralism vision and cultural essentialism that is held by many critics of multiculturalism including many influential sociologists as this chapter has shown. Although it should be noted that the essentialist critique of multiculturalism has been recently challenged by Kymlicka (2014). Nevertheless, the dynamic nucleus approach would ensure civic pluralist multiculturalism and integrative pluralism. Canadian public-policy discourse in the 1990s and mid 2000s used catch-words and phrases like "two-way street," "inclusive citizenship" and "identity" (Metropolis, 2007; Kunz, 2007) to suggest a leaning toward a dynamic nucleus approach. Beyond the public-policy discourse recent Canadian empirical research on young adult Muslims reveal that they maintain a dual Canadian-Muslim identity by utilizing the ideology of multiculturalism despite being stigmatized for their religion (Nagra & Peng, 2013). However, since the election of a Conservative government in Canada in 2006 the reality is one of a retreat to the immutable core approach. One of many examples of this retreat is the Conservative government's revamped Canadian citizenship guide launched in 2009 and entitled *Discover Canada: The Rights and Responsibilities of Canadian Citizenship*. This guide, as Beenash Jafri (2012, p. 1) notes, has exclusionary ideas about what constitutes Canadian identity and imagines multiculturalism in ways that "advance a thesis of culture clash and reinforce the ostensible superiority of 'Western Civilization.'" The fundamental question now is whether there will be the return of a political will in Canada to encourage and facilitate a dynamic nucleus and interactive pluralism.

NOTES

[1]   The term ethnic pluralism is utilized in this chapter as being synonymous with the term cultural pluralism and multiculturalism. Li (1999, p. 148) rightly points out that "multiculturalism" while a nebulous concept has been also adopted by academics for various analytical interpretations and thus have added more confusion to the term.

[2]   This work was completed by Paul Lawton a graduate student in sociology at the University of Calgary. Examples of search terms include: "post, anti, critique, problem, fragmentation" combined with "multiculturalism, pluralism, cultural pluralism, ethnic pluralism, diversity." Of the 46 articles, 18 were specifically on European countries, 16 on Canada, 5 on other countries (mostly U.S. and Australia), and 7 were not country specific but more theoretical in nature.

[3]   This work was completed by Stefan Lewis, a graduate student in sociology at the University of Calgary.

[4]   More specifically a classical sociology of knowledge approach is used here where the view is that the production of knowledge is shaped by social structures and the social locations of individuals (who are producing the knowledge) within those structures (Mannheim, 1936, p. 282; Meja & Stehr, 1999, Introduction).

[5]   A crude discourse analysis of the words in title of this book suggests that the mosaic or multiculturalism is pathological and deviant ("madness" and "pluralism (as in rebel) without a cause") although Bibby may not have meant it to be interpreted this way.

[6]   These obviously include such values as those concerning abortion, capital punishment, gun control, the welfare state, same-sex marriage, and many others. Satzewich and Liodakus (2007, p. 133) point out that those critics of multiculturalism who appeal to the 'national' character of Canada are

usually vague in describing what constitutes Canadian culture, where they usually mean Anglo-tradition, and also vague on defining what Canadian values are.

[7] See Figures 2 and 3. The other visions of assimilationism and cosmopolitanism, while important, are not the focus here. Assimilationism would involve the "strategy of privatization" of cultural differences and conflict (Barry, 2001, chapter 2) and is part of the recent liberal critique of multiculturalism. Cosmopolitanism remains an important conceptualization and recent work by Delanty and He (2008), for example, link critical cosmopolitanism to Asian and European transnationalism.

[8] The actual descriptions of these two approaches were described by Metropolis as follows:

> The first approach revolves around the belief that a strong immutable core – often defined as national identity – is essential for the successful integration of newcomers. Indeed, this approach maintains that integration is only possible when newcomers and those in the "host" society understand and adhere to the component parts of the core .... In this first approach, an exclusive national identity, or immutable core, is strongly articulated through shared values, a shared language, shared ethnicity and culture, or, in the most extreme form, racial or religious homogeneity. Newcomers must accept and conform to this core and its articulations to be granted citizenship .... Proponents of this approach fear that a country with a weak sense of national identity is prone to fractures and fault-lines .... They may also believe that immigration-fuelled diversity challenges a stable national identity and may threaten the core values of the "host" society.

> The other approach revolves around the belief that the core can, and indeed must, evolve by including citizens and newcomers in ongoing discussion on the construction of the national identity. This, proponents suggest, ensure support for shared responsibilities, values and goals ... the composition of a national identity is viewed as an on-going process that engages newcomers and fosters a sense of shared citizenship ... and acts as the dynamic nucleus that holds a diverse citizenry together. Proponents of this approach maintain that the social compact is renewed and reinforced when national identity is allowed to evolve through discussions between newcomers and "host" societies that allow them to redefine and re-articulate the values and responsibilities that comprise their shared citizenship. (Metropolis, 2003)

REFERENCES

Abbas, T. (2005). Recent developments to British multicultural theory, policy and practice: The case of British muslims. *Citizenship Studies, 9*(2), 153-166.
Abu-Laban, Y., & Gabriel, C. (2002). *Selling diversity: Immigration, multiculturalism, employment equity, and globalization.* Peterborough: Broadview Press.
Abu-Laban, Y., & Stasiulis, D. (1992). Ethnic pluralism under siege: Popular and partisan opposition to multiculturalism. *Canadian Public Policy, 18*(4), 365-386.
Angus Reid Public Opinion. (2010). Canadians endorse multiculturalism, but pick melting pot over mosaic. Retrieed from: http://www.angusreidglobal.com/polls/canadians-endorse-multiculturalism-but-pick-melting-pot-over-mosaic/
Banting, K., & Kymlicka, W. (2010). Canadian multiculturalism: Global anxieties and local debates. *British Journal of Canadian Studies, 23*(1), 43-72.
Banting, K., & Kymlicka, W. (2013). Is there really a retreat from multiculturalism policies? New evidence from the multiculturalism policy index. *Comparative European Politics, 11*(5), 577-598.
Barry, B. (2001). *Culture and equality.* Cambridge: Polity Press.
Bauböck, R. (2002). Farewell to multiculturalism? Sharing values and identities in societies of immigration. *Journal of International Migration and Integration, 3*(1), 1-16.
Bibby, R. (1990). *Mosaic madness: Pluralism without a cause.* Toronto: Stoddart.
Bibby, R. (1991, October 9). Toward dignifying diversity. *The Globe and Mail.*

Bibby R. (2008, March 1). Whatever happened to mosaic madness? [Web Log Post] Retrieved from: http://reginaldbibby.blogspot.com/

Bisoondath, N. (1994). *Selling illusions: The cult of multiculturalism in Canada*. Toronto: Penguin.

Buchignani, N. (1982). Canadian ethnic research and multiculturalism. *Journal of Canadian Studies, 17*(1), 16-34.

Chua, A. (2003). *World on fire: How exporting free market democracy breeds ethnic hatred and global instability*. New York: Anchor Books.

Delanty, G., & He, B. (2008). Cosmopolitanperspectives on European and Asian transnationalism. *International Sociology, 23*(3), 323-344.

Fleras, A., & Elliott, J. (2002). *Engaging diversity: Multiculturalism in Canada* (2nd ed.). Toronto: Nelson.

Goodhart, D. (2004). Too Diverse? *Prospect, 95* (Feburary). Retrieved from: http://www.prospect-magazine.co.uk/article_details.php?id=5835

Gozdecka, D., Ercan, S., & Kmak, M. (2014). From multiculturalism to post-multiculturalism: Trends and paradoxes. *Journal of Sociology, 50*(1), 51-64.

Gregg, A. (2006). Identity crisis. *The Walrus, 3*(2), 38-47.

Hall, S. (2000). Conclusion: The multi-cultural question. In B. Hesse (Ed.), *Un/settled multiculturalisms: Diasporas, entanglements, 'transruptions'* (pp. 209-241). London: Zed Books.

Hartmann, D., & Gerteis, J. (2005). Dealing with diversity: Mapping multiculturalism in sociological terms. *Sociological Theory, 23*(2), 218-240.

Huntington, S. (1993). The clash of civilizations? *Foreign Affairs, 72*(3), 22-49.

Huntington, S. (1996). *The clash of civilizations and the remaking of world order*. New York: Simon and Schuster

Jafri, B. (2012). National identity, transnational whiteness and the Canadian citizenship guide. *Critical Race and Whitenesss Studies, 8*(1), 1-15.

Jedwab, J. (2005). Neither finding nor losing our way: The debate over Canadian multiculturalism *Canadian Diversity, 4*(1), 95-102.

Joppke, C. (2004). The retreat of multiculturalism in the liberal state: Theory and policy. *The British Journal of Sociology, 55*(2), 237-257.

Kallen, E. (1982). Multiculturalism: Ideology, policy and reality. *Journal of Canadian Studies, 17*(1), 51-63.

Kirkham, D. (1998). The reform party of Canada: Discourse on race, ethnicity and equality. In V. Satzewich (Ed.), *Racism & social inequality in Canada* (pp. 243-267). Toronto: Thompson Educational Publishing.

Kundnani, A. (2002). *The death of multiculturalism*. London: Institute of Race Relations. Retrieved from: http://www.irr.org.uk/2002/april/ak000001.html

Kunz, J. (2007). Multicultural Canada in the 21st century: Harnessing opportunities and managing pressures. *Cultural Diversity*. Retrieved from: http://www.policyresearch.gc.ca/page.asp?pagenm=rp_mult_bkg

Kymlicka, W. (1998). *Finding our way: Rethinking ethnocultural relations in Canada*. Toronto: Oxford University Press.

Kymlicka, W. (2010). The rise and fall of multiculturalism? New debates on inclusion and accommodation in diverse societies. *International Social Science Journal, 61*(199), 97-112.

Kymlicka, W. (2012). *Multiculturalism: Success, failure, and the future*. Washington, DC: Migration Policy Institute.

Kymlicka, W. (2014). *The essentialist critique of multiculturalism: Theories, policies, ethos*. EUI Working Paper RSCAS 2014/59. Badia Fiesolana: European University Institute.

Latour, B. (2002). *War of the worlds: What about peace?* Chicago, USA: Prickly Press LLC.

Lentin, A., & Titley, G. (2012). The crisis of 'multiculturalism' in Europe: Mediated minarets, intolerable subjects. *European Journal of Cultural Studies, 15*(2), 123-138.

Levrau, F., & Loobuyck, P. (2013). Is multiculturalism bad for social cohesion and redistribution? *The Political Quarterly, 84*(1), 101-109.

Lewis, B. (1990). The roots of muslim rage. *The Atlantic Monthly, 266*(3), 47-60.

Li, P. (1999). The multicultulturalism debate. In P. S. Li (Ed.), *Race and ethnic relations in Canada* (2nd ed., pp. 148-177). Don Mills: Oxford University Press.

Li, P. (2003). Deconstructing Canada's discourse of immigrant integration. *Journal of International Migration and Integration, 4*(3), 315-333.

Mannheim, K. (1936). *Ideology and utopia*. New York: Harcourt, Brace and Company.

Meja, V. & Stehr, N. (1999). Introduction. In V. Meja & N. Stehr, *The sociology of knowledge* (pp. xiii-xxi). Northampton, MA.: Edward Elgar.

Metropolis. (2003). *Metropolis presents: Shared citizenship: Immutable core of dynamic nucleus?* October 14, 2003, Ottawa, Canada. Retrieved from: http://canada.metropolis.net/events/metropolis_presents/shared_citizenship/index_e.htm

Metropolis. (2007). *Metropolis phase III (2007-2012) annexes A-L, memorandum of understanding between social sciences and humanities research council and citizenship and immigration Canada.* Retrieved from: http://canada.metropolis.net/policypriority/citizenship_e.htm

Modood, T. (2005, September 29). Remaking multiculturalism after 7/7. *Open Democracy.* Retrieved from: http://www.opendemocracy.net/conflict-terrorism/multiculturalism_2879.jsp

Modood, T. (2013). Multiculturalism and religion: A three part debate. Part one: Accommodating religions: Multiculturalism's new fault line. *Critical Social Policy, 34*(1), 121-127.

Nagra, B., & Peng, I. (2013). Has multiculturalism really failed? A Canadian Muslim perspective. *Religions, 4*(4), 603-620.

Porter, J. (1965). *The vertical mosaic*. Toronto. University of Toronto Press.

Porter, J. (1972). Dilemmas and contradictions of a multi-ethnic society. *Transactions of the Royal Society of Canada, 10*(4), 193-205.

Porter, J. (1975). Ethnic pluralism in Canadian perspective. In N. Glazer & D. Moynihan (Eds.), *Ethnicity, theory and experience* (pp. 267-304). Cambridge, Mass.: Harvard University Press

Porter, J. (1979a). Ethnic luralism in Canadian perspective. In J. Porter (Ed.), *The measure of Canadian society* (pp. 103-138). Toronto. Gage Publishing.

Porter, J. (1979b). Melting pot or mosaic: Revolution or reversion? In J. Porter (Ed.), *The measure of Canadian society* (pp. 139-162). Toronto. Gage Publishing.

Prins, B., & Slijper, B. (2002). Multicultural society under attack. *Journal of International Migration and Integration, 3*(3-4), 313-328.

Richmond, A. H. (2000). Immigration and policy research in Canada: Pure or applied. *Journal of Ethnic and Migration Studies, 26*(1), 109-125.

Satzewich, V., & Liodakis, N. (2007). *Race and ethnicity in Canada: A critical introduction.* Don Mills: Oxford University Press.

Silverman, M. (1992). *Deconstructing the nation: Immigration, racism, and citizenship in modern France.* London: Routledge.

Singh, G., & Cowden, G. (2011). Multiculturalism's new fault lines: Religious fundamentalisms and public policy. *Critical Social Policy, 31*(3), 343-364.

Soutphommasane, T. (2005). Grounding multicultural citizenship: From minority rights to civic pluralism. *Journal of Intercultural Studies, 26*(4), 401-416.

Stein, J., Cameron, D., Ibbitson, J., Kymlicka, W., Meisel, J., Siddiqui, H., & Valpy, M. (2007). *Uneasy partners.* Waterloo: Wilfrid Laurier University Press

Taylor, C. (2001). Democracy, inclusive and exclusive. In R. Madsen, W. Sullivan, A. Swindler, & S. Tipton (Eds.), *Meaning and modernity: Religion, polity and the self* (pp. 181-194). Berkeley: University of California Press.

Vertovec, S. (2010). Towards post-multiculturalism? Changing communities, conditions and contexts of diversity. *International Social Science Journal, 61*(199), 83-95.

Uberoi, V. & Modood, T. (2013). Has multiculturalism in Britain retreated? *Soundings: A Journal of Politics and Culture, 53*(Spring), 129-142.

Uitermark, J., Rossi, U., & Van Houtum, H. (2005). Re-inventing multiculturalism: Urban citizenship and the negotiation of ethnic diversity in Amsterdam. *International Journal of Urban and Regional Research, 29*(3), 622-640.

Wieviorka, M. (1998). Is multiculturalism the solution? *Ethnic and Racial Studies, 21*(5), 881-910.

Wieviorka, M. (2014). The end of multiculturalism? Retrieved from: http://wieviorka.hypotheses.org/321

Winter, E. (2011). *Us, them, and others: Pluralism and national identity in diverse societies.* Toronto: University of Toronto Press.

Lloyd Wong
Department of Sociology
University of Calgary

SOURAYAN MOOKERJEA

5. MULTICULTURALISM AND EGALITARIANISM

MULTICULTURALISM TODAY?

What has happened to multiculturalism now, forty plus years after it entered Canadian public cultural and political life? I propose to address this question by asking what the recent Reasonable Accommodation Debate and the Hérouxville Affair[1] tell us about the way both Multiculturalism and racism in Canadian society are changing. In doing so, I will approach the issues from the perspectives of historical sociology, transnational feminism and cultural studies.

What is multiculturalism today? What is racism today? These two questions have to be linked. As we shall see, racism and multiculturalism are fundamentally connected. Not because the two can be reduced to each other (they can't), not because anti-racist critique in Canada has long argued (correctly) that multiculturalism failed as an effective, comprehensive anti-racist strategy, but rather because of what made that critique necessary in the first place. For racism is more than a mere individual moral failing (it may be that, too); more significantly, it is a mode of politics. As such, it is one dimension of the changing aesthetic or ideology of Canadian nationalism and this is what connects it to multiculturalism. Here it may be useful to register the usual clarifications. The term multiculturalism, we are often reminded, is sometimes used to describe the empirical social fact of diversity. In itself this is a banal observation, if it is not merely the panic that grips white privilege on those occasions when the stance of colour-blindness fails it. For the more deeply we understand human history, the more we understand how hybrid and multicultural the human condition has usually been and how homogeneity of identity has been the artefact of political domination. Whatever people's official or avowed identifications may be, history teaches us that the cultural forms, media, practices, rituals, texts, repertoires and strategies out of which identities are constructed are themselves much traveled and deeply diasporic (Bayly, 2004; Goody, 1996; Robertson, 2003). "Deep diversity" runs deep indeed and certainly does not map neatly to the paperwork of the world system of nation-states nor its myriad fracture lines of legitimacy, the so-called ethnic minorities. This multiculturalism of culture is, in its material effectivity, enduring. It is time-biased, as Harold Innis (1951) would say, and in this respect it undermines every kind of linear spacing we impose upon history through our technologies of measuring time. So marking the anniversary of multiculturalism in this sense is especially pointless. Moreover, if there is a social fact of multiculturalism, it is a fact of the imagination, since multiculturalism, otherwise, is a matter of differing identifications with the deep diversity of human history

S. Guo & L. Wong (eds.), Revisiting Multiculturalism in Canada, 91–106.

itself. This returns us to the topics of politics and ideology. Still, it would be good to know the range and proportions of different birthplaces, languages spoken, religious affiliations and the like, especially since Prime Minister Stephen Harper's Conservative Government has made this more difficult to know. But this would tell us only a small and not very important part of what now is at stake with our multiculturalism. This recent 40th anniversary is more properly that of the governmental policy, of course, the second distinct reference of the term. But it has been widely noted how peculiar a policy it is, almost a non-policy in comparison with healthcare, trade, science and technology, immigration, etcetera, insofar as no governmental programs and services are mandated by it, save small change funding to this or that community organization. One wouldn't want to overlook the influence it has had in other policy domains, especially in arts and cultural policy, and even in healthcare. But this only underscores the symbolic rather than administrative and organizational character of the policy. Its symbolic character, however, does not mean the policy plays no role in governing or social engineering the polity, far from it. Consequently, multiculturalism qua politics and ideology – that is to say, hegemony, the third sense with which the term is used – is the crucial dimension of what is at stake here on this anniversary. So then also at stake is the question of racism with which it is useful to begin.

Afterwards forty plus years of multiculturalism, are we struggling today against another new racism? This question is being asked with increasing urgency around the world. The normalization of racial profiling, the "securitization" of immigration policy but especially the Reasonable Accommodation Debate in Quebec and beyond raises this question for us in Canada as well. This question, however, prompts another. What were the specifically Canadian features of what we once called by the names of "the new racism," "cultural racism," and "democratic racism" during the conjuncture spanning the late 1960s to some hard to pin down point over the horizon of the recent past? The question of another new racism would have to address this question as well.

HÉROUXVILLE'S AFGHANISTAN

The racism of the Hérouxville Declaration's provocation cannot be kept within the letter of the Declaration's guidelines, nor even the list's hyperboles.[2] It will be remembered that there was a groundswell of popular support for a policeman who faced disciplinary action for his racist song lyrics as well as innumerable other incidents, racist and Islamophobically so, which form a chain of events out of which the Declaration appeared and through which it rippled on. What requires particular attention in this regard is the unrelenting Islam-baiting of American hawks and their Canadian proxies on talk radio, cable news and the blogosphere. The Hérouxville Declaration was soon enough grist for the mill of their hate-mongering. Speech act theory can then help us describe the racist dimension of this event with precision. As symbolic actions performed by texts and utterances, speech acts are analyzed by Austin (1962) in terms of their representational sense, their illocutionary force and their perlocutionary effects. Thus the utterance "it's cold in here" has a representational or constative sense insofar as it describes a state of affairs. Its illocutionary force could be either that of a description, a command, or request (to close a window, for example), or some other such verbal act. The utterance's perlocutionary force would then involve how the illocutionary possibilities actually play out, whether the utterance ends up being taken as a request and a window gets closed or some other chain of consequences follow. The racist dimension of this event, then, turns on what speech act theory would call the Declaration's perlocutionary effect, an analysis that, moreover, underscores racism's tactical and political character. I want to name this familiar aspect of the Declaration's communicative force – where signifiers of "culture" perform as a racializing code – with the following formula: one speaks of "culture" and it – the signifier – signifies "race." I will call this the spectral effect of the old nineteenth century racisms as they return as "culture": as a racialized field of affect, image, stereotype and sense. (But the past, as we shall see, returns as culture in more ways than this.)

A second crucial consideration to register regarding the Reasonable Accommodation Debate and the Hérouxville Declaration has to do with the fact that we have been at war. The more war is normalized as faraway but routine, among the necessities of letting the mundane, every day run as it will, the more will everyday ordinary interactions brim with felt violence. This is precisely the situation that anti-imperialist scholarship theorizes as a systematic relationship between hot and cold war and the everyday ordinariness of class struggle. David Harvey's (2003) analysis of "accumulation by dispossession" outlines several important aspects of this systemic link. Harvey suggests that we generalize Marx's account of primitive accumulation: Genocide in the Americas, Atlantic slavery and the plantation system, and the enclosures of commons all formed the historical conditions of the possibility of modern colonial state formation, industrial capitalism, and biopower. But this accumulation by violent dispossession continues, Harvey argues, as an ongoing systemic feature of capitalist social reproduction, the political violence through which spatial-temporal fixes are sought. The intense waves of privatization and commodification we have endured over the last few decades are thus explained as the transnational capitalist class' attempt to retard the declining rate of profit in Northern economies especially.

Harvey's analysis is relevant in two ways: if everyone now takes offence more quickly, this is because of a symptomatic accumulation of contradictions within the liberal ideological symbolic universe as a result of the wars. For the United States' barbaric misadventures in Afghanistan, Iraq and, finally, its fatal hesitations in Egypt, have thoroughly discredited democratic ideology in the eyes of the world's subaltern masses, leaving no doubt that "democracy" is only something that the geopolitical West will lecture them about as an excuse for bullying and interfering without meaning a word of it. As such, democracy can only amount to mere American representative democracy, yet another thing for the wealthy to buy. This, then, is another crucial aspect of our conjuncture's relationship to the global human past. This barbarism has uncoupled from each other what Laclau and Mouffe (2001) conceptualize as the egalitarian and democratic imaginaries. Rehearsing a set piece of Eurocentric historiography, indeed, the key version of the rise of the West story, Laclau and Mouffe argue that an egalitarian, democratic imaginary comes into being through European modernity and its "democratic invention," which their theoretical interventions seek to defend and radicalize. Be that as it may, what is of interest to us here is the conjunctural fate of this last residue of essentialism underlying the democratic imaginary of politics today. From the unspeakable brutality of the West's sanctions against Iraq to that of the wars themselves in both theatres, what has become effectively operative for all locations of subalternity through this new assemblage of war is the enhancement, retrieval, reversal and obsolescence (McLuhan & Fiore, 1968) of the democratic imaginary by an egalitarian counter-environment. Along with everything else the War on Terror amounts to being, it has been a techno-economical symbolic act meant to communicate a message over the ramparts of the fortress. But among its many unintended consequences is that of a cultural realignment of the firmament such that a radically new relationship of the present to the human past has become temporarily accessible. This is the radical contingency of historical counter-environments to the symbolically ratified official path through which the present is authoritatively said to emerge – not only from the so-called "end of history" at the close of the cold war back into history again with more war and crisis following in train but also the dominant "textbook" narratives of how we arrived at this last episode in the first place. In this situation, the ground becomes a figure, and counter-environmental contingency scrambles the compass readings for the American Empire's triumphant march into the future. For example, Anthony Hall's (2003, p. 212) study of the transmission of aboriginal egalitarian critiques of European social inequality from the Baron de Lahontan's Fur Trade colleague and Huron interlocutor (known to the historical record variously as Kondiaronk, the Rat, and as Adario) to the dawning French Enlightenment takes on a new kind of global political importance too great to remain buried as an obscure footnote in the historiography of New France. So it is that this conjuncture has seen the flourishing of renewed theoretical and practical experiments with various forms of deliberative or participatory democracy, Bolivarian circles, legan sha'beya, barrios asembleas, and cooperatives – especially in the global South – that establish new tactical relationships to the world system of nation-states rather than working in conformity to its coloniality of power. Such struggles against accumulation by dispossession and the new enclosures embody contingent counter-environmental passageways from disparate historical struggles against primitive accumulation and the old enclosures that gave rise to a capitalist world economy. They emerge through what might be understood via McLuhan's (2009) idea of a resonating interval – an echo – of subjective processes of becoming egalitarian that such struggles, past and present, entail.

Secondly, "accumulation by dispossession" also refers to the contingency that the world we live in is characterized by the duration of the difference between overdevelopment and underdevelopment, and that the duration of this difference is one of the ways the past violently remains alive in the present and so contradicts it. The last thirty years have seen a sharp increase in social inequality in Canada as well as around the world, as has been robustly documented by the social sciences (Green & Kesselman, 2006; Korzeniewicz & Moran, 1997; Singer, 1999; United Nations Development Program, 2000). It needs to be emphasized that this accelerating social polarization is neither an accidental outcome of the course of events, nor a moral or natural consequence of social changes, but the creation of policy, public and private; which is to say that it is the result of the exercise of class power. Sklair (2001) and others have theorized these developments as the emergence of a transnational ruling class. The consequences of this for the way immigration policy has been reframed during this time is self-evident enough, but the Hérouxville Affair makes it clear that there are consequences also for multiculturalism as an ethical framework for immigrant integration and settlement, since migration flows follow overall net capital flows from periphery to core.

In this situation, the under-theorization of class politics by intersectionality researchers is especially debilitating. We risk misunderstanding everything through a critique of racialization that remains confined entirely within the binary logic of racialization, as happens with Thobani's (2007) manicheistic and moralizing oppositions between racialized and exalted subjects. Walby's (2007) intervention in the current debates on intersectionality breaks important ground in this respect by shifting the focus of the problematic back from false problems of identity to the question of how we can understand (and struggle against) historically contingent articulations of different systems of domination and exploitation. Drawing on chaos theory's primary axiom that any system is constituted by its borderline differentiating it from its environment, and that therefore no system can ever saturate its environment, Walby argues that intersectionality can be more clearly conceptualized as the relationship any singular system of domination or exploitation has to its environment, now understood as a multiplicity of other systems of domination and exploitation. To extend this line of critique opened by Walby, I have argued elsewhere (Mookerjea, 2010, 2013) that the concept-metaphor of intersectionality can then be rendered more useful if the problematic is reconstructed in terms of a dialectic of multitude and subaltern, enabling us to give theoretical primacy to the agency of political struggles against intersecting systems of domination and exploitation. This dialectic of class politics keeps reification at bay on three crucial issues, allowing us to make analytic distinctions while grasping empirical-historical relationships. In this dialectic, the concept of the subaltern names the non-identity of the multitude with itself, thereby differentiating the multitude from the transnational class. Whereas, the concept of the multitude names the non-identity of the subaltern with itself, thereby underscoring that it is the commonality of subaltern struggles in defence of the common against new and old enclosures that enables subaltern struggles to stop reproducing the war of all particularities against all. On the one hand, then, both "multitude" and "subaltern" are thus re-inscribed as narrative characters, rather than as referential categories. On the other hand, class politics is then more clearly understood as a political struggle over the historically contingent content of the universal in politics. Any singular subaltern resistance engages in a politics of the multitude when it struggles for the abolition of all and every form of domination and exploitation (including the environment). In doing so, another search begins for an egalitarian mode of social reproduction. Lastly, the concept of the subaltern allows us to get past the reification of chaos theory's spatial figure of "environment" by drawing our attention to the egalitarian counter-environments of subaltern revolt and insurgency that form the historical ground over and against which contemporary systems of oppression have been established.

I want to bring these considerations regarding the reproduction of social inequality and the intersection of systems of oppression together under a concept of "accumulated violence" and suggest that intersectional politics needs to be understood as a politics that emerges out of and through egalitarian counter-environments. The widely noted and discussed mobilization of ethnic and religious identifications of recent times can be understood better in its light. Particularist identification hardens for people not because the universal is inhospitable in principle, but because people have had to depend on such enclaves and networks more and more in order to make for themselves an inhabitable "concrete universal," as common projects serving historically determinate needs are devalued, privatized and commodified outright.

These are the main conjunctural developments that form the broader relevant political context for the new strategies of racism that have crystallized through the Reasonable Accommodation Debate and the Hérouxville Affair. As we shall see, they involve an articulation of racist populism with class politics, such that the ideological innovations of the transnational ruling class find their popular, local imitations. Nonetheless, these new formations of racism have not fallen from the sky but have had to be worked through and out of pre-existing ideological, cultural and political raw materials. They involve, in other words, some kind of structural transformation of multiculturalist discourse. This transformation cannot be grasped without re-examining multiculturalism's role in the hegemony of a bygone historic bloc that the Harper Conservatives have finally succeeded in burying. It is to this issue that I now turn.

MULTICULTURALISM, OR, ALLEGORIES BETWEEN EMPIRES

Rather than juxtaposing and opposing multiculturalism with some putative real anti-racist policy we wanted and have never got, as the common critique of multiculturalism proposes, or simply denouncing it as the logic of global capitalism as Slavoj Zizek (1997) does, it is better to grasp how multiculturalism, as a particular historical form taken by Canadian nationalism over the last forty years, is a contradictory site of both a specific and unique form of racism and Utopian antiracism.

While it is a commonplace to note that Canadian multiculturalism emerges as a compromise in the face of prairie immigrant resistance to the Trudeau government's plans for pursuing a policy of "bilingualism within a bicultural framework," the significance of this outcome is missed if we do not attend to the historical, conjunctural situation in which this policy came to be negotiated. Postwar decolonization and the collapse of the British Empire (from 1947 into the

1960s) leaves the post-confederation, "Red Ensign" British Dominion of Canada identity of the postcolonial hegemonic historic bloc without a future, especially as the United States supercedes the British Empire as the superpower hegemon organizing the conditions of possibility for capital accumulation on a world scale (Mookerjea, Szeman, & Faurschou, 2009). Indeed, the Quiet Revolution itself – the immediate background to the rise of the "three wise men" within the establishment of the Liberal Party and, with them, of bilingualism as a policy priority – has often enough been understood as being cut from the same anti-systemic cloth as the decolonization movements of the long twentieth century (Dumont, 2009). In any case, "the change from British imperialism to American imperialism," as Harold Innis (2008) put it, had been "accompanied by friction and a vast realignment of the Canadian system." Canada's multicultural national identity can thus be understood as the uncertain and ambiguous outcome of the ruling elite's long quest to reconstitute a hegemonic historic bloc in this conjunctural passage between empires.

Multiculturalism, then, is one genre of stories of national belonging among several others – the founding nations genre, and the genre of the Rise of the West – that we would come to tell about ourselves by the 1970s. In order to understand how these different genres of nationalist narrative worked together to perform hegemonically, let us begin by considering first the place of racism in the specifically ideological operations of nationalist narrative. As we have noted earlier, the postwar conjuncture inaugurates a break with the nineteenth century formation of pseudo-scientific racism. The combined moral authority of the decolonization movements' critique of colonialism, the war against fascism and revelations of the Nuremberg Trials, and then the civil rights movement in the U.S. together puts in place a new set of taboos in enlightened liberal public culture regarding on-record expression and law such that the racist "structure of feeling" along with its rationalities and juridical implements from before the Second World War are both marked as belonging now to the past and subjected to censure for that reason. The belated arrival of this enlightenment in Canada can be symbolically designated by the immigration reforms of 1962 that formally ended the White Canada policy dating from 1910; and then by the introduction of the immigration points system in 1967. As racism did not thereby magically disappear, we have had, since then, several different theories of racism to work with in order to come to grips with this new situation – polite racism, structural racism, cultural racism and so on. Even though Frances Henry's (2006) account of what she calls "democratic racism," one such theory of the new racism, has been deservedly criticized for the severe problems with the way she presents her ideas, I want to argue that her concept of democratic racism nonetheless registers a crucial insight regarding the way racism articulated the new nationalism of the post-1967 era (Fleras & Elliot, 2006). Henry, it will be recalled, argues that democratic racism is to be understood as a way that contradictions in the meritocratic values of Canadian society are rationalized. I want to suggest that this is where we confront the ideological operation in its purest form.

Recall also that after Althusser's (1971) retheorization of the problematic of ideology, underscoring its importance to the processes of social reproduction, ideology is to be henceforth understood to involve the question of identity (and therefore hegemony) as well as epistemology (so that denunciations of false consciousness as error is shown to miss the point of it all – and ditto the commonplace dismissals of the problematic on that account). Thus the famous Althusserian formulation – ideology is a symbolic representation of a subject's imaginary relation to the real social and historical conditions of one's existence – not only gives the subject center stage in the definition but, indeed, amounts to an account of the "subject effect" of becoming interpellated as the center of your "own" social and symbolic universe and thereby coming to be recognized, located and included in social relations. Fredric Jameson (1981) and Slavoj Zizek (1989) then introduce two important further refinements to the Althusserian theory by drawing on its psychoanalytic borrowings. Jameson rewrites the old epistemological theme of false consciousness in terms of Marx's own account of the fetishism of the commodity form (involving not error but a structural transformation) and points out how such ideological mystification must first gratify the subject's "political unconscious" by offering some Utopian wish-fulfilling aesthetic fantasy and disguised daydreaming unconscious political enjoyment in order to sweeten the pot and seal the deal. Zizek works these Jamesonian elaborations out in Lacanian theoretical language into a theory of ideological fantasy, emphasizing the dialectic of desire and pleasure in closing all the loopholes in the ideological interpellation of the subject. For our purposes here, then, these refinements of the theory of ideology allow us to grasp the key role ideology plays in mediating the relationship between self and other and, therefore, in any process of othering. With this in mind, let us return to Henry's observation about the links between the new "democratic racism" and Canadian meritocracy.

Our so-called "meritocratic values" articulate a Utopian element of ideology insofar as they carry a libidinal and affective charge from the egalitarian counter-environment, but the promised lightning strikes of which they nevertheless tame and limit into the well-known normative principle: rewards ought to be distributed on the basis of the "content of your character, not the colour of your skin" (in Martin Luther King's memorable formulation), as the outcome of a competition predicated on an equality of opportunity. This rule-book neutralization of egalitarian political desire owes itself to the fact that as a normative principle, the meritocratic image of equality can readily be inverted into an empirical assertion that ontologizes and naturalizes one's historically contingent but structured privileges and advantages: "all the ladders are of equal length, I climbed to the top all by myself." In this way, meritocracy relieves one of any obligation to right historical injustices and level playing fields. This is ideology at work in its purest form. The flames of political desire may thereby be dimmed but, as Wallerstein observes, they are not therefore quenched (Balibar & Wallerstein, 1991). The very fact that meritocracy depends upon the egalitarian counter-environment for its seductive appeal ensures that meritocracy's depoliticization of one's relationship to an other is always open to the possibility of repoliticization. For nothing guarantees that those left to fend for themselves in some condition of subalternity will, in fact, swallow such self-congratulatory moralizing. However, the valuable insight in Henry's theory of "democratic racism" enables us to see clearly that it is racism that enables the self-deception involved in playing the shell-game switch of the empirical for the normative in the first place. What is more, it also makes clear the formal symmetry between racism, sexism, homophobia and any other accumulated and symbolically violent gesture of othering, since any of these indifferently are also capable of flipping meritocratic principle into self-justifications of inequality.

So we are now better positioned to understand how multiculturalism has worked as a historically specific form of hegemony (which, for shorthand, I will call Trudeau Nationalism), of the post-war historical bloc that, in recent years, has completely unravelled, crisis by crisis.

Trudeau Nationalism brought together several narrative grammars – multiculturalism, the Two Founding Nations, and The West – together into an ideological formation, an ink blot which allowed a different national narrative to be told variously depending on the constituency and the situation. This constellation of narrative possibilities can be understood, following Fredric Jameson's studies of culture and ideology, to be allegorical in form. Jameson's theory of ideological meaning production takes its point of departure from the vertical allegories of medieval narrative poetry and biblical exegesis which posit fixed correspondences between different levels of meaning enabling, for example, the translation of stories of the foreign culture of the Holy Land into the lived world view of Europe undergoing Christianization through the interpretative key provided by stories of Jesus' life. Ideology also involves telling several different stories at once, except that such allegories are "horizontal" insofar as there is no "master narrative" that establishes correspondences from some transcendent position outside the ideological text. Rather, ideological allegories involve the slippage of signification from one narrative to another (Jameson, 1981). For ideology to become a hegemonic ideology, it must elaborate an allegorical system of narratives insofar as a multiplicity of interests and subject positions need to be articulated together. Thus Trudeau Nationalism involved the elaboration of an allegorical system telling the stories of multiculturalism, the founding nations and the paradigmatic supremacy of the West through each other, enabling it to work as a hegemonic ideology, as not any one of these narrative possibilities could have kept this postwar historic bloc afloat by itself.

How then did this allegory work? The ambiguity in the title of George Bowering's (1974) poem from the same period nails the crucial rhetorical dodge precisely: "At War With the U.S." For each of these narratives of national identity – whether multiculturalism, the two founding nations, or the West –allowed a different mode of identification with the universal, a different mediation of our capitulation to our dependence on American economic and political leadership. Multiculturalism and the Two Founding Nations narratives served as two anti-American and subtly pseudo-anti-capitalist mediations that enabled us to live our consent to American imperialism and the emerging multinational character of capitalism while allowing us to pretend that this was not what we were doing. The relationship between these two identifications is described aptly by Etienne Balibar's (Balibar & Wallerstein, 1991) analysis of the supplementary relationship between nationalism and racism. Our multiculturalist identification could always be mediated by our identification with the other two narratives. This is precisely how the race-culture spectre could be invoked to appear. But this also explains why appeals in the Canadian context to the Birmingham anti-racist critique missed the crucial point. The multiculturalist position could always mediate the other two when it was necessary (hence the affirmations of Kymlicka, 2001, and Taylor, 1994). Rather than hiding a secret British, French, or White essence, the racism of Trudeau nationalism was racism emptied of all positive content but still occupying the privileged empty point of universality (as, indeed, Zizek suggests in a different context). But this is the point at which the crucial third narrative of the West becomes decisively important and holds the clue to how this allegorical system is now changing.

For the West is as impossible an Ethnic Thing as the other two. Rather, the identity flag of "the West" is a geopolitical alliance, strictly speaking, among specific ruling classes. Even though the core strategic mission of the humanities from the late nineteenth century was to create the rhetorical content of Western Culture that could serve as a stain of particularity, the rise of the multinational corporation as the dominant institutional form of capitalism ensures that the world's "transnationalized" ruling classes will undermine whatever might remain of their own particularist allegiances. As Zizek (1997, p. 46) puts it, "the horror is not the [particular, living] ghost in the [dead, universal] machine, but the [dead, universal] machine in the very heart of each [particular, living, and diasporic] ghost." Thus it is that we now confront a key contradiction of this ideological discourse that is alleged to extrude a substantial Western cultural identity.

Samuel Huntington's (1993) widely discussed re-writing of the cold war formation of the Western discourse in terms of the paradigm of the "clash of civilizations" provides the telling clue. For in Huntington's imaginary theatre of culture war, "the West" is reduced to a Judeo-Christian tin soldier facing off against various stereotypes and clichés, such that the cardboard intellectual shoddiness of the exercise drew the wide derision it so richly deserved. Nonetheless, this set the stage so that the Bush administration needed to only declare a crusade briefly for rifles to be cocked across the homeland, making the subsequent retractions and recalls moot. This instrumentalization of religion into the most elementary form of Schmittian (2007) identity politics, of course, is also characteristic of what goes by the name of religious fundamentalism of all kinds, as it is also of the offense that now gets so easily taken whenever one or another form of unexamined self-absorption is disturbed by the existence of some other. In the course of ideological struggle during the cold war, the discourse of the West needed to outbid egalitarian communist Utopianism item by item. Huntington's rewrite of it in terms of religion qua culture, then, inadvertently clarifies its subsequent fate. Since no one (and, least of all, its advocates) believes in democracy talk nor, for that matter, truly free markets, the supremacy of the Western civilizing mission today amounts to risk management plus corporate social responsibility, capitalism with an insurance salesman's face; or, alternatively, the chance to win it all back in the state lottery.

MULTICULTURALISM AT FORTY

Against the backdrop of this shift in the ideological values of Western discourse, what then are we to make of the Reasonable Accommodation Debate's renewal of the battle to safeguard the separation of church and state? How should we interpret this symptom of the underlying transformations of multiculturalist national allegory? I should put my cards on the table here and confess my admiration for the principled defence of one of the key victories of the Quiet Revolution – the struggle against obscurantism – that Hérouxville also represents.

But the thrust of Hegel's critique of Kantian secularism cannot be so easily escaped, namely that it is all very well to claim to have chased religion from the public world into the domain of individual conscience and private life. For the fact remains that either such confessions of secular convictions are patent hypocrisy, the religion of the dominant group marching by in sensible shoes, or else religion is thereby turned into a cynical exercise in commodity fetishism, since the whole point of my personal relationship to my god is that the cultural-ethical content of this relationship mediates my relationship to you in the public world, rather than my consumption choices doing so. As any kind of genuine spiritual insight today recognizes, however, secularism itself has been thoroughly co-opted by postmodern cynicism. This world culture seems to have only one temporal project, accumulation by dispossession and environmental destruction, and which consequently greets every affirmation of the bliss of being ironically, in order to maintain a distance of class distinction and state security when it does not find it necessary to punish the other existence and impose on it a regime of lack-scarcity. But any such faithful critique of secularism is thereby a social critique: it then entails the multicultural recognition that the very universality of any religion's myth can only be renewed by historicizing and secularizing its narratives, thereby particularizing and relativizing the counter-environmental truth-test of its egalitarianism among a multiplicity of desubjectifying, critical, paths to grace, which is precisely how the critique of secularism becomes Utopian. Otherwise, it merely amounts to yet another kind of cynical and offended egotism waging a war of all against all, as well as surrendering to obscurantism. The sudden nostalgia for souvenirs and memorabilia of Catholicism in the most distinctly secularized society of the federation embodies just this ambiguity.

Our current conjuncture has only ratcheted up the grip of such double binds. With the conjunctural preponderance of finance capital, the self-preservation of capital has required the invention of ever new ways to turn a determinate quantity of money into a larger quantity of money (Arrighi, 2010; Harvey, 2003). The result has been the immediate commodification of various ethical social bonds – promises, obligations, commitments, instructions, trust, etcetera – in the form of the so-called "specialized investment vehicles," including the collateralized debt obligations and subprime mortgages much discussed in the aftermath of the global financial crisis of 2008. As the various ponzi schemes came tumbling down, and the cynicism of public authority became ever more apparent, the pleas of the political unconscious have only grown more plaintive for the sacred to re-enter the public stage as an avatar of the Utopian with all the unpredictability and sublime drama of revolutionary desire.

If anti-racist multicultural allegory undergoes such a transformation through the ideological-political forcefield of the current conjuncture, then what about multiculturalist democratic racism? Or more precisely, how should we then understand the current wave of "Islamophobic feminism" whereby various patriarchal authorities and offices set aside their habitual sexism in order to wage some high profile campaign to liberate women from their veils? Is there not a better way to understand this than the standard identity politics reading "white men saving brown women from brown men" which neither illuminates anything nor escapes the racialized logic of the situation. Since the U.S.-led invasion of Afghanistan, examples keep multiplying, but the latest round in both France and Canada involve rituals of compulsory civic participation – holding public office, school attendance, and court appearances or obtaining formal citizenship. For example, the (once upon a time, leftist) Parti Québecois government of Québec, until it was swept from power in a landslide electoral defeat in April 2014, had launched a series of legislative initiatives against the veil culminating in the proposal of a new charter of values that would have banned hijabs, niqabs, kippas, turbans and other so-called "indiscrete" religious symbols from any publicly funded institution, including government offices, hospitals, and schools. In December 2011, the Government of Canada proclaimed an order-in-council announcing that Muslim women who wear burkas or niqabs must remove them while taking the oath of citizenship. Embracing the media limelight, then Minister of Citizenship and Immigration, Jason Kenney, explained that showing one's face while taking the oath is apparently a matter of "deep principle." The citizenship oath is "a quintessentially public act. It is a public declaration that you are joining the Canadian family and it must be taken freely and openly" which apparently burkas and niqabs prevent. Kenney furthermore justified this order-in-council with the crucial punchline: "we want women to be full and equal members of Canadian society" (Mackrael & Perreaux, 2011, p. A7). What do we make of this kind of Canadian multiculturalism now? Judith Timson (2011, p. L2), writing in the *Globe and Mail*, put it this way: "Mr. Kenney is not exactly known as a feminist ... so here you have a Conservative government, the same Conservative government that moved to defund any agency that would provide abortion services to imperiled women in Third World countries, striking a blow for women's equality ... what a rich stew indeed, what a quandary for us, who think highly of ourselves as tolerant Canadians."

To make our way through this quandary then, consider how in a time of deepening crises, given the urgency of the situation from the ruling class' point of view, racism becomes even more important in the arsenal, especially since it is crucial to the primary class strategy of divide and rule. Islamophobic hate-mongering is crucial because if you can be crudely racist in this specific instance, you lower the threshold of liberal tolerance established over the immediate postwar decades and give license and permission for all kinds of overt expressions and symbolic-affective acts of hate and violence, a role effectively played by homophobia in the intervening years. So these are the stakes. Given the postwar liberal overcoming of the racism of the British Empire's glory days by the post-civil rights, multicultural democratic racism of the American neo-Empire, racism today, we have already noted, is spectral, a return of the repressed. The task is then to work up racism – around the taboos set up against it – to return not only as cosmopolitan culturalist tolerance (a stance which Taylor and Kymlicka have blown up into whole political philosophies) but especially now also as hate, as a blow that can be tactically effective in the present conjuncture. However, in order to mobilize affect as racist hate, the Right must first find a way to render this affect political and therefore meaningful. This is the moment, then, when Jason Kenney discovers that he is a feminist in full bloom. Let us try to understand why and how.

Insofar as the Harper government, like most governments in the core of the world-system, does not pursue any collective-historical project of any kind but demands (as such governments have ever since Reagan and Thatcher) that the public make sacrifice after sacrifice for the absolutely unquestionable cause of accumulation, it must opportunistically make bits and pieces of the egalitarian counter-environment its own. This is because the accumulation process of capitalism – the transformation of a determinate quantity of money into a larger quantity of money, by any means necessary, whether through (post)-industrial production or through the casino capers of high finance – is entirely a meaningless drive, and as such, it is not, in itself, a collective project at all.

As Andrew Coyne (2012) notes in a different debate about citizenship, national belonging is, among other things, a moral project. Indeed, most would agree that it ought to be. In which case, as it is often pointed out, the telos of the process of accumulation would be to serve as the infrastructure or foundation for the higher ends of human moral and political freedom, happiness, and, if you like, love of God. But as Karl Polanyi (2001) cogently formulated it, the "post-ideological" and "post-political" political task economic liberalism set for itself involves putting the cart before the horse and subsuming the whole of social life under the market mechanism; so it has been for the neo-liberals of our conjuncture as well. Though this is a class political task, it is by no means an easy one for a special interest government, then, to convince its subjects to tighten their belts, work longer hours at precarious jobs, destroy the environment, and keep their noses to the grindstone only to further enrich the rich.

No subjective investment or interpellation is possible with the contingent "necessity" of the accumulation of capital itself. As Zizek (2012) observes, accumulation is, in this way, a drive in the precise Lacanian psychoanalytic sense and so needs displacement by desire if there is to be subjective engagement with its myriad forms of necessary political violence and if the demanded sacrifices are to be dutifully made by those who will be shaken down the most for the sake of corporate profitability and ever higher executive compensation benchmarks. Thus the non-sequitur of Jason Kenney's sudden feminism, as though someone inexplicably briefed him with a powerpoint presentation on the writings of Emmanuel Levinas. This credit drawn from the egalitarian counter-environment lends meaning to the post-political governance of society reduced to a series of risk calculations. It provides political direction and purpose to the mobilization of affect, indeed, renders the baseness of racist hatred sublime by alloying it with righteous indignation. In doing so, this hypocritical feminism very surgically but politically strikes a violent blow in the ongoing class struggles of our times by issuing a valid permit for violence to be done to some subaltern other, a project that has a proven historical track record. Governments by capital for capital that we now have, as sexist as ever, cannot therefore be feminist without being racist or be racist without being feminist.

NOTES

[1] After months of hyperbolic media controversy in Quebec over the summer and fall of 2006 regarding the accommodation of religious and cultural minorities (which came to be known as the Reasonable Accommodation Debate) and incidences of anti-immigrant racism, the town council of Hérouxville, a small village in central Quebec (population 1338), adopted a "declaration of norms for immigrants," which it posted on the town's web-site in January 2007. At the time, none of the inhabitants of Hérouxville were recent immigrants. In the months to follow, several other municipalities adopted similar declarations. The Reasonable Accommodation Debate took place during a provincial election campaign in which a new right-wing party, the Action democratique du Québec leapt out of obscurity and did surprisingly well at the polls by scapegoating immigrants.

[2] The declaration read as follows:

1. At Christmas, children sing Christmas songs.
2. No stoning women.
3. No burning women with acid.
4. No ceremonial daggers in school even if you're a Sikh.
5. Boys and girls can swim in the same pool whether Muslims like it or not.
6. Men can drink alcohol whether Muslims like it or not.
7. No walking around with your face hidden except on Halloween.
8. Female police can arrest male suspects even if it troubles their egos.
9. Women are allowed to dance.
10. Women are allowed to drive.
11. Women are even allowed to make decisions on their own.

REFERENCES

Althusser, L. (1971). *Lenin and philosophy and other essays*. Ben Brewster, Trans. New York: Monthly Review Press.

Armitage, D. (1998). *Theories of empire. 1450-1800. Vol. 20*. Aldershot, Great Britain; Brookfield, VT: Ashgate/Variorum.

Arrighi, G. (2010). *The long twentieth century: Money, power, and the origins of our times*. London: Verso.

Austin. J. L. (1962). *How to do things with words*. Oxford: Clarendon.

Balibar, E., & Wallerstein, I. (1991). *Race, nation, class: Ambiguous identities*. London: Verso.

Bayly, C. A. (2004). *The birth of the modern world, 1780-1914: Global connections and comparisons*. Malden, MA: Blackwell.

Bowering, G. (1974). *At war with the U.S.* Vancouver: Talonbooks.

Coyne, A. (2012, January 19). Leader's allegiance should be to Canada only; Dual citizenship sends a less-than-inspiring message from NDP hopeful. *Edmonton Journal*, p. A25.

Delanty, G. (2006). *Europe and Asia beyond East and West*. Vol. 8. London: Routledge.

Dumont, F. (2009). Of a hesitant Quebéc. In S. Mookerjea, I. Szeman, & G. Faurschou (Eds.), *Canadian cultural studies: A reader, x-y*. Durham: Duke University Press.

Fleras, A., & Elliot, J. L. (2006). *Unequal relations: An introduction to race and ethnic relations in Canada* (5th ed.). Toronto: Pearson Educational Press.

Goody, J. (1996). *The East in the West*. Cambridge: Cambridge University Press.

Green, D. A., & Kesselman, J.R. (Eds.). (2006). *Dimensions of inequality in Canada*. Vancouver: University of British Columbia Press.

Hall, A. 2003. *The American empire and the fourth world*. Montreal: McGill-Queens University Press.

Harvey, D. (2003). *The new imperialism*. Oxford: Oxford University Press.

Henry, F. (2006). *The colour of democracy: Racism in Canadian society* (3rd ed.). Toronto: Thomson Nelson.

Huntington, S. (1993). The clash of civilizations. *Foreign Affairs, 72*(3) (Summer), 22-49.

Innis, H. A. (2008). *The bias of communication*. Toronto: University of Toronto Press.

Jameson, F. (1977). Ideology, narrative analysis, and popular culture. *Theory & Society, 4*(4), 543-559.

Jameson, F. (1981). *The political unconscious: Narrative as a socially symbolic act*. Ithaca, NY: Cornell University Press.

Korzeniewicz, R. Z., & Moran, T. P. (1997). World economic trends in the distribution of income, 1965-1992. *American Journal of Sociology, 102* (January), 1000-1039.

Kymlicka, W. (2001) *Politics in the vernacular: Nationalism, multiculturalism, and citizenship*. Oxford: Oxford University Press.

Laclau, E., & Mouffe, C. (2001). *Hegemony and socialist strategy: Towards a radical democratic politics*. London: Verso.

Mackrael, K., & Perreaux, L. (2011, December 13). Muslim women must lift veils during oath. *The Globe and Mail*, p. A7.

McLuhan, M., & Fiore, Q. (1968). *War and peace in the global village*. New York: Bantam.

McLuhan, M. (2009). Canada as counter-environment. In S. Mookerjea, I. Szeman, & G. Faurschou (Eds.), *Canadian cultural studies: A reader*. Durham: Duke University Press.

Mielants, E. (2007). *The origins of capitalism and the "rise of the west."* Philadelphia: Temple University Press.

Mookerjea, S. (2010). Subaltern biopolitics through the networks of the Commonwealth. *Journal of Alternative Perspectives in the Social Sciences*, Special Issue on Globalization, Development and Education in Africa and Asia/Pacific: Critical Perspectives, *2*(1), 245-278.

Mookerjea, S. (2013). Paths through the utopian forest: Politics of community and the Athabaskan tar sands. *Canadian Journal of Sociology*, Special Issue on Tar Sands Development in Northern Alberta, *38*(2), 233-254.

Mookerjea, S., Szeman, I., & Faurschou, G. (Eds.) (2009). Between empires. In S. Mookerjea, I. Szeman, & G. Faurschou (Eds.), *Canadian cultural studies: A reader*. Durham: Duke University Press.

Negri, A. (1999). *Insurgencies: Constituent power and the modern state*. Minneapolis: University of Minnesota Press.

Polanyi, K. (2001). *The great transformation: The political and economic origins of our time*. Boston: Beacon Press.

Robertson, R. T. (2003). *The three waves of globalization: A history of a developing global consciousness*. Black Point, NS: Fernwood.

Schmitt, C. (2007). *The concept of the political* (Expanded Edition, 1932). G. Schwab, trans. Chicago: University of Chicago Press.

Singer, D. (1999). *Whose millenium? Theirs or ours*. New York: Monthly Review Press.

Sklair, L. (2001). *The transnational capitalist class*. Oxford: Blackwell.

Taylor, C. (1994). *Multiculturalism: Examining the politics of recognition*. Princeton: Princeton University Press.

Timson, J. (2011, December 16). I don't like segregation in any religion. *The Globe and Mail*, p. L2.

United Nations Development Program. (2000). *Overcoming human poverty*. New York: United Nations Development Program.

Walby, S. (2007). Complexity theory, systems theory, and multiple intersecting social inequalities. *Philosophy of the Social Sciences, 37*(4), 449-470.

Žižek, S. (1989). *The sublime object of ideology*. London: Verso.

Zizek. S. (1997). Multiculturalism, or, the cultural logic of late capitalism. *New Left Review, 225*(September-October), 28-51.

Zizek. S. (2012). *Lacan's four discourses*. Retrieved from: http://www.lacan.com/zizfour.htm

Sourayan Mookerjea
Department of Sociology
University of Alberta

HO HON LEUNG

6. CANADIAN MULTICULTURALISM IN THE 21ST CENTURY

Emerging Challenges and Debates

INTRODUCTION

Official multiculturalism policy was adopted by the Canadian federal state in 1971 and was entrenched in the 1982 constitution. This policy has attracted many controversies and heated debates, not only in Canada but also in the rest of the world. Yet multiculturalism has also earned Canada a leadership role in the world's eye in an attempt to create a nation with a higher level of inclusion. Multiculturalism turned forty in 2011. As Canada takes this issue seriously, it is meaningful and necessary to revisit its policy periodically so that the goals and the implementations of the policy may be evaluated and improved for the future. The purpose of this chapter is to re-examine the value of multiculturalism and develop an argument that it is a key policy not only for nation-building, but also for ensuring a more inclusive, equal, and democratic society for the citizens. First, this chapter introduces the historical development of multiculturalism, emphasizing the meaning of multiculturalism that has been evolving along with the political, economic, social and cultural developments of the Canadian society. In order to engage in a meaningful evaluation of multiculturalism, we need to reframe the policy in the twenty-fist century Canadian context where the domestic and international situations have changed tremendously in the last forty years. With this context in mind this chapter explores in the directions multiculturalism should move in conjunction with other Canadian values such as equality and democracy. Finally a working argument is put forward with a vision to broadening the scope of multiculturalism, bearing strong and strict notion on ethno-religious diversity, to include all types of cultures, so that every citizen is drawn into an inclusive and collective process in which Canada charts its discourse of national identity and nationalism.

THE HISTORICAL CONTEXT AND THE MEANING OF MULTICULTURALISM

It is difficult to aim at a moving target. Multiculturalism is neither a static concept nor a simplistic idea. It is not only a moving target, but also a multidimensional entity. In order to understand what it is and criticize its policies, there is a need to acknowledge its complexity. The ontological meaning of multiculturalism may not be as straightforward as desired. Its initial defined meanings and purposes were

S. Guo & L. Wong (eds.), Revisiting Multiculturalism in Canada, 107–119.

contextualized in the specific historical, political, social, and cultural conditions at the time it was created. The establishment of multiculturalism, proposed by Prime Minister Pierre Trudeau forty years ago, was situated within a bilingual framework of the English and French speaking elements of Canada. Trudeau stated his position on the multiculturalism in the House of Commons on October 8, 1971:

> It was the view of the Royal Commission, shared by the government and, I am sure, by all Canadians, that there cannot be one cultural policy for Canadians of British and French origin, another for the original peoples and yet a third for all others. For although there are two official languages, there is no official culture, nor does any ethnic group take precedence over any other. No citizen or group of citizens is other than Canadian, and all should be treated fairly ... Sometimes the word 'bi-culturalism' is used, but I don't think that it accurately describes this country. I prefer 'multiculturalism.' (as cited in Fleras & Elliott, 1992a, p. 281)

At the time, the demographic composition of the Canadian population contained only 3% of non-European origin (Jansen, 2005, p. 26). Therefore, some scholars view this policy as an attempt to manage the ethnic relations between the English- and the French-Canadians for the best (Jansen, 2005, p. 26); some view it as a policy to undermine the Quebecois claim to a special status in Canada (Uberoi, 2009, pp. 807-809). Although the 1971 version of multiculturalism could and should include the aboriginal population, this minority group was largely excluded from the making of this policy. This version of multiculturalism at the time could be understood as bi-culturalism.

As the Canadian immigration policies changed in the 1960s from race-based to a merit- based point system that welcomes immigrants who can meet the economic development needs according to their level of education, occupational skills, knowledge of English and French and other merits, immigrants from non-traditional sources (other than Europeans) have been added to the Canadian ethnic landscape. The official website for Toronto, the most populated city in Canada, proudly announces the fact that it is one of the most multicultural cities in the world and is still ranked as the safest large metropolitan area in North America by Places Rated Almanac. The city is also home to residents who speak over 140 languages and dialects, and half of Toronto's population (1,230,720) was born outside Canada, up from 48% in 1996 (Toronto's Racial Diversity, n.d.). Although minority cultures and differences were recognized and celebrated within the bilingual framework during the multiculturalism policy in 1970s, minorities continue to be excluded from full equality and equal participation in the mainstream society. Racial and ethnic stratification remains. Fleras and Elliott observe: "...compared with whites, people of colour occupied an unequal status in society above and beyond the "initial adjustment" [original] phase. Therein lay the discriminatory component: discrimination was institutionalized in that it was supported by cultural values and social practices, reflected normal functioning of societal structures, and persisted as pervasive feature of interpersonal contact" (1996, pp. 115-116). Racial discrimination becomes the obstacle in Canada that prevents citizens from actualizing themselves. This does not meet Canada's commitment to individual rights and formal equality as prerequisites for national unity and identity (Fleras & Elliott, 1996, p. 115).

A position put forward under the rubric of the multiculturalism focused on combating racial discrimination. This was evident in a shift in program emphasis from language and culture to group understanding, declared by the Honorable John Munro who was Minister of Multiculturalism in 1975. It was a response to spokespersons for visible minorities that included Chinese, West Indians, and south Asians. These spokespersons argued that the earlier implemented programs under the multicultural policy did not put enough emphasis on eradicating racism in Canada (Kallen, 2004, p.88). This was a shift in policy focusing on the needs of visible minority immigrants from the European orientation (Driedger, 1996, p. 56).

Furthermore, Canada institutionalized multicultural policy in the 1980s. Multiculturalism was made reference in the Canadian Charter of Rights and Freedoms, adopted in 1982. Section 27 of the Charter states: "this Charter shall be interpreted in a manner consistent with the preservation and enhancement of the multicultural heritage of Canadians." As Dewing states, "it empowers the courts to take Canada's multicultural reality into account at the highest levels of decision-making. In the words of a former Human Rights Commissioner, it provides a useful 'interpretative prism' [original] to assist the courts when balancing individual and multicultural (and often collective) [original] rights" (2009, p. 5).

In addition, Section 15 (1) in the Canadian Charter of Rights and Freedoms states: "every individual is equal before and under the law and has the right to equal protection and equal benefit of the law without discrimination and, in particular, without discrimination based on race, national or ethnic origin, colour, religion, sex, age, or mental or physical disability." In other words, the Section 15 (1) guarantees both equality and fairness to all under the law, regardless of race and ethnicity.

In the spring of 1995 multiculturalism policy continued to develop to meet the needs in the evolving and increasingly diverse society. A review of the Department of Canadian Heritage's multiculturalism programming activities pointed to new directions that included three fundamental goals: (1) Identity: recognizing and reflecting a diversity of cultures so that people of all backgrounds feel a sense of belonging and attachment; (2) Civic participation: developing active citizens who have the opportunity and capacity to participate in shaping the future; and (3) Social justice: ensuring fair and equitable treatment that respects the dignity of people of all origins (Canadian Heritage, 2001, as cited in Jansen, 2005, p. 27).

Fleras and Elliott (1996, p. 335) summed up the development of the multiculturalism in the 1990s. They stated that the focus of multiculturalism in the 1970s was on celebrating cultural differences that stressed cultural sensitivity; in the 1980s multiculturalism accommodated the needs of the ethnically diverse society at the institutional level by emphasizing equity; and in the 1990s, multiculturalism emphasized society building focusing on inclusion in the form of participation and citizenship.

Thus the concept and the execution of federal multiculturalism, implemented at different provincial and municipal levels, are never static. Many programs, such as integration of immigrants, support of new arrivals, professional accreditation, fighting against racism, to name a few, have been developed in the context of multiculturalism in order to meet the challenges generated from different political, social and cultural changes in the Canadian society. When questioning the existence of multiculturalism we must understand the twenty-first century version of multiculturalism and consider the challenges Canada now faces. This will help us decide which elements from the past should be kept, eliminated, modified, and developed.

THE TWENTY-FIRST CENTURY CANADIAN MULTICULTURALISM

Before examining the notion of multiculturalism in the twenty-first century Canadian context, the reality of this policy's goals requires some investigation. The first dimension is the continuous decline of French as a spoken language, the decline in numbers of the English/British cultural group (Dupont & Lemarchand, 2001, p. 321). This is due to current Canadian immigration policies that continue to recruit immigrants from non-traditional sources so multiculturalism is now one of the most important polices that "manages" the most ethnically and religiously diverse population in the history of Canada (Fleras & Elliott, 1992a, p. 280; Nancoo, 2000).

The other dimension relates to the relations between Canada and the rest of the world. Globalization facilitates the flow of commodities, images, information, migrants from all corners in the world in the intersecting political, economic, social, cultural, and environmental domains in everyday life (Leung & Hendley, 2009, p. 2). Canada is politically and economically more globally integrated than in the past. An example of political involvement would be Canada's peace-keeping role in the world (Jansen, 2005, p. 28). In addition, Canada's membership in the global trade organizations of NAFTA and WTO indicates economic integration into the global economy. Communication with other countries via the conducting of political and economic business requires intense cultural exchange. In other words, Canada is more intensely connected to the rest of the world; and the nation has become more global in terms of the ethnical and religious diversity. How can Canada be a strong nation if it does not prepare itself well to face the challenges in the twenty-first century reality? Without a doubt, the earlier version of "bi-culturalism" in the guise of multiculturalism created forty years ago is no longer applicable to the new reality. It would be unrealistic for any critic to attempt to preserve Canada's previous course of action in the traditional English way of life and values (Magsino, 2000, p. 327), because the increase in the intensity of cultural exchange within Canada and with the global world is irreversible. What is suggested here is that in order to effectively manage internal and international ethnic relations, multiculturalism, if not the only way, is one of the most useful lighthouses for the future of Canada. In this sense, one of the dimensions of multiculturalism is that it can be understood as an ideology. Its goal is to reach a genuine, meaningful cultural understanding and exchange. Canadians are nurtured in a multicultural environment and ready to engage in meaningful and productive intercultural communication in the global village.

MULTICULTURALISM IN RELATION TO OTHER CANADIAN VALUES

The discourse of multiculturalism indicates that it does not just manage ethnic relations but intends to produce some desirable outcomes, such as equality, equity, and inclusion which, by and large, are consistent with the values in democracy (Fleras & Elliott, 1996; Ryan, 2010). The meaning and practice of these values change across time. Equality is an excellent example. The concept of equality has different meanings for distinct gender and racial groups before and after the civil rights movement in the U.S. Furthermore, the concept of democracy evolves as time passes and brings changes. No one would deny that Canada is proud to be one of the most democratic societies in the world. At the same time, the reality of democracy in Canada has evolved after the civil rights movement so that the democracy of Canada in the twenty-first century is more inclusive than in the past. However, studies (Bloemraad, 2000; Henry & Tator, 1994) indicate that many visible minorities in Canada have been marginalized due to different forms of prejudice and discrimination and are not able to fully participate in the political process in mainstream society. If democratic values are the driving forces behind Canada, why cannot multiculturalism be part of the engine? If multiculturalism must be understood in terms of ethnic relations (indicting that there are other ways of understanding the term such as sexuality, class, gender and so on), its policies must ensure that visible minorities can fully participate in political, economic, and social sectors in this democratic society.

In summary values, such as equality and democracy discussed above, are constantly being re/interpreted according to the times and spaces where the political, economic, social and cultural circumstances change. Hopefully, the re/interpretation is heading in the right direction for humanity. Canada and its citizens should continue to adopt these values as ideologies that define and guide the development of the nation and the people.

MULTICULTURALISM: DOWN TO EARTH FROM IDEOLOGY

Dupont and Lemarchand (2001, p. 310) observe that multiculturalism, as a virtue for Canada, is not sufficient. How multiculturalism exists in everyday life needs to be examined. One of the major concerns is that multiculturalism, supported by the insertion of Section 27 in its Canadian Charter of Rights and Freedoms, encourages preservation and enhancement of the multicultural heritage of Canadians. Therefore visible minority groups might tend to retain their cultures and segregate themselves from the mainstream society. In this way, some critics argue that the lack of a dominant culture within the framework of several diverse cultures undermines the national unity and identity.

However, Sahadat (2000) explores a way to seek unity in diversity without requiring uniformity in religious diversity. He argues, "dialogue should lead us from the attitude of segregation and discrimination to complementarity, the richness of which should be felt in a consolidated drive toward harmony in diversity without the threat of uniformity" (p. 357). He further states, "[pluralism] will make our complex society more viable as we move beyond the threshold of the 21st century. It will continuously be a source of enrichment to the life of our nation; and our sense of unity without the threat of uniformity will be good reason for hope of a brighter future with deeper understanding and trustworthy relationships" (p. 357). In other words, multiculturalism that celebrates, protects, and nurtures diversity can be a Canadian ideology that leads a unified, but not uniform, nation.

The survival of the ethno-religious cultures among Hutterites and Hasidic Jews might shed some light on how unity in diversity works. Boldt (1985) found that Hutterites are not as "orthodox" as they wish. Although this group has maintained its culture and religious practice to a very high degree that manifests itself behaviorally in a very clear and distinctive way, this maintenance has required sacrifice and compromise. In order to keep the cohesion of the colonies and minimize defection of young adults religious leaders must have to interpret the rules flexibly and be sensitive to the wishes and desires of the members. As a result, a small degree of materialism has been tolerated. The rationale behind this flexibility is that the leaders have the authority to distinguish between the "essentials" and "nonessentials" of their culture. As long as the nonessentials do not threaten the survival of the religious and cultural practices, some nonessentials are allowed. Examples are the use of cameras and individualized residences far beyond what their traditions tolerate (Boldt, 1985, pp. 98-99).

A recent visit to an Amish colony in Lancaster, Pennsylvania, confirms what Boldt described and analyzed. An Amish tour guide, who was just about to hop into some visitors' vehicle for touring the colony, was inquiring, via a mobile phone, when the other guide would come to greet other visitors. When asked about the permission for phone use, he responded that it depended on the leaders of different colonies. Yet, in general, public phones by the roadside were allowed, particularly for medical emergency. Before setting off with his group, he handed out his business card with his email address printed on it. He admitted that he used a computer at home. Such transformation of Amish culture is well documented by Hurst and McConnell's recent study on the world's largest Amish community (2010). Another study of Amish communities (Nolt & Meyers, 2007) articulates "conversation" as the philosophy, similar to Sahadat's "dialogue" (2000) that sustains the Amish culture and identity. They document that contemporary Amish settlements are indeed a rich and diverse culture that is a result of the interaction of migration history, church discipline, ethnicity in the community life, and their existence in the world but not fully of it. Nolt and Meyers state, "engaging the Amish community as conversation reorients the questions and presuppositions that spring from such notions about unity. The Amish remain distinct – and united –

not by demanding total conformity or papering over deep historical, ethnic, and churchly difference" (2007, p. 192).

Some Hasidic Jews in Montreal face different types of pressure, but they have to use "flexibility" and "conversation" to ensure the survival of their communities. Similar to Hutterites and Amish, Hasidic and ultra-orthodox Hasidic Jews have the highest level of adherence to the traditions and laws of the Holy Scripture, the Torah. Unlike Hutteries and Amish who are more rural dwellers, they tend to segregate themselves in their urban communities which are isolated from other groups. Leung (2001) found that, similar to any community, the members of these orthodox communities are forced to deal with common social problems in the families and schools such as employment issues, challenges in learning in school, family violence, and alcoholism. And, intervention with families by social service professionals was considered as a threat. However, the well-being of both the family and the community could not be neglected. With limited specialized social service skills and resources, more liberal rabbis were willing to seek help from the Jewish family service agencies. The concepts and practices of social services, therapy, and counseling, although relatively new to the group, had been slowly accepted by the rabbis and the community members.

In examining Canadian Jewish life, Weinfeld (2001) explores their history and diversity, their work and family lives, their various communities and religious divisions, and the politics of their culture. He argues that "Today, within the Montreal or Toronto Jewish communities, there are formal organizations representing Sephardi, Israeli, Ethiopian, and Russian Jews. These organizations are seen as best able to meet certain needs of the sub-community members, not only by speaking the language, but by empathizing with their problems....Hasidic or ultra-Orthodox Jews need even more specialized services. In providing them, is the Canadian Jewish community acting responsibly, or risking further fragmentation?" (2001, pp. 180-181). His answer to the latter question is "no." What keeps a culturally and linguistically diverse community with different practices of Judaism united is their engagement in dialogue amongst the community members and between the sub-communities. The rabbis, like the leaders in Hutterites and Amish communities, exercise flexible interpretation of the rules, and are sensitive to the needs of the members. The Jewish communities reach out to help with sensitivity and empathy. Weinfeld then redirects the question that he posed (above) to Canada by stating, "this is precisely the same question that Canada must ponder, regarding the limits of multiculturalism and the balance between diversity and social cohesion" (2001, p. 181). The lesson learned here is that diversity, whether cultural, ethnic or other types, should not be a threat to unity. Rather, unity should be sought in diversity, not uniformity.

If the orthodox groups have to 'yield' to a certain degree in order to maintain their cultures and identities, other immigrants and their subsequent generations from visible minority groups would display an even higher level of assimilation or integration into the mainstream society. Weinfeld (1994, 1981; Kymlicka, 1996) conducted a very thorough survey of the existing literature on ethnic assimilation and the retention of ethnic cultures by using language retention, ethnic intermarriage and social networks, ethnic self-identification and ethnic culture as indicators. It was found that "by most accepted definitions and measures, ethno-cultural assimilation is proceeding, notwithstanding the rhetoric of multiculturalism, and is more pronounced among the later generations in Canada" (Weinfeld, 1994, p. 261). Peach (2005) also questioned whether the mosaic model and the melting pot model had any impact on the residential patterns. His study concluded, "… the Canadian and US data seem to indicate a situation in which all groups except African Americans pursue settlement patterns related to their own agency rather than to the constraints of national policies of their respective countries" (Peach, 2005, p. 23). All in all, the Peach statement can be understood in light of the aforementioned review of literature that concludes that assimilation of minorities depends less on the state polices than on their ability to live well within their own religious and cultural constraints. Multiculturalism has not halted the erosion of ethnic differences and assimilation is proceeding apace (Boldt, 1985, p. 101); then to what extent does multiculturalism live up to its claims and principles? This chapter maintains the position that multiculturalism is still an imperative policy that guides Canada to be a more inclusive democratic nation.

THE INTERPLAY OF MULTI-DIEMENSIONS OF MULTICULTURALISM IN NATION-BUILDING

Multiculturalism involves much more than just supporting the retention of minority cultures. As the concept and policies of multiculturalism are evolving, it becomes a multi-dimensional entity. Fleras and Elliott (1992b) discussed the concept in the following nine dimensions: (1) policy constructed for restricting government-minority relations, (2) economic resources in advancing national and minority interests, (3) collective process in reshaping Canada's symbolic and social order, (4) fundamental component in Canadian nation-building, (5) distributive ideal in allocating reward and resources, (6) political instrument for managing racial and ethnic diversity, (7) social experiment for promoting diversity as a unifying forces, (8) ideology for national discourse and decision-making, and (9) key metaphor in shaping Canadian identity. It is important to see each dimension as an integral part of the well-being of a nation. It is difficult to rank the level of importance or the priority of each of these nine dimensions. It is not productive to criticize one point without taking other points into consideration. Therefore, a more holistic approach to the understanding of multiculturalism is essential.

It is not difficult to understand the consequences of marginalizing visible minorities who become a more substantial part of the population. Based on the past Canadian criteria for immigrant selection immigrants' skills and education are the national economic resources (Fleras & Elliott, 1996, pp. 338-340) and their cultures from different parts of the world are the national and civic treasures. If they cannot maximize their talents, skills, and resources (devaluation of their credentials in mind), who is going to pay the price? If ethnicity is taken out of the nation-building equation, the growing gap between the rich and the poor should be regarded as a threat to the well-being of a nation. Multiculturalism policies of equality, equity, and inclusion are indispensable principles when allocating reward and resources.

The demands for full participation in nation-building via democratic practices in the recent uprisings in some African and Middle Eastern regions should have sent a strong signal to the more developed democratic societies like Canada. Ideal nation-building should be a collective process. Critics and supporters of multiculturalism come from both minority and majority groups. All these groups should appreciate the political and social platform created by multiculturalism on which national issues are discussed and debated. Opposition and support are drawn into the collective process in which Canada charts its discourse of nationalism. This effect is securely in place. In the absence of any consensus on what Canadian identity or culture is, "multiculturalism fills a void, defining Canadian culture in terms of the legitimate ancestral cultures which are the legacy of every Canadian defining the whole through the sum of its parts...which all Canadians are to assimilate is seen as a national strength, and as a key force differentiating Canada from the United States" (Weinfeld, 1981, p. 97).

THE BECOMING OF CANADIAN CULTURE AND IDENTITY

A nation, a culture, and an identity are never static. The nations of China and Greece before World War II are so different from their existence in the twenty-first century. Although their strong ethno-national identities remain strong, their Chineseness and Greekness, the practices of their cultures, have been evolving. This concept is not difficult to understand. The DNA, the hereditary material, of a person remains the same from birth to death. As a person grows from an infant, to a teenager and then an adult, s/he stays as the same person as the DNA of the person. However, the person's values, outlook on life, and experience develop along with the changes in his/her living environment. Such is the personality of Canada. Canada, like many other nations in the world, remains as the same nation by name but constantly evolves; the Canadianness, the practices of Canadian culture, changes constantly[1]. Although Canada continues to be a member of the Commonwealth, it has much weaker ties to Britain than in the past. Loo (2011, p. 61) made a case in point, "In fact, historically, being Canadian meant having an abiding attachment to another country – namely, Britain. Imperialism was at the heart of Canadian nationalism." However, the twenty-first Century Canada is charting a new course. It is going to be a challenge to articulate the developing Canadian identity and culture. This is no different in other nations. Nations may be regarded as named and self-defining communities that are repeatedly formed and reformed by their citizens through cultivating shared symbols, values and traditions, memories, and myths (Smith, 2009, 49) and are at the same time being de/re/constructed (Leung et al., 2009). In other words, nation, nationalism, national identity, and culture always include contests and conflicts as they are in the process of developing. Multiculturalism, a Canadian symbol and value, is an ingredient of nation-building that will always entail controversies and contests.

Of the many challenges in the shaping of a multicultural Canadian society, one concern has emerged in the power group that still dominates the Canadian political, economic, social and linguistic arena. This power group consists of English descendants and other white Europeans whose trace of ethnicity had long disappeared prior to official multiculturalism (Dupont & Lemarchand, 2001, p. 310). While official multiculturalism encourages preservation of ethnic minority cultures, what culture(s) can the power group preserve? A sense of being ignored in this cultural pursuit has developed. However, an egalitarian notion of civic and democratic culture practiced in Canada is not only a product of western civilization, but also a specific creation of this power group. Looking for an authentic, namely pure, culture as a comfort zone to which an ethnic group can belong is unrealistic. As argued above, even religious orthodox groups are constantly adapting in social environments for survival. This is equally applicable to the power group and other minority groups in Canada. The contemporary Canadian civic, democratic, and egalitarian culture is a development from a white, Christian, male-dominant tradition that was gradually expanded to include all citizens. The white group's practice is a cultural practice that is also shared and valued by many immigrants and minority groups (Frideres, 1997), and such practice has been hybridized in many parts of cultures in the world (Pieterse, 2009). The connotation and understanding of the multiculturalism in the twenty-first century Canada is ingrained with the white group culture that now begins to incorporate other world cultures brought by immigrants to Canada. While we celebrate minority cultures under the system of multiculturalism, we are also celebrating the transformed white culture that is also diverse in nature (see Magsino, 2000, p. 334 for the latter point). This multiculturalism has already assumed a form of synthesization and hybridization.

Furthermore, multiculturalism is a policy to deal with ethno-religious diversity and celebrates multi-cultures (Fleras & Elliott, 1992a). The concept of multiculturalism should transcend to diverse- (a synonym of "multi") culturalism in which we celebrate all types of cultures that include gender, sexuality, political differences, subcultures, and personal differences. In other words, the whole is the sum of the parts. The transcended version of multiculturalism is a new entity that has a global component (the aboriginal, the European, and immigrants from all over the world) which is what Canada is now. All Canadian citizens are engaging in a mapping exercise that explores the essence of multiculturalism, national identity, and culture. This process seeks to validate maps. At the same time, the limited and contingent status of any kind of map is realized (Pieterse, 2009, p. 121).

<h2 style="text-align:center">CONCLUSION</h2>

This chapter attempts to show that multiculturalism, like any other concept and ideology, is not static, and constantly evolves. While Canada is striving toward a more inclusive and democratic society in the last forty years, multiculturalism is certainly not contradictory to these values, and should be a very complementary ideology. Although critics continue to question whether Canada can strive for a better, more inclusive, more equal society without multiculturalism, since the successful Canada's record of integration can be explained by other factors (Kymlicka, 2010). The answer is affirmative. There are other ways. However, Canadian multiculturalism has made tremendous contributions to a more inclusive and equal society (Kymlicka, 2010). There is no reason to pluck the sprout prematurely. Multiculturalism has laid the foundation for forty years. As argued earlier, the principles and values endorsed in multiculturalism are parallel and complimentary to a liberal and democratic society. Multiculturalism strengthens the Canadian political, economic and social system. Multiculturalism has given Canada a reputation and an international image that we are in the vanguard of acknowledging and managing a national and global reality where cultural diversity is flourishing. This mission is clearly stated throughout different developments of multiculturalism (Uberoi, 2009). The move to recognize diversity in the nation and officially address the needs to manage the relationship between visible minorities and the mainstream society is most admirable. Multiculturalism has already created a platform for the making of the unity of the nation notwithstanding its challenges. The assertion of the principles in this legislation offers a choice to Canadians who can determine how they identify themselves ethnically and to what degree they retain their ethnic cultures within a lawful, respectful and democratic political and social framework.

Of all challenges faced in the execution of multiculturalism policies a point about lifelong learning needs to be addressed. No matter how good a system is created, the effectiveness of the system ultimately relies on the hearts of the actors in the system. They are the interpreters and the executors of the rules. The challenge to the Canadian society is how to nurture its citizens to develop a global mindset sensitive to all cultures and peoples, cognitive skills, and the passion to achieve the goals advocated in multiculturalism. While pondering this question, Guo (2010, p. 159) raised concerns of structural barriers that deny immigrants opportunities to learn how to live together in the newly adopted countries. As a consequence, these immigrants are marginalized from fully participating in the mainstream society. Dib et al. (2008) concluded that different levels of governments play important roles in removing structural barriers and fostering common multicultural spaces for Canadians to come together. What is equally important is that citizens in the mainstream society should actively engage themselves in learning from the resources brought by the immigrants in these spaces. Loo (2011) observed that the success of multiculturalism is a result of successful integration, a two-way learning facilitated by the particular economic, social, political, and institutional context of a civil society and state intervention. The success of Canada relies on a mutual respect in conversations through which "multiculturalism is the nurturing of multiculturally nurtured cultures" (Ryan, 2010, p. 218).

REFERENCES

Bloemraad, I. (2002). Citizenship and immigration: A current review. *Journal of International Migration and Integration 1*(1), 9-37.

Boldt, E. D. (1985). Maintaining ethnic boundaries: The case of the Hutterites. In M. Dewing (Ed.), *Ethnicity and ethnic relations in Canada* (pp. 87-104). Toronto: Butterworths.

Dewing, Michael. (2009). *Canadian multiculturalism*. Retrieved from: http://www.parl.gc.ca/Content/LOP/ResearchPublications/2009-20-e.htm

Dib, K., Donaldson, I., & Turcotte, B. (2008). Integration and identity in Canada: The importance of multicultural common spaces. *Canadian Ethnic Studies/Etudes ethniques au Canada, 40*(1), 161-187.

Driedger, L. (1996). *Multi-ethnic Canada: Identities & inequality*. Toronto: Oxford University Press.

Dupont, L., & Lemarchand, N. (2001). Official multiculturalism in Canada: Between virtue and politics. In G. H. Cornwell & E. W. Stoddard (Eds.), *Global multiculturalism: Comparative perspectives on ethnicity, race and nation* (pp. 29-50). New York: Rowman & Littlefield.

Fleras, A., & Elliott J. L. (1992a). *The challenge of diversity: Multiculturalism in Canada*. Scarborough, Ontario: Nelson Canada.

Fleras, A., & Elliott J. L. (1992b). *Unequal relations: An introduction to race, ethnic and aboriginal dynamics in Canada*. Scarborough, Ontario: Prentice Hall Canada Inc.

Fleras, A., & Elliott J. L. (1996). *Unequal relations: An introduction to race, ethnic and aboriginal dynamics in Canada* (2nd ed.). Scarborough, Ontario: Prentice Hall Canada Inc.

Frideres, J. S. (1997). Edging into the mainstream: A comparison of values and attitudes of recent immigrants, their children and Canadian born adults. In W. W. Isajiw (Ed.), *Multiculturalism in North America and Europe: Comparative perspectives on interethnic relations and social incorporation* (pp. 537-562). Toronto: Canadian Scholars' Press.

Guo, S. (2010). Toward recognitive justice: Emerging trends and challenges in transnational migration and lifelong learning. *International Journal of Lifelong Education, 29*(2), 149-167.

Henry, F., & Tator, C. (1994). The ideology of racism – Democratic racism. *Canadian Ethnic Studies/Etudes ethniques au Canada, 26*(2), 1-14.

Hurst, C. E., & McConnell, D. L. (2010). *An Amish paradox: Diversity & change in the world's largest Amish community*. Baltimore: Johns Hopkins University Press.

Jansen, C. J. (2005). Canadian multiculturalism. In C. E. James (Ed.) *Possibilities and limitations: Multicultural policies and programs in Canada* (pp. 12-20). Halifax: Fernwood Publishing.

Kallen, E. (2004). Multiculturalism: Ideology, policy and reality. In E. Cameron (Ed.), *Multiculturalism & immigration in Canada* (pp. 47-58). Toronto: Canadian Scholars' Press Inc.

Kymlicka, W. (1996). Social unity in a liberal state. In E. Paul, F. Miller, & J. Paul (Eds.), *The communitarian challenge to liberalism*. Cambridge: Cambridge University Press.

Kymlicka, W. (2010). *The current state of multiculturalism in Canada and research themes on Canadian multiculturalism 2008-2010*. Citizenship and Immigration Canada. Retrieved from: www.cic.gc.ca/english/pdf/pub/multi-state.pdf (accessed August 25, 2012).

Leung, H. H. (2001). *Cultural sensitivity in the context of ethnic polities: Comparison of two family service agencies*. McGill, Quebec: Faculty of Graduate Studies: McGill University.

Leung, H. H. & Hendley, M. (2009). Imagining globalization through changes in places. In H. H. Leung, M. Hendley, R. W. Compton, & B. Haley (Eds.) *Imagining globalization: Language, identities, and boundaries*. New York: Palgrave Macmillan.

Leung, H. H., Hendley M., Compton R. W., & Haley B. D. (Eds.). (2009). *Imagining globalization: Language, identities, and boundaries*. New York: Palgrave Macmillan.

Loo, T. (2011). Hotel Canada. *Canada's History, 91*(4), 60-61.

Magsino, R. F. (2000). The Canadian multiculturalism policy: A pluralist ideal re-visited. In S. E. Nancoo (Ed.), *21st century Canadian diversity*. Mississauga: Canadian Educators' Press.

Nancoo, E. S. (2000). Managing diversity. In S. E. Nancoo (Ed.), *21st century Canadian diversity*. Mississauga: Canadian Educators' Press.

Nolt, S. M. & Myers, T. (2007). *Plain diversity: Amish cultures and identities*. Baltimore: The Johns Hopkins University Press.

Peach, C. (2005). The mosaic versus the melting pot: Canada and the USA. *Scottish Geographical Journal, 121*(1), 3-27.

Pieterse, J N. (2009). *Globalization & global melance* (2nd ed.). Toronto: Roman & Littlefield Publishers, Inc.

Ryan, P. (2010). *Multicultiphobia*. Toronto: University of Toronto Press.

Sahadat, J. (2000). Unity in diversity: Not uniformity. In S. E. Nancoo (Ed.). *21st century Canadian diversity*. Mississauga: Canadian Educators' Press.

Smith, A. D. (2009). *Ethno-symbolism and nationalism*. New York: Routledge.

Toronto's Racial Diversity. (n.d). Retrieved from: http://www.toronto.ca/toronto_facts/diversity.htm.

Uberoi, V. (2009). Multiculturalism and the Canadian charter of rights and freedoms. *Political Studies, 57*(4), 805-827.

Weinfeld, M. (1981). Myth and reality in the Canadian mosaic: "Affective ethnicity." *Canadian Ethnic Studies/Etudes ethniques au Canada, 13*(3), 80-100.

Weinfeld, M. (1994). Ethnic assimilation and the retention of ethnic cultures. In J. W. Berry & J. A. Laponce (Eds.), *Ethnicity and culture in Canada: The research landscape*. Toronto: University of Toronto Press.

Weinfeld, M. (2001). *Like everyone else ... but different: The paradoxical success of Canadian Jews*. Toronto: McClelland & Stewart Ltd.

Ho Hon Leung
Department of Sociology
State University of New York College at Oneonta

SECTION II

MULTICULTURALISM, ETHNICITY AND BELONGING

SHIBAO GUO AND YAN GUO

7. RETHINKING MULTICULTURALISM IN CANADA

Tensions between Immigration, Ethnicity and Minority Rights

INTRODUCTION

Despite Canada's rich history in immigration and the strategic role that immigration plays in Canada's future, the tension between immigration, ethnicity, and minority rights is still prominent. Some of the tension focuses on the existence of ethno-cultural organizations. Despite the rhetoric that Canada relies on immigrants to help ameliorate its labour shortages and aging population, the very ethnicity that many immigrants are associated with is often treated with suspicion. In particular, ethnic organizations are often criticized for threatening national unity, diluting Canadian identity, and promoting ghettoization and separatism. In particular, ethnic organizations are often criticized for threatening national unity, diluting Canadian identity, and promoting ghettoization and separatism. This chapter therefore examines the tension between immigration, ethnicity and minority rights with a focus on how multiculturalism facilitates or hinders the development of ethnic community organizations in Canada. Drawing from two case studies, the chapter explores the role of Chinese ethnic organizations in responding to changing community needs in Edmonton and Calgary. The findings suggest that ethno-specific organizations can be an effective alternative in providing accessible and equitable social services for immigrants because they are more closely connected with and responsive to ethnic community needs. The study also reveals the salience of ethnicity as both an important resource, and a liability. On the one hand, ethnicity was utilized by the state as a way to mobilize ethnic political support to serve an ethnic-specific community; on the other hand, the same ethnicity also became a device for the state to legitimize its political agenda in multiculturizing ethno-specific organizations with an ultimate goal of assimilation. To build an inclusive society, it is imperative to treat ethno-specific organizations as an integral part of Canadian society and to adopt minority rights that recognize and accommodate the distinctive identities and needs of ethno-cultural groups and their ethnic communities.

THE MULTICULTURALISM DEBATE

Immigration has played an important role in transforming Canada into an ethno-culturally diverse and economically prosperous nation. One of the major mechanisms for accommodating immigrants' cultural differences and diversity is

S. Guo & L. Wong (eds.), Revisiting Multiculturalism in Canada. 123–139.

multiculturalism. In fact Canada was the first country to formulate an official policy for multiculturalism and to give it full legal authority. Multiculturalism was formalized in 1971 by the Liberal government of Canada, in response to the report of the Royal Commission on Bilingualism and Biculturalism in the mid-1960s, and the Official Language Act of 1969, which granted equal status to both French and English as the official languages of the Parliament and government of Canada. The main goal of the multicultural policy was to: (1) assist cultural groups with their cultural development; (2) help members of cultural groups to overcome cultural barriers to full participation in Canadian society; (3) promote creative encounters and interchange among all cultural groups in the interest of national unity; and (4) help immigrants to acquire at least one of Canada's official languages (House of Commons, 1971, p. 8546).

Though multicultural policy evoked enthusiasm and attracted attention of some groups in Canada, reactions were generally mixed (Fleras & Elliott, 2002; Moodley, 1983). Concerns have rested on three critical points. First, the multicultural policy neutralizes the special claims of the French and the First Nations Canadians by putting them on an equal footing with numerous others (Fleras & Elliott, 2002). Aboriginal people argue that multiculturalism does nothing to help them with their land claims and forgotten treaty rights, and French Canadians view multiculturalism as a device "to reduce the importance of the French fact in Canada to that of an outsized ethnic minority" (Taylor, 1993, p. 162). Second, the multiculturalism policy is based on a depoliticized and static definition of culture and ethnicity. The focus of multicultural policy on expressive and instrumental aspects of cultural diversity "trivialises, neutralizes, and absorbs social and economic inequalities" (Moodley, 1983, p. 326). A third noted flaw of multicultural policy lies in the separation of culture and language. Canadian Bilingualism defined English and French as the official languages of Canada. This policy, by deemphasizing languages of other cultural groups, helped to create a cultural and linguistic hierarchy in Canada. Multiculturalism, Moodley argues, must presuppose multilingualism. Cultural preservation without language protection becomes ephemeral and artificial, she posits, and is bound to fail. Moodley suggests the jettison of the very notion of 'mainstream culture.'

The above views largely represent the perspective of critical multiculturalism. Other critics of multiculturalism, such as Bissoondath (1994) and Gwyn (1980; 1995), claim that multiculturalism undermines Canadian 'core values' and 'traditions.' "In eradicating the centre, in evoking uncertainty as to what and who is a Canadian," Bissoondath states, "it [multiculturalism] has diminished all sense of Canadian values, of what is a Canadian" (p. 71). Instead of promoting integration, Bissoondath maintains, multiculturalism encourages ethnic 'ghettoization' and separatism. Therefore, he continues, maintenance of ethnic heritage and identity is injurious to national allegiance and unity. Also according to Bissoondath, the very practice of supporting ethnic organizations is problematic. He rejects using taxpayers' money to fund ethnic organizations. He argues that allocating special resources to support such organizations will undermine Canadian democratic principles and erode norms and practices of democratic citizenship. In his vision, multiculturalism should not aim at preserving differences but at "blending them into a new vision of Canadianness, pursuing a Canada where inherent differences and inherent similarities meld easily" (p. 224). It is apparent that Bissoondath's vision of Canadianness resembles the American Melting Pot and the cult of ethnicity as advocated by Schlesinger (1991).

Proponents of multiculturalism have fought back. In response to the above attacks, Kymlicka (1998) contends that the assertion that multiculturalism has increased 'ghettoization' and decreased the rate of integration of immigrants is flawed and bizarre. He maintains that multiculturalism is a "coherent, defensible, and indeed successful approach" to the integration of ethnic groups in Canada, which was supported by the following points. First, notes Kymlicka (1998), naturalization rates have increased since the adoption of Multiculturalism in 1971. Second, ethnic groups participate actively in the political life of Canada. Third, the demand for classes in English and French as second languages (ESL, FSL) has never been higher. Fourth, intermarriage rates have consistently increased since 1971 (Kymlicka, 1998). Kymlicka believes that "Canadians do a better job of respecting ethnic diversity while promoting societal integration than citizens of any other country" (p. 22). In commenting on Bissoondath's claim that multiculturalism encourages separatism, Kymlicka (1998) contends that it is "an immensely ambitious and arduous project" to maintain a separate societal culture in Canada. Unlike the Quebecois who have the basic conditions for sustaining a separate societal culture, it is almost impossible for immigrant groups to achieve such a goal. Reviewing multiculturalism policies and programs, Kymlicka claims that in practice multiculturalism is "a response to the pressures that Canada exerts on immigrants to integrate into common institutions," and provides "a framework for debating and developing the terms of integration" (p. 40). Integration does not happen overnight; it is usually a long, difficult, and often painful process. Sometimes special institutions and programs are required to help immigrants with this process. Supports include certain services in an immigrant's mother tongue, and special support for immigrant organizations that assist in the settlement and integration process. According to Kymlicka, these institutions do not represent unjust privileges for immigrants, nor do they promote ethnic separatism. They function as a transition and they are honest attempts to accommodate diversity and distinctive problems facing particular ethno-cultural groups. The ultimate goal is to facilitate greater participation in and integration into mainstream society.

The debate over multiculturalism and immigrant settlement and adaptation has been extended to the rights of ethno-cultural minorities, or minority rights in short. Kymlicka and Norman (2000) define minority rights as "a wide range of public policies, legal rights, and constitutional provisions sought by ethnic groups for the accommodation of their cultural differences" (p. 2). Minority rights extend beyond the common provisions of civil and political rights of individual citizenship in a liberal democratic society, and the adoption of any minority rights is intended to recognize and accommodate the distinctive identities and needs of ethno-cultural groups. Minority groups seek these rights to allow them to do things or gain access to services which members of the majority culture already enjoy. They seek special provision because of culturally specific disadvantages, or because the desired common activity is out of the reach of members of non-dominant groups. The adoption of minority rights is intended to promote fairness and justice by correcting the disadvantages that minorities suffer within difference-blind institutions. Kymlicka and Norman (2000) claim that refusal to grant recognition and autonomy to such minority groups is likely to provoke even more resentment and hostility, alienating them further from their identity as citizens of the larger state, and discouraging them from becoming full members of the community.

To contextualize this hot debate over multiculturalism and minority right, cases studies were conducted with two ethnic Chinese community organizations in Calgary and Edmonton. The study investigated of the founding and historical development of the Edmonton Chinese Community Services Centre (now ASSIST Community Services Centre) and the Calgary Chinese Community Service Association. The following sections present the research findings, followed by an analysis of the complexities and paradoxes of ethno-specific organizations.

BRIDGING THE GAP

From the Confederation of Canada in 1867 to the 1960s, the selection of immigrants in Canada was based on racial background, with the British and Western Europeans being the most 'desirable' citizens, the Asians the 'unassimilable' and, therefore, 'undesirable.' With the postwar boom in the mid-1960s, Canada needed skilled labour to help build its expansionary economy. This led to the introduction of the 'point system' in 1967, which based the selection of immigrants on their "education, skills and resources" rather than their racial and religious backgrounds (Whitaker, 1991, p. 19). By the mid-1970s, there were more immigrants arriving from developing countries than from the developed world, the largest number coming from Asia, followed by the Caribbean, Latin America, and Africa. Among the Asian group, many were Chinese immigrants from Hong Kong (Li, 1998). According to Li, between 1968 and 1976, about 90,000 Chinese immigrants came to Canada; between 1977 and 1984, another 80,000 arrived. When they arrived in Canada, these immigrants needed assistance with language, employment, housing, daycare, health, counseling, and legal services. They were likely to encounter barriers in accessing such services, including those related to language, lack of information about services, cultural patterns of help seeking, lack of cultural sensitivity by service providers, financial barriers, and lack of service availability (Bergin, 1988; Leung, 2000; Reitz, 1995; Stewart et al., 2008).

In 1977, Edmonton Chinese Community Services Centre (ECCSC) was established in response to the cultural and language barriers faced by Chinese immigrants in accessing social services in Edmonton. The organization began as a Summer Student Community Project, an initiative of the Chinese Graduates Association of Alberta (CGAA), and was coordinated by Kim Hung out of a basement in Chinatown. With funding from the Secretary of State, three full-time students and one part-time student were employed to conduct city-wide surveys to assess the needs of social services of the Chinese population in Edmonton. As part of the project, a drop-in centre with library and referral services was established and programs for Chinese seniors were also provided. When the summer project ended, the Centre continued to operate, using volunteers comprising mainly university students with donations from local businesses for the rent and operating expenses. The first two years following its establishment were the most difficult time for the Centre.

The Chinese Graduates Association of Alberta (CGAA) played a pivotal role in the founding and initial development of ECCSC, so it warrants some special words here. Only two years older than ECCSC, CGAA itself was founded in 1975 by Chinese students, primarily from Hong Kong, who were attending the University of Alberta. The aim of the group was to provide mutual support and foster social development in the Chinese community. Soon after their graduation from the University, many of the original members entered the Edmonton community and became community activists. The very first project the Association took on upon its inception was to organize a panel discussion and forum in 1975 on the Green Paper on immigration policies. Subsequently, the Association submitted a brief to the Minister of Manpower and Immigration on the concerns of the Chinese community about discriminatory recommendations in the Green Paper. Another important project for the Association, with a grant from the federal Multiculturalism program, was to produce a bilingual Social Services Directory of Alberta in both English and Chinese. Furthermore, the Association organized a committee in 1976 to respond to the proposed two-tiered fee structure for foreign students at the University of Alberta. Within two years of its establishment, membership in the CGAA had increased to seventy. When the association started its ECCSC project in 1977, it had already established credibility with the Chinese community and the three levels of government (Kwan, 1983a).

During 1979-1980, Canada took over 60,000 refugees out of the 900,000 who were resettled, flowing out of Vietnam, Cambodia, and Laos following the Communist victories there. This was the largest single refugee movement in Canadian history (Whitaker, 1991). Among those resettled in Canada, Whitaker states, 54% were privately sponsored by community voluntary organizations. ECCSC was one of such organizations in Edmonton that provided resettlement services to the Vietnamese refugees of Chinese descent, including housing, clothing, employment, English classes, and medical referrals. In 1980, the Centre received a grant of $15,000 from the City of Edmonton to continue its resettlement programs. The Centre's programs and services were further expanded with funding from the federal government in 1981. Its contributions to the community had laid the foundation for the Centre to be formally incorporated under the Societies Act of the Province of Alberta in January 1983 with Kim Hung as the Chair.

The founding of Calgary Chinese Community Service Association (CCCSA) had much in common with ECCSC. Like ECCSC, CCCSA was founded in 1978 by a group of enthusiastic students led by Julia Tao and Teresa Woo-Paw, and was a response to the failure of government and mainstream organizations to provide accessible social services to Chinese immigrants in Calgary. In an interview with Woo-Paw, she recalled that the organization emerged "I think primarily out of the need of first the recognition that there's no service, no accessible service for people of Chinese descent and those who cannot speak English well." Some of the services, primarily provided by bilingual volunteers who spoke English and Cantonese, included: information services, translation and interpretation, English classes, basic counseling services, and assistance with forms. Stated Woo-Paw, "We actually also escorted people to different places in addition to those hours we were in the Centre. We would set up appointment and go out when they had to see a lawyer, a doctor, or a service provider ... So we tried to do what we can." People who accessed the Centre's services were a mixture of those who had been in Canada for some time as well as new immigrants from Hong Kong and Guangdong Province of China. Like those of ECCSC, most clients were Cantonese-speakers, and included many Vietnamese refugees of ethnic Chinese origin. Unlike ECCSC which received small government funding at its inception, CCCSA only received limited funding from the Chinese community to help with its rent.

It was clear that the initial founding of ECCSC and CCCSA, in addition to responding to clear needs in the communities, were partly inspired by the multiculturalism policy, which encouraged ethnic groups to maintain their cultural identities by developing ethno-cultural organizations while integrating into the new society.

RESPONDING TO CHANGING COMMUNITY NEEDS

Canadians tend to adopt a difference-blind approach when it comes to servicing immigrants. Henry et al. (2006) argue that failure to provide immigrants with services that are "racially sensitive, culturally appropriate, and linguistically accessible" can be attributed to the liberal universalism which assumes that "people are essentially the same" (p. 223). Despite obvious differences in the cultural backgrounds and racial identities of clients, the underlying assumption is that all people share common needs and, therefore, require similar modes of service and intervention. Although some mainstream agencies have attempted to provide more accessible services by introducing a multicultural organizational model, the changes often appear to be 'cosmetic' rather than substantive, because "the needs and interest of minorities are dealt with on an *ad hoc* basis rather than being integrated into the structure, policies, programs, and practices of the organization" (p. 191). As an alternative, ethno-racial organizations have undertaken the responsibility of providing more effective, responsive, and equitable services to minority communities. The experience of SUCCESS in Vancouver (Guo, 2008) and the experience of the Jewish community of Montreal (Weinfeld, 2000) provide good examples.

An analysis of the development of ECCSC and CCCSA indicates that ethno-racial organizations were more effective than mainstream organizations because they were more closely connected with and responsive to ethnic community's needs. In Edmonton, ECCSC continued to provide accessible social services throughout the 1980s to help Chinese immigrants overcome barriers to their settlement and adaptation. According to Allan Kwan (1983b), who was involved in the early stages of the organization's development as a board member, the most popular programs during this time were ESL (English as a Second Language), citizenship classes, information and referral services, language interpretation and translation, and legal services. During this time most of their clients were Vietnamese refugees. "We still did have Chinese immigrants, but not as many as Vietnamese refugees at that time," recalled Kwan in a personal interview. They came to ECCSC because many of them were Vietnamese of Chinese descent. By mid-1980s, it had "unfolded fully," according to Yvonne Chiu, who was the Executive Director of ECCSC from 1984-1985. She also pointed out that "[i]t was still small in the sense it has a small team and staff, no more than five people." To build up the profile of ESSCS, Chiu and her colleagues spent a lot of time "building bridges" at this stage. Chiu had this to say in her interview:

> So I remember during those years, it was a lot of building bridges to key funders like Canadian Heritage, to the City of Edmonton. I really tried to build up a profile and tried to position us even though I don't think we were formally recognized as a formal agency. We will invite ourselves to conferences and meetings with other settlement agency presidents ... So we were trying to showcase when you're ethnic specific, there are some particular roles that are really important, and that it should be recognized.

The change of international climate in the mid-1980s also helped ECCSC raise its profile. In 1984, Britain and China signed the Sino-British Joint Agreement on the future of Hong Kong, which declared that the colony was to become a special administrative region under the rule of China in 1997. Many of the residents who were worried about their future began to leave Hong Kong (Wong, 1992). Among them, a large number found home in Canada. According to the Landed Immigrant Data System (Citizenship and Immigration Canada, 2003), from 1980 to 2001 Calgary and Edmonton became the fourth and fifth largest cities respectively in Canada in terms of receiving Chinese immigrants, accepting 29,868 in Calgary, and 24,245 in Edmonton (Guo & DeVoretz, 2006a). Chinese immigrants came primarily from three regions – PR China, Hong Kong, and Taiwan. In Edmonton, in response to the substantial increase of Chinese immigrants in the late 1980s and early 1990s, ECCSC expanded its settlement services with funding from the Immigrant Settlement Program (ISP). To this point, settlement serviced had been provided by volunteers. In the mid-1990s, the organization restructured its programming, moving beyond basic settlement and ESL services to emphasize family development and support, including programs for youth, parents, seniors, and women. According to Yvonne Chiu, who was involved in this restructuring as a board member, they were "very explicitly resonant with the ISP program," but with a special effort to demonstrate "how holistic ASSIST was, more than a settlement agency. It was really a community service centre."

The early development of CCCSA was not as smooth as ECCSC, unfortunately. In 1982, the organization had to be folded temporarily because "[f]inancial support had been difficult to obtain, many funding sources did not understand nor see the value in the role of ethno-specific organizations" (CCCSA, 2006, p. 6). The organization was revived in 1984 by Teresa Woo-Paw, who was completing a university degree in social work at the University of Calgary. At this stage CCCSA was mainly providing education and cultural programs for immigrant children, the most popular of which was the summer camp program. Joanne Yee, former Executive Director of CCCSA, recalled that in the 1980s and early 1990s "there were a lot of kids that would live in Chinatown, a lot of new immigrants families with young children." These were also the most difficult years for the organization because they were not successful in receiving any government funding. In her interview, Woo-Paw stated that basically they were providing services "with no pay, no money, no profile." She also added: "I was rejected by every level of government. I was rejected by every single funder in town, because we're Chinese. So I came to realize at that time it's going to be very, very difficult for us to get financial support to do our work."

Eventually the organization evolved, although changes came much later than for ECCSC. Starting from early 1990s, the demographics of the Chinese community in Calgary had changed. With 1997 approaching, an increasing number of Hong Kong Chinese immigrants made Calgary their new home. There was an increasing demand for bilingual services in the Chinese community. In 1990, CCCSA secured $15,000 from Canadian Heritage to provide heritage language program for immigrant children. The year 1990 thus marked an important turning point for the organization. Following its first success in obtaining funding, in 1992, CCCSA received $30,000 from the United Way of Calgary, after three previous rejected applications. Teresa Woo-Paw called this a major 'breakthrough' for the Chinese community in Calgary, which made its counterpart in Edmonton admire because they had been trying to become a member of the United Way of Edmonton for years, but without success. This grant provided the Calgary community with badly needed funding to pilot a counseling program; to support a family program and a women's support group; and to start a Scouting program, and after-school tutorial sessions for school-aged children. This success came about only with much lobbying, alliance building, and educating funders about the unique role of ethno-specific organizations in Calgary.

THE ROLE OF VOLUNTEERS

In *Ethnic Associations and the Welfare State*, Jenkins (1988) examines the role of ethnic organizations in five countries – Australia, Israel, the Netherlands, the United States, and the United Kingdom. She distinguishes ethnic associations from ethnic agencies. While viewing the former as a special type of voluntary association, she defines the latter as established social agencies with a primary commitment to members of one or more ethnic groups with both public and voluntary funding. Characteristics associated with both types of organizations described by Jenkins could be found in ECCSC and CCCSA. In 2005, ECCSC reached a membership of 150 and a volunteer base of 200, while CCCSA had 30 voting members, 200 non-voting members, and 200 volunteers. With such a large membership and volunteer base, both organizations could be described as ethnic associations. On the other hand, they also provided professional services with paid staff, using public funding, and administered by a board of directors. In 2005, ECCSC had a team of twenty-two professional staff while CCCSA had eleven, most of them holding bachelor's degree in social work, education, and psychology and some with master's degree. The latter traits were clearly identified with ethnic agencies. This study shows clearly that Jenkins' distinction between ethnic associations and ethnic agencies has been blurred in the case of these two organizations.

Regarding the role of volunteers, this study found that the special qualities and commitment of volunteers played an important part in the development of ECCSC and CCCSA. Volunteers were regarded as an integral part and a vital component of their teams. All people interviewed, including board members, administrators, and staff, were once volunteers for their organizations. They shared common experiences as immigrants with the people they helped. They recognized the importance of facilitating adaptation through settlement programs and services. They understood that their contribution would make a difference to the organization and, most importantly, would benefit immigrants. Volunteering was also the best way to get involved in a community. Games Choy, Vice-Chair of ECCSC, started to volunteer for ECCSC in 1979 upon his landing in Edmonton as an immigrant. He commented on what motivated him to volunteer:

I found when I moved to Edmonton, to Canada, this new country I knew nothing. I knew nothing about it. So if I wanted to have a bit of knowledge about the society, the city, this community, I had better get involved. I think it is mutual benefit. I can help people, I can help myself. That's how I started. As you get more involved, you feel helping people is one of the joy.

Volunteers contributed different kinds of expertise, and played an instrumental role in the daily operation of the organization. They fulfilled many roles, including child care worker, interpreter, teaching assistant, youth mentor, program facilitator, fundraiser, data entry work, answering phones at the front desk, and assisting with special events. According to the 2004-2005 CCCSA Annual Report, 90% of the organization's programs and services were delivered with the help of volunteers in 2005, totaling 12,123 hours (CCCSA, 2005). Volunteers alleviated the shortage of staff, and also contributed financially. Jeff Huang, Project Manager of ECCSC, started as a volunteer for the organization, then worked as an outreach worker in the Immigrant Settlement Program (ISP), and later was promoted to volunteer coordinator and project manger. He discussed the process of recruiting and preparing a volunteer. First, when they needed volunteer, they would post a recruitment message in the Chinese newspapers, and on the Web. As a volunteer coordinator, Jeff was responsible for recruitment, interviewing, screening, orientation, training, and assignment placements with the aim of matching the volunteer's interests and strengths with the organization's needs. He also organized an annual volunteer fair to publicize volunteer opportunities with the presence of potential volunteers and non-profit agencies in Edmonton. What emerges as important from this process is the bridging role that ECCSC has played in creating 'the space' for volunteers and organizations to participate effectively. By engaging immigrants in volunteer activities, ECCSC and CCCSA were instilling the Canadian value of voluntarism among immigrants. Volunteering also encouraged community participation and mutual support, and collectively sought answers to community problems. The organizations have helped many immigrants to become independent and democratic citizens.

THE COMPLEXITIES AND PERPLEXITIES OF ETHNO-SPECIFIC ORGANIZATIONS

When it comes to ethno-specific organizations, we need to consider a number of important questions: What is ethnicity? How do we assess ethnic affinity? What constitutes ethno-specific organizations? Do members of such organizations come from the same country, speak the same language, and hold the same citizenship? A brief survey of the existing definitions of ethnicity discerns that ethnicity, for the most part, is conceived as being ascribed or given at birth (Isajiw, 1985; Jandt, 1998; Weber, 1978, as cited in Driedger, 1996). Very often the definition of ethnicity has relied heavily on culture such that these terms are all too often treated as overlapping or coterminous. Many researchers challenge the primordialist and essentialist emphasis of such definitions (Li, 1999; Moodley, 1983; Satzewich & Liodakis, 2007). Li (1999) points out that "people of the same ethnicity do not necessarily share a common culture" (p. 11). Moodley (1983) argues against depoliticized and static conceptualizations of ethnicity and questioned those viewing ethnicity as "having an intrinsic vitality regardless of the context" (p. 321). Satzewich and Liodakis (2007) emphasize the social relational aspects of ethnicity, representing the lived experiences of individuals and groups as important dimensions of social inequality.

Meanwhile, primordialist views of culture have been identified as a common problem inherent in ethnic studies in Canada. In the context of studies in the history and development of the Chinese in Canada, Li (1998) argues, the focus was primarily on the cultural adaptation of the Chinese as a racial minority coming from an ancient culture. He further points out that research on Chinese voluntary associations in particular was influenced by this approach. Scholars coming from this perspective were interested in exploring how the Chinese used an ancient traditional culture as the basis for the development of various culturally unique social organizations in the receiving society. He posits that this approach woefully ignored the social context within which the history of Chinese Canadians was constructed, and the social relationship between the Chinese and the dominant majority.

This study contextualized the concept of ethnicity by unpacking the complexities and perplexities of ethno-specific organizations. From an early description of the founding and historical development of the two organizations, it seems clear that most of the clients who came to their services may be called Chinese. However, the study has clearly demonstrated that it was no longer a homogeneous group consisting of Chinese from the rural areas of Mainland China; there were substantial sub-group differences. The new immigrants were diverse in origin, socio-economic status, educational background, and settlement needs, which aligns with the composition of Chinese immigrants at a national level (Guo & DeVoretz, 2006a). A more in-depth analysis of the profiles of the clientele reveals that in fact Chinese immigrants in both Calgary and Edmonton came from different parts of the world (i.e., People's Republic of China, Hong Kong, Taiwan, Vietnam, Laos, Cambodia, Malaysia, Singapore, Philippines, etc.), representing different citizenship (Chinese, Vietnamese, Laos, British), different world religions (Buddhism, Christianity, and Islam), and different social and political systems (Communism, Capitalism, and a combination of the two). Clients and members of the two support organizations studied here did not necessarily shared the same language or culture, let alone notions of nationhood, motherland, or hometown. Can thus ECCSC and CCCSA still be counted ethno-specific organizations? Allan Kwan described the diversity of their clients at ECCSC:

> From the time perspectives, it seems the 70s and 80s were Vietnamese, and people from Hong Kong. But the shift in client origin is lately mainly from Mainland China. Their educational background is much higher. But of course if you look at the Hong Kong group, they have money. The early refugees really came with nothing, right? No kids. Not much education. So quite interesting. As time goes on, how things have changed!

To respond to the diverse needs of various groups of Chinese immigrants from different parts of the world, the organizations had to constantly adapt. One big challenge facing the two organizations was when the Mainland Chinese arrived in large numbers since late 1990s, bringing with them differences in language and dialects. While both organizations were originally founded to serve primarily Cantonese-speaking Chinese immigrants, recent arrivals from Mainland China speak Mandarin Chinese, using simplified characters in written forms. Some of the organizations' staff members may speak Mandarin, but do so with an accent because it is not their first language. As a solution both organizations hired Mandarin-speaking staff members, expecting their staff to be trilingual at least, speaking English, Cantonese, and Mandarin. In a five-year Strategic Plan, CCCSA identified this as among its service priorities for 2006-2010: "use of simplified Chinese in our service pamphlets instead of only traditional Chinese; Mandarin classes for staff; where possible, recruit staff that represents the diverse needs of the community" (CCCSA, 2006, p. 18).

More importantly, recent newcomers have come with different expectation, challenges, and needs. Jim Wong, Co-Chair of CCCSA in 2005, commented on the expectations of immigrants from China, where the state plays a larger role in taking care of its citizens: "A lot of them come over expecting the government to give them a house or a place to stay, expecting they will have a job here. They don't know they have to go out for an interview. It is a whole different culture here. Some of them are highly educated professionals and they don't understand why they can't get jobs here as doctors or as engineers." Employment prospects are another major challenge facing recent immigrants from China. Despite the fact that recent Chinese immigrants have arrived in Canada with substantial human capital compared to that of their early counterparts, their prior learning and work experiences are frequently unrecognized in Canada. As a consequence, many have suffered from unemployment, underemployment, and downward social mobility (Guo & DeVoretz, 2006b). This also seems the case for Edmonton and Calgary. Serena Ma, Executive Director of ASSIST from 2001-2004, pointed out, "what they want is how they can apply their skills and find a job here. That's the No. 1 priority." As organizations serving immigrants, ECCSC and CCCSA have found it necessary to constantly shift their priorities and reinvent themselves in response to immigrant's changing needs. The diverse backgrounds and changing needs of Chinese immigrants as well as the consequent shifting of these organizations illustrate the complexities and perplexities of ethno-specific organizations.

THE TENSIONS AND PARADOXES

Despite the fact that ethno-specific organizations play a valuable role in immigrants' settlement and adaptation, they are not always seen as benign, self-motivated, or altruistic institutions. Often they are viewed as threatening national unity, diluting Canadian identity, and promoting ghettoization and separatism (Bissoondath, 1994; Gwyn, 1995). Critics also question whether the state should use taxpayers' money to fund such organizations. They argue that all Canadians should be treated equally, and that allocating special resources to support such organizations undermines Canadian democratic principles.

An analysis of the funding difficulties experienced by both ECCSC and CCCSA demonstrates how the above view has influenced the policies and attitudes of funding bodies toward ethno-specific organizations. Some participants in both the Edmonton and Calgary communities discussed in great length about how the state has used funding requirements to navigate its political goals away from a centered, liberalized direction toward a narrowly-defined culturally restrained approach toward ethno-specific organizations. They commented on how suspicious funders were about the collective goals of ethno-specific organizations in providing a community support network for newcomers. One participant, Lan Chan-Marples, the Executive Director of ECCSC from 1998-2001, had this to say: "In the 1980s and 1990s we had a very difficult time accessing funding, because funders do not fund single ethnic groups... I kept getting these doors slammed because we were a single ethnic group." As a consequence, the organization was underfunded and understaffed, in turn leaving many community needs unmet. To survive, in 2001, ECCSC had to change its name to ASSIST Community Services Centre, dropping Chinese from its original name so that they would appear to the funders that they were a multicultural service agency.

The name change did help ASSIST meet many of its funding requirements, but this came at a heavy price. It created tension, controversy, and backlash in the Chinese community. Many Chinese leaders accused of ASSIST abandoning the Chinese community; donors threatened to withdraw donations to the organization; even ASSIST's own staff members started to question its new shift. Serena Ma, the Executive Director of ASSIST from 2001-2004, commented: "We were getting backlash from the Chinese Benevolent Association, all the other Chinese associations, because they felt that by serving other immigrants and changing our name, we were abandoning them. We were no longer serving the Chinese community." Clearly it created division in the community. In the end, the organization decided to keep the Chinese version of the original name, which seems a compromise. In an interview with Allan Kwan, who served as the Vice-Chair of ASSIST in 2001, we asked him about the criticism that his organization promoted 'ghettoization.' He noted:

> I am not sure I would agree with that statement. The fact of the matter is, when newcomers come, they need psychological and social support. If they don't have our support, it can be a problem. I think we offer services to assist them to achieve integration. It just makes them much better to go to the mainstream. So actually I think the funding agencies have very good return on their investment, on their funding. I don't see it's a criticism, but I think it's misinformation. I will put it this way.

It seems evident that the name change and the discriminatory funding practices speak to the paradox of ethnicity. On the one hand, ethnicity has been used as a vehicle by the state to mobilize ethnic community resources and to support immigrant settlement and integration – responsibilities that fall under federal jurisdictions. On the other hand, the same ethnicity became a liability in applications for federal funding because it was also used as a device by the state to legitimize its political agenda in multiculturizing its programs with an ultimate goal of assimilation. This paradox confirms Ng's (1996) argument that ethnic organizations may also be seen to function as an extension of the coordinated activities of the state, through funding requirements and accountability procedures, in which the state exercises a form of social control. The negative attitudes and behaviours toward ethno-specific organizations seem to contradict with Canada's national policies toward immigration, which are seemingly welcoming. They also seem to be in conflict with Canada's commitments to democratic principles such as justice, equality, and fairness. The co-existence of these conflicting practices and ideologies are referred to as 'democratic racism' by Henry et al. (2006). Democratic racism prevents the government from fully embracing differences or making any changes in the existing social, economic, and political order, and from supporting policies and practices that might ameliorate the low status of immigrants because these policies are perceived to be in conflict with and a threat to liberal democracy.

CONCLUSION

This chapter was set out to examine the tension between immigration, ethnicity and minority rights through an investigation of the founding and historical developments of two organizations in Edmonton and Calgary: the ASSIST Community Services Centre, and the Calgary Chinese Community Service Association. The study reports that both organizations were founded in late 1970s to bridge the gap in social services for Chinese immigrants in both communities, and to help immigrants become full, participating members of Canadian society. Both organizations had austere beginnings, and were primarily staffed by volunteers owing to lack of funding. In their early stages, they provided basic settlement and information services, language translation and interpretation, and English classes. With the demographic changes and the increasing demand for their services in the late 1980s and early 1990s, both organizations found it necessary to evolve in response to changing community needs, including those of both newly arrived immigrants and established citizens. By the late 1990s, both organizations had become well-established community organizations, providing both immigrant settlement programs, and family development and support services. As transitional institutions, they helped ease the process of immigrant settlement and adaptation. Furthermore, they had become important bridges between the immigrant community and Canadian society at large. The history of ASSIST and CCCSA has demonstrated that ethno-cultural organizations can be an effective alternative in providing accessible and equitable social services for immigrants because they are more closely connected with and responsive to ethnic community needs. Their community actions represent a collective effort in pursuing social justice and have raised their level of social consciousness transforming them into social activists.

Through an account of the founding and historical development of the above two ethno-specific organizations, this study contextualizes the concept of ethnicity by examining its complexities and paradoxes in detail. It is evident that their founding was partly inspired by the multiculturalism policy, which encouraged immigrants to integrate into Canadian society without sacrificing their ethnic identity. When an increasing number of immigrants and refugees of Chinese descent arrived in Canada, ethnicity was utilized by the state as a way to mobilize ethnic political support through the provision of resources, mutual help, self-help, and volunteerism to serve ethnic-specific communities, in this case the Chinese. However, the study has clearly demonstrated that the Chinese were no longer a homogeneous group consisting of people from the rural areas of Mainland China, and that in fact there were substantial sub-group differences. The new immigrants were diverse in origin, socio-economic status, educational background, and settlement needs. These diverse backgrounds, along with changing needs, and the constantly shifting responses of the organizations have shown the complexities of ethnicity. Ethnicity is dynamic concept, which is constantly changing. This study suggests that in understanding an ethno-specific organization, one cannot assume a simple correspondence between people, culture, and language among its group members. What united members of an ethnic group like ASSIST and CCCSA was not a common culture, but common experiences as newcomers to Canada, a shared goal to succeed in a new society, and their interdependent support relationships. Ethnicity represents a process of constant negotiation and construction of immigrant's adjustment and integration to a new environment. It is the social relational features rather than the primordial features of ethnic formations which informed this study.

It is perplexing and paradoxical to reveal that the same ethnicity also became a device for the state to legitimize its political agenda in multiculturizing ethno-specific organizations with an ultimate goal of assimilation. Through funding mechanism that set the criteria for which programs, groups and organizations were eligible, the state exercises a form of social control reshaping the structure and operation of ethno-specific organizations. In the case of ASSIST and CCCSA, lack of funding left the organizations ill-funded, understaffed, and operating in inadequate facilities. In this context, ethnicity has become a liability. Furthermore, the study demonstrates that multiculturalism has eroded from a centered, liberalized direction to a narrowly-defined culturally restrained approach. The negative attitudes and behaviours toward ethno-specific organizations can be attributed to the existing ideologies of 'democratic racism' and liberal universalism, which refuse to fully embrace differences or to make any substantive changes in the existing social, economic, and political order because these changes are perceived to be in conflict with and a threat to liberal democracy.

This discussion is particularly important in the current international context where there has been a growing assault on and subsequent retreat from multiculturalism in Australia, the US, and Western European countries. Will Canada follow their footsteps? To what extent have the recent international developments influenced debates in Canada? This study has clearly demonstrated that Canada is moving backwards toward more assimilative and coercive multicultural policies and practices, which were discouraged by its official multiculturalism. If Canada intends to reclaim its original goal of helping immigrants with their full participation in Canadian society without sacrificing their ethnic identity, it needs to go beyond the superficial rhetoric of difference and diversity by adopting a framework which truly reflects Canada's social and cultural realities. More importantly, to build an inclusive society, it is imperative to treat ethno-specific organizations as an integral part of Canadian society, to redistribute resources equitably, and to adopt minority rights that recognize and accommodate the distinctive identities and needs of ethno-cultural groups and their ethnic communities.

REFERENCES

Bergin, B. (1988). *Equality is the issue: A study of minority ethnic group access to health and social services in Ottawa-Carleton*. Ottawa: Social Planning Council of Ottawa-Carleton.

Bissoondath, N. (2002). *Selling illusions: The cult of multiculturalism in Canada*. Toronto: Penguin.

Calgary Chinese Community Service Association. (2005). *2004-2005 annual report*. Calgary: Calgary Chinese Community Service Association.

Calgary Chinese Community Service Association. (2006). *Strategic plan: For the period of 2006-2010*. Calgary: Calgary Chinese Community Service Association.

Citizenship and Immigration Canada. (2003). *Landed immigrant data system: 1980-2001*. Ottawa: Citizenship and Immigration Canada.

Driedger, L. (1996). *Multi-ethnic Canada: Identities & inequalities*. Toronto: Oxford University Press.

Fleras, A., & Elliott, J. L. (2002). *Engaging diversity: Multiculturalism in Canada*. Toronto: Nelson Thompson Learning.

Guo, S. (2008). The promotion of minority group rights as the protection of individual rights and freedoms for immigrants: A Canadian case study. *Interchange, 39*(2), 259-275.

Guo, S., & DeVoretz, D. (2006a). The changing face of Chinese immigrants in Canada. *Journal of International Migration and Integration, 7*(3), 275-300.

Guo, S., & DeVoretz, D. (2006b). Chinese immigrants in Vancouver: Quo vadis? *Journal of International Migration and Integration, 7*(4), 425-447.

Gwyn, R. (1980). *The northern magus.* Toronto: McClelland and Stewart.

Gwyn, R. (1995). *Nationalism without walls: The unbearable lightness of being Canadian.* Toronto: McClelland and Stewart.

Henry, F., Tator, C., Mattis, W., & Rees, T. (2006). *The colour of democracy: Racism in Canadian society.* Toronto: Thompson Nelson.

House of Commons. (1971). *Debates.* Ottawa: Government Printer.

Isajiw, W. W. (1985). Definitions of ethnicity. In R. M. Bienvenue & J. E. Goldstein (Eds.), *Ethnicity and ethnic relations in Canada: A book of reading* (pp. 5-18). Toronto: Butterworths.

Jandt, F. E. (1998). *Intercultural communication: An introduction* (2nd ed.). Thousand Oaks: Sage Publications.

Jenkins, S. (1988). *Ethnic associations and the welfare state: Services to immigrants in five countries.* New York: Columbia University Press.

Kwan, A. (1983a). *A brief history of CGAA, 1975-1982.* Edmonton: Edmonton Chinese Community Services Centre.

Kwan, A. (1983b). *A look at the Chinese community service centre.* Edmonton: Edmonton Chinese Community Services Centre.

Kymlicka, W. (1995). *Multicultural citizenship: A liberal theory of minority rights.* Oxford: Clarendon Press.

Kymlicka, W. (1998). *Finding our way: Rethinking ethnocultural relations in Canada.* Toronto: Oxford University Press.

Kymlicka, W., & Norman, W. (2000). *Citizenship in diverse societies.* New York: Oxford University Press.

Leung, H. H. (2000). *Settlement services for the Chinese Canadians in Toronto: The challenges toward an integrated planning.* Toronto: Ontario Administration of Settlement and Integration Services.

Li, P. S. (1998). *The Chinese in Canada.* Toronto: Oxford University Press.

Moodley, K. (1983). Canadian Multiculturalism as ideology. *Ethnic and Racial Studies, 6*(3), 320-331.

Ng, R. (1996). *The politics of community services: Immigrant women, class and state.* Halifax: Fernwood Publishing.

Reitz, J. (1995). A review of the literature on aspects of ethno-racial access, utilization and delivery of social services. Retrieved from http://ceris.metropolis.net/virtual%20library/other/reitz1/reitz1.html

Satzewich, V., & Nikolaos, L. (2007). *'Race' and ethnicity in Canada: A critical introduction.* Don Mills, ON: Oxford University Press.

Schlesinger, A. M. Jr. (1998). *The disuniting of America: Reflections on a multicultural society.* New York: W.W. Norton

Stewart, M., Anderson, J., Beiser, M., Mwakarimba, E., Neufeld, A., Simich, L., & Spitzer, D. (2008). Multicultural meanings of social support among immigrants and refugees. *International Migration, 46*(3), 123-159.

Taylor, C. (1993). Shared and divergent values. In G. Laforest (Ed.), *Reconciling the solitudes: Essays on Canadian federalism and nationalism* (pp. 155-186). Montreal & Kingston: McGill-Queens' University Press.

Weinfeld, M. (2000). The integration of Jewish immigrants in Montreal: Models and dilemmas of ethnic match." In D. J. Elazar & M. Weinfeld (Eds.), *Still moving: Recent Jewish migration in corporative perspective* (pp. 285-98). New Jersey: Transaction.

Whitaker, R. (1991). *Canadian immigration policy since confederation.* Ottawa: Canadian Historical Association.

Wong, S. L. (1992). *Emigration and stability in Hong Kong.* Hong Kong: The University of Hong Kong.

Shibao Guo
Werklund School of Education
University of Calgary

Yan Guo
Werklund School of Education
University of Calgary

MORTON WEINFELD

8. CANADIAN JEWS, DUAL/DIVIDED LOYALTIES, AND THE TEBBIT "CRICKET" TEST

DIASPORAS AND DUAL/DIVIDED LOYALTIES IN CANADA AND IN GENERAL

This chapter will explore the controversial issue of dual or competing/conflicting loyalty, with reference to Canadian minorities in general, to Jews, and to the Canadian Jewish case in particular. To illustrate some of the themes explored, the last section will examine how a small sample of Canadian Jewish leaders wrestle with a Canadian version of the "Tebbit cricket test" (this test wondered whom immigrant minorities in England would support in a cricket match between their current country and ancestral homeland). This study will analyze the loyalty issue within the broader frame of the relevance – or irrelevance – of the Jewish case in the broad field of diasporic or transnational studies.

Sheffer distinguishes between dual and divided loyalties (2003, pp. 225-26). The former, inevitable among immigrant or ethno-religious minorities, are relatively benign. In some cases they can lead to difficult choices between competing cultural or social obligations. In others they can offer an enriching set of cultural and communal options, including creative hybrid cultural contexts. But they ought not to be confused with the possibilities of divided loyalties, with their potential national security implications. In general the evidence suggests that interest by Canadian immigrants and minorities in a homeland's welfare or policies does *not* impede political integration or participation (Black, 2011; Black & Leithner, 1988; Wong, 2007/08). This could be considered as good news. But these studies generally refer to routine diasporic instances, and the research focuses on variables such as voting rates. This research less commonly looks at the content or objectives of the political participation of minorities. Thus, political participation to persuade the Canadian polity to accept, say, seemingly illiberal gender practices, or to re-orient a foreign policy, would be far more challenging. Moreover, this transnational connection can become particularly problematic during the occasional periods of acute geo-political tension or conflict between Canada and that homeland, when dual loyalties can change to divided ones.

The possibility of dual or divided loyalty in cases of real, perceived, or potential conflict between the country of residence and another homeland or religious commitment, has long been used to stigmatize and seriously victimize minorities, and notably Jews. The argument is that ties to a homeland by immigrants or their descendants, or to a wider diaspora, inevitably weaken the commitments in times of tension to Canada, its values and sense of national and social cohesion. In this view diasporic minorities might engage in a range of activities opposed to the so-

S. Guo & L. Wong (eds.), Revisiting Multiculturalism in Canada, 141–158.
© 2015 Sense Publishers. All rights reserved.

called "national interest." These can range from legitimate domestic mobilization and aggressive lobbying to promote a specific domestic or foreign policy, to unlawful cases of espionage, treason, terrorism, or acting as a "fifth column" generally (Granatstein, 2007).

These issues are of course not new to Canada. During World War One, "enemy aliens," notably Ukrainians and Germans, suffered abuse, prejudice, discrimination, and internment in Canada (Kordan, 2002). Better known are the tribulations of those Canadians of Japanese, German, and Italian ancestry during World War Two (Adachi, 1976; Hilmer, Kordan, Luciuk, 1988; Iacovetta, Perrin, Principe, 2000). These cases today are most often remembered for their clear racist undertones, as well as the mass violation of civil liberties of Canadian citizens, notably Japanese Canadians. And of course the shadow of these events has hung over the response, in Canada and other western nations, to the events of 9/11 and the general phenomenon of actual or thwarted terrorist incidents associated with militant Islamist or other organizations in the west. These issues are often framed analytically within the competing discourses of national security on the one hand, and Islamophobia on the other, similar to our understanding of the violations of liberty during the two world wars (Arat-Koc, 2006; Youssif, 2008). Islamic communal organizations in Canada, like counterparts in the United States and Britain, would take care to articulate condemnations of terror while at the same time lobbying for causes, such as the Palestinian case, which would minimize internal group divisions (Ross, 2013). Both a concern for national security, and a concern for equality and the right to dissent, are now considered legitimate, and indeed must be balanced. Canadian Tamils were recently wrestling with the perceptions of being suspect minorities following the designation of the Tamil Tigers as a terror group by the government, and protested publicly in Toronto in 2008 against this Canadian policy (Ashutosh, 2013; Thurairajah, 2011; 2014).

The holding of dual citizenship is growing in Canada and the west generally (Bloemraad et al., 2008). But this has become suspect in some sections of Canadian society. Many Canadians opposed using Canadian funds and resources to repatriate absentee dual Canadian and Lebanese citizens caught during the 2006 clash between Israel and Hizbollah (Nyers, 2010). Lebanese Canadians themselves would resort to discourses which distinguished between authentic and pseudo citizens, to navigate this dilemma (Harder & Zhyznomirska, 2012). More generally, even respected political leaders have faced some suspicion or skepticism for holding dual citizenship. Stephane Dion, former leader of the Liberal party, Michaelle Jean, former Governor General of Canada, and Thomas Mulcair, NDP and parliamentary opposition leader, each have held French citizenship. These dual citizenships provoked significant press commentary, much of it critical (Jedwab, 2007/2008). Indeed, Ms. Jean renounced her French citizenship prior to becoming Governor General. In any event, some of the skepticism concerning dual citizenship, with an undertone of doubt about possible conflicting loyalties, is captured by the recent comment of Prime Minister Harper, referring to the Mulcair case: "In my case, I am very clear: I'm a Canadian and only a Canadian" (Davis, 2012).

The dominant frame for the study of these cases of alleged dual loyalty has been one of victimization and injustice. Less attention has been paid to the challenges faced and decisions taken by these suspect minorities themselves and their Canadian communal leaders, in these delicate situations. Thus, an examination of the situation of Japanese, German, and Italian Canadian communities before, during, and most interestingly *after* World War Two has revealed findings that are more nuanced than the binary of national security vs. unfair victimization. To very varying degrees, Canadians of these ancestries shared sympathies with the fascist or nationalist homeland governments in the 1920s and 1930s (Bassler, 1999; Granatstein & Johnson, 1988, pp. 108-109; Principe, 1999). These sympathies in fact only became problematic with the outbreak of World War Two (Massa & Weinfeld, 2010).

After the war, these groups and their communal organizations and leaders adopted two postures to achieve full reintegration back into the Canadian social fabric. At first the communities emphasized rather deferentially the imperatives of re-establishing their acceptance as patriotic Canadians, and reintegrating fully into Canadian society. Any thought of reparations or apologies was premature, and indeed, inconceivable in the first three post-war decades. As one Italian Canadian leader put it: "We needed to prove we were good Canadians." This posture reflects the prevailing social and political inequalities, and constitutes an accommodationist *paradigm*. In contrast, the subsequent attempt to seek compensation and apologies for these wartime injustices relied on a legalistic and more assertive and even militant posture grounded in more entrenched notions of equal rights (Massa & Weinfeld, 2010). The second approach, which reflects *an equal rights paradigm*, is sustained by the Canadian Charter of Rights and Freedoms and the general embrace of equal citizenship for all. It now dominates the discourse of all minorities.

THE JEWISH CASE

This militancy has also been embraced strongly by diasporic Jewish communities. A legacy of the Holocaust has been a determination for militant opposition to anti-Semitism in all its forms, crystallized in the motto of "Never Again." This implies learning from the mistakes of the past, when Jewish organizations in the west – and Canada – were allegedly insufficiently militant in pressuring their governments for rescue and resettlement of Jewish refugees before, during, and after World War Two (Abella & Troper, 1982). For Canadian Jews, it has been argued that this period of new self-confidence as equal citizens began in the 1960s (Troper, 2010).

The Holocaust has set subconscious limits to the degree of loyalty some Jews can maintain to their host societies. They recall the gathering storm before World War Two, appeasement of the Nazi threat, and the "abandonment of the Jews" (Wyman, 1984). For many Jews the weeks before June 1967 seemed to be a replay of those events. The lesson learned was not to rely on others, but to take unilateral, assertive, or pre-emptive action – whether in the June 1967 war, the raid on Entebbe in 1976, organizing for the emigration of Soviet and Ethiopian Jews in distress, the Israeli air raid on the Iraqi nuclear reactor in Osirak in 1981, or the alleged Israeli attack on a secret Syrian nuclear facility in 2007.

Discussions of contemporary cases of dual loyalty are well situated within the framework of diasporic studies and transnationalism. This chapter situates diaspora Jewry and suspicions of dual/divided loyalty as an important case study of relevance to this framework (see Sheffer, 2003, ch. 9). In an earlier time, the Jewish case was indeed seen as central in these areas. The entry on "diaspora" in the 1937 edition of the *Encyclopedia of Social Sciences* was written by Simon Dubnow. Dubnow was one of the major specialists in the field of Jewish history, and specifically the history of eastern European Jewry. Dubnow's entry was about five pages in length. It devoted about a half a page to a discussion of the Armenian and Greek diaspora cases; the entire rest of the article focused on the Jewish case. The Jewish case was then recognized as archetypical (Dubnow, 1937; Safran, 2005).

The Jewish case was still seen as important, though far from central, as the field of diasporic studies emerged in the 1990s. In one major overview the Jewish case was recognized as historically relevant but with less contemporary salience. "... scholars of diaspora recognize that the Jewish tradition is at the heart of any definition of the concept. Yet if it is necessary to take full account of this tradition, it is also necessary to transcend it" (Cohen, 1997, p. 21). And indeed, the origin of the Jewish conception of diaspora is the experience of exile, and hence suffering and the imperative of return to Zion. This can be seen as somewhat limiting given the range of contemporary experiences, even that of Jews who have found in North America a far more congenial diasporic option (Vertovec, 2009, pp. 129-135). In any case, the centrality of the Jewish case has continued to erode. This disengagement has been more pronounced in European work. The following examples of conferences, institutes, and books are illustrative:

Every year a conference dealing with Diasporas and Multiculturalism is held by the Centre for Research on Nationalism, Ethnicity, and Multiculturalism, (CRONEM) at the University of Surrey, England. Among the 180 papers and posters at the 2009 conference, attended by the author, not one, at least as judging by the titles, dealt with Jews, or Israelis – not in Britain, or the Middle East, or anywhere. In the fall of 2011, there was an academic conference in Warsaw, also attended by this author, sponsored by International Migration, Integration, and Social Cohesion in Europe (IMISCOE). Scores of papers were presented, and none mentioned – by title – anything relating to Jews or Israelis. And around the same time, also in September of 2011, the 16th annual International Metropolis Conference, dealing as always with issues of migration, integration, and diversity, took places in the Azores, at the other end of Europe. From an estimated 350 presentations, only one dealt explicitly with the Jewish case (comparing Moroccan Jews in France, Quebec, and Israel).

The Centre on Migration, Policy, and Society (COMPAS) is a respected research institute associated with Oxford University. As of this writing in 2012, COMPAS had published in total 93 working papers. None dealt explicitly with any Jewish/Israeli case. Some of the papers and writings, notably by then Centre director Steven Vertovec, did address the political complications arising for homelands and hostlands from the proliferation of diasporas (Vertovec, 2006; 2009). Two of the 93 working papers focus on issues of "diasporic engagement policies" and thus could deal with the political organization of diasporic communities, links to homelands, and potentially issues of dual or divided loyalties (Gamlen, 2006; 2008). Indeed, Gamlen identified 70 states that have clear diaspora engagement policies. What is of note is that while Israel is listed as one of those 70 countries at no point in these two working papers is there any discussion of the Jewish/Israeli diaspora, nor any item among the references in both papers that deals with the Jewish/Israeli case. Yet perhaps no country is so heavily invested in maintaining and analyzing links with a relevant diaspora than is Israel. No diasporic community has likely developed the extensive arrays of communal institutions – local, national, and international – as have Jews (Breton, 1991; Elazar, 1976).

As a final example of the marginality of the Jewish case, consider the edited book *the Transnational Studies Reader*, published by Routledge (Khagram & Levitt, 2008). This reader includes 50 articles. They are all of high quality. Yet as seen in their titles, not one of these articles, many of them case studies, refers to Jews/Israelis in any way. So the field is perceived, as seen by many researchers and editors, as one in which the Jewish case is peripheral or irrelevant.

This kind of academic segregation seems not to exist to the same extent, in Canada. The first major edited volume on the subject –*Transnational Identities and Practices in Canada*, contains 13 chapters, and one of them does indeed deal with the Jewish case (Wong & Satzewich, 2006). Moreover, a recent conference sponsored by the Canadian Ethnic Studies Association and the Association for Canadian Studies in the fall of 2011, on the 40th anniversary on Canadian Multiculturalism, featured 79 presentations, and three of those dealt with a Jewish topic. On the other hand, the two most recent national Canadian Metropolis conferences taken together, in 2012 and 2011, present a different picture. Out of hundreds of workshop and roundtable presentations, only one focused directly on the Jewish case, in Canada or elsewhere (see www.metropolis.net).

These examples do not represent a definitive analysis. But things have clearly changed. How to explain this drifting of the Jewish case to the periphery and beyond, notably in the European case, but even in Canada? First one should note that this marginalization can be found for all the older and established white, migrant groups. And Jewish migration to Canada, while still significant, is far less numerous than for other non-white groups. Moreover, the roster of current issues of concern to researchers in these areas, such as asylum seekers, Islamophobia, remittances, racism, discrimination and socio-economic inequalities, are no longer seen as issues relating to Jews. And finally, the negative political assessments of Israel with regard to Palestine which prevail in much of European and Canadian academe may make the Jewish case ideologically less welcome.

SCHOLARSHIP ON THE JEWISH DIASPORA

Jewish diasporic communities are effectively studied as "polities" and this Jewish polity, which reflects a degree of cradle to grave institutional completeness, could almost be construed as being a "state within a state" (Elazar, 1976). This work occurs within the academic field of modern Jewish Studies, and more directly the social scientific study of contemporary Jewry. Much of this work is produced by Jewish/Israeli scholars, and is published in general disciplinary social scientific outlets, or Jewish studies journals such as *Contemporary Jewry,* which is published by the Association for the Social Scientific Study of Jewry, and in scholarly books (e.g., Ben-Rafael et al., 2009, ch. 11-20). The Israeli based Jewish People Planning Institute, or JPPI, associated with the Jewish Agency for Israel, has produced a variety of papers and studies on precisely these areas, many data driven and social scientific (see www.jppi.org.il). Studies of the "distancing debate, as to whether North American Jews retain their strong ties with Israel, or if youth trips to Israel impact on Jewish identity, are other examples (Beinart, 2010; Sasson, 2014; Saxe et al., 2009)

An example of this type of research, which stands in stark contrast to the Routledge volume described above, is a large edited work published by Brill (Ben Rafael et al., 2009). This book has 34 chapters. But ten deal with the Jewish case. This is not surprising, since 22 of the 40 authors work at Israeli universities, or on Jewish/Israeli topics. And thus we see another example of academic segregation. The earlier mentioned Routledge reader has 66 authors. Both volumes deal precisely with social scientific studies of diasporas and transnationalism. The subject matter is identical. Yet the two books have only one author in common.

Divided Jewish loyalties – real or potential – have been studied. A common American perspective argues that the pro-Israel lobby is excessively powerful, promotes the interests of Israel over the United States, and in general distorts Middle East policy (Mearsheimer & Walt, 2007). Indeed, there have also been studies of the Canadian Jewish or Israel lobby, and the policy activities of the Canadian Jewish polity (Barry, 2010; Goldberg, 1990; Sasley & Jacoby, 2007; Taras & Goldberg, 1989; Taras & Weinfeld, 2010). One detailed study compared the Jewish and Ukrainian polities and their efforts on the issue of alleged Nazi war criminals in Canada (Troper & Weinfeld, 1998). A different literature but also dealing with challenges of divided loyalties evolved as part of the early debates on Zionism, in the late 19th and 20th century (for an overview, see Hertzberg, 1969). It has been reshaped in the post-war period as the impact of Israel on diasporic Jewish identity, and indeed on the actual and desirable nature of the linkage between diaspora Jewry and Israel, including conceptions about post -Zionism. This literature is in part polemical and in part analytical.

These debates on Zionism – about whether Jews would be better off in their ancestral homeland or living as a diasporic minority – in turn flow out of debates about the Jewish encounter with modernity, with liberal democracy, and with modern anti-Semitism. These were historically interconnected and understood as "the Jewish Question." (This question is in fact a precursor of the multicultural dilemma of how liberal democratic societies can remain rooted in equal individual rights while at the same time recognizing group rights in one form or another). One element in these debates, certainly in the democratic west, related to potential divided loyalties. In the post-1948 period this was crystallized in a famous exchange of letters between Israeli Prime Minister David Ben- Gurion and Jacob Blaustein, head of the American Jewish Committee, beginning in 1950. Much and perhaps most of the communal leadership of American Jewry in the period around 1948 was non-Zionist or anti-Zionist. They were concerned that the establishment of Israel might raise concerns about divided loyalty, and thus hamper the struggle for American Jews for full acceptance in their new homeland. Blaustein was a non-Zionist, though supportive of the state of Israel, and wanted to clarify to Ben-Gurion that American Jews' first loyalties were and would remain with the United States. Israel would not be interfering in the life of American Jewry, and vice versa (Liebman, 1974).

The idea of the Jews as a people is rooted in the Bible, first in the Old Testament, where Jews are described first and foremost as a nation, or as a collection of tribes. Subsequently, Jews in Palestine were part of a Kingdom. And with the expulsion by the Romans 2000 years ago, they became transnational. Today this focus on Jews as a people is reflected in such institutes as the JPPI, in Jewish think tank reports, and in many scholarly volumes such as *Jewish Peoplehood: Change and Challenge* (Revivi & Koplewitz, 2008). The world- wide Jewish polity today operates on the premise that Jews have an interdependence of fate, and thus a transnational responsibility for each other. For many Jewish communal leaders this dates back to a rabbinic injunction that *kol yisrael arevim zeh ba-zeh,* or "all Israel are bound up one with another." What seems clear is that the suspect issue of dual/divided loyalty, and the more benign notion of solidarity and mutual responsibility, are two sides of the same coin.

Points of contact between the general diasporic literature, and the Jewish diasporic literature, are virtually non-existent. Some analysts of diasporas and transnationalism with Israeli ties, who also focus on the Jewish case, are exceptions (see Sheffer, 2003; Shain, 2002). But it is clear that the issues under discussion for the Jewish diaspora – the debates on Zionism, Israel, and Jewish peoplehood – are very similar to issues which have arisen and will likely arise for all other diasporic and transnational communities, in Canada and elsewhere. Almost all these diasporic groups seek to strike a balance between some form of communal cohesion and cultural maintenance on the one hand, and equal participation and integration into the host society on the other. Of course that balance will differ for different groups, and in different contexts. But given their long and varied diasporic experience, the Jewish case may be a useful and still relevant template, since they have managed to minimize tradeoffs in both those objectives. It seems certainly worthy of inclusion in the broader conversation. In Canada, for example, the Canadian Jewish Congress, and the weekly Canadian *Jewish News,* were models for similar efforts by other minority groups (Weinfeld, 2001, pp. 205-206). Moreover, the international Jewish polity includes quasi-political organizations such as the World Jewish Congress, or the International

Association of Jewish Parliamentarians, which seek to defend and promote Jewish concerns. Taken as a whole, this extensive national and international Jewish polity may parallel or prefigure developments for other diasporic communities.

The Jewish tradition as represented in the Bible reveals how the allegation of dual/divided loyalty was a primary source of anti-Semitism. The very first example of "recorded" anti-Semitism, it can be argued, is the chilling command by Pharaoh in Exodus 1:10, "Come let us deal wisely with them, lest they multiply, and if war break out they join our enemies and fight against us..." So this foundational myth of anti-Semitism is not based on any assumption of Jewish racial inferiority, or religious error, but on a fifth column-like fear of suspect loyalty Later, the famous Talmudic dictum of "*dina de'malchuta dina*" states succinctly that "the laws of the kingdom in which you live are the laws" (Nedarim 3:3). In this same spirit, one finds today in most North American and Western European synagogues formal and sincere prayers for the welfare of the host country and its rulers.

This emphasis on deference and obedience begins to change the modern period, in the 17th and 18th centuries, for Jews and other minorities. Minorities now seek to integrate as equals into host/majority societies, while retaining to the degree they wish, identities and ties linked to other traditions or former homelands. Synthesizing these two objectives poses a challenge to all liberal-democratic diverse societies, whether or not they are officially "multicultural." This synthesis proves difficult enough when the issues at hand are cultural differences or economic inequalities. Political differences are far more challenging. Liberal theorists argue that in fact competing rights of individuals, groups, and the liberal state can be accommodated (Taylor & Guttmann, 1994; Kymlicka, 1998). In general minorities, as equal citizens have the right to dissent from, challenge, and attempt to change government policy. Yet this exercise of rights may also alienate the majority Canadians who support those policies. Thus members and leaders of minority cases must engage in trade-offs when negotiating an optimum response to such delicate oppositions.

Jews have for a long time wrestled with the canard of divided loyalty as one of several motifs of modern anti-Semitism. This concern dates back in Canada at least to the debate about the acceptance of the Jewish Ezekiel Hart into the parliament of Lower Canada, following his election by the voters of Three Rivers in 1807. Newspapers of the day printed letters opposing his entry into the Assembly, and the fear of disloyalty was clearly an issue: "By what right can a Jew who is only worried about himself and his sect expect to look after the interest of the whole nation? And what reason is there to expect that such a man would work in the interests of the common good?" (Tulchinsky, 1992, p. 25). With the rise of the Zionist movement, dual loyalty charges were the foundation of the conspiracy theories of *The Protocols of the Elders of Zion* and subsequent formulations. In the United States the prominent American Zionist (and Supreme Court Justice) Louis d. Brandeis sought to negate this danger by asserting that in fact Zionism and Americanism were symbiotically related and mutually reinforcing (Brandeis, 1942). In Canada, where Reform Judaism was far weaker, the Zionist movement enjoyed greater support, and the fears of dual loyalty were relatively muted.

Zionism became a central feature of Canadian Jewish identity (Tulchinsky, 1992, pp. xxii-xxiii; 1998, pp. 145-146). As early as World War One, 300 Jewish Canadians volunteered for the Jewish legion, to fight alongside British soldiers to liberate Palestine from Ottoman rule. In 1947-49 a disproportionate number of Canadian Jews went to fight for an independent Jewish state (Bercuson, 1984). And after the creation of the state, the percentage of Canadian Jews who emigrated to Israel (the Hebrew term is to make *aliyah* or go up, to Israel) was higher than the United States, though comparable to or less than Britain and South Africa (Statistical Abstract of Israel, 2011). In short, the Canadian Jewish link to Israel is strong. About two thirds of Canadian Jews have visited Israel, compared to about one third of American Jews (Weinfeld, 2001, p. 361).

This popular strength has had its organizational dimension. The Canada Israel Committee (CIC) was formed in 1970 by the Canadian Jewish Congress, B'nai B'rith, and the Canadian Zionist Federation. It was hoped the CIC would advance the case for Israel in a more professional manner, following the trauma of the 1967 war. In 2011 the Centre for Israel and Jewish Advocacy was created by Canadian Jewish communal leaders (and not without a good deal of controversy), as a replacement of the CIC and the venerable Canadian Jewish Congress, to further professionalize and centralize advocacy on behalf of Israel in Canada. In general, Canadian Jewish organizations have sought to advocate for Israel using a blend of liberal values shared by all Canadians, with pragmatic concerns for national security (Sucharov, 2011). This activism has created a context where Canadian Jewish ties to Israel have on occasion caused comment and criticism. Consider:

In 1988 then Minister of External Affairs Joe Clark caused a stir among Canadian Jewish supporters of Israel when he criticized alleged human rights violations by Israel during the first intifada, at a gathering of the CIC. This prompted a hostile reaction from his audience. And that in turn prompted press criticism, most strongly from the *Toronto Star,* which editorialized about Clark's comments: "It was also a necessary reminder to members of the Jewish community of Canada that they are citizens of Canada, not Israel." In a responding letter on March 15, two officials of the Ontario Canadian Jewish Congress replied: "The Star by questioning the loyalty of Jewish Canadians to Canada, has crossed the line from unrelenting criticism of Israeli government policy into anti-Semitism." (Weinfeld, 2001, p. 259)

Subsequently, allegations or suspicions of dual loyalty were leveled against high profile Canadian Jews. Norman Spector, former chief of staff to Prime Minister Brian Mulroney, was appointed to be the first Jewish ambassador from Canada to Israel in 1992. (In fact he was the first Jewish diplomat of any sort sent to Israel). Following his appointment, an Arab group condemned the appointment of "a Zionist, who was close to the Bronfmans." And veteran foreign affairs analyst Peyton Lyon claimed that among the professional foreign affairs community there was resentment of "the lobbying that has distorted what they believe best for Canada, the United States, and even Israel" (Weinfeld, 2001, pp. 259-260).

The career of former Canadian Justice Minster Irwin Cotler also raised the issue. Cotler, a McGill Law professor for many years, was also a well- known Jewish communal leader, and had served as President of the Canadian Jewish Congress from 1980-83. Cotler would argue repeatedly that divided loyalty and related clashes were an impossibility. When campaigning for the CJC presidency, and well before he entered federal politics, he said "the agendas, Jewish and Canadian, not only interlock more than ever before, but impact upon each other in ways that hitherto have not been experienced...There is no distinction between being a good Jew and being a good Canadian" (Lazarus & Burkham, 1980). A more pointed episode concerned a case where Mossad agents had used Canadian passports in a botched assassination attempt. The Canadian government angrily recalled the ambassador to Israel, David Berger, who happened to be Jewish. Indeed, according to news reports several Jewish Canadians reported being approached by Mossad agents to use their passports (Weinfeld, 2001, pp. 260-61).

THE TEBBIT OR CRICKET TEST, CANADIAN STYLE

In 1990, British MP and former Conservative Cabinet Minister Norman Tebbit made headlines by speaking about what he called the "cricket test" as a measure of the integration of immigrants to Britain. The loyalties of sports fans were thought to be relevant. Speaking in a *Los Angeles Times* interview in April 20 of 1990, he said: "A large proportion of Britain's Asian population fails to pass the cricket test. Which side do they cheer for? It's an interesting test. Are you still harking back to where you came from or where you are?"

The cricket test became the subject of wide and repeated discussion for several months. It was attacked as being racist in inspiration and consequence. But gradually, over the years, it became more an object of ridicule and seeming irrelevance. A British "State of the Nation" poll carried out in 2011 by IPSOS Mori for a new think tank, British Future, found 60% of people agreed with the statement: "People from abroad who settle in Britain should be able to choose to support the sporting teams of the countries they came from, even against British teams, without people saying this shows they aren't willing to fit in here." Only 15% agreed that "People from abroad who settle in Britain should support our sporting teams, even when they are competing against the countries they come from, to show they want to fit in here" (Jolley & Katwala, 2012). The consensus in Britain therefore is that the Tebbit test is not a meaningful indicator of immigrant integration, and certainly not of loyalty. The current view seems to be that Britons of any background could root for their homeland team while remaining fully loyal and patriotic Britons (Fletcher, 2011).

With this context I decided to use a version of the innocuous Tebbit test simply as an icebreaker when beginning interviews with Canadian Jewish leaders. These individuals included elected politicians, leaders of Jewish communal organizations, rabbis, intellectuals, and journalists. They were chosen as a purposive sample through reputational criteria, not to be representative of Jews with some public or communal profile, but to illustrate a range of profiles and postures. The idea was to pose a trivial, engaging and likely fun question in the opening of interviews, one that the respondents would enjoy answering and talking about. This question would ease the discussion into the more serious issues of exploring and reconciling any possible competing and conflicting loyalties: "Suppose that Israel and Canada are competing in a Gold medal Olympic soccer game. For whom would you root, and why?" This question was not even considered as a part of the formal interview, and had been omitted from any drafts of the open ended questionnaire and pretest. The goal was to focus subsequently on more serious matters; it was assumed that this question would set a positive tone with interviewees.

That assumption was wrong. What was surprising was the degree of consternation and discomfort, even if fleeting, that the question elicited, for most of the respondents. Most in fact felt this question posed a serious challenge to their presumed loyalty, and many engaged in fence-sitting and obfuscation in attempting to come up with a "satisfactory" answer. And this discomfort emerged despite the fact that they all knew the interviews were confidential and they could explicitly go off the record for any question. The discomfort was evident not only in the large group that refused to choose one answer, or in the text of the reasoning they offered, but also in the irritation that could at times be seen in their tone, their facial expressions, and their body language.

Of seventeen respondents, ten refused to choose or to declare a clear preference in this hypothetical match. Two indicated support for Canada, and five indicated support for Israel. One respondent "solved" the dilemma by declaring support for Israel if the match was soccer, and support for Canada if the match was in hockey! This respondent, an academic, was then asked to speculate about a preferred outcome for a volleyball game, but still no luck. The academic explained further: "It's a tough choice, like choosing amongst members of your family, who do I love more, my father or my mother, I love them each differently and in different ways, it's the same between Israel and Canada ... but in most instances I would be rooting for Canada and in some I might be rooting for Israel."

Of the majority who would not or could not choose, many somehow hoped it would be a tie – which of course is impossibility in any final game. As one academic put it: "I would be thrilled that they're playing against each other and probably I would hope it was going to be a tie." Another academic responded: "I couldn't give a shit about soccer," but then also refused to choose when the hypothetical question was changed to a debating tournament. In the words of yet another academic: "I really don't know, I have a deep emotional attachment to both, it is not a tough question, but tough to explain the answer."

A Jewish communal leader explained "I would be thrilled they both got to that point and I would be thrilled with either one....the winning is the fact that they are playing each other at that level in sports. That Israel made it to that level, that Canada made it to that level, and whichever team won, two great teams, two great countries having that opportunity to interact, so it would be one over the other ... that was hard. That's how I would relate to it. Another communal leader succinctly argued in a similar vein ..., "I would root for both, a no lose situation." A communal leader who wound up refusing to choose nonetheless offered another

Solomonic approach to splitting a vote, based not on the sport but on geography: "It's a tough question, I don't know. Especially since I don't follow soccer. No it's a tough call. If the game is in Canada I'd probably be rooting for Canada. If the game is in Israel, I would be rooting for Israel ... I really can't tell you off the top of my head. It's a tough one, yeah. And yet another respondent, a politician, refused to be pinned down claimed "I would just enjoy the game, as a Canadian I would be disposed to support Canada, but on a psychological level, I would support Israel."

One intellectual who refused to choose launched into a socio-political critique of soccer and indeed all sports, particularly at the elite level. This is not unusual in the sociology of sport, which includes commonly post-modern and highly critical perspectives, often within a cultural studies framework (Carrington & Macdonald, 2001; Crawford, 2004; Hylton, 2009). As this respondent explained: "I feel there is a kind of scary background to the nationalism that emerges around soccer, and in particular I think there is a fascinating kind of anti-colonialism that happens ... so Canada to me as well as Israel in different ways represent a colonial project. So if I were seeing this soccer match, I would be thinking of it in that framework ... you know, this idea of the nation state as a collection of communities ... this is sort of how Canada talks about itself. That would be on my mind. And sort of – would I be rooting for Canada? I don't know, I would be interested. And for Israel, a country I have a lot of ideological issues with, a lot of spiritual and religious connection to, and community based connection to ... I'd be disturbed. I think no matter what soccer match I was watching I would have this colonial discourse going on in my head ... so that's how I would define it, I would be watching it in a kind of disturbed state ... I couldn't answer the question on who I would be rooting for. That would be too binary for me. I don't have a yes or no answer."

Another respondent, a member of the media, agonized over the question at even greater length. Some highlights: "I'd probably be rooting for Canada as a Canadian and be delighted if Canada won and I would be delighted if Israel won too ... I would absolutely root for Canada and I would absolutely probably root for Israel ... I would be somewhat conflicted because I would be happy either way. ... it's like Keats' 'negative capability' ... the art of poetry is the ability to simultaneously hold two contradictory ideas in your mind without diminishing the value of the other .... In dual citizenship or religious loyalty you have to have a certain kind of negative capability.... So as a Jew I am loyal to being Jewish and the notion of Israel as the apotheosis of thousands of years of searching, is meaningful to me .... But Israel's not my home ... and if it was I would simply move there ... I don't, I have never really had that strong urge to make *aliyah*. So clearly my identity is here, my primary identity is Canadian. My home is Canada, my sense of place is Canada and my sense of meaning is derived from Canada but it profoundly intermingles with Israel." This may well be the first time that Keats' "negative capability" has been used in a discussion of soccer preferences.

Of those five who clearly were rooting for Israel, one Jewish communal leader claimed s/he would in public answer with a diplomatic answer and hope for a tie, but off the record admitted that s/he would support Israel. The argument was that it was more difficult for a Jew to say in public that they would root for Israel, so best to keep the Israel support private. Another respondent, a rabbi and educator, also supported Israel, but claimed that if the game were in a public space in Canada, they would bring two flags... "I would feel the need to affirm the Canadian piece as well. I don't know that I would be comfortable in a public role identifying myself as a Jewish Canadian through my dress, such as wearing a *kippa* (skullcap), in a Canadian stadium, rooting against Canada."

A Jewish communal professional argued that support for Israel was strategic; it was more important for Israel to win. Another would support Israel because they are an underdog in world public opinion. And an academic argued: "Israel. If Canada won, I'd also be happy, but I imagine I would root for Israel." The respondent elaborated: "I have both Canadian identity and Israeli identity, even though I am not an Israeli citizen ... it's possible that my identification with Jewish values is stronger than any other form of identification .... It's also possible that Israel is more of the underdog. In sports one tends to go with the underdog ... so I think that would influence my decision."

The two respondents who would root for Canada were the most direct, perhaps feeling their choice required little elaboration. These were the respondents who would pass the infamous Tebbit test with flying colors. One Jewish communal official would root clearly for Canada, but "would want a hard fought 2-1 game and not a 10-0 blowout." The other respondent, a media personality, was the more forceful for Canada, and perhaps had the most decisive answer of any of the respondents:

Q. Who are you rooting for?

A. Canada.

Q. Yeah, no hesitation?

A. None. That one's easy.

Q. Can you elaborate? Why is it so easy?

A. It's easy for me because first and foremost I am a Canadian citizen and I'm always cheering for Canada when it comes to a sporting event. And I would have no hesitation and trepidation. I'd probably be one of the few people who when the Maccabi team came over here to play the Raptors, I would have been cheering for the Raptors.

CONCLUSION

In sum, only two of the seventeen respondents were clear that they would support Canada. This suggests a strong degree of identification with Israel among the other respondents, which is likely among many other Canadian Jews. Most respondents did not like the question, and had difficulty arriving at a comfortable response. They were enmeshed clearly in versions of dual, divided, and ambiguous loyalties. These competing identifications were pronounced when dealing with sports events, which in the grand scheme of things are relatively trivial. One can imagine that if real conflicts of interest were to arise, whether dealing with Israel or some basic issue regarding the welfare of the Canadian Jewish community, these feelings of ambivalence would be even more acute. But in the past, certainly in the 1970s and 1980s, some Canadian Jewish leaders had felt that Canadian governments might have been more staunchly supportive of Israel on the occasion of UN votes during the Trudeau years targeting Israel, or positions on specific Middle East policy questions. A shift to a more consistent posture supportive of Israel is detected with the succession of Paul Martin as Liberal Prime Minister, and then later under the Conservative Harper government (Barry, 2010; Goldberg, 1989).

What is perhaps surprising is that the high degree of observed ambivalence is found in these Canadian Jewish leaders. For Jews, there are not serious homeland conflicts with Canada. In fact the Stephen Harper government may be the most pro-Israel government in Canadian history. And it might be noted that recent poll data indicate that a majority of Canadians support this current Middle East policy, and only 23% find it "too pro-Israel" (Martin, 2012). And even the Liberal government which preceded it was supportive of Israel. Moreover, Canada is a liberal democratic society, where minority rights enjoy constitutional protection, and where the ideas of multiculturalism are also entrenched in the Constitution and government programs and departments. Thus, Canadian Jews have become successful poster children for multiculturalism, seemingly able to maximize full participation in Canadian life with a meaningful retention of a cultural heritage (Adelman & Simpson, 1996; Brown, 2006; Weinfeld, 2001).

Nevertheless, despite these facts, there may be a reservoir of marginality which lies dormant in many Canadian Jews. (This may apply not only to Canadian Jews, but to other groups, and for different historic and contemporary reasons. One thinks of Quebecois, First Nations, Muslims, Arabs, and some – but not all – visible minority groups). There have been questions raised about the loyalties of Jewish Canadians in the public sphere. Tensions in the Middle East routinely pose challenges to those Canadian Jews who seek to maximize Canadian government support for Israel. These tensions have also begun to sway voting patterns of Canadian Jews, at least according to some reports. The Conservative government of Stephen Harper has systematically increased its level of support for Israel, and this action has been appreciated by significant segments of the Canadian Jewish population (Merkley, 2011). Indeed, one exit poll has confirmed a marked shift to the right, finding that in the federal election of 2011 52% of Canadian Jews voted for the Conservatives, and only 24% for the Liberals and 16% for the NDP (Simpson, 2011). This overturns a long, documented post-war affinity of Canadian Jews for the centre/left, and the Liberals (Laponce, 2010). Jewish Canadians with a profile in either the general or Jewish communities wrestle with conflicting loyalties even at the minimally consequential level of sports. And even some who supported Israel in the soccer match indicated they were reluctant to display that support in public! This insecurity was a reflected in the discomfort which many respondents felt in even addressing the trivial sports question. As these interviews have shown, underneath the seeming picture of Jews as having "made it" in

Canadian life, there persist ongoing internal doubts and negotiations of status in these responses. ("If everything is so good, why is everything so bad?"). If this can be found for Jews, it can be found for many other Canadian minority groups. And thus in changing circumstances, benign dual loyalties can become more serious divided ones.

ACKNOWLEDGEMENTS

The author wishes to thank the Social Sciences and Humanities Research Council for funding this research. And thanks are also due to Dr. Randal Schnoor for invaluable assistance with the interviewing process, and Ms. Gabrielle Jacobs for library research.

REFERENCES

Abella, I., & Troper, H. (1982). *None is too many.* Toronto: Lester, Orpen, and Dennys.

Adachi, K. (1976). *The enemy that never was: A history of the Japanese Canadians.* Toronto: McClelland and Stewart.

Adelman, H., & Simpson, J. (Eds.). (1996). *Multiculturalism, Jews and identities in Canada.* Jerusalem: Magnes Press.

Arat-Koc, S. (2006). Whose transnationalism? Canada, 'clash of civilizations' discourse, and Arab and Muslim Canadians. In L. Wong & V. Satzewich (Eds.), *Transnational identities and practices in Canada* (pp. 216-240). Vancouver: UBC Press,

Ashutosh, I. (2013). Immigrant protests in Toronto: Diaspora and Sri Lanka's civil war. *Citizenship Studies, 17*(2), 197-210.

Barry, D. (2010). Canada and the Middle East today: Electoral politics and foreign policy. *Arab Studies Quarterly, 32*(4), 191-217.

Bassler, G. 1999. Germans. In P. Magosci (Ed.), *The encyclopedia of Canada's people,* (pp. 587-612). Toronto: University of Toronto Press.

Beinart, P. (2010, July 12). The failure of the American Jewish establishment. *New York Review of Books.* Retrieved from: http://www.nybooks.com/articles/archives/2010/jun/10/failure-american-jewish-establishment/?pagination=false

Ben-Rafael, E., & Sternberg, Y. (Eds.). (2009). *Transnationalism: Diasporas in the advent of a new (Dis)order.* Boston: Brill.

Bercuson, D. (1984). *The secret army.* Toronto: Stein and Day.

Black, J. (2011). Immigrant and minority political incorporation in Canada: A review with some reflections on Canadian-American comparison possibilities. *American Behavioral Scientist, 55*(9), 1160-1188.

Black, J., & Leithner, C. (1988). Immigrants and political involvement in Canada: The role of the ethnic media. *Canadian Ethnic Studies, 20*(1), 1-20.

Bloemraad, I., Korteweg, A., & Yurdakul, G. (2008). Citizenship and immigration: Multiculturalism, assimilation and challenges to the nation-state. *Annual Review of Sociology, 34,* 153-179.

Brandeis, L. D. (1942). *Brandeis on Zionism: A collection of addresses and statements.* Washington DC: Zionist Organization of America.

Breton, R. (1991). *The governance of ethnic communities.* New York: Greenwood.

Brown, M. (2006, July 16). From binationalism to multiculturalism to the open society: The impact on Canadian Jews. Jerusalem Center for Public Affairs.

Carrington, B., & McDonald, I. (2001). *Race, sport and British society.* London: Routledge.

Cohen, R. (1997). *Global diasporas: An introduction.* London: University College London Press.

Crawford, G. (2004). *Consuming sport: Fans, sport, and culture.* London: Routledge.

Davis, J. (2012, January 18). Citizenship issue hits Mulcair. *The (Montreal) Gazette.*

Dubnow, S. (1937). Diaspora. In *Encyclopedia of the social sciences* (Vol. 5, pp. 126-130). New York: Macmillan

Elazar, D. (1976). *Community and polity: The organizational dynamics of American Jewry.* Philadelphia. Jewish Publication Society.

Fletcher, T. (2011). Who do "they" cheer for? Cricket, diasporas, hybridity, and divided loyalties among British Asians. *International Review for the Sociology of Sport,* July, 1-20. doi: 10.1177/1012690211416556.

Gamlen, A. (2006). *Diaspora engagement policies: What are they and what kind of states use them?* Working Paper 06-32. Oxford: COMPAS.

Gamlen, A. (2008). *Why engage diasporas?* Working Paper 08-63. Oxford: COMPAS.

Goldberg, D. (1989). Keeping score: From the Yom Kippur war to the Palestinian uprising. In D. Taras & D. Goldberg (Eds.), *The domestic battleground, Canada, and the Arab-Israeli conflict* (pp. 102-122). Montreal: McGill Queen's Press.

Goldberg, D. (1990). *Foreign policy and ethnic interest groups: American and Canadian Jews lobby for Israel.* New York: Greenwood.

Granatstein, J. (2007). *Whose war is it? How Canada can survive in the post 9/11 world.* Toronto: HarperCollins Publishers.

Granatstein, J., & Johnson, G. A. (1988). The evacuation of the Japanese Canadians: A realist critique of the received version. In N. Hillmer, B. V. Kordan, & L. Y Luciuk (Eds.), *On guard for thee: War, ethnicity, and the Canadian state, 1939-1945* (pp. 101-130). Ottawa: Canadian committee for the history of the Second World War.

Harder, L., & Lyubov, Z. (2012). Claims of belonging: Recent tales of trouble in Canadian citizenship. *Ethnicities, 12*(3), 293-316.

Hertzberg, A. (1969). *The Zionist idea: A historical analysis and reader.* New York. Atheneum.

Hillmer, N., Kordan, B. V., & Luciuk, L. (Eds.). (1988). *On guard for thee: War, ethnicity, and the Canadian State, 1939-1945.* Ottawa. Canadian Committee for the History of the Second World War.

Hylton, K. (2009). *Race and sport: Critical race theory.* London: Routledge.

Iacovetta, F., Perrin, R., & Principe, A. (Eds.). (2000). *Enemies within: Italians and other internees in Canada and abroad.* Toronto: University of Toronto Press.

Jedwab, J. (2007/2008). Dually divided? The risks of linking debates over citizenship to attachment to Canada. *International Journal, 63*(1), 65-77.

Jolley, R., & Katwala, S. (2012). *The British future: State of the nation report.* London: British Future.

Khagram, S., & Levitt, P. (Eds.). (2008). *The transnational studies reader.* London: Routledge.

Kordan, B. (2002). *Enemy aliens, prisoners of war: Internment in Canada during the Great War.* Montreal: McGill-Queen's University Press.

Kymlicka, W. (1998). *Finding our way: Rethinking ethnocultural relations in Canada.* Toronto: Oxford University Press.

Laponce, J. (2010). Left or centre: The Canadian Jewish electorate, 1953-83. In R. Brym, W. Shaffir, & M. Weinfeld (Eds.), *The Jews in Canada* (pp. 270-292). Toronto: Oxford University Press.

Lazarus, S., & Burkham, D. (1980, April 3). Candidates for CJC presidency present views on its objectives, operation and organization. *Canadian Jewish News,* 5.

Liebman, C. (1974). Diaspora influence on Israel: The Ben-Gurion--Blaustein "exchange." *Jewish Social Studies, 36*(3-4), 271-290.

Martin, P. (2012, Jan 31). Nearly half of Canadians say Ottawa's policy on Arab Palestinian conflict shows the right balance. *The Globe and Mail,* n.p.

Massa, E., & Weinfeld, M. (2010). We needed to prove we were good Canadians: Contrasting paradigms for suspect minorities. *Canadian Journal for Social Research, 3*(1), 15-28.

Mearsheimer, J., & Walt, S. (2007). *The Israel lobby and U.S. foreign policy.* New York: Farrar Straus Giroux.

Merkley, P. C. (2011). At issue reversing the poles: How the pro-Israeli policy of Canada's conservative government may be moving Jewish voters from left to right. *Jewish Political Studies Review, 23*(1), 39-60.

Nyers, P. (2010). Duelling designs: The politics of rescuing dual citizens. *Citizenship Studies, 14*(1), 47-60.

Principe, A. (1999). *The darkest side of the fascist years: The Italian-Canadian press. 1920-1942.* Toronto: Guernica

Revivi, M., & Kopelowitz, E. (2008). *Jewish peoplehood: Change and challenge.* Brighton. Academic Studies Press.

Ross, L.R. (2013), Muslim interest groups and foreign policy in the U.S., Canada, and the U.K.: Identity, interest, and action. *Foreign Policy Analysis, 9*(3), 287-306.

Safran, W. (2005). The Jewish diaspora: A comparative and theoretical perspective. *Israel Studies, 10*(1), 36-60.

Sasley, B. E., & Jacoby, T. A. (2007). Canada's Jewish and Arab communities and Canadian foreign policy. In P. Heinbecker & B. Momani (Eds.), *Canada and the Middle East in theory and practice* (pp. 185-204). Waterloo: Wilfrid Laurier University Press.

Sasson, T. (2014). *The new American zionism.* New York: New York University Press.

Saxe, L., Phillips, B., Sasson, T., Hecht, S., Shain, M., Wright, G., & Kadushin, C. (2009). *Generation birthright Israel: The impact of an Israel experience on Jewish identity and choices.* Waltham: Cohen Center for Modern Jewish Studies, Brandeis University.

Shain, Y. (2002). The role of diasporas in conflict perpetuation or resolution. *SAIS Review, 22*(2), 115-144

Sheffer, G. (2003). *Diaspora politics: At home abroad.* Cambridge: Cambridge University Press

Simpson, J. (2011, September 28). How the political shift among Jewish voters plays in Canada. *The Globe and Mail,* n.p.

Statistical Abstract of Israel. (2011). Jerusalem: Central Bureau of Statistics.

Sucharov, M. (2011). Values, identity, and Israel advocacy. *Foreign Policy Analysis, 7*(4), 361-380.

Taylor, C., & Guttmann, A. (1994). *Multiculturalism: Examining the politics of recognition* Princeton, NJ: Princeton University Press.

Taras, D., & Goldberg, D. (1989). *The domestic battleground: Canada and the Arab Israeli conflict.* Montreal: McGill-Queen's Press.

Taras, D., & Weinfeld, M. (2010). Continuity and criticism: North American Jews and Israel. In R. Brym, W. Shaffir, & M. Weinfeld (Eds.), *The Jews in Canada* (pp. 293-310). Toronto: Oxford University Press.

Thurairajah, K. (2011). The shadow of terrorism: Competing identities and loyalties among Tamil Canadians. *Canadian Ethnic Studies. 43*(1), 129-152.

Thurairajah, K. (2014). *Caught between the bleeding homeland and the save haven: Negotiating loyalties in times of conflict.* McGill, Montreal: Department of Sociology, McGill University.

Troper, H. (2010). *The defining decade: Identity, politics and the Canadian Jewish community in the 1960s.* Toronto: University of Toronto Press.

Troper, H., & Weinfeld, M. (1999). *Ethnicity, politics and public policy in Canada.* Toronto: University of Toronto Press.

Tulchinsky, G. (1992). *Taking root.* Toronto. Lester Publishing.

Tulchinsky, G. (1998). *Branching out.* Toronto: Stoddart.

Vertovec S. (2009). *Transnationalism.* London: Routledge.

Vertovec, S. (2006). *Diasporas good? Diasporas bad?* Working Paper 06:41. Oxford: COMPAS.

Weinfeld, M. (2001). *Like everyone else but different: The paradoxical success of Canadian Jews.* Toronto: McClelland and Stewart.

Wong, L. (2007/08). Transnationalism, active citizenship, and belonging in Canada. *International Journal, 63*(1) (Winter), 79-99.

Wong, L., & Satzewich, V. (Eds.). (2006). *Transnational identities and practices in Canada.* Vancouver: University of British Columbia Press.

Wyman, D. (1984). *The abandonment of the Jews: America and the Holocaust.* New York, Pantheon.
Yousif, A.E. (2008). *Muslims in Canada: A question of identity.* Ottawa: Legas.

Morton Weinfeld
Department of Sociology
McGill University

REBECCA MARGOLIS

9. YIDDISH AND MULTICULTURALISM

A Marriage Made in Heaven?[1]

INTRODUCTION

Yiddish has made the transition from a Jewish immigrant language to a Jewish heritage and ethnic language within the rubric of Canadian multiculturalism. It has done so within a broader engagement between Canadian Jewry and multiculturalism. This chapter will examine the interplay between four decades of multiculturalism and the changing place of Yiddish within Canadian life. It will argue that multiculturalism has ultimately had a mixed impact for Yiddish in Canada. On the one hand, it has encouraged the maintenance of Yiddish in the preservation of a distinct Jewish identity within a matrix of Canadian diversity. The notable beneficiaries have been Yiddish writers in the secular realm. On the other hand, multiculturalism has also promoted the integration of Yiddish into the wider fabric of Canadian cultural life as a marker of ethnic identity, which has resulted in the privileging of accessibility over linguistic and cultural cohesiveness. In this role, Yiddish has become one expression of symbolic ethnicity among Canadian Jews who have integrated linguistically but sought to preserve a distinct identity. This tension stems from the shift of Yiddish from a shared immigrant language to one increasingly imbued with symbolic meaning, a mode that American scholar Jeffrey Shandler has termed "postvernacular" (Shandler, 2006). In contrast, a growing population of Haredi (highly traditional, "God-fearing") Jews employ Yiddish as an ethnic marker to deliberately separate themselves from a pluralistic Canadian society. This study explores the ways in which Yiddish has intersected with Canadian concepts of multiculturalism.

YIDDISH IN CANADA

Within the last century, Canadian Jewry has undergone many changes as successive waves of immigrants arrived in the country. After 250 years of continual Jewish settlement in Canada, the country's Jewish population expanded from several hundred individuals in the mid-nineteenth century, who were largely of British origin and integrated into the English milieu, to some 16,000 in 1901 due to the beginnings of a mass immigration of Eastern European Jews fleeing violence and persecution. This immigrant group would augment Canada's Jewish population to some 125,000 by 1921, after which restrictive immigration policies severely curtailed Jewish immigration until the end of the 1940s. Despite wide

S. Guo & L. Wong (eds.), Revisiting Multiculturalism in Canada, 159–170.

political and ideological diversity among the newcomers, the Jewish immigrant community was unified by its shared lingua franca of Yiddish. In 1931, when the Jews formed the eighth largest ethno-linguistic group in Canada, Yiddish was identified as mother tongue by some 96% of 156,000 Canadian Jews on the census (Rosenberg, 1993, p. 12). As the primary language spoken among Jews, Yiddish spanned multiple venues, including the home and street, the political arena, the picket line, the theatre stage, the daily newspaper, the classroom, the synagogue, and the traditional Jewish study hall.

Since that time Yiddish has faced steady attrition within the mainstream Jewish community in Canada. The linguistic integration of Yiddish-speakers has been but one root of a sharp global decline of the language as a shared vernacular in the second half of the twentieth century. Other contributing factors are: the decimation of Jewish life and the murder of half of the world's speakers in the Holocaust; the suppression of Yiddish culture in the Soviet Union; and the privileging of Hebrew in the State of Israel. Yiddish has moved from the daily language of some eleven million speakers comprising three-quarters of world Jewry in the late 1930s, to one spoken today by an estimated one million people worldwide, a growing majority of them Haredi Jews who reject mainstream culture. While this decline has been tempered in Canada by a strong institutional commitment to Yiddish, notably in systems of schools that teach the language as well as in the area of performance, the 2001 census reported a mere 37,000 Yiddish speakers among some 350,000 Jews. Meanwhile, with the rising centrality of the State of Israel in Jewish life, Israeli Hebrew (Ivrit) has assumed a place of growing prominence in Jewish education and communal life, with twice as many speakers as Yiddish. Canadian Jews have historically expressed a strong commitment to Israel and its culture, and the prominence of Ivrit has more recently been augmented by Israelis who have settled in Canada and maintained strong ties to their home culture (Gold & Cohen, 1996). While Yiddish has increasingly shifted from a vernacular to a heritage language in the Jewish mainstream, Hebrew has emerged as the unifying, communicative language of Jewish life in addition to its traditional role as language of prayer and sacred text (Davids, 2010-11). Further, the centrality of Yiddish has declined due to successive of waves of Jewish immigrants to Canada with no connection to Yiddish, notably a sizable population of Jews from North Africa.

The survival of Yiddish, a language that first emerged among Jews in Germanic lands in the tenth century and developed into a distinct, extraterritorial tongue with eastward migration into Slavic lands, has historically been contingent upon the exclusion of its speakers from the mainstream. Opportunities for Jews to participate in the dominant culture in countries that emancipated their Jewish populations such as France or Germany entailed abandoning their distinctiveness, notably their Yiddish language. Conversely, in the Russian Empire, where Jews remained unemancipated and marginalized even after generations of residence, the 1897 census indicated that 97% of Jews had Yiddish as mother tongue while only a quarter claimed Russian literacy (Fishman, 2005, p. 6). Mainstream Canadian society was largely closed to Yiddish-speaking newcomers in the first decades of the twentieth century, in particular in the largest Jewish population centre of Montreal. There the Jews formed a "third solitude" alongside French-Catholic and English-Protestant communities, each with their own institutionally complete infrastructures. Because of agreements predating their arrival, Jews were streamed into the Protestant schools and incorporated into the English milieu, albeit incompletely as they continued to face exclusion from many facets of Canadian political, economic and social life (Stevenson, 1999, pp. 45-46). With linguistic integration into the country's dominant English culture, Yiddish usage declined rapidly in the decades leading up to multiculturalism. By the time the policy came into effect, the transition from Yiddish as Jewish lingua franca to marker of Jewish ethnic identity was complete, at least outside of Haredi enclaves.

CANADIAN JEWISH AND MULTICULTURALISM

Multiculturalism has had significant impacts on Canadian Jewish life in both theory and practice. Randal Schnoor's recent article, "The Contours of Canadian Jewish Life," states, "Canadian Jews have been successful in comfortably integrating into the larger Canadian society while retaining a vibrant internal Jewish religion and culture. In this way they can be considered Canada's multicultural community par excellence" (Schnoor, 2011, p. 196). Menkis writes that Canadian Jews have increasingly employed multiculturalism to "legitimize their attachment to the more particularistic Jewish practices, and their resistance to 'innovations'" (Menkis, 2013, p. 305). Koffman and Weinfeld's study, "Recent Developments in the Social Scientific Study of Canadian Jews," refers to "the much-vaunted Canadian multiculturalism, which many Canadians and much of the international community see as perhaps the most distinctive feature of Canadian life" and which, both as public policy, and a shared cultural value, has had extensive influence on the Canadian Jewish experience. Further, they suggest that the rhetoric around multiculturalism frames core community debates around controversial issues such as assimilation in very different ways from the neighbouring United States (Koffman & Weinfeld, 2011, pp. 201-202). The opening line of Carol Zemel's study of Jewish Canadian performance and installation art exemplifies the ways in which Jews have come to be identified as the embodiment of multiculturalism: "In a nation that trumpets its pride in diversity, Jewish experience exemplifies the success of the Canadian mosaic" (Zemel, 2013, p. 13).

However, the early Jewish encounter with Canadian multiculturalism was fraught with ambivalence. While Jews have, since their arrival in Canada in the colonial era, maintained a group identity distinct of the country's English and French founding nations, their own understanding of this identity was influenced by the precariousness of their political and social status. As historian Michael Brown has suggested in his study, "Canadian Jews and Multiculturalism: Myths and Realities," Canada has in practice been a multicultural country since the mass immigration of Yiddish-speaking Jews to Montreal and Toronto beginning in the late nineteenth century, which created a community infrastructure independent of the two charter groups. However, Brown posits, the period before the advent of official multiculturalism was an "era of multiculturalism manqué" (Brown, 2006), with little room for Jewish distinctiveness within the dominant Canadian English and French milieus. Rather, the Jewish immigrant community maintained its own set of institutions rooted in Yiddish language and religious culture. The results were two-fold. On the one hand, Jews were excluded from the dominant culture, which limited their economic and social mobility in Canadian society. On the other, their relative cultural isolation encouraged the cohesion of Jewish communal life and the maintenance of markers of distinctiveness such as Yiddish language usage.

Canadian Jews did not immediately embrace the discourse of multiculturalism that emerged in the early 1960s. As Richard Menkis has argued, the Canadian Jewish Congress (CJC) – the chief representative body for Canadian Jewry – was cautious in its encounter with the Royal Commission on Bilingualism and Biculturalism and unwilling to identify the Jews as an ethnic group (Menkis, 2011). Established in 1919 and reconstituted in 1934 in response to rising anti-Semitism in Europe as well as in Canada, by the 1960s the CJC served a Jewish community that had transitioned from a predominantly Yiddish-speaking immigrant community to a minority group that was in the process of defining itself. In contrast to vigorous participation by representatives of other Canadian linguistic and cultural groups, notably Ukrainians, the CJC made a single appearance at a preliminary hearing of the Commission in 1963 to protest its mandate; the CJC stated its commitment to maintaining Canada's Jewish heritage and, unlike other minority groups, made no demands for public support of its cultural institutions. One explanation lies in the "status anxiety" of the Canadian Jewish community, in particular in Quebec – home to more than half of the country's Jews and the headquarters of the CJC – where the CJC sought to avoid alienating the French community. Further, census statistics from 1961 indicated a major discrepancy between those who identified Jewish by ethnic origin (173,000), and those who identified as Jewish by religion (254,000), and the CJC leadership hoped to promote the status of Canadian Jews by advocating for the concept of religious pluralism with Jews as a religious group, rather than Jews being identified as one of many ethno-linguistic groups.

The issue of Yiddish language represented a further deciding factor in the reluctance of the CJC to identify the Jews as an ethnic group. The 1961 census pointed to ongoing declining numbers of Yiddish speakers, with a drop in Yiddish mother tongue statistics from 51% in 1951 to 32% in 1961. As demographer Leo Davids has pointed out, "In 1951, the majority of Jews still reported Yiddish as their mother tongue and younger Jews had a passive mastery of Yiddish; although they didn't speak it very often, they understood it fully and had no problem receiving communication from older Jews who would speak to their children and grandchildren in Yiddish. At the same time (in the 1950s and later), the home use of Yiddish was increasingly mixed with English" (Davids, 2000, p. 97). This linguistic attrition was problematic given the Commission's emphasis on the place of language among ethnic groups. However, at the same time, among the many internal meetings held by CJC were two addresses in Yiddish by Jewish leftist organizations promoting secular Yiddish culture that argued for a place for cultural pluralism within the framework of biculturalism. They criticized the CJC for limiting Jewishness to a religious category and not mentioning Yiddish and the concept of Jewish national culture (*folkskultur*), and called for government support of "cultural institutions of different ethnic groups, such as schools, libraries, choirs" (Menkis, 2011, p. 289).

Much has changed since the 1960s. Despite a post-Second World War influx of Holocaust survivors – an estimated 35,000 individuals in total – many of whom were Yiddish speakers committed to the language and culture, Yiddish could not be relied upon in the longterm as a shared marker of distinctiveness among Canadian Jews. Yiddish use among Canadian Jews would continue to drop rapidly into the 1970s and beyond as English became the dominant lingua franca among Jews (Davids, 2010-2011). The political underpinnings of Yiddish culture, where the language was promoted as core component of Jewishness because of its historical role as the vernacular of the Eastern European Jewish masses, in particular in conjunction with leftist ideologies, has given way to voluntary engagement with Yiddish as an expression of identity. Rather than serving as a common vernacular among Canadian Jews, Yiddish has entered a postvernacular mode, where "the symbolic level of meaning is always privileged over its primary level: the very fact that something is said (or written or sung) in Yiddish is at least as meaningful as the meaning of the words being uttered – if not more so" (Shandler, 2006, p. 22). Further, Yiddish usage has become polarized within a rhetoric of Jewish identity maintenance among two groups: (1) secular Jews who identify with Yiddish culture but who more often than not lack linguistic facility in it, and (2) Haredi Jews, mainly Hasidim, for whom Yiddish serves as a vernacular and marker of ethnic distinctiveness in their quest for separation from the mainstream.

Despite the initial reticence of the Jewish leadership to endorse participation in multiculturalism, the outcome of the 1971 Multiculturalism Policy of Canada has had a positive impact on the continued institutionalization of Jewish life in Canada. Schnoor points to "Canada's new climate of multiculturalism" in the 1970s as the backdrop to easier Jewish integration into Canadian life and "significant socio-economic success" (Schnoor, 2011, p. 183). The provisions of the 1988 *Canadian Multiculturalism Act* – which recognize cultural diversity among Canadians, and encourage groups of all origins to "enhance and share their cultural heritage" as "fundamental characteristics" of Canadian society – have translated into a confidence among Jews to preserve and promote their various cultural heritages (Canadian Multiculturalism Act). As Schnoor states, "the new ethos of multiculturalism, whether symbolic or real, brought about a new confidence and comfort level in developing a comprehensive parochial school system for one of Canada's minority groups (Schnoor, 2011, p. 192), thereby legitimizing and promoting Jewish day school education. It has led to public funding for educational and cultural programs such as book fairs and film and music festivals as well as Jewish studies programs in Canadian universities. All of these developments have directly benefitted Yiddish. One tangible result has been the high rate of Jewish day school attendance, including a small number of secular Jewish schools where Yiddish has historically formed an integral part of the curriculum alongside Hebrew (Brown, 2006). For-credit university courses at a handful of institutions across the country are attracting students from a wide variety of backgrounds (Brown, 2006). Yiddish within academia marks part of a professionalization of Yiddish teaching and scholarship that has impacted Canada as well as a host of other countries. The ethos of cultural preservation that forms an integral part of multiculturalism has manifested itself in adult Yiddish education, which represents an area of growth. A variety of Jewish community centres and synagogues offer courses in Yiddish that offer exposure to the language and literature. These programs generally attract individuals with some prior exposure to Yiddish seeking opportunities to converse or read Yiddish in an informal setting. Films with Yiddish content are shown at Jewish film festivals and books about Yiddish or translations from the Yiddish are featured at book fairs. Toronto's Ashkenaz Festival, a multi-day event that showcases Yiddish culture founded in 1995 that attracts thousands of participants.

However, the present and future of Yiddish as a communicative language in these secular sites is not guaranteed by multiculturalism, in theory or practice. Despite public funding, the future of Yiddish instruction in Canada's schools has become increasingly precarious in recent years; the country's largest remaining network of secular Jewish schools, Montreal's Jewish People's and Peretz Schools, which have been at the fore of a continued commitment to teaching Yiddish at the elementary and high school levels, have been sacrificing mandatory language instruction in favour of other subjects (Fishman & Shaffir, 2004).

The area where the direct impact of multiculturalism on Yiddish culture is most clearly evident is Yiddish publication and translation. Polish-born writer Sholem Shtern offers an example of a writer who embraced and embodied the spirit of Canada's policy on multiculturalism. Shtern immigrated to Canada in 1926 as a young man and become active in Canadian Jewish leftist circles as well as in the literary community. After the Holocaust, he deliberately adjusted the dominant focus of his writing from a European to a Canadian context, and produced four Yiddish novels in verse portraying the experiences of Jewish working class immigrants (Margolis, 2007). Like much of his cohort of Yiddish writers in Canada, Shtern funded these projects through support within the Jewish community. At the same time, the aging and lack of replenishment of his Yiddish readership resulted in Shtern's efforts to locate sources of state funding both for Yiddish-language projects as well as ventures to render Yiddish literature accessible to a wider reading public. From the early 1970s through the late 1980s, Shtern maintained an ongoing relationship with government offices associated with official multiculturalism, and support through Canadian multiculturalism resulted in a flurry of publication and translation activity. A grant from the Minister of State, Multiculturalism in 1980 subsidized the English and French translations of three of his works – *In Canada: A Novel in Verse; The Family in Canada: A Novel in Verse*; and *The Household of Professor Sidney Goldstein: A Novel in Verse* – by a team of translators under the direction of Montreal publisher Guy Maheux.[2] All of these published translations acknowledged funding from the Multicultural Program Department of the Secretary of State of Canada.

Both parties expressed goals of preserving Yiddish as part of a distinct Jewish ethnic identity. For example, the letter informing Shtern of a grant for his Yiddish project, "Memoirs and Essays of Yiddish Writers in Canada," stated, "It is my hope that the financial support of projects such as this one will augment our appreciation of the cultural richness of Canadian society"; this line would be repeated in future letters.[3] Likewise, when Shtern received funding from the Multiculturalism Sector toward a cassette recording of excerpts from *The Family in Canada*, the adjudicating committee decided to support the project if it were prepared on both Yiddish and English and marketed to Canadian Yiddish language schools, with following rationale: "such a project merits support because it would help keep the Yiddish language alive." The committee suggested that if the recording were completed entirely in Yiddish, it would recommend additional support from the Cultural Enrichment Program budget.[4] This project was used as a precedent for recordings of poetry and prose in heritage languages.[5]

Shtern thus became an embodiment of the values of multiculturalism. He was a writer within a prominent ethnic group who was dedicated to the promotion of literature and culture both within his community and to the wider Canadian public in translation. His projects to disseminate minority ethnic literature that centred on the immigrant experience in Canada in both of the country's official languages exemplified the richness of a multicultural Canada.

While Shtern was the most industrious in his efforts, a number of other Yiddish writers were showcased in volumes published in the 1970s and 1980s with funding via Canada's policy of official multiculturalism Canada, in particular in collective anthologies. The first of these, *Canadian Yiddish Writings*, offered samples poetry and prose by seven Yiddish writers in English translation: Jacob Zipper, Chava Rosenfarb, Rochl Korn, J.I Segal, Melech Ravitch, and Sholem Shtern (Boyarsky & Sarna, 1976.). Published in 1976 with assistance from the Secretary of State, Multiculturalism Program, this was a pioneering introduction of Yiddish literature for a broad, non-Yiddish readership. Its foreword emphasizes both the specificity and the universality of this body of letters: "Canadian Yiddish Literature is a collection which reflects the experiences of men and women of diverse dispositions who have witnessed the destruction of a world. As such they offer the Canadian reader a body of literature cohesive [sic] themes and related in its portrayal of powerful and timeless themes" (5). In addition to rendering a body of ethnic literature accessible, the volume created a first canon of Canadian Yiddish letters even though it featured only a tiny fraction of the country's active Yiddish writers. The work was soon followed by other anthologies that included the works of Yiddish writers, albeit as a small minority among English-language Jewish writers. *The Spice Box*, a collection of poetry and prose by some three-dozen Canadian Jewish writers published in 1981 with support from the Multiculturalism Program, includes a handful of works by poets J.I. Segal and Rochl Korn (Sinclair & Wolfe, 1981). The volume underlines the accessibility of this body of literature as it "invites you to join us in following the many voices of Canadian Jews as they make their sometimes funny, sometimes poignant journeys from the *shtetls* of Europe into the mainstream of modern Canadian life" (p. ix). *Mirror of a People*, published in 1985 with the assistance of the Multiculturalism Directorate, includes Yiddish memoirs of immigrant farmer Michael Usiskin and verse by J.I. Segal and Rokhl Korn, in addition to a host of anglo-Jewish writers (Oberman & Newton, 1985). Newton's brief foreword employs a rhetoric of multiculturalism to characterize the collective experiences of Canada's Jews: "they carved a hyphenated identity for themselves as Canadian-Jews, then sought full assimilation, then reinstated their 'ethnicity' as a badge of selfhood within the pluralistic mosaic" (p. xiv). These English-language anthologies present Yiddish literature mediated by translation and aimed for a wide readership. Their function was not to promote or preserve the language and culture but rather to introduce it to a non-Yiddish audience; in these anthologies, Yiddish ceded its place to English as a vehicular language. Further, these various ventures were not coordinated by any overseeing organization; rather, they marked the efforts of individual editors. In contrast, the trilingual *Kanader yidisher zamlbukh/ Canadian Jewish Anthology/ Anthologie Juive du Canada*, published under the aegis of the Canadian Jewish Congress's National Committee on Yiddish in 1982, is dominated by Yiddish-language essays, poetry and prose, with only short abstracts provided in English and French (Spilberg & Zipper, 1982). While the volume includes a few original works in English and French, its stated aim was to "acquaint the reader with the contributions and accomplishments achieved by the pioneers of Yiddish culture in Canada" (p. 14).

The efforts of writers as well as translators and editors to broaden the readership for Yiddish literature via translation intersected with the ethos of multiculturalism: to recognize and preserve cultural diversity in Canada. These ventures negotiated two forces: the particularism of Yiddish literature, with its thematic focus on the European Jewish past and more recent immigrant experience; and the shared mosaic of ethnic identities comprising Canadian multiculturalism. These publications also highlighted the inherent limitations of multiculturalism: the rich diversity of Canada's Jewish ethnic literature was ultimately expressed not in the Yiddish in which they were originally written but in translation into Canada's official languages.

With the passing of Shtern's cohort – the last generation of European-born native Yiddish speakers – the rhetoric around cultural ventures to promote Yiddish have become firmly situated within a discourse of multiculturalism. Usage of Yiddish as a daily language lies in the past for most Jewish Canadians, but the roots of the culture still resonate. For example, a recent initiative to promote Yiddish culture in Toronto was characterized as follows: "A vibrant Yiddish culture was planted within our borders, beginning in the early 1900s and ending with an influx of Holocaust survivors in the late '40s and '50s. The multicultural fabric of Canada has been profoundly impacted by Yiddish, which is still being taught, sung and read today" (Gasner, 2008). Much of the activity around contemporary Yiddish culture in Canada is performative in nature, centered in particular around music (Margolis, 2010). Mainstream Canada's Yiddish legacy is manifest in a largely symbolic capacity rather than as a communicative language.

In recent years, Yiddish has emerged as an object of heritage and memory in the area of installation and performance art, which bring together visual art and theatre. For example, Vera Frenkel's installation, "... *from the Transit Bar*" (Frenkel, 1992) which has been mounted in Ottawa, Toronto as well as internationally, features an art deco train station bar at which visitors pause and watch other "travelers" on a nearby monitor. As Zemel writes, "But allusions to greater losses echo through a mix of languages. The monitor interviewees speak Yiddish and Polish – the languages of Frenkel's grandparents, voices of family long gone – while subtitled translations of their speech appear in English, French, and German, hegemonic languages of the West." Here Yiddish thus serves as a symbol of a vanished past and the losses of the Holocaust (Zemel, 2013, p. 15).

One area where Yiddish has gained ground since the advent of multiculturalism is in Haredi communities. The language serves as vernacular for a significant proportion of Canadian Hasidim, most of who reside in the Montreal area in densely populated enclaves, where their distinctive dress and deliberate Yiddish usage contribute to their forming a highly visible minority (Shaffir, 1995). These communities, which have created mechanisms to self-consciously create boundaries that separate them from the mainstream, have – perhaps paradoxically – benefitted from state support for their cultural institutions, notably schools, provided they are willing to adjust their curricula to state-sanctioned requirements. Further, certain groups have negotiated with Canadian government bodies for the benefit of their communities. For example, sociologist Randal Schnoor discusses how the Hasidim of Outremont, Quebec, have developed innovative strategies to address economic problems within their community with funding from a government that promotes the values of multiculturalism (Schnoor, 2002, p. 64). On the other hand, discourse around multiculturalism has been employed to protest practices among Hasidic Jews that facilitate the way of life that separates them from modern society. An example is opposition to the *eruv*, a legal fiction negotiated with the secular state that allows ritually observant Jews to carry on the Sabbath, which they would not otherwise be able to do. Ardently secular opponents of the *eruv* have employed the argument that the structure compromises an area's multiculturalism by "granting one group a privileged claim on the public space" (Stoker, 2003, p. 20). According to Koffman and Weinfeld, situations such as these present "Jews as test cases for the limits and flexibility of Canadian multiculturalism" (Koffman & Weinfeld, 2011, p. 211). However, unlike in mainstream, secular contexts, multiculturalism has not directly impacted on the expanded usage of Yiddish in these closed communities. While Hasidic leadership may seek out state support for the community's institutions, Yiddish usage has expanded in Canada due to internal trends elevating its status as a language of daily use within the international Hasidic community, notably in formal instruction in schools (Soldat-Jaffe, 2010), rather than Canadian government policies on multiculturalism per se. In Canada, as in other countries such as Great Britain, Yiddish is taught in these Hasidic schools as an insider language rather than a cultural or heritage language within a pluralistic society (Fishman & Shaffir, 2004).

CONCLUDING REMARKS

Despite the strides for Canadian Jewish life that have been associated with it, a fundamental ambivalence about multiculturalism and its lasting impact of Jewish life in Canada remains. As Koffman and Weinfeld suggest, "In some respects, we might consider Jews the poster children for the possibilities of multiculturalism in Canada, though the jury is still out on just what this means for the story of ethnicity in Canada more broadly (Koffman & Weinfeld, 2011). The actual impact of multiculturalism as policy and cultural ideal on Jewish life in Canada are difficult to measure.

Canadian multiculturalism has been a mixed blessing for Yiddish. On the one hand, scholars Joseph Lévy and Yolande Cohen suggest in their study of Moroccan Jews: "The politics of multiculturalism favoured in Canada have helped the maintenance of a stronger ethno-cultural identity at the expense of a real political integration into the host country" (Lévy & Cohen 1995, p. 117). For Yiddish, this maintenance has translated into strong institutions to promote a distinct culture. This infrastructure has endured, as has a commitment to the culture within the broader Jewish community. More broadly, Yiddish in Canada has been buoyed by the legitimization of pluralism as a positive value as well as state support to fund heritage and educational programs. On the other hand, as Brown posits, multiculturalism has rendered the Jews part of a Canadian mainstream: "In less concrete terms, multiculturalism has meant that in strengthening their own institutions and culture, Jews were no longer acting as outsiders but rather as exemplary Canadians" (Brown, 2007, 19). This has enabled Yiddish to become an integral part of Canadian culture but also to become diffused within the wider pluralism of contemporary Jewish culture. A telling example of this tendency towards inclusiveness is the Ashkenaz Festival, which is broadly billed as "one of the world's largest public celebrations of Yiddish and Jewish culture" (Ashkenaz). With actual Yiddish use sporadic at the event, the programming has also broadened significantly in recent years to include a variety of Jewish ethnicities, with its spokespeople emphasizing the diversity of its offerings within a multicultural context (Kates, 2010). In sum, for Yiddish, Canadian multiculturalism amounts to a "catch-22": once a distinct language and culture are embraced as part of Canada's national diversity, the framework that created that distinctiveness and the impetus for maintaining it weakens. Multiculturalism has brought translation projects and performance to showcase Yiddish into the public sphere, but the language itself is actually spoken primarily among a group of Jews – Hasidim – for whom the very concept of cultural pluralism is antithetical to the maintenance of their community identity.

NOTES

[1] Research for this chapter was funded by a research grant from the Social Sciences and Humanities Research Council of Canada.

[2] LAC, R11806-0-8-E, box 8, Guy Maheux, Guy Maheux to The Jewish Community Foundation, 14 September 1982. According to correspondence from Maheux, despite the government grants, losses resulting from a lack of funds for this project ultimately caused him to lose his business. Guy Maheux to Sholem Shtern, 12 December 1983; 22 December, 1983; 7 February 1984.

[3] LAC, R11806-0-8-E, box 8, Minister of State Multiculturalism, Jim Fleming to Sholem Shtern, 1 June 1981; David M. Collenette to Sholem Shtern, 16 March 1984.

[4] LAC, R11806-0-8-E, box 8, Minister of State Multiculturalism, [Second page with signature missing] to Sholem Shtern, 25 July 1985.

[5] LAC, R11806-0-8-E, box 8, Minister of State Multiculturalism, Barbara Preston to Sholem Shtern, 24 April 1986.

REFERENCES

Ashkenaz festival offers the best in Jewish and Yiddish culture. (n.d.). Retrieved from: http://www.jewishtoronto.com/page.aspx?id=183124.

Boyarsky, A., & Sarna, L. (Eds.). (1976). *Canadian Yiddish writings*. Montreal: Harvest House.

Brown, M. (2006). *From binationalism to multiculturalism to the open society: The impact on Canadian Jews*. Jerusalem Center for Public Affairs No. 10.

Brown, M. (2007). Canadian Jews and multiculturalism: Myths and realities. *Jewish Political Studies Review, 19* (Fall), 3-4.

Canadian multiculturalism Act. (1985). Department of Justice (c. 31, assented to 21st July, 1988). Retrieved from: http://laws.justice.gc.ca/eng/acts/C-18.7/page-1.html

Davids, L. (2000). Yiddish and Hebrew in Canada: The current situation. *Canadian Ethnic Studies, 32*(2), 95-106.

Davids, L. (2011-11). Hebrew and Yiddish in Canada: A linguistic transition completed *Canadian Jewish Studies/Études juives canadiennes, 18*(19), 39-76.

Fishman, D. E. (2005). *The rise of modern Yiddish culture*. Pittsburgh, PA. University of Pittsburgh Press.

Fishman, G. A., & Shaffir, W. (2004) Commitment to a language: Teaching Yiddish in a Hasidic and secular school. In J. Sherman (Ed.), *Yiddish after the Holocaust* (pp. 149-178). Oxford: Boulevard Books, The Oxford Centre for Hebrew and Judaic Studies.

Frenkel, V. (1992). "*... from the Transit Bar*." Retrieved from www.yorku.ca/BodyMissing/barspace/Bar1a.html

Gold, G., & Cohen, R. (1996). The myth of return and Israeli ethnicity in Toronto. In H. Adelman & J. H. Simpson (Eds.), *Multiculturalism, Jew and identities in Canada* (pp. 179-191). Jerusalem: The Magnus Press.

Gasner, C. (2008, June 26). New project to promote Yiddish in Toronto. *Canadian Jewish News*. Retrieved from: http://www.cjnews.com/index.php?option=com_content&task=view&id=14884&Itemid=86

Kates, K. (2010, August 26). Ashkenaz festival features broad range of traditions. *Canadian Jewish News*. Retrieved from: http://www.cjnews.com/index.php?option=com_content&task=view&id=19729&Itemid=86

Koffman, D., & Weinfeld, M. (2011). Recent developments in the social scientific study of Canadian Jews. *Contemporary Jewry, 31*(3), 199-221.

Lévy, J., & Cohen, Y. (1995). Moroccan Jews and their adaptation to Montreal life. In I. Robinson & M. Butovsky (Eds.), *Renewing our days* (pp. 95-118). Montreal: Véhicule Press.

Margolis, R. (2007). Sholem Shtern: Bridging the gaps. In P. Anctil, N. Ravvin, & S. Simon (Eds.), *Traduire le Montreal Yiddish/New readings of Yiddish Montreal* (pp. 93-102). Ottawa, ON: University of Ottawa Press.

Margolis, R. (2010). Yiddishism in Canadian garb. In J. Fogel & K. Weiser (Eds.), *Czernowitz at 100: The first Yiddish language conference in historical perspective* (pp. 165-177). Lanham, MD: Rowman and Littlefield.

Menkis, R. (2011). Jewish communal identity at the crossroads: Early Jewish responses to Canadian multiculturalism, 1963-1965. *Studies in Religion / Sciences Religieuses, 40*(3), 283-292.

Menkis, R. (2013). Reform Judaism in Canada. In I. Robinson (Ed.), *Canada's Jews: In time, space and spirit* (pp. 294-307). Brighton, MA: Academic Studies Press.

Oberman, S., & Newton, E. (Eds.). (1985). *Mirror of a people: Canadian Jewish experience in poetry and prose*. Winnipeg: Jewish Educational Publishers of Canada.

Rosenberg, L. (1993). *Canada's Jews: A social and economic study of the Jews in Canada in the 1930s* (M. Weinfeld, Ed.). Montreal and Kingston: McGill-Queen's University Press. (Originally published in 1939)

Schoenfeld, S. (1999). Reluctant cosmopolitans: The impact of continentalism, multiculturalism, and globalization on Jewish identity in Canada. In S. M. Cohen & G. Horenczyk (Eds.), *National variations in Jewish identity: Implications for Jewish education* (pp. 137-156). Albany, NY: State University of New York Press.

Schnoor, R. F. (2002). Tradition and innovation in an ultra-Orthodox community: The Hasidim of Outremont. *Canadian Jewish Studies, 10*, 53-74.

Schnoor, R. F. (2011). The contours of Canadian Jewish life. *Contemporary Jewry, 31*(1), 179-197.

Shaffir, W. (1995). Safeguarding a distinctive identity: Hassidic Jews in Montreal. In I. Robinson & M. Butovsky (Eds.), *Renewing our days: Montreal Jews in the twentieth century* (pp. 75-94). Montreal: Véhicule Press.

Shandler, J. (2006). *Adventures in Yiddishland: Postvernacular language and culture*. Berkeley, CA: University of California Press.

Sinclair, G., & Wolfe, M. (Eds.). (1981). *The spice box: An anthology of Canadian Jewish writing*. Toronto: Lester & Orpen Dennys.

Soldat-Jaffe, T. (2010). Yiddish without Yiddishism: Tacit language planning among Haredi Jews. *Journal of Jewish Identities, 3*(2), 1-24.

Spilberg, C., & Zipper, J. (Eds.). (1982). *Kanader yidisher zamlbukh/Canadian Jewish Anthology/ Anthologie Juive du Canada*. Montreal, QC: National Committee on Yiddish, Canadian Jewish Congress.

Stevenson, G. (1999). *Community besieged: The Anglophone minority and the politics of Quebec*. Montreal, QC: McGill-Queen's.

Stoker, V. (2003). Drawing the line: Hasidic Jews, eruvim, and the public space of Outremont. *History of Religions, 43*(1), 18-49.

Zemel, C. (2013). In the mosaic: Jewish identities in Canadian performance and installation art. *Canadian Theatre Review, 153*, 13-19.

Rebecca Margolis
Department of Modern Languages and Literatures
Department of Classics and Religious Studies
University of Ottawa

KALYANI THURAIRAJAH

10. CANADIANS UNDER SUSPICION

Sri Lankan Tamil Diasporic Community as a Suspect Minority Group

INTRODUCTION

Fear of terrorism has become particularly rampant since the tragic events of 9/11. However, concern about where the allegiances of various ethnic and immigrant groups lie has been present for as long as there has been immigration. The apprehension regarding immigrant loyalty is not so much to do with the fact that immigrants have dual loyalties, but rather with the fear that immigrants may, in fact, be more loyal to their homeland or country of origin than they are to their country of settlement. If such a hierarchy of loyalty were to exist, then, at times of conflict between the homeland and country of settlement, immigrants may choose to side with their countries of origin, thereby posing a threat to their country of settlement. For example, such concerns of disloyalty led to fears of the presence of a "fifth column" during World War II, whereby it was believed that there were enemies of the state posing as citizens in order to infiltrate the nation in order to do a hostile take-over (MacDonnell, 1995).

In protecting "national interests," fears of terrorism have led to heighted security and immigration measures since 9/11. For example, Canada and the United States signed the Smart Border Declaration and Action Plan as a security measure to protect the two nations from any suspicious travel. There are four primary aims of this Action Plan: to secure flow of people; to secure flow of goods; to invest in secure infrastructure; and to coordinate and share information in the enforcement of these objectives (Public Safety Canada, 2008). According to Public Safety Canada, "the secure flow of people is about separating low risk travellers from high risk travellers and facilitating the movement of those who pose little risk to our security." However, the website does not describe what would constitute a "high risk traveller," and what characteristics would distinguish them from a "low risk traveller."

Changes have not only been made to security policies in Canada, but also to immigration policies. Canada has become more vigilant in terms of requiring appropriate documentation including visas from those wishing to enter the country (Adelman, 2002), and has also become much more stringent in terms of the qualifications that are required for immigration. While these changes are meant to secure the nation's borders from external threat, those who are within the borders have also been viewed with trepidation – particularly when they are believed to

S. Guo & L. Wong (eds.), Revisiting Multiculturalism in Canada, 171–185.

have ties to an external homeland that may be perceived as threatening to the country of settlement.

The changes in immigration and security policies since the tragic events of 9/11 demonstrate that the loyalties of certain diasporic and immigrant communities are not just being questioned. Their loyalties are being assumed. They have become "suspect minorities," whose loyalties to their homelands are assumed will be inevitably prioritized above their loyalties to their hostlands. Therefore, a perceived imperative of countries of settlement is one of implementing policies to protect themselves against any acts of terror or harm that may be committed by these diasporic and immigrant communities.

While there have been examples of when members of immigrant and diasporic communities have endangered their countries of settlement in the interests of their countries of origin, can all immigrant and diasporic communities be labelled as "suspect minorities"? What is the process through which these communities negotiate between their dual loyalties and identities? Furthermore, when the community is labelled as a "suspect minority" group, and their loyalties are questioned, do these diasporic communities reframe their identities? Do they move away from the country of settlement that labels them in such a way? Do they, in fact, construct a homeland identity and loyalty that endangers their country of settlement?

In order to tackle these questions, the Sri Lankan Tamil diaspora in Canada will be utilized as a case study. This population was chosen because tension was introduced in the relationship between their country of settlement (Canada) and their homeland (Sri Lanka/Tamil Eelam) following the labelling of the Liberation Tigers of Tamil Eelam (LTTE, also known as Tamil Tigers) as a terrorist organization. The members of this diasporic community have also been very actively engaged in homeland politics, as evidenced by the mass protests they staged in 2009 in Toronto and Ottawa during the months leading to the end of the ethnic conflict in Sri Lanka.

While the community is from Sri Lanka, they primarily identify with the Tamil provinces, which collectively form Tamil Eelam, their desired nation-state. The LTTE was the insurgency group that fought for the establishment of an independent Tamil State in Sri Lanka. For decades the LTTE had been engaged in ethnic conflict with the Sri Lankan government, and for decades Tamil Canadians were involved in these homeland politics. Whether they supported the actions of the LTTE or whether they desired the establishment of a separate Tamil state, the political allegiances of Tamil Canadians to their homeland was not in conflict with their political allegiances to Canada. However, this changed in 2006, when the Canadian government officially labelled the LTTE as a terrorist organization.

The LTTE was the 39th group to be labelled as a terrorist group under Canada's Anti-Terrorism Act. It was the first group that the Conservative government added to the list of banned terrorist organizations when the Conservative Party came into power. The banning of the Tamil Tigers meant that it would be considered a criminal offence to support any activities of the Tamil Tigers, including financial contributions through Tigers' "war taxes." In fact, on May 14, 2010, a Tamil

Canadian became the first man to be charged under the Anti-terrorism financing legislation for raising funds for the World Tamil Movement (WTM), an organization that has been widely believed to provide financial support to the LTTE (Carter, 2010). Prior to the LTTE being labelled as a terrorist organization, members of the Sri Lankan Tamil diaspora were able to support the secessionist movement in Sri Lanka without feeling torn regarding their affiliations with Canada. While many may not have supported the Tigers, there were others who considered them to be "freedom fighters," soldiers who were fighting to protect the rights of the Tamils. However, after 9/11, and the war on terror, the actions of militant groups could no longer be ignored, and there was a crackdown on insurgency groups around the globe. It was not long before the LTTE was officially labelled as "terrorist," and organizations that supported this group were also declared to be "terrorist organizations" (CBC, 2008). In labelling the Tamil Tigers as terrorists, Canada was taking an official stance on the ethnic conflict in Sri Lanka. Suddenly, Tamil Canadians were faced with the challenge of determining whether their support for Tamil Eelam and for the LTTE was a betrayal of their allegiance to Canada, while also struggling to decipher what this act by the Canadian government meant in terms of its loyalties to the diasporic homeland.

Canada had been home to Sri Lankan Tamils for years, and was considered a primary destination for those who fled the civil war that had ravaged the island of Sri Lanka. The Civil War in Sri Lanka spanned over two decades and triggered a mass exodus of its population, particularly Sri Lankan Tamils who fled from the violence and persecution of the war. Despite their leaving, many Sri Lankan Tamil immigrants continued to foster a relationship with their country of birth while also developing a relationship with their new host country. These immigrants travelled around the globe searching for homes, settling across Europe, Australia, and Singapore. But the country that welcomed them in droves was Canada – particularly Toronto – placing it as the home to the largest Sri Lankan Tamil diaspora in the world – a population estimated to be just over 200,000 people.

Despite immigrating to a new country, the Sri Lankan Tamil diasporic community continued to feel connected to their homeland. This connection further strengthened the resolve of Tamil Canadians to be involved in the politics of Sri Lanka. Between January and May of 2009, tens of thousands of members of the diaspora participated in several protests in Toronto and Ottawa to highlight what they believed was the genocide of the Tamils in Sri Lanka (Ferenc, 2009). In May 2009, the LTTE was defeated by the Sri Lankan government, and the ethnic conflict was declared to be over. However, despite the official declaration that the war in Sri Lanka had ended, and that the LTTE had been defeated, this diasporic community continued in its efforts to intervene in homeland politics.

In order to understand this political engagement, this study draws on 37 in-depth interviews conducted among members of this population in Toronto. All participants were between the ages of 18 and 30, and were either born in Canada or had immigrated to Canada prior to the first grade. Participants were intentionally drawn from the 1.5 and second generation of the diasporic community in order to determine how those who had primarily grown up within the country of settlement without significant physical presence in the homeland negotiated the process of loyalty and identity formation. The study was made up of 22 females and 15 males. The average age of the participants was 25. Pseudonyms for participants were used.

TIGERS: TERRORISTS OR FREEDOM FIGHTERS?

For Sri Lankan Tamil diasporic community members, there may be some distinctions between whether they identify with being Sri Lankan or Sri Lankan Tamil. There may be very complicated feelings regarding their support for a separate Tamil Eelam. The creation of Tamil Eelam would remove any identification with the Sri Lankan nationality in favour of that of Tamil Eelam, creating significant shifts in their definitions of nationality. While the process of determining where their loyalties lie with respect to Sri Lanka is complex and multifaceted, it became even more challenging following Canada's declaration that the LTTE was an official terrorist group in 2006.

The labelling of the Tamil Tigers as a terrorist organization was met with a myriad of reactions from second-generation Sri Lankan Tamils. However, the majority of the participants fell within two very distinct camps: one of disappointment and the other of acceptance. With respect to the first, participants expressed frustration regarding the Canadian government's decision to label the LTTE as terrorists. They felt that the government had not done its research, and was simply jumping on the "war on terror" bandwagon without having a comprehensive understanding of the history of the LTTE, and the philosophies of the organization. Nagesh, a 27 year-old male, was explicit in his belief that the Canadian government was uninformed in its decision:

> I don't know if they were educated on what was going on, I think they did it just 'cause the US did it. That's how I felt. 'Cause I guess we have close ties with the US, we don't wanna piss them off. And then now I think even after that when Harper came to power, he had some kind of dinner with people that were associated with the Tigers. It didn't really make sense. The government just wants kind of ... they do whatever to get more votes.

Participants were disappointed in the Canadian government for not taking the time to really understand the problem, and they shared that it would be a sign of good faith if the government removed the Tigers from this list. Ranjini, a 26 year-old female said:

> I felt bad. I felt sad when that happened. I was like, wow, like, you people don't even take the time to consider what happened to us, and what's happened to us. It's like, you just automatically, by the word of the government, the Sri Lankan government, you've put us – you've listed us. And yeah, it's just a list, it's just a label, but, I mean, it's a label .... And it was sad that the government was promoting that by putting us on that list. I mean, we're not. We're not terrorists. We didn't go into any other country

and cause any sort of havoc. I mean, we were in our own country fighting for our own rights. I mean, basic human rights .... No, we're asking for the right to study, and the right for food, and the right for, you know, equality. How does that make us terrorists? And it was ridiculous. It was sad. And it just made it more obvious to me that politics is just, that's what it is. It's people kissing each other's butts. Governments doing whatever is necessary to protect their own, and you know, like, trying to get whatever they can from another country .... It was sad that, even Canada, a peace-loving nation or whatever it is, um, decided to follow that and actually do that to our cause. But it happened. It was sad. It was a sad day.

Ranjini was born in Europe and immigrated to Canada when she was three years old. She had never been to Sri Lanka, and yet, she did not separate herself from the LTTE. With the Tamil Tigers being labelled as terrorists she felt that she was also being labelled as a terrorist. She did not proclaim that "they are not terrorists," but, instead, vehemently asserted in the interview that "we're not terrorists." Therefore, the act of placing the LTTE on the official list of terrorist organizations was not seen simply as labelling a militant group, but instead was considered to be an act of labelling an entire diaspora with the brand "terrorist."

The Canadian Tamil Congress released a press release shortly after the Tamil Tigers were listed as a terrorist organization, articulating their disappointment in the Canadian government (Canadian Tamil Congress, 2006), echoing some of the frustration expressed by participants:

> The Canadian Tamil community is deeply shocked and saddened of the decision by our Canadian government to list the Liberation Tigers of Tamil Eelam (LTTE) as a Terrorist organization under Bill C-36. The Canadian Tamil Congress, the representative organization of Canadian Tamils, considers this decision to be harmful as both the LTTE and the government of Sri Lanka are currently engaged in an internationally brokered peace process as equal partners. This decision, at such a sensitive time, will tip the delicate balance which has brought both parties to the negotiating table and hinder the prospects for long term peace and stability in the region.

However, while the statement released by the Canadian Tamil Congress was certainly representative of the views of many participants, it did not embody the attitudes of all members of the diasporic community. While there were participants who were as disgruntled as Ranjini, others were much more pragmatic in their views of the banning. Whether they supported the Tamil Tigers or not, they were able to understand the difficult position in which the Canadian government found itself, and stated that they could comprehend why the LTTE was labelled in such a way. Participants spoke of how, even if the Tamil Tigers may have a just cause, their means could not be justified, particularly following the events of 9/11. Venkatesh, a 26-year-old who had never been to Sri Lanka and was born and raised in Canada, claimed that it was not impossible to understand why Canada would feel the need to define the LTTE as terrorists. He was one of many participants who declared that the diasporic community should have been more strategic at the protests, and should not have brought flags that represented the Tamil Tigers:

> I mean, if you took a step back, and took a more intellectual look at the story, you'd say, 'you know what, it makes sense that they would be labelled.' It's because they [the LTTE] are not the government, and our government having political – and this is again based on not having a great knowledge of political science – would have to call them a terrorist organization. So bringing those flags and recognizing they've been labelled as such is just detrimental, it's taking two steps backwards …

Neither Ranjini nor Venkatesh have been to Sri Lanka. They are both the same age, and are both young professionals. Despite these similarities, however, they were very different with respect to their views on the labelling of the LTTE. Whereas Ranjini understood the labelling of the Tamil Tigers as an error of judgment made by the Canadian government, and as something that was completely inappropriate, Venkatesh declared that he was able to understand the politics that would have driven the actions of Canada, and he felt that it was important that the diasporic community act accordingly. The sentiments expressed by this diasporic community echo the challenges that Nadarajah and Sriskandarajah (2005) observed behind labelling the LTTE as a terrorist group. These authors suggest that the naming of the Tamil Tigers as terrorists despite the fact that others may view them as freedom fighters demonstrates the political agendas of the Sri Lankan government, the LTTE, and the diasporic communities, and the complex ways in which they interact to inform international foreign policies.

While Venkatesh and Ranjini represent the two more common perspectives that were offered by the second-generation participants with respect to Canada's stance on the LTTE, all participants were unanimous in stating that the government's decision to label the LTTE did not alter their own opinions of the insurgency group. If they had supported the Tamil Tigers prior to 2006, they continued to do so even after the group was labelled as a terrorist organization. They did not stop supporting the group because Canada had branded it as a terrorist organization. It did not appear as if the opinion of the country of settlement could alter the opinions of the members of the diaspora – what did become apparent was that while some were pragmatic and were more understanding of the rationale behind Canada's decision to ban the LTTE, others saw this move as an act of betrayal. They felt that the Canadian government had sided with the Sri Lankan government rather than listening to the pleas of the diasporic community. Therefore, labelling the Tamil Tigers as terrorists did not bring anyone closer to the country of settlement; it either maintained their relationship to Canada or it distanced them.

TIGERS, TERRORISTS AND THE TAMIL IDENTITY

The defeat of the Tamil Tigers did not suspend engagement in homeland politics because, while the Tamil Tigers may have been the insurgency group representing the Tamils in Sri Lanka, they did not represent the Tamil identity. Therefore, when asked if the defeat of the Tigers altered their understanding of their Tamil identity, the majority of participants proclaimed that it did not. They were just as certain of their Tamil identity after the LTTE was dismantled as they had been before the war ended. However, participants felt that while they were able to distinguish between being Tamil and being a Tamil Tiger, they found that non-Tamil Canadians were unable to do the same. Participants expressed that, following the protests, it was not always easy to be Tamil in Canada.

Second-generation Sri Lankan Tamils commented on how, despite everything that had happened, and the attempts that had been made to educate the public, they often experienced situations in which non-Tamil Canadians would treat "Tamil" as being synonymous with being "Tiger," which was then in turn synonymous with being "terrorist." They commented on how, when they mentioned that they were Tamil, they were often asked if they were a Tamil Tiger. While some were asked this in jest, others found themselves in a situation in which they had to explain that being Tamil did not automatically imply that they were members of the LTTE.

Nearly every participant that was interviewed had a story to share where they found themselves being equated to the Tigers or to terrorists because of their Tamil identity. A few participants explicitly compared the experiences of the Tamil community and the Muslim community, referring to the suspicion that is cast on both groups due to fears of terrorism.

While some participants expressed that they understood that the comments were being made in jest by friends and colleagues, and some found it an opportune way to educate people on Sri Lankan history and the ethnic conflict, others expressed a keen disappointment in their fellow Canadians for not taking the time to consider the impact of their words. The blame for this insensitivity was placed on the media for not educating Canadians correctly on the subject matter. As Haran, a 28-year-old male, proclaimed:

> Well, the way other people look at Tamils, when they look at Tigers they think of terrorists ... 'cause I guess that's how the media put it .... That's what they learned. Like, they look down at Tamil people, I noticed that. Especially after all the protests ...

During the time of the protests in Toronto, much media attention was centered on the Tamil diaspora and the ethnic conflict in Sri Lanka. News articles discussed the impact of the protests on the citizens of Toronto, the intent of the protesters, and the implications of these protests (Ferenc, 2009; Taylor, 2009). Journalists questioned how the protests reflected the level of tolerance of Canada and whether Canada should be tolerant. An editorial by Haroon Siddiqui in the Toronto Star (2009) addressed how the protests highlighted some of the questionable edges of multiculturalism and tolerance in Canada, addressing the question of whether it's appropriate to bring homeland politics into the country of settlement:

> Tamil Canadians are not the only ones to bring baggage to this debate. In the last few days we've heard, over and over again, an old Canadian myth: Let the immigrants not import their old country troubles to Canada. Except that

they always have: the British and the French, to start with, and the Irish, the Ukrainians, the Serbs, the Sikhs, etcetera, etcetera. Canadian politics and the Canadian character have been shaped, in some ways, by "old country" politics.

Margaret Wente of the Globe and Mail (2009) further questioned engagement in homeland politics, by asking the critical question: "Can you belong to more than one nation?" She wrote that while it is evident that Tamil Canadians appear to be engaged in both contexts, she remained uncertain of whether it was indeed possible to maintain a "transnational citizenship," and concluded by stating that "there are many mini-nations in our midst. And we don't know anything about them."

It is a weighty statement on which to conclude an article that took great pains to point out the level of political engagement practiced by Tamil Canadians, including second- and third-generation diasporic community members. Her conclusion implies a threat that is borne from uncertainty. If there are so many mini-nations in our midst and we do not know anything about them, then how confident can we truly be in their loyalty, and in their citizenship? It is this uncertainty that breeds distrust and opens space for the creation of 'suspect minority' groups.

As shown with the Sri Lankan Tamil diasporic community, they were disappointed to discover that they were being viewed with suspicion. The community was not just perceived to support the Tamil Tigers, an officially labelled terrorist organization, they were actually believed to be Tigers themselves. In being Tamil, they were also Tiger, and hence 'terrorist,' further demonstrating that they were suspect minorities. This phenomenon of collapsing a minority population into a terrorist faction when the minority population had not posed any notable threat to the country of settlement raises questions about whether the country of settlement is actually as open and tolerant to immigration as might have been believed. Furthermore, in the case of Canada, a country that is internationally recognized for its multicultural policies, the questions of the extent to which multiculturalism actually exists and works are raised.

MULTICULTURALISM AND SUSPECT MINORITIES

The protests that took place in Toronto began a dialogue on the implications of multiculturalism in Canada. While the fact that an ethnic minority group felt confident enough in their rights as Canadians to stage a protest in the core of the busiest city in Canada speaks volumes to how successful multiculturalism has been in promoting the rights of a diverse population, the perceived reactions of the wider Canadian community suggests that multiculturalism has not been successfully implemented on an individual citizen basis. The extent to which participants felt that they were not being understood or accepted by the larger Canadian population because of their Tamil identities and allegiances reveals that there are aspects of multiculturalism that have yet to be fully addressed by Canadian policy makers.

In feeling as if they had to justify their involvement in homeland politics, and needing to defend their support for the Tamil Tigers or the creation of a separate Tamil state, the members of this diasporic community were placed in a very vulnerable situation. While they may have staged the protests in hope of garnering sympathy and support for the civilians who were dying in the ethnic conflict, the protests actually appeared to play another role, demonstrating a very sharp edge of multiculturalism in Canada. The protests provided the platform on which Canadians that had an allegiance to a country or identity that was different from their country of settlement needed to prove that their passion and sense of urgency was both appropriate and warranted. They needed to not only explain why they were protesting, they had to explain why any protest of the ethnic conflict would demand some mention of the Tamil Tigers, which inevitably led to conversations about terrorism instead of conversations about the right to protest and advocate.

The participants of this study were very staunch Canadians, often expressing their appreciation and gratitude for the country that allowed them to escape the war in Sri Lanka. However, their experience of the protests, and the reactions that the protests seemed to evoke among their fellow Canadians, caused them to wonder about just what it meant to be Canadian, and whether Canada still deserved the label of being a 'multicultural' nation. They had assumed that multiculturalism meant tolerance and sensitivity, and this was not what many experienced. Karen, a 21 year-old female noted:

> Students were sitting down on the road, they had the roads closed off, but students were sitting on it and right beside them, not even two meters away there was horse manure ... right? And even being raised here, there's a lot of students who were Canadians who were born here that were voicing their opinions, and Canada's a place where, you know, there's multiculturalism, it's open to freedom, open voice, it's democracy, and everyone has a say in what they believe in. And why they were restrained, and compressed into a little area and they were ignored. And that's kind of disappointing from a Canadian perspective.

Perhaps these experiences should not have come as a surprise. As Ryan (2010) points out, Canadians often live with a 'multicultiphobia,' a worry regarding the consequences of multiculturalism and issues of loyalties and identities. Ryan argues, however, that this anxiety is due to the ways in which various events are presented by the media, often skewing the views of the general population with errors in facts and interpretation. These inaccuracies and overgeneralizations may lead the average Canadian to question the integrity of multiculturalism and fear various ethnic groups, when, in fact, these concerns may not be warranted.

The protests staged by the Sri Lankan Tamil diasporic community in Canada presents a very important and timely opportunity to consider the implications of not only how multiculturalism is being understood and implemented by Canadians, but also how these policies affect transnational communities who continue to engage with their homelands.

179

The reactions from the media and other Canadians regarding the protests and Tamil Canadians were felt keenly by the diasporic community. Some participants spoke of comments they heard and read from other Canadians, where members of the diaspora were encouraged to go "back home" if they were so anxious to engage in homeland politics. Their right to belong to Canada was being questioned and an implicit message that they belonged to Sri Lanka was also being conveyed.

During the time of the protests, not only were there a number of articles addressing the protests and the diasporic community, there were also hundreds of online posts from Canadians. While there was a range of reactions to the protests, including an attitude of support for the protesters and their rationale for protesting, there were also several posts that highlighted the belief that this diasporic community consisted of immigrants who were not Canadian, and who should actually be considered as suspect minorities:

> Canadians protesting about Sri Lanka? Or are you displaced Sri Lankans holding another country hostage for a few hours and should be moved home. Pick your loyalty. You chose Canada, the fight is not here. (Lewington & Makin, 2009: Online comment posted by user "Bob London")

> Let's give them their Tamiltopia in CANADA. The civil war seems to be lost for these poor people and it seems that there is no chance of them ever getting their home land in Sri Lanka. As there are a lot of media supporters for their cause at the Toronto Star and other media outlets how would it be if they began lobbying for a TAMILTOPIA in CANADA??? We could offer them Prince Edward county!! Nice island area that is clean and quiet. Then the likes of Siddiqui and other Canadians could donate a portion of their nice salary to the advancement of this new country!!! After all, as been stated in many articles, the inconvenience we CANADIANS have suffered at the hands of these terrorist supporters is tiny compared to the conditions suffered by the Tamils in Sri Lanka. It seems to me therefore that a small inconvenience for the residents in the part of Canada that would host this new Tamiltopia would show what great people we really are!!! Anyone agree?? (Siddiqui, 2009: Online commented posted by user "blogexpert")

These are but two of the posts that demonstrate the real concern that some Canadians appear to have regarding the Sri Lankan Tamil diasporic community. The concern is not only that the members of this diasporic community are not really Canadian, since they appear to be so actively invested in the politics of their homeland, but also that they may eventually bring these politics to the country of settlement and move beyond "simple" protests. User 'blogexpert' articulates the concern that in allowing a suspect minority group to go unchecked in their support of their homeland, it would not then be surprising for this group to one day demand a separate Tamil state within Canada itself.

While this online respondent was perhaps being facetious, there are several interesting points made in their comment. They equate the protesters with "terrorist supporters," and separates Tamils from other Canadians. And by speaking of a "Tamiltopia," there is a level of mockery about the desire to establish a Tamil

Eelam in Sri Lanka. This comment highlights the idea that the Sri Lankan Tamil diasporic community does not belong in the nation of Canada, and that if they are given any support, they may in fact lobby to separate Canada into smaller ethnic communities – such as a "Tamiltopia." These comments are indicative of the fear that is often felt in association to immigrant populations who are perceived to have dual identities. These different identities mean that Canada cannot take the allegiances of these community members for granted, and if there is ever tension between the country of settlement and the homeland, these community members may side with their homeland, thereby posing a very real threat to Canada.

It is important to note, however, that while there were Canadians who expressed a lack of support for the protests and who viewed the diasporic community through a lens of suspicion, the actions of the Canadian government for the most part did not demonstrate this. While the LTTE had been banned as a terrorist group, the diasporic community were still allowed to protest. In fact, Foreign Affairs Minister Lawrence Cannon staunchly claimed that he would not put an end to the protests: "'It's not up to me to put an end to protest. People are allowed to protest in Canada. We live in a democracy'" (Potter, 2009). Andrew Potter suggests in his Maclean's article, however, that the reason that the Tamil protests were "tolerated" was because it is not considered to be as significant a concern for Canadians as issues in the Middle-East. However, while Potter may argue that Canada generally showed a tolerance for the Tamil protests, the comments posted in response to this article, as well as the previous comments demonstrate that even if the protests were tolerated by the Canadian government, Canadians were not all so tolerant.

As shown among the second-generation Sri Lankan Tamil diasporic community members, they demonstrate a very strong connection to their homeland, and expressed a very heavy disappointment in Canada for their lack of support for both the diasporic community and their "cause" in the homeland. These factors, therefore, may lead one to presume that if they were ever faced with the challenging position of having to choose between their two national loyalties, the Sri Lankan Tamil community in Canada would lean more towards their Tamil allegiances, thereby justifying the worries of Canadians who perceive this diasporic community to consist of 'suspect minorities.' However, it was found that this was not the case.

THE BOUNDARIES OF SUPPORT

While Tamil Canadians were protective of the homelanders, and understood that it was now their responsibility to speak up for them, there were certain lines that they would not cross in order to advocate for the homeland. Namely, when asked if they would engage in any acts of violence on Canadian soil in order to increase awareness of the situation in Sri Lanka, participants claimed that they would not. They acknowledged that there may be extremists who would engage in these behaviours, but these acts would not be condoned by the vast majority of the diasporic community. Participants shared that they felt that Canada was their home, and they would not do anything to jeopardize their positions in this country.

Therefore, while they are loyal to the homeland, and while they do feel a sense of responsibility to the homelanders, this responsibility is not eclipsed by their gratitude to Canada and their desire to maintain their Canadian citizenship. As Pooja, a 23-year-old female, stated:

> If it [the Canadian government] became like, I don't know, the Iraqi government or something like that, then it would be easier to engage in violence. But the diaspora in general, I think, I don't know, I just feel like, maybe – it's hard for me to kind of distance myself since I'm a member of the diaspora – but just in general, there's much love for their adopted land ... I just feel like, there's a general gratitude. Like, the fact that we're able to have television stations, radio stations, the funding, the fact that they allowed us to come at the beginning ...

While Tamil Canadians, for the most part, accepted their role as advocates following the defeat of the LTTE, feeling a responsibility to the homelanders, and a sense of connection to the Tamils in Sri Lanka, it is important to note that this connection was not left completely unchecked. The members of the diaspora may recognize their roles as defenders and lobbyists, but they were unwilling to advocate if it meant it would affect their positions in Canada. Participants commented on the difficulties that the Muslims faced following 9/11, and they were unwilling to do anything that would paint their entire community with the same "terrorist" brush. They would not engage in any act of terror on Canadian soil. While several participants explained that this would not be an effective strategy and therefore should not be considered, many also added that they would not risk their positions and the security they had in Canada. Onisha, a 21 year-old female, articulates this perspective, when she says:

> I absolutely would not, and I ... don't think anyone in the right of mind should, or would, feel that way ... I would find that scary if anyone would be like, yeah, let's, let's make ourselves heard by, you know, having suicide bombs, like, in another country or somewhere like that. No, absolutely not. And I think ... anyone would be able to understand that hypothetical example – if the LTTE were to have a suicide bomber in Canada or something like that, we would not – we'd be a lot farther from having peace and having people listen to us, so I don't think anyone would agree to that ...

However, their willingness to dismiss violence as a tactic to be used in Canada also appeared to stem from the fact that they had a general understanding of politics and international relations. Whereas their level of knowledge in terms of Sri Lankan politics varied, they were appreciative of the fact that condoning violence on foreign soil would not actually be beneficial to the Tamil cause, and that in addition to not being helpful to Tamils in Sri Lanka, it would also effectively ostracise the diasporic community. Their ability to step back and react to the conflict from a matter-of-fact perspective does not necessarily suggest that second-generation members of the diaspora are not emotional about the cause, but rather indicates that they are able and willing to be strategic regarding the future directions of the conflict.

Although the second-generation diasporic community members may need to be convinced to terminate their political engagement in the homeland, they did maintain strong boundaries with respect to how they exercise this political activism. Participants shared that the end of the ethnic conflict has left room to consider other means of supporting the homelanders and achieving rights and freedoms for the Tamils in Sri Lanka. Second-generation diasporic community members did not condone violence, and argued that the defeat of the LTTE, while tragic, also means that more peaceful and humanitarian efforts must be made in assisting the homelanders, such as the development of infrastructure in Sri Lanka. When participants were asked how they would react if the LTTE or another insurgency group were to rise again, they argued that they would not be able to support these groups if violence was the primary means through which they planned to achieve their objectives.

CONCLUSION

The manner in which diasporic communities determine where their loyalties lie, and how they construct their relationships with both their homelands and their countries of settlement, is not a simple one. The process is not static, and it is certainly not one-dimensional. Several factors must be considered in this process of negotiation, and what is particularly challenging is that these factors must be reconsidered each time the relationship between the homeland and the country of settlement shifts. When the members of the diasporic community know that the country of settlement and the homeland are on friendly or neutral terms, then they can maintain a relationship with both the homeland and the country of settlement without feeling as if it is in any way betraying one for the other. It is when any form of tension is introduced into the relationship between the country of settlement and the homeland that diasporans may find themselves experiencing the challenging situation of needing to actively negotiate loyalties.

As observed here among the second-generation members of the Sri Lankan Tamil diaspora, the perspective the country of settlement may take, in terms of the homeland, does not unilaterally determine the strength and direction of loyalty experienced by the diaspora. Labelling the Tamil Tigers as terrorists did not weaken the diaspora's ties with the homeland. Participants in this study demonstrated that their relationship with the homeland did not change as a result of Canada's position on terrorism and the LTTE. However, while their relationship with the homeland may not have altered as a result of the banning, this study showed that there were members of the diasporic community whose connection to the country of settlement was weakened by the Canadian government's decision to ban the LTTE. For those who disapproved of the terrorist label, Canada's decision to label the LTTE as terrorists was seen as an example of how the Canadian government was uninformed on the topic of the Sri Lankan ethnic conflict, and was unconcerned about the position of the Sri Lankan Tamil diasporic community in Canada.

When the needs of the homeland were most severe, and there was a call for action, the diasporic community was moved to engage more actively in homeland politics. However, while the members of the diasporic community seemed to take their job as advocates seriously, their support was not unconditional. The extent to which they would engage in homeland politics was limited by their loyalty and gratitude for the country of settlement. Despite their interests in homeland politics, participants spoke of how they did not feel that the diasporic community would ever act in a way that would cost them their own rights and freedoms in their country of settlement. Their support for a resolution to the conflict in Sri Lanka would not extend to supporting violent actions in Canada.

As such, while the Sri Lankan Tamil diasporic community may be considered with misgiving in the country of settlement, as they are a "suspect minority group," and while their loyalties may be questioned, the findings reveal that despite their high level of support and engagement in homeland politics, this community still maintains strong boundaries around their support. They understand the need to act through non-violent means in their efforts to support the homeland, and they have also learned through the experiences of the Muslim population how detrimental it could be to bring homeland politics into the country of settlement. In addition to not wanting to jeopardize their own position in the country of settlement, the diasporic community also recognizes that strategies utilizing violence and terror will not benefit the homelanders and the political agenda of the homeland.

These findings illustrate that several different factors, including the political climate of the homeland, the level of understanding and tolerance of the country of settlement, and the personal experiences of the country of settlement, all influence how the diasporic community negotiates its ties between both the country of settlement and the homeland. The process by which the second-generation members of the diaspora determine their national allegiances is dynamic and is constantly shifting. In order for Canada to be assured that the diasporic community is continuing to be loyal, it must be able to demonstrate that it too feels a strong sense of connection to its immigrant population, and it must foster space for diasporic communities to engage with all aspects of their identity. While fear of terrorism and betrayal has affected how immigrant populations are treated in their countries of settlement, this study reveals that diasporic community members are not all uniform in terms of their attachments, and that their loyalties cannot be assumed or dismissed at times of tension between the homeland and Canada.

REFERENCES

Adelman, H. (2002). Canadian borders and immigration post 9/11. *International Migration Review*, *36*(1), 15-28.

Canadian Tamil Congress. (2006, April 10). *Canadian Tamils disappointed by LTTE listing*. Press Release.

Carter, S. S. (2010, May 14). Man convicted in first terrorism financing case. Retrieved from: http://www.antiterrorismlaw.ca/

CBC. (2008, June 16). Canada lists World Tamil Movement as terrorist organization. *CBC News*. Retrieved from http://www.cbc.ca/news/canada/story/2008/06/16/day-tamil.html

Ferenc, L. (2009, March 17). Human chain of Tamils circles city core. Protestors explain why they're demonstrating. *The Toronto Star*. Retrieved from http://www.thestar.com/printArticle/603446

Lewington, J., & Makin, K. (2009, May 11). Tamil protest surprises Toronto. *The Globe and Mail*. Retrieved from: http://v1.theglobeandmail.com/servlet/story/RTGAM.20090510.wtamilprotest0510/BNStory/Front/News/

MacDonnell, F. (1995). *Insidious foes: The axis fifth column and the American home front*. New York: Oxford University Press.

Nadarajah, S., & Sriskandarajah D. (2005). Liberation struggle or terrorism? The politics of naming the LTTE. *Third World Quarterly, 26*(1), 87-100.

Potter, A. (2009, April 21). Tamil protesters, yes. George Galloway? Keep out. *Maclean's*. Retrieved from: http://www2.macleans.ca/2009/04/21/tamil-protesters-yes-george-galloway-keep-out/

Public Safety Canada. (2008). Smart border declaration and action plan. *Public Safety Canada*. Retrieved from: http://www.publicsafety.gc.ca/prg/le/bs/sbdap-eng.aspx

Ryan, P. (2010). *Multicultiphobia*. Toronto: University of Toronto Press.

Siddiqui, H. (2009, May 16). Tamil protests a test of our tolerance. *The Toronto Star*. Retrieved from: http://www.thestar.com/columnists/article/635385

Taylor, L. C. (2009, January 31). Thousands protest Tamil 'genocide'; As many as 45,000 line downtown streets to beg for help in Sri Lanka's escalating civil war. *The Toronto Star*, GT-1.

Wente, M. (2009, April 23). Can you belong to more than one nation? *The Globe and Mail*. Retrieved from: http://v1.theglobeandmail.com/servlet/story/RTGAM.20090422.wcowent23/BNStory/International

Kalyani Thurairajah
Department of Sociology
MacEwan University

SECTION III

YOUTH, IDENTITY AND RACIALIZATION

EVANGELIA TASTSOGLOU AND SANDY PETRINIOTI

11. MULTICULTURALISM AND THE FORGING OF IDENTITIES BY LEBANESE-ORIGIN YOUTH IN HALIFAX

INTRODUCTION

This chapter focuses on the process of identity negotiation and formation by Canadian-born youth of Lebanese descent in Halifax, a middle tier city in Atlantic Canada. If multiculturalism, as collective identity and normative framework for national identity building (Kymlicka, 2004), involves a negotiation between "us, them and others" (Winter, 2011), how does identity negotiation and formation for the Canadian born of Lebanese descent take place and how does it partake in the collective multicultural identity? Our research sought information about the multicultural experience of this youth group. Essentially, this chapter deals with the question whether and how multiculturalism has become part of the lived experience of second-generation, Canadian-born youth of Lebanese origin – in school, family, labour market and community – in the city of Halifax. This research continues the exploration of the experiences of immigrant and second-generation Canadian-born youth in smaller urban centres which began with the pilot study of the negotiation of ethnocultural identity by Greek and Jewish youth in Halifax (Byers & Tastsoglou, 2008).

Halifax has had comparatively (with other Canadian cities) small immigrant settlement (31,245 or 8.1% of the population of Halifax were foreign-born immigrants in 2011) – notwithstanding its port being a major entry gate of immigrants to Canada in the 20th century. Provincial government efforts in recent years have focused on increasing Nova Scotia's ability to attract and retain immigrants for demographic and economic reasons, reflecting, at the same time, the official multicultural ideology, policy and public discourse. Following the footsteps of cultural theorists and social geographers, we assume that place has a fundamental influence on the lived experience of multiculturalism. Thus, it is through examining the lived experience in the specificity of place that we can draw out in relief how social relations, both informal and institutionalized (family, education system, labour market, the civic and political citizenship frameworks) in a particular locality, contribute to the construction of subjectivity and collective identities (Agnew, 1993).

The chapter derives from a research project which aimed to explore the Lebanese and Canadian identity formation by sixteen Canadian-born youth living in Christian Lebanese households in Halifax,[1] as revealed by their views on the

S. Guo & L. Wong (eds.), Revisiting Multiculturalism in Canada, 189–205.

meaning of being a young man or woman in the city, the forging of ethno-religious and cultural identity, the intergenerational tension between individual, family and social values and expectations, and the negotiation of parental and community goals with individual desires.

We begin by drawing the broad lines of the historic presence of Lebanese immigrants in Nova Scotia and Halifax and by summarizing statistical data of their numbers. We then proceed to theoretical considerations focusing on the central concepts of multiculturalism, ethnic identity, hybridity, lived experience, place and second generation. Following a brief description of research methodology, we discuss our findings of our participants' identities, mostly hyphenated, and the meanings of such identities to them. Subsequently, we discuss ethnicity and ethnic identity both as "option" and as "imposition" in the context of the lived experience of Lebanese-Canadian youth in Halifax.

THE LEBANESE IN NOVA SCOTIA/THE LEBANESE IN CANADA

Nova Scotia has had a long history of Lebanese immigration that can be traced back to the mid-1880s. The early immigrants were Christian Syrians, fleeing Syria and what is today Lebanon, as a result of particular political and economic conditions at the time (Abu-Laban, 1980). The post-World War II Arab immigration, by contrast, was more heterogeneous, involving more countries of origin from the Arab world, and included a larger proportion of non-Christians (Abu-Laban, 1980). However, it was a small movement overall. Restrictive immigration laws in the post-World War II period resulted in a hiatus that lasted until the mid-1970s. The Lebanese Civil War, which erupted in 1975 and lasted for 16 years, caused a surge of emigration. During this time, immigration to Canada rose during times of intense violence and slowed down during times of relative peace. A *Lebanese Special Program* was created in Canada's immigration policy for those Lebanese fleeing violence who did not fit the definition of a refugee (*Encyclopedia of Canada's Peoples: Lebanese*).

The Lebanese in Halifax are predominantly of Christian faith but some are Sunnite Muslims. Maronite Christians comprise the largest denomination of Christian Lebanese but there is also an Eastern Orthodox parish in the city. The 2011 National Household Survey (Statistics Canada, 2014a) states that there were 190,275 persons in Canada who reported Lebanese ethnic origin (single and multiple-origin responses), with 7,245 of them living in Nova Scotia and 4,550 in the Halifax CMA. The respective figures for Canada in 2006 were 164,840 and 6,535 in Nova Scotia (Statistics Canada, 2009).

It is important to note that today's Lebanese newcomers encounter a more ethnically diversified Halifax, than was the case for Lebanese arriving earlier. Nova Scotia has recently been actively seeking more immigrants and the Lebanese are not the only immigrants in Halifax from the Middle East. Of the immigrants living in Halifax in 2011, 8,300 came to Canada between 2006 and 2011. These recent immigrants made up 26.6% of the immigrants in Halifax (Statistics Canada, 2014b). More immigrants now arrive from East and South Asia and the Middle

East. As a result of these developments, Arabic has now become the most spoken, non-official language at home (Mohammad, 2004). The 2011 National Household Survey also reports that the first of the most often non-official languages spoken at home in Halifax is Arabic (the second is Chinese and the third is Farsi) (Statistics Canada, 2014b). Responding to these changes, some hospitals are printing their patient instructions (in public areas) in Arabic. According to the 2011 National Household Survey (Statistics Canada, 2014c) of the Lebanese in Halifax, 1495 reported they belonged to the first generation, 1390 to the second and 1665 to the third generation. These numbers show that immigration has kept pace with the past and possibly accelerated in recent years.

In a classic monograph on Arabs in Canada, Abu-Laban (1980) explains the conceptual challenges of speaking about Arab ethnicity in Canada in particular. There are multiple dimensions of it on linguistic, religious and national-origin grounds which echo complex geopolitical developments, nascent nationalisms and modern state formation in the broader Middle East and confirm the socially constructed character of ethnicities. With respect to Canada, the conceptual challenges of speaking about "Arabs" are intertwined with those of speaking about the "Lebanese." The pioneer immigrants from the Arab Middle East to Canada in the latter part of the 19th century originated from Syria and were classified as "Syrians." In the 1901 Canadian Census though, they were combined with Turks ("Syrians and Turks") because, at the time, Syria was under Turkish control. In the five decennial Censuses from 1911-1951, the Syrians and Lebanese were grouped as "Syrians," while with the emergence of Lebanon as an independent state in the 1940s, Arab Canadians began to increasingly identify with either Syria or Lebanon until the 1961 Canadian Census utilized the designation "Syrian-Lebanese" to reflect this reality. Since 1962 official Canadian immigration statistics grouped all the new arrivals, Arab or otherwise, from the broader Middle East according to the country of their last permanent residence, while since 1971 the Canadian Census excluded the Arabs from the list of ethnic groups who were considered for detailed demographic analysis. There are limited data available based on language, i.e., Arabic as mother tongue in this Census. But the use of mother tongue for defining ethnicity underestimates the size of the Arab-Canadian community (Abu-Laban, 1980, pp. 20-26) and does not provide any information about the Lebanese. The 1976 Canadian Census provides no information by "home language," "place of birth," "citizenship" or "ethnic origin" (Statistics Canada, 2014d). However, the 1976 Census utilizes the category "Lebanese" when it refers to immigrants by "country of last permanent residence" (Statistics Canada, 2014e). Subsequent Censuses (1981, 1986, 1991, 1996, 2001, 2006 and 2011) all provide information about "ethnic origin" and apply the category "Lebanese."

According to the Statistics Canada (2007), a large majority of Lebanese – origin Canadians have a strong sense of belonging to Canada. In 2002, 89% of all those aged 15 and over reporting they had Lebanese ethnic roots said they had a strong sense of belonging to Canada. At the same time, 50% said that they had a strong sense of belonging to their own ethnic or cultural group. This finding echoes the results of the Ethnic Diversity Survey for all second-generation ethnic groups in that the ones with the strongest sense of ethnic identity report the strongest sense of belonging in Canada.[2] Canadians of Lebanese origin are also involved in various capacities in the public sphere, with high turnout in voting or participating in sports teams or churches. According to the Statistics Canada (2007), in 2002 about one quarter of Lebanese-origin Canadians reported having experienced discrimination or unfair treatment based on their ethnicity, race, religion, language or accent in the past five years, or since they arrived in Canada. A majority of those who had experienced discrimination said that they felt it was based on their race or skin colour (Statistics Canada, 2007).

THEORETICAL CONSIDERATIONS

Based upon the work of Fleras and Kunz (2001), we can identify five levels of meaning attributable to the concept of multiculturalism in Canada: fact, ideology, policy, practice, and critical discourse. According to Kymlicka's somewhat different grouping of these meanings (2004), there is a three-partite distinction of levels of multiculturalism: as a social fact, as a policy, and as a normative framework for society-building and national identity. The youth of our sample were born in their majority in the early nineties, that is, at the time of what Winter calls the "differentialist" turn of multiculturalism (2011, pp. 6-7) from a more group-rights approach to a stronger and more openly acknowledged emphasis on individual choice. With temporary exceptions in support of multiculturalism and reformulations as a result, and despite criticisms of offering lip service, being motivated by the neo-liberal agenda of "selling diversity" and/or attracting votes from minorities (Abu-Laban & Gabriel, 2002), or being blamed for lower levels of integration of contemporary, mostly non-European immigrants, Canadians today are proudly multicultural and multiculturalism has become part of Canadian identity (Winter 2011, p. 16). The Lebanese youth of our study conceive of multiculturalism as their experience of the demographic and social fact in Halifax, but also of the ideology and normative framework of the broader Canadian society. However, these two experiences may be at odds with one another, especially when it comes to minority cultures in Canada's regions where minority numbers are still very low and multiculturalism as policy, practice and critical discourse is cast into question. Atlantic Canadian provinces are grappling with questions of the sustainability of their founding peoples' cultures, languages and traditions in the face of their diminishing demographic weight within Canada's population. Their stance on multiculturalism policy- as it affects latecomers' claims to preserve their ethnocultural identity- is also influenced by a long standing outmigration because of economic stagnation and lack of employment opportunities for youth.

Ethnic or ethnocultural identity is taken to signify a fluid, negotiated, socially constructed, historically variable, relational and situational outcome which involves a compromise between selected, essentialized elements of an immigrant/ethnic culture and equally selected and essentialized elements of Canadian society, including such from its various "others." Ethnic identity and pan-Canadian identity are often portrayed as a zero-sum nexus. We argue here, echoing other researchers (e.g., Winter, 2011), that pan-Canadian identity is not a "national identity" but a multicultural one, which comfortably includes a variety of ethnic identities. Such ethnic identities are also inflected by gender, age, race, religion, and other forms of social division and inequality (Tastsoglou, 2001) which also play a role in the making of ethnic identities. The inflections unavoidably produce unique experiences, as do individual and group-based political choices of identification. The element of "choice" in the negotiation of ethnic identities in particular is highly variable, ranging from cases where ethnicity is an option (Waters, 1990) to ones where ethnocultural identity is totally imposed. A Lebanese, Greek, or Italian ethnic identity is a way of looking at pan-Canadian identity from particular angles. Having more "Lebanese characteristics" does not reduce one's attachment or commitment to Canada. Our subjects in everyday life choose, often situationally, from a range of identities available to them, producing their own variable syntheses or "hybrid identities."

"Hybridity" is one of the most widely used and criticized concepts in cultural studies and post-colonial theory. From its original racialized connotation, the term was displaced to cultural studies by Homi Bhabha (1994) and post-colonial work on borderlands (e.g., Anzaldua, 1987). Cultural hybridity suggests a creative, open and flexible way of being "in-between," not fully belonging to an "either/or" oppressive dichotomy, a "third space" where cultures overlap and new creative syntheses emerge. For Bhabha, it is these indeterminate spaces in-between subject positions that serve as sites of disruption and displacement of hegemonic cultural practices. Hybrid identities and a multiplicity of cultural borders are permanent features of contemporary societies.

Furthermore, we see hyphenated identities as markers of hybridities, verbally entrenching them. Scholars of culture and identity have extensively discussed their significance (Hoerder et al., 2005). As Byers and Tastsoglou have discussed (2008) the hyphen underscores the complex relationship between the desire to mark oneself as different and the desire to mark oneself as just like everybody else. Researchers have pointed to the hyphen as a point of resistance against assimilation (Brody, 1995), or a boundary where people can hide and pass when they need to, or strategically cross and reveal their mixed-race origin in order to confront and disrupt essentialized mainstream assumptions (Mahtani, 2005).

The concept of the "lived experience" refers to the practical activities of people's – youth in this case – daily lives. Practical activities in the everyday world are social in that they are worked out in the course of working together with others. As we engage in them, we confirm and recreate for ourselves a shared world of objects and people (Smith, 1987). The lived experience is accessed by the researchers of this study through youth narratives centering on family, friends, schools, ethnic community, and jobs.

"Place," according to Agnew, is comprised of three interwoven elements: *locale,* or the setting of social relations; *location,* or the impact that socio-economic processes on a wider scale have on locale; and the *sense of place,* or the cultural mediation produced by everyday practices (Agnew, 1993, p. 263). According to Massey, the specificity of place is continually reproduced, and derives from a number of sources. One such source is a distinct mix of wider and more local social relations (Massey, 1991). In this definition, linkages of a place with the wider world are important aspects of the history of place. The importance attributed to linkages augurs well for the study of ethnocultural identity of migrants as it articulates well with the theme of transnational lives and diasporic communities.

The focus on locality not only presupposes the recognition of the social construction of space but posits that uneven globalization processes (including migration) shape local economies, local politics, and local culture (Glick-Schiller & Caglar, 2008). Migration and success of immigrant integration clearly impact on the rank of a city in the global and national hierarchy of wealth and power, but also the particular economic and socio-cultural matrix of locality (Agnew, 1993, p. 263) affects the experiences of immigrants creating the sense of place or "local structures of feeling" (Agnew, 1987; Williams, 1958) which constitute the particularity of Halifax as opposed to that of Hamilton, Regina or Trois Rivieres.

Immigration in Atlantic Canada presents unique challenges for ethnocultural identity maintenance due to low numbers of immigrants and low densities of immigrant concentration. Immigrants in Halifax represented 7% of the total population according to 1986, 1996, and 2001 Census data (CIC, 2005) rising slightly to 8.1% in 2011. Contrast that with 20.6% immigrants in Canada's total population in 2011 (NHS Focus on Geography Series – Halifax) Halifax' status as a city, partly as a result, is contested in the literature between a "second tier" (McIsaac, 2003) and a "third tier" (Frideres, 2006) one.

The present study builds on the problematic raised in the earlier study of Greek and Jewish descended second-generation youth in Halifax (Byers & Tastsoglou, 2008), i.e., the dynamic of growing up and building identities outside of Canada's primary urban centres. It was argued in that study that the lower densities of immigrant concentration placed unique pressures and higher levels of "acculturative stress" (Tonks & Panjpe, 1999) on young people in Halifax to both maintain their distinct cultures and integrate into the dominant culture. Even if such youth practised their ethno-religious identification as an "option" (Waters, 2006), lower densities of immigrant populations were more likely to render the youth practicing ethno-religious options stand out in their group, and thus "other." As a result, the second-generation youth of smaller urban centres and lower diversity levels, practicing ethnicity "symbolically" (Gans, 1979), might be likely to struggle more trying to balance peer demands and cultural expectations of families and communities of origin. This study's youth can also be considered "new generation youth" (Yan et al., 2008) a term that refers to the children of visible minority immigrant families, as the Canadian youth of Lebanese parentage are often constructed as visible minorities[3] in the context of Atlantic Canada.

Finally, the choice of second-generation youth in the study of identity formation is very significant in that it emphasizes multiple transitions on a continuum of migrant mobility. A mobility which is, at the same time, spatial (family migration from specific places in Lebanon to specific places in Canada, Nova Scotia and Halifax); temporal/generational, as it is widely recognized that the experiences of the immigrant second generation are different from those of their parents (Hébert et al. 2008; Tastsoglou & Byers, 2009); and, above all, socioeconomic (Ray, 2011). Migration and settlement studies focus on these transitions, questioning whether integration is taking place and how; whether social cohesion is promoted; and whether new forms of collective identity have evolved, and of what kind. This implicitly means that one accepts that ethnic identities are not essential or fixed in time, but are constructed, multiple, and evolving (Hall, 1988, p. 257). Turning to specific localities means being able to contextualize these social processes of integration, social cohesion and formation of national identities, and, thus, being indirectly able to study the loci where transnational notions of self and becoming play out. In this sense, studies of identity formation of the second generation in specific localities present an important advance over earlier ethnographic research.

METHODOLOGY

This is a qualitative study of sixteen (8 male, 8 female) Lebanese-origin youth in Halifax. Our participants were identified through personal acquaintance and word-of-mouth and interviewed by our Christian Lebanese research assistant in 2009. The interviews were audio-taped, transcribed and analyzed with Nu*dist. The youth were born between 1983 and 1990, with most being born around 1987. The majority were born in a city and identified themselves as Christians of various denominations. The overwhelming majority had lived in Halifax for most of their lives, with a few having lived in Lebanon or elsewhere for a few years. Fifteen of the youth were single and lived with their parents and siblings. Thirteen were not in a relationship at the time of the interview. The three who were in relationships had Lebanese-origin partners. Twelve youth were attending university and the rest had graduated and/or were continuing with their education in professional programmes.

HYPHENATED ETHNIC IDENTITIES

The majority of respondents appeared to adopt a hyphenated identification, with "Canadian" or "Lebanese" coming first in an equal split and depending on which component they felt was more dominant. Nevertheless, a number of participants identified as simply Lebanese born in Canada or simply Lebanese or even "Canadian" "by choice" – that is, despite the fact, as they explain, that they were cast in the broader society as "others." This interesting finding speaks to the agency and political choice, the "politics of belonging" of individuals (Tastsoglou, 2006). Jeremy (a 20 year-old male born in Halifax) identified himself as just

> Canadian, but of course, the rest of society knows I'm not just Canadian, so I consider myself Canadian because I feel like I'm Canadian. I was born in Canada, I was brought up Canadian, so I consider myself Canadian.

By contrast, Elle had accepted the mainstream definition of her as "other" and adopted it, though strategically and situationally, as she introduced herself differently in Lebanon – which speaks to the fluidity of ethnic identification, and the individual's agency and identity politics:

> Yeah. Well, I say I'm Canadian, and then they say, well, you don't look like you're from Canada, where are you originally from (laughs)? So, I say I'm Lebanese, I was born in Canada, but I'm Lebanese .... In Canada, I say I'm Lebanese, but in Lebanon, like I'm not exactly like the Lebanese in Lebanon, so I say Canadian.

An important part of the "Lebanese" component of the youth's identity was the overwhelming agreement on the importance of maintaining the Arabic language. The reason for the importance they ascribe to being able to understand Arabic was that language was seen as a quintessential part of culture, showing their pride in the Lebanese culture and their desire to maintain it. On the other hand, few of the respondents admitted to being proficient in Arabic (especially reading and writing). Communication with family, both in Canada and Lebanon, was a more utilitarian expression of the same desire to maintain culture and links to roots.

> ... I love visiting there, and being able to speak the language when you go, makes it that much more convenient ... to interact with the family, cousins, aunts and uncles that are all still in Lebanon because their English is very limited (Chris).

Our young participants explained that they learned the "Lebanese" part of their identities through a number of activities and from different individuals. Among these individuals were, first and foremost, their parents and grandparents and, second, their friends:

> My parents are first-generation moving to this country, so they brought a lot of tradition with them. And, uh, we try to, uh, try to adapt them to Canadian things, but still, the way they grew up was definitely different from the way we grew up, and they try to enforce some of those traditions at home (Chris).

Last but not least, the organized Lebanese community with its church, celebrations, kin and community gatherings "taught" these young people how to be Lebanese. Periodic trips to Lebanon and direct immersion in the culture and extended family there also helped:

> There's a strong Lebanese community here. You learn a lot through them. It's more, like, you learn through your culture, what your people are like. (Anthony)

> Being involved in the church, and we have festivals every year. We have dance groups, Lebanese dance groups, and we all hang out at the Lebanese community, outside of school .... (Nancy)

MEANING OF BEING LEBANESE IN HALIFAX: BELONGING TO A DISTINCT ETHNIC GROUP

Almost all of the respondents felt that being Lebanese in Halifax meant belonging to a group which was perceived as being different from mainstream society. This sense of uniqueness had been prevalent among the Jewish and Greek-origin second-generation youth in Halifax (Byers & Tastsoglou, 2008). In the words of one young man of Lebanese descent:

> So, I feel like being Lebanese in Halifax means being part of a select group, um, that we look out for each other, and we understand each other. (Alex)

And from a young woman:

> Definitely identifiable, and being a part of a society like that, a community, it really distinguishes [us] from being Canadian. (Sarah)

The Lebanese identity for these youth was primarily expressed as belonging to a community sharing common descent and common cultural understandings, and as a framework of references to be drawn upon in the effort to negotiate their loyalties and belongings.

One such understanding was religious practice: the interviewees were Christian of various denominations (primarily Orthodox and Catholic) and practised in various degrees by going to Church with their families, participating in religious ceremonies, attending Sunday school, teaching Sunday school, and so forth. A common pattern was that of practising families, with the children gradually drifting away, but still connecting with the Church from time to time.

> Um, growing up, I went every single Sunday, and attended Sunday school, and I took part in the church events and all that. But as I grew up a little more, I, uh, strayed from the church a little bit. It's not that I lost my faith, I just didn't really find the time to go to church anymore, and I, uh, had things going on with athletics and school .... (Alex)

These patterns coincide with the findings from the Greek-origin second-generation youth in Halifax (Byers & Tastsoglou, 2008). As in the case of the Greek and Jewish communities, the very foundations of the two Lebanese communities (Christian Orthodox and Maronite) were religion and religious institutions. It was the latter that organized community life, so that secular Lebanese cultural experiences were difficult or even impossible to sustain.

Our participants used the term "Lebanese," however, to refer exclusively to their own group of Christian Lebanese, and in particular, their own narrower Christian denominations of Maronite or Orthodox Christians. Their ethnic identity centred on their Christian religion and place of origin (or that of their families). It was not uncommon for ethnicity to be intertwined with religion and place of origin, though what was unusual here was the total claim of "Lebanese" for the Christian Lebanese.

Furthermore, the respondents were able to pinpoint several differences between mainstream society and the Lebanese community which forged the uniquely Lebanese features of their collective identity. Foremost among such features was the strength of family ties which, they avowed, held transgenerational importance, and, of immediate relevance to them, the manner in which they were raised within Lebanese households as opposed to how they perceived their Canadian counterparts were raised. Sweet (1974) had underscored the same strength of family ties and kinship in her ethnographic study of the reconstitution of the Druze village of "Ain ad-Dayr" in Edmonton. Ahdab-Yehia's study (1974) of the Detroit Maronite community yielded similar findings among the Maronite Lebanese (first and second generation, at least) at the time. Among our youth of Lebanese origin in Halifax, Chris phrased it this way:

> I mean, family, uh, it's a big tradition, Sunday lunches, we still live at home, basically it's very difficult for us to be allowed, if we want to move away to go to university. Um, parents are very strict, and want to keep the family tight knit and close together. So, I think that, uh, there are definitely different experiences that I would have shared, than people who are Canadian.

Elle (raised in Lebanon) focused on the self-reliance ethic that she perceived was the norm for her Canadian peers. By contrast, Lebanese youth maintain ongoing ties, emotional and material, with their families:

> Well, just the thought of when you're eighteen, you know, parents tell you …
> go and make a life for yourself. In Lebanese communities, that's not the case.
> I mean, your parents don't tell you, now it's time to support yourself, time to
> make a living. Maybe it's a bad thing. More or less, we can live at our
> parents' house until we get married (laughs).

Although they cherished their family, few of the respondents lived in an extended family arrangement which included grandparents or uncles, aunts and cousins. Kinship was valued and respondents visited with their relatives in Lebanon but the nuclear family was the norm in Halifax. This may be a characteristic of Muslim Lebanese communities as well, as indicated by the Lebanese community of Lac La Biche, Alberta (Barclay, 1968).

Most youth were aware that parental control of their life outside of school, parental interest in who they meet and socialize with, steering the youth to activities organized by the church groups and the Lebanese community school, and encouraging intra-community friendships, was their parents' way of maintaining a distinct cultural identity and passing it on to their offspring.

> I remember growing up and crying with my mom because she wouldn't let
> me hang out with my friends. I'd have to be home, or my Lebanese friend
> could come over. But, if I was like, my Non-Lebanese friends were always
> out, and having sleepovers, and I was never allowed, no (laughs). (Mona)

Chris reiterated that his (Canadian) teenager friends' practices such as sleepovers were not permitted by his (Lebanese) parents, this being something completely alien to them and, therefore, to be rejected: "In Lebanon, our parents aren't used to those things, you know? They don't have a name for them."

It was in the domain of associating with the opposite sex – dating, courtship and marriage – that the young people related that their apartness from their Canadian peers was most felt. Dating was not permitted for Lebanese girls and frowned upon for Lebanese boys. Similarly, fathers in the Muslim Lebanese community of Lac La Biche, without exception, denounced the practice of dating, although a few of the most prosperous and most assimilated businessmen were willing to yield to dating arrangements under proper supervision (Barclay, 1968, p. 154). Alex presented the dilemma of dating a Lebanese girl in ways that echo the study of Greek and Jewish youth (Byers & Tastsoglou, 2008, p. 18):

> It doesn't look good that you're dating a Canadian girl because you're not expected to marry her so what are you doing with her besides sex, sexual relations? So, um, I think that, uh, it comes right back to presenting your family well, and not going out and doing it, and uh, being more respectful towards women as a whole, and if possible, you know, try dating some of the Lebanese. But, uh, that becomes complicated, because if you're dating a Lebanese girl, she comes with a Lebanese family and a Lebanese father. And you can't really mess up with a Lebanese girl ….

From the point of view of a young woman:

> Uh, well, young guys and girls, you know, if a Lebanese guy and Lebanese girl were dating, like, three months down the road, someone would say, "so it's time to get married." I find that a Lebanese guy will not date a Lebanese girl unless he is going to marry her.

It was on the topic of marriage that both men and women converged in their recognition that both their family and community expected that they should marry within the ethnic-religious community. Both the Greek and Jewish communities study (Byers & Tastsoglou, 2008) and the study of the Muslim Lebanese community of Lac La Biche (Barclay, 1968, p. 153) confirm as well these communities' emphasis on endogamy. As one young man from our sample phrased it:

> … it is an unwritten rule in the Lebanese community that you're supposed to marry, or even date, a Lebanese girl and, I mean, the end goal would be, for a Lebanese man to marry a Lebanese woman.

Laura, in her response to the question of whether and how she negotiated with members of her family her expectations and desires as regards to her future spouse, explained that valuing family closeness was a trait which, in her mother's mind, was particular to the Lebanese:

> Actually, I was just talking to my mom this morning that some people think that it doesn't matter who you marry, as long as they are a good person …. And she said, well, you know, in the long run, they might think differently.

Will you see them at Sunday lunch every Sunday? Like, that's a big thing. Like, can you see them sitting at the table with us? Can you see them being comfortable with our family, or do you see them as pushing away from the family, which would make you push away from the family. We want to keep our family close together; we don't want to push it apart, and bring someone who doesn't have strong family values who then it will push our family apart.

ETHNIC IDENTITY: FROM OPTION TO IMPOSITION

For the Lebanese youth of this study, ethnicity was generally an "option" (Waters, 1990). Although Lebanese identity was ascribed through (positive) reinforcement from within the family and the local community and through visits to Lebanon, sometimes it is instances of racism, discrimination, or stereotyping, that transformed a distinct ethno cultural identity into "otherness" in a city which is predominantly "white." Mona recalled:

When I was growing up a lot of people pick on you because you are different ... You're known as Arab.

Here is how one young man phrased it:

I think [being Lebanese] it makes me kind of unique and identifiable more so, kind of sometimes a minority. I don't feel it, personally, especially when I've gone to university. I feel there are more people like me. But I also got classified like that, even when I didn't want to be. (Jack)

Another young man admitted to being the object of a little "friendly racism" that was projected by his "White-Canadian" friends:

Even now, some of my friends are White-Canadians, and they will just joke around or something. Like, as friendly racism, if that's what you want to call it. It hurts me a little more than what I project out to the rest of the people, so. I've been dealing with that for a while now, but I'm sorta used to it .... (Jeremy)

John felt that, as a child, he was an object of stereotypical reactions to his Lebanese identity:

One is to have a corner store. Like to especially have a corner store. I mean not anymore, because the role has developed, right? But when we were little kids, we were like, "do you have a corner store"?

It is not certain whether these experiences of racism, discrimination or stereotyping are universally experienced by Lebanese immigrants and their offspring throughout the Canadian urban landscape or were especially poignant in Halifax due to the small population base, the relative ethnocultural homogeneity of Nova Scotia and the small size of the Lebanese community. It is, however, interesting that the respondents stated that they felt that there has been an "evolution" for the better in this regard ..., "... the role has developed, right?" This evolution could be understood as a positive change from a culturally imposed ethnic identity to an "option." One should not exclude, however, the possibility that evolution could also mean that they have accepted this "friendly racism" as "the way things are" in "white" Halifax.

It seems that of the social institutions that these Lebanese youth have experienced in Halifax, they felt that they became the objects of discrimination in elementary and junior high school where children arrived with their identity and personality primarily shaped by their family and social situation. As higher grades of education were achieved, a socialization of egalitarianism and tolerance for difference as well as exposure to students of diverse origins, as in university, seemed to make peer groups more accepting. This finding had been mirrored in the Greek youth (Byers & Tastsoglou, 2008).

Nevertheless, this may not be the case in the inherently competitive realm of employment. Laura was more direct about feeling excluded by her co-workers:

Sometimes I feel like I'm an outcast, like all those Canadians will kinda group together. And kinda, solidify. Sometimes I feel that way with jobs.

The situation in the labour market was apparently more complex. One respondent stated that there may be advantages to being a member of a minority population for government employment while another believed that knowledge of Arabic may be a good thing to put in his resume. Some youth perceived advantages in being identified as Lebanese with employers with an ethnic clientele. Another one felt "… that there are lots of Lebanese with companies that may help you get a job" (Amira), while two young men stated they may be hired because of personal relationships which have developed between families in the community. These findings resonated similar ones among the Greek youth in the 2008 study of Byers and Tastsoglou.

CONCLUSION

In this chapter we examined, through the narratives of second-generation youth of Lebanese descent living in a middle-size Atlantic Canada city, how social institutions – the family, schools, community, the labour market – in the setting of a specific place, Halifax, interact to shape their experiences and identities. Our examination of the experiences of locality brought out the feeling of alienation felt by the youth in school and up to university. It is in the school setting and the all-important participation in and acceptance by peer groups that the young people interviewed most acutely felt their "otherness."

Being in alternative (to the mainstream), culturally segregated spaces are encouraged so that children and teenagers can socialize within their ethno-religious community at Church, language schools, parish organized sports, dance groups and community festivals. The community thus is important to these young people as a frame of reference, especially in their formative years, to help them learn to be Lebanese. Ethnocultural maintenance is practiced later in adolescence and young adulthood in courtship rituals and in marriage with discouragement of cross-cultural dating and pressure to marry within the ethno-religious community.

The hybridity of their identity is "set" by both the negatively coloured ascription of "difference" expressed by mainstream society and the reinforcement of the feeling of a different distinct identity by the family and the community. The young Lebanese feel and express the tension generated by these two forces especially acutely because they are in a life stage where "belonging" is especially valued as teenagers and young adults endeavour to situate themselves in society. However, as transitions occur and they progress from elementary school to higher levels of education, as they learn how to be male or female and what is expected of them in their gender roles, and as they transition from the formal education system to acquiring their first paid work experiences, they seem to develop a hybrid ethnocultural identity – more coherent at its core and less so on the fringes where situational factors are at play – selecting and accepting certain attributes from both local mainstream and parental cultures. This pattern of acculturation seems to be one which produces "better" personal and social outcomes: higher levels of personal satisfaction and adaptation and more successful social integration and resulting social cohesion (Sykes, 2008, pp. 10-12).

A vital component of this selective hybridity is recognition of their parents' migratory journey. Thus, generational conflict is tempered by their understanding of their parents' different circumstances and different experiences as well as a basic acceptance of "Lebanese" core values. While parents act as "pilots" in their children's learning their ancestors' traditions, their children blaze trails of learning to be "like Canadians" and to help parents learn how to be parents "in Halifax."

Identity formation is complex and contingent on context as defined by place. Lebanese youth in Halifax seem to have an extensive cultural knowledge of possible self-identities and the concomitant specific places where these identities may be assumed in variable syntheses. The fluidity of their hybridity may be explained not only by the transition to the second generation as well as by their stage in the life cycle, but also by the situational character of identity itself. The fluidity of hybridity facilitated by the vernacular fluency in various cultures confirms the idea that ethnic identity/Canadian identity is not a zero sum game, but the two co-exist and collaborate, inform and shape each other.

Challenges to the active citizenship of others exist despite government policy and, to some extent, a public discourse that acknowledges the Canadian multicultural ideal. However, in a world of transnational migrations where "individuals are more connected globally but are increasingly divergent locally across ethnicity, religion and culture" (Sykes, 2008), Halifax has to imagine ways by which divergent groups can live together while maintaining multidimensional belongings, and ways in which individuals may acquire a sense of place, which will allow them to feel that the city belongs to them as much as they belong in the city.

NOTES

1   The project was entitled *Negotiating Ethnocultural Identity among Halifax Youth: The Lebanese Second Generation and Beyond* and was funded by the Atlantic Metropolis Centre through a grant in 2009. We are grateful to Ellie Lawen for conducting the interviews in the Lebanese community.
2   See Jack Jedwab's (2007) analysis.
3   Defined as Non-Caucasian in race and non-white in skin colour by Canada's *Employment Equity Act*.

REFERENCES

Abu-Laban, B. (1980). *An olive branch on the family tree: The Arabs in Canada*. Toronto: McClelland and Stewart Ltd. with the Multiculturalism Directorate, Department of the Secretary of State and the Canadian Government Publishing Centre, Supply and Services Canada.

Abu-Laban, Y., & Gabriel, C. (2002). *Selling diversity: Immigration, multiculturalism, employment equity and globalization*. Peterborough: Broadview.

Agnew, J. A. (1987). *Place and politics: The geographical mediation of state and society*. Boston, MA: Allen and Unwin.

Agnew, J. A. (1993). Representing space: Space, scale and culture in social science. In J. Duncan & D. Lev (Eds.), *Place, culture, representation* (pp. 252-272). London: Routledge.

Ahdab-Yehia, M. (1974). The Detroit Maronite community. In B. C. AswadArabic (Ed.), *Speaking communities in American cities* (pp. 137-153). New York: Center for Migration Studies of New York.

Anzaldua, G. (1987). *Borderlands/la frontera: The new mestiza*. San Francisco: Aunt Lute.

Barclay, H. B. (1968). An Arab community in the Canadian northwest: A preliminary discussion of the Lebanese community in Lac La Biche Alberta. *Anthropologica New Series, 10*(2), 143-56.

Bhabha, H. K. (1994). *The location of culture*. London-New York: Routledge.

Brody, J. D. (1995). Hyphen-nations. In S. Case, P. Brett, & S. L. Foster (Eds.), *Cruising the performative* (pp. 148-162). Indianapolis: Indiana University Press.

Byers, M., & Tastsoglou, E. (2008). Negotiating ethnocultural identity: The experiences of Greek and Jewish youth in Halifax. *Canadian Ethnic Studies Special Issue on the Experiences of Second-Generation Canadian Youth* (guest-edited by Evangelia Tastsoglou), *40*(2), 5-33.

Citizenship and Immigration Canada. (2005). *Recent immigrants in metropolitan areas: Halifax – A comparative profile based on the 2001 census*. Retrieved from: http://www.cic.gc.ca/english/resources/research/census2001/halifax/parta.asp

Encyclopaedia of Canada's Peoples: Lebanese. Retrieved from: http://multiculturalcanada.ca/Encyclopedia/A-Z/l4/2.

Fleras, A., & Kunz, J. L. (2001). *Media and minorities: Representing diversity in a multicultural Canada*. Toronto: TEP.

Frideres, J. S. (2006). Cities and immigrant integration: The future of second and third-tier centres. *Our Diverse Cities, 2* (Summer), 2-3.

Gans, H. (1979). Symbolic ethnicity: The future of ethnic groups and cultures in America. *Ethnic and Racial Studies, 2*(1), 1-20.

Glick-Schiller, N., & Caglar, A. (2008). *Migrant incorporation and city scale: Towards a theory of locality in migration studies*. Willy Brandt Series of Working Papers in International Migration and Ethnic Relations 2/07. Malmö, Sweden: Malmö Institute for Studies of Migration, Diversity and Welfare (MIM) and Department of International Migration and Ethnic Relations (IMER) Malmö University.

Hébert, Y., Wilkinson, L., Ahmad Ali, M., & Oriola, T. (2008). New modes of becoming in transcultural glocal spaces: Second-generation youth in Calgary, Winnipeg, and Toronto. *Canadian Ethnic Studies, Special Issue on the Experiences of Second-Generation Canadian Youth* (guest-edited by Evangelia Tastsoglou), *40*(2), 61-87.

Hoerder, D., Hébert, Y. & Schmitt, I. (Eds.). (2005). *Negotiating transcultural lives: Belongings and social capital among youth in comparative perspective*. Toronto: University of Toronto Press.

Jedwab, J. (2007). *The young and the rootless: Measuring ethnicity and belonging to Canada*. Retrieved from: http://www.acs-aec.ca/_media/polls/11882297694378.pdf

Kymlicka, W. (2004). Marketing Canadian pluralism in the international arena. *International Journal, 59*(4), 829-852.

Mahtani, M. (2005). Mixed metaphors: Positioning "mixed-race" identity. In J. Lee & J. Lutz (Eds.), *Situating "race" and racisms in space, time, and theory* (pp. 77-93). Montreal-Kingston: McGill-Queen's University Press.

Massey, D. (1991, June24-28). A global sense of place. *Marxism Today*. Retrieved from: http://www.amielandmelburn.org.uk/collections/mt/index_frame.htm

McIsaac, E. (2003). *Nation building through cities: A new deal for immigrant settlement in Canada*. Ottawa, ON: The Caledon Institute of Social Policy.

Mohammad, S. (2004, October 14). Halifax's Arabic community says media ignoring it. *King's Journalism Review*. Retrieved from: http://older.kingsjournalism.com/kjr/journalism_3673_5331.html

Ray, B. (2011, March 30). Does "where" matter? Comparing the labour market experiences of second-generation women and men in Toronto and Montreal. Public lecture conducted at the Atlantic Metropolis Centre, Halifax, N.S. Retrieved from http://community.smu.ca/atlantic/events_e.html

Smith, D. E. (1987). *The everyday world as problematic: A feminist sociology*. Toronto: University of Toronto Press.

Statistics Canada. (2014a). *2011 National Household Survey: Data tables (Canada; Nova Scotia; Halifax)*. Retrieved from: http://www12.statcan.gc.ca/nhs-enm/2011/dp-pd/dt-td/Rp-eng.cfm?LANG=E&APATH=3&DETAIL=0&DIM=0&FL=A&FREE=0&GC=0&GID=0&GK=0&GRP=1&PID=105396&PRID=0&PTYPE=105277&S=0&SHOWALL=0&SUB=0&Temporal=2013&THEME=95&VID=0&VNAMEE=&VNAMEF=

Statistics Canada. (2014b). *2011 National Household Survey, focus on geography series – Halifax*. Retrieved from: http://www12.statcan.gc.ca/nhs-enm/2011/as-sa/fogs-spg/Pages/FOG.cfm?lang=E&level=4&GeoCode=1209034

Statistics Canada. (2014c). *2011 National Household Survey: Data tables (Halifax; ethnic origin; single and multiple-origin responses; generation status)*. Retrieved from: http://www12.statcan.gc.ca/nhs-enm/2011/dp-pd/dt-td/Rp-eng.cfm?TABID=1&LANG=E&APATH=3&DETAIL=0&DIM=0& FL=A&FREE=0&GC=0&GK=0&GRP=0&PID=105396&PRID=0&PTYPE=105277&S=0&SHOWALL=0&SUB=0&Temporal=2013&THEME=95&VID=0&VNAMEE=&VNAMEF=

Statistics Canada. (2014d). *Historical statistics of Canada, Section A: Population and migration, immigration* (Series A350-416). Retrieved from: http://www.statcan.gc.ca/pub/11-516-x/sectiona/4147436-eng.htm#4

Statistics Canada. (2014e). Immigration to Canada by country of last permanent residence. *Historical statistics of Canada, section A: Population and migration, immigration*. Table A385-416. Retrieved from: http://www5.statcan.gc.ca/access_acces/archive.action?l=eng&loc=A385_416-eng.csv

Statistics Canada. (2009). *2006 Census*. Population by selected ethnic origins, by province and territory. Retrieved from: http://www.statcan.gc.ca/tables-tableaux/sum-som/l01/cst01/demo26d-eng.htm

Statistics Canada. (2007). Profiles of ethnic communities in Canada. *The Lebanese community in Canada 2001*. Catalogue no: 89-621-XIE – No. 15. Ottawa: Ministry of Industry.

Sweet, L. E. (1974). Reconstituting a Lebanese village society in a Canadian city. In B. C. Aswad (Ed.), *Arabic speaking communities in American cities* (pp. 39-52). New York: Center for Migration Studies of New York.

Sykes, S. (2008). *Life on the reef in the Canadian ocean: The "new" second generation in Canada*. Discussion Paper, PRI Project Cultural Diversity. Ottawa: Government of Canada.

Tastsoglou, E. (2001, November 1-2). *Re-appraising immigration and identities: A synthesis and directions for future research*. Report commissioned by the Department of Canadian Heritage for the Ethnocultural, Racial, Religious and Linguistic Diversity and Identity Seminar, Halifax, N.S. http://canada.metropolis.net/events/ethnocultural/publications/tastsoglou_e.pdf

Tastsoglou, E. (2006). Gender, migration and citizenship: Immigrant women and the politics of belonging in the Canadian Maritimes. In E. Tastsoglou & A. Dobrowolsky (Eds.), *Women, migration and citizenship: Making local, national and transnational connections* (pp. 201-230). Burlington, VT: Ashgate Publishers.

Tonks, R. G., & Paranjpe, A. C. (1999, January). *Two sides of acculturation: Attitudes toward multiculturalism and national identity amongst immigrant and Canadian born youth.* Paper presented at the Third National Metropolis Conference, Vancouver, Canada.

Waters, M. (1990). *Ethnic options: Choosing identity in America.* Berkeley: University of California Press.

Williams, R. (1958). Culture is ordinary. In R. Gable & R. Williams (Eds.), *Resources of hope: Culture, democracy, socialism* (pp. 3-14). London: Verso.

Winter, E. (2011). *Us, them and others: Pluralism and national identity in diverse societies.* Toronto, ON: University of Toronto Press.

Yan, M. C., Lauer, S., & Jhangiani, S. (2008). Riding the boom: Labour market experiences of new generation youth from visible minority immigrant families. *Canadian Ethnic Studies. Special Issue on the Experiences of Second-Generation Canadian Youth* (guest-edited by Evangelia Tastsoglou), *40*(2), 129-148.

Evangelia Tastsoglou
Department of Sociology and Criminology
Saint Mary's University

Sandy Petrinioti
Department of Sociology and Criminology
Saint Mary's University

205

DAN CUI

12. MULTICULTURALISM AS AN INTEGRATIONAL POLICY

Lessons from Second Generation Racialized Minorities

INTRODUCTION

Canada has the largest foreign-born population (20.6%) among the G8 countries, and this figure is only second to Australia (26.8%) across the world (Statistics Canada, 2011). Compared with many other countries, Canada's distinctive immigration and integration model characteristic of large-scale skill-based immigration policy and integration policy of multiculturalism has been regarded as relatively successful in that Canadian public holds a general positive attitude towards mass immigration (Reitz, 2012). And the multiculturalism policy is believed to serve as an important social cause for such popular views. It helps Canada garner international prestige and attract a large number of new immigrants to build their homes in this country. Over forty years have passed since multiculturalism's inception in 1971, this policy has fueled ongoing debates among academics, politicians, media, and Canadian public, particularly on its role in promoting social justice and equity for racialized minorities. One of the critiques is that racialized minorities have yet to be treated as "real" Canadians or as equal partners with the White dominant group, although multiculturalism claims all cultures in Canada enjoy equal status (Ali, 2008; Bannerji, 2000). The term of second generation racialized minorities refers to racialized immigrants' descendants. Their lived experiences will be a truer reflection of the long-term integration problems in Canada than their parents who may struggle with language and adaptation issues over time (Reitz & Somerville, 2004). Therefore, research on second generation racialized minorities will have important implications for us to develop a better understanding of the multiculturalism as an integration policy. This book chapter begins with a theoretical review of multicultural debates, followed by an introduction of my research project and data used in this study. I will then discuss three themes regarding the lived experiences of second generation racialized minorities. Finally, I conclude by discussing the implications of this study for multicultural debates.

REVIEW OF CANADIAN MULTICULTURAL DEBATES

Multiculturalism has triggered a variety of debates over the years. There are two major themes that attracted more academic attention than others. In the past, the debate focused on multiculturalism as a politics of recognition and its cultural pluralist assumptions. More recently, academics have disagreed with one another about whether multiculturalism is a divisive force that leads to national fragmentation or one which can lead to national unity.

For many political philosophers, such as Charles Taylor, multiculturalism is an alternative political philosophy used to address the weakness of liberalism and to deal with an increasingly diverse population in contemporary Western industrial society (Abu-Laban, 2002). For Taylor (1992), a form of liberalism that emphasizes individual rights, state neutrality and the value of difference blindness that treats everyone as equal regardless of one's background is "highly discriminatory," and "impractical in tomorrow's world" (p. 43). In his widely-cited work, "Politics of Recognition," he argues that it is crucial "we all recognize the equal value of different cultures; that we not only let them survive, but acknowledge their worth" (p. 64). His model of multiculturalism as a politics of recognition has sparked debate. Abu-Laban (2002) criticizes this model's essentialized understanding of culture and argues that it is impossible to categorize human beings according to which cultural groups they belong to because individuals may identify with more than one culture and thus have multiple and shifting identities. As well, Li (1999) points out that multiculturalism is mistakenly used by academics as a synonym of cultural pluralism to analyze racial and ethnic relations. In so doing, ethnic groups are defined as members of a group who share a homogenous and primordial ethnic culture rather than one constructed from and through unequal power relations. Li argues that the maintenance of ethnic distinctiveness may not result from ethnic groups' own choices and preference, but rather as a response to their subordinated position in relation to the dominant group. Bannerji (2000) also questions Taylor's politics of recognition by pointing out that it treats difference among people simply as an issue of cultural diversity, and the multicultural state as a power-neutral entity and thus is devoid of social relations based on "race," gender, class and other social indicators. As she argues: "Speaking here of culture without addressing power relations displaces and trivializes deep contradictions. It is a reductionism that hides the social relations of domination that continually creates 'difference' as inferior and thus signifies continuing relations of antagonism" (p. 97). In a similar vein, Fraser (2000) identifies two problems associated with Taylor's politics of recognition: reification and replacement. The problem of reification means that through a politics of recognition, homogenous and simplified group identity is imposed on individual members, which denies the complexity and multiplicity of individual identification. As well, it treats one's identity formation as an "auto generated auto-description" rather than resulting from social interaction with other groups (p. 112). Further, Taylor's (1992) politics of recognition tends to displace a more important issue of distribution by treating misrecognition simply as a problem of cultural depreciation rather than as an inequality based on distribution of limited social resources. In this regard, misrecognition should be viewed as status subordination i.e., one is denied status as a full partner in social interaction through systemic and institutional racism such as laws, government policies or long-standing customs. The debate on multiculturalism as a politics of recognition has significant implications for understanding the integration of second generation racialized minorities. An important question arising from this debate is: Are they recognized and treated as equal partners by the dominant White group in a multicultural society?

A second important debate about multiculturalism focuses on whether it is a divisive force which creates racial and ethnic enclaves, encourages multiple identities and divided loyalties, and hinders the production of a singular Canadian civic culture, a common national identity and consequently, social cohesion (Garcea, Kirova, & Wong, 2008). *Canadian Ethnic Studies* published a special issue (2008) that critiques the anti- or post-multiculturalism discourse that regards multiculturalism as a segregating force. For example, Garcea (2008) argues that the alleged fragmentary effect of multiculturalism is not evidence-based. Likewise, Wong (2008) points out that there is no clear definition of what constitutes societal fragmentation and that a one-dimensional approach – multiculturalism as either being about unity or fragmentation – is problematic. He notes that difference and diversity does not necessarily lead to fragmentation given the fact that "Canadians diverge on many social issues and values, which is certainly deemed acceptable in a democracy" (p. 26). In fact, if we examine the initiation and evolution of multiculturalism as an integration policy, such fragmentation discourse is obviously not tenable. It has been argued that from the very beginning multiculturalism policy has been used by the federal government as a political strategy to counteract Quebec nationalism, to appease the political demands of various social forces, and to sustain order and unity of the nation (Li, 1999). Despite its claim for cultural diversity, multiculturalism policy within a bilingual framework has been criticized for being assimilation-oriented by separating language rights from cultural rights. By denying the vital link between language and culture, it is difficult for ethnic groups to maintain culture without official support for ethnic language learning (Day, 2000). What federal multicultural policy did achieve is to legalize the hegemonic position of English and French languages while only offering a symbolic endorsement of cultural diversity. Given the fact that official languages are connected to key cultural, educational, and political institutions, cultural and linguistic conformity has remained strong. Li (2003) argues that, over time, there will be a substantial rate of ethnic language loss among immigrant descendants who resemble the White dominant group rather than their immigrant parents in terms of linguistic and social patterns. Further, this multiculturalism debate about unity is also reflected in an emerging research interest among academics in examining ethnic identity, national identity, and sense of belonging among second generation racialized and ethnic minority youth. Literature reviews show that a number of researchers argue that youth's ethno-cultural identifications do not undercut or diminish their national identity and attachment to Canada (Jedwab, 2008; Jurva & Jaya, 2008; Wilkinson, 2008). More empirical research is needed to examine the ethnic language and cultural maintenance among second generation racialized minorities, as well as their sense of belonging to Canada in relation to the multiculturalism policy within a bilingual framework.

SECOND GENERATION RACIALIZED MINORITY YOUTH PROJECT

In Canada, research on second generation racialized minority youth is relatively new (Kobayashi, 2008). Asia remained Canada's largest source of immigrants (56.9%) between 2006 and 2011; and Chinese were identified as the second largest visible minority group (21.1%) after South Asian (25%) and accounted for 4% of the total Canadian population (Statistics Canada, 2011). The 2006 survey shows that among the second generation "visible minority" groups, Chinese is the largest category and is a significant young age group with 76% between 15-34 years old (Jantzen, 2008). However, research on second generation Chinese youth has yet to be fully developed. Data used for this chapter was drawn from a larger project on the social and cultural integration of the second generation Chinese-Canadian youth in Alberta. The term of second generation used here generally refers to the first generation foreign born immigrants' descendants regardless of whether they were born in Canada or not. Thirty-six second generation Chinese youth were interviewed, including nineteen males and seventeen females. Twenty-five youth had immigrant parents from mainland China, ten from Hong Kong and only one from Taiwan. Fifteen youth were either born in Canada or immigrated to Canada before the age of six, while the rest came to Canada after the age of six. Their ages ranged between 15-25 years old. With only a few of them still in senior high school, the majority of research participants were university students. The average age of participants was 19.2 years old. These participants came from diverse family backgrounds. Some of their parents were successful business people, professors, and engineers, while others were housekeepers, restaurant cooks, bus-drivers or unemployed. During the interview, participants were asked to talk about their lived experiences at school, within family and through their formative contact with Canadian mainstream media. Interview questions also include their ethnic language and cultural maintenance in Canadian multicultural society.

RACIALIZED MINORITIES AT CANADIAN SCHOOLS

Living in present-day Canada where the discourses and ideology of multiculturalism have been prevalent for decades, most Chinese-Canadian youth, at the beginning of their interviews, were reluctant to talk about their experiences of racial discrimination. However, as the interviews continued and trust was built between the researcher and the participant, such stories emerged. M3 left mainland China at the age of eight. He recalled his school experiences in a small town in Alberta:

> S is a city of descendants of the French colonialists so it's basically a very White city. The general population is Caucasian. I am the only Asian in junior high. So the White kids I don't think they've ever met an Asian person before in their life so they are a bit nervous in a way but also cautious in their

attitude toward me. Also at the same time, they are a bit discriminatory. Because just by appearance I look different from them and also by academic achievement, I differ from them quite a bit too.

He noted he has been excluded from school projects and addressed with racial slurs.

There was one time in the social studies class we all had to assemble into groups. Basically all the White kids got into groups and I was basically forced to be excluded from any of the groups ... eventually I got into a group and then they started piling all the work to me .... They sometimes incorporate racial slurs in there. Like *Chinaman, chink* ... those words would sometimes be used but not often. Mostly it's indirectly. I remember also in music class there was one guy who was pretty good with the guitar. Every so often when the teacher wasn't around, he starts playing (singing a tune) on the guitar and everybody in the class would start laughing. That was a little oriental tune ... Basically in a society where they are not exposed to multicultural, their thinking is very discriminatory and very White centered.

By comparison, M3 found a bigger city, such as Edmonton, more accepting of different cultures compared with this small town he once resided in. Similarly, in their research with youth of Greek and Jewish origins in Halifax, Byers and Tastsoglou (2008) note that it is more likely for youth who follow ethno-religious practices to stand out among peers in smaller urban centres, thus they experienced a higher level of "otherness" (e.g., anti-Semitism). M3's story demonstrates that multiculturalism, as providing equal statuses in social interaction, was not fully supported in Canadian peripheral regions where minority numbers are low. This is not to say racism only exists in small towns or rural areas. In fact, racism as a discourse has been deeply embedded in Canada's value system, in the language people use and in jokes they share. It has been maintained and reproduced in people's everyday life. For example, F6, who completed all of her schooling in Edmonton, recalled:

There were always teasing from students. The low chances are like, *Me Chinese Me no Dumb*. I cannot remember what other part of the teasing was but that always bugs me. They do actions. It really, really bugs me because it made fun of Chinese people.

When such things happened, the only thing she could do was to ignore it, "because the more you confront them about it, the more they are going to do it to you." Surprisingly, discriminatory beliefs and discourses are not just restricted to several aberrant students; rather, they are also taken up by some well-educated teachers. M3 noted such a teacher in his biology class:

I remember this one class about all the herbivores, there is no current war to keep that population down. The population of herbivores will eventually peak and fall. And the teacher will make comments like, while, looks like we were heading to, with all the immigrants coming in, the world will come to the end because all the immigrants come in. People here start losing jobs. Immigrants are having so many kids, now they move here and there, so they have more kids so we will run out of supplies. So the end of world. It was spread out the whole semester. That's the message.

Such remarks that treat immigrants as foreigners and competitors, rather than as Canadian citizens and contributors to nation building are not something new, but a discursive reproduction of the racist discourses in Canadian history. Early Chinese immigrants were blamed for grabbing limited employment opportunities from White workers during the economic downturn. In so doing, Western states use immigrants as scapegoats to distract public attention from the real economic problems of capitalism (Li, 1998; Pfzelzer, 2007). Further, evidence from empirical research has proved the assumption that immigrants bring extra burdens to Canadian social welfare was incorrect. As Li (2003) notes: "On the contrary, most studies indicate that immigrants have contributed to Canada in a variety of ways, and the weight of evidence suggests that Canada has benefited from immigration" (p. 99). As well, contemporary racism is also characteristic of ignorance and marginalization. F6 recalled her mother's experience at parent-teacher meeting:

I had a teacher that discriminated against Chinese people. It's just open hostility. Even to [my] mom, when we go to parent-teacher meetings, she would like to ask certain parents for help and she would never ask my mom and she was just open discrimination.

Such embarrassing experiences made F6's mom decide to enroll her in a Catholic school simply because she believed "they are more accepting of different ethnicities." Further, racial stereotypes such as "Chinese students are not good at sports or do not have a good command of the English language" affect how Chinese youth perceive themselves. M18, a university student specializing in physical education, observed how racial stereotypes worked in his class. As he stated:

A lot of students weren't expected to reach the same level as a lot of the White kids just like for resistance training, they were pushed further than we were. The teacher was basically like their expectation of you wasn't as great.

Teachers' stereotyped assumptions about Chinese students were also found in English class. F2, a Canadian-born Chinese, on the one hand, was quite proud of her enrollment in an English International Baccalaureate (IB); on the other hand, she acknowledged:

I don't know if they [teachers] did it consciously but I guess they did make a distinction between the different races, I guess kind of by expectation. Like they expect the Chinese students to do well but they also expect them to be bad in English and stuff. I'm pretty sure like in Social and Humanities, I think they kind of come in with the perception that you're going to do bad because you don't really speak the language ... I think White teachers are probably the worst for it. They can be a little more prejudiced especially for classes like English and Social and World Literature and everything. They kind of pick on the people that they don't think are as good too. I think a lot of people don't like those kind of classes. The teacher has a lot of control and they can pick on you.

Both M18's and F2's experiences demonstrate how racial stereotypes can work through a "hidden curriculum" to affect Chinese-Canadian youth's self-perception. Hidden curriculum refers to the tacit way that students learn school norms and values as well as their places in school and social hierarchies (Apple, 2004; Wotherspoon, 2009). It is the unintended outcomes of the schooling process (McLaren, 2003). As Henry, Tator, Mattis, and Rees (2006) point out, "one of the most difficult aspects of racism to isolate and identify is the hidden curriculum" (p. 204). For example, hidden curriculum can be found in school calendars in terms of which holidays are celebrated, and which are given days off. It can also be manifested in the constant "gaze" that African Canadian students experienced by White school authorities that treat them as potential trouble makers (Kelly, 1998). In the case of Chinese students, hidden curriculum is exemplified in some teachers' low expectation on their potentials and abilities in the Phys-Ed and English classes. Through hidden curriculum, teachers deliver messages such as "you won't do well in my English class" through tone, eye contact, body language, and marking that may discourage Chinese students to excel in such types of classes. As a result, students are very likely to fall into a trap of self-fulfilling prophecy, and end up with a bad performance or grade. James (2003) calls for educators to critically examine the reasons why African Canadian students believe that they can only fulfill their educational needs and aspirations through sports (as cited in Henry et al., 2006). Through this logic, Canadian teachers also need to engage in self-reflection as to why many Chinese students believe they can only excel in science, rather than in English and sports.

MIS-REPRESENTATION IN CANADIAN MEDIA

Historically, racialized minorities have long been denigrated by mainstream media as a "problem" or "social threat" to Canadian society. Despite the implementation of multiculturalism policy for forty years, Canadian media institutions have often been criticized for their reluctance to reflect multicultural commitments of Canada, and their continued insistence on negative coverage of minorities. Particularly, in November 2010 Canada's leading newsmagazine *Maclean's* published a provocative article entitled "Too Asian?" (Findlay & Kohler, 2010). In this article, Asian students are depicted as only academically focused while lacking social skills. Their competiveness and work ethic not only deprives their White counterparts of postsecondary opportunities, but also ruins their social life, characterized by sports, parties and alcohol. The article quotes a White mother who complains that the reason her son did not get a space in university is mainly because it is taken by Asian students. During the interview, participants were asked to read the "Too Asian?" article and voice their opinions. M19 refuted the media misrepresentation of Asian students as advantaged competitors:

One thing they gotta keep in mind is that a lot of Chinese people, before they come to Canada, they didn't even know a word in English, ok. Like me, when I first came, I was standing in front of McDonald's, and I was trying to order something, and I look at the picture and I didn't know a word in English. How did I make it to university at the same time? Because I spent triple amount of time in studying, in looking through the dictionary, until this got ripped. I spent triple amount of time learning a language that I'm not even familiar with. And I got into university and got a higher mark than you .... And you guys, ok, English is your first language. How come you don't get in, got a lower mark? you know, they are denying your effort.

Similarly, F16 did not agree with the "Too Asian?" article's attempts to interpret entrance into post-secondary institutions along a racial line. As he said:

It's just racist. Um, I think Asian students do work hard, like the majority of the people I know, they work hard. But I also have Caucasian friends who also work really, really hard. And so I think it's a fair game, it doesn't matter if you're White or not White.

In "Too Asian?," Findlay and Köhler (2010) argue that Asian students' academic achievements were accompanied by an incomplete and one-dimensional lifestyle. At the same time, Asian students were represented as advantaged as a result of receiving more help from their parents than their White peers.

The focus on academics was often to the exclusion of social interaction. 'The kids were getting 98 per cent but they didn't have other skills,' she [a guidance counselor] says. 'Their parents would come in and write in the résumé letters that they were in clubs. But the kids weren't able to do anything in those clubs because they were academically focused' (Findlay & Köhler, 2010, p. 78).

Such representations, however, did not capture the reality of Chinese youths' lived experiences in Canada. For example, M1 is a top student in a very academically competitive high school in Edmonton. He noted that he seldom saw his father at home, who works on a night shift in a local Chinese restaurant, during the whole school year. His father has neither time nor ability to provide the academic support *Maclean's* suggested gives Asian students the competitive edge. In fact, many participants revealed their parents experienced a difficult time in finding professional jobs after immigration due to language barriers, credential devaluation, or lack of Canadian work experience and discrimination. Many of them, therefore, have had to work several part-time jobs in the service industry as bus drivers, dishwashers, waitresses, cooks and housekeepers, in order to support their families.

In response to the stereotyped image of Asian students as "nerds" who lack interest in social or extracurricular activities, F16 argues that: "When I first read this, my feeling was that a lot of the comments are stereotypical Asian, not all of us are like that, like not all of us just study and have no social life at all." M12, a member of school volleyball team echoed this point: "I think for myself, one of the reasons I started going to the gym with friends is because … I just want to break stereotypes." Many participants indicated their involvements in various extracurriculum and social activities such as basketball, volleyball, music band, clubs, student organizations, and church, as a counter-discourse to the stereotyped "nerd."

The mis-representation of Chinese people by Canadian mainstream media shows that racism as an institutional and systemic problem needs to be addressed seriously before Canada can truly fulfill its multicultural promise where everyone is treated equally. The current reality, however, is that Canadian media continues to construct social issues along racial lines, reinforcing racial stereotypes, vilifying racialized minorities with deficit lifestyles and deviant personalities, or as competitors who come to Canada to grab limited resources from White Canadians. Given the role of media in constructing "common sense" understandings, manufacturing consent, and influencing how people think about racialized minorities (Cui & Kelly, 2013), such biased media representations will have harmful impacts on developing a truly democratic and multicultural society as well as promoting social cohesion and harmony among different ethnic groups.

ETHNIC LANGUAGE AND CULTURAL MAINTENANCE

Although multiculturalism policy encourages ethnic groups to maintain their language and culture, in reality English and French as the dominant official languages inevitably lead to a process of linguistic and cultural assimilation, which is often associated with a loss of ethnic language acquisition in terms of reading, writing, and speaking to varying degrees. During interviews, participants were asked to talk about their language use in both public and private spaces, such as in school and at home. Most of them indicated English was the primary language used in their daily life. M3, who came to Canada with his parents at the age of nine, noted:

> I have been raised in an English world, when speaking; my Chinese vocabulary is very limited. I can say basic things, but when it comes to discussion or anything more than just daily stuff, I cannot find the exact word. And anytime there is an idiomatic expression used, chances are that I may not be able to understand.

When it came to language use at home, it was very common for participants to speak simple Mandarin or Cantonese with their parents and English with their brothers or siblings: "English with brother and Chinese with my parents" as told by M3. However, for those Canadian-born who know little Chinese, they communicate with their parents in a unique "bilingual" way: "at home, they [her parents] usually speak in Cantonese so I just reply back in English," F5 revealed. Without the language skills, many participants are prevented from accessing

Chinese websites, movies, music, community organizations and activities. In other words, their limited knowledge of ethnic language affects the maintenance of ethnic culture as well as the possibility of developing a substantial connection with their parents' home country. For example, M3 explained why he did not surf Chinese websites: "I cannot understand non-literary meaning. I can talk [Chinese] but I cannot read and write." F2 described the difficulty she experienced in getting involved in local Chinese church activities: "If I know the language better, I will feel more connection [with Chinese community]."

Not surprisingly, a lack of ethnic language proficiency results in a symbolic connection with China, even though some of them self-identify as Chinese-Canadian. As F4 noted: "I just think of myself as Chinese-Canadian. Just because the way I grew up, because of the fact that I have been surrounded by so many Chinese friends." However, when being asked, "Where do you think you belong to?" she replied,

> I think I belong in Canada. I would like to say the Chinese community in Canada but it's not really true .... There is a lot more, I guess, the fact that I cannot even really speak the Cantonese language technically pushes me away from the ability to be even a part of that. So I would probably consider myself pretty much Canadian especially in terms of beliefs in my inability to speak Cantonese properly.

Interview data shows one's ethnic identity and sense of belonging are not in a simplistic linear and causal relationship. In other words, one's strong ethnic identification does not entail a lower sense of belonging to Canada. This finding has particular implications for the ongoing debate that multiculturalism is a divisive force by encouraging multiple identities. For example, M14 argues,

> Like if anybody stepped up to me now and asked me oh what ethic background are you from? It's unlikely I would say Canadian because you kind of assume that being in Canada that you'd be Canadian so I say Chinese but I mean when somebody asks you your ethnic background or whatever, I don't really do a lot of Chinese things and the customs have kind of dropped off through the generations ... but [my connection with China], I think it's more symbolic. I don't really associate with China. I don't go and check everything. Like when something happens in the news and you hear it's related to China, it does kind of pique my interest because I'm Chinese right? but I don't feel there's a super strong connection. I don't associate all the time with it ... I'd say like I would tell people I'm Chinese Canadian but I would feel more strongly for Canada.

In this sense, multiculturalism within a bilingual framework acts as an assimilating force rather than as a divisive one. Although it encourages ethnic cultural maintenance, it maintains the hegemonic position of English and French as official languages. Through school education and socialization, English becomes the primary language for many Chinese Canadian youth in both public and private spaces. Research participants revealed that speaking fluent English without a

Chinese accent was often viewed as a sign of Canadian membership and linked to various privileges and power in social interactions at school and other public institutions. This becomes one of the main reasons that they have little interest in learning Chinese. Therefore, although some of them have been sent by their parents to Chinese bilingual school or Saturday language school, they were not fully committed. Even though some of them have to speak Chinese for the needs of daily communication at home, because their family members know little English, many of them indicate they are only functional speakers that can only talk about basic day-to-day topics. As Louie (2006) points out, the lack of ethnic language skills among Chinese second generation youth contributes to the distancing between children and parents as they cannot communicate with their parents about complex personal or political issues. In other words, language barrier functions as a divisive factor between second generation Chinese and their non-English speaking immigrant parents. More importantly, Portes and Rumbaut (2001) argue that language is more than a means of communication but a crucial component in the development of the self, that is, of one's identification. People use language to define the boundaries of communities, nations and ethnic solidarities, a sense of "we-ness." In this point, despite some youth's ethnic identification as "Chinese Canadian," their connection with China is more symbolic than substantial, due to the lack of ethnic language proficiency. In addition, Growing up under the strong pressures of linguistic and cultural assimilation, it is more likely for them to build a sense of belonging to Canada than to their parents' home country, which many participants indicate they seldom go back to visit, are unfamiliar with its language and don't see it as a place associated with their daily lives.

CONCLUSION

This chapter examined two major themes of multiculturalism debates: multiculturalism as a politics of recognition and multiculturalism as a divisive force. One debate centers on the critique of viewing difference between people as simply cultural diversity rather than as unequal power relations between dominant and subordinate groups. The second debate focuses on an anti-multiculturalism discourse that views multiculturalism as a divisive force which fosters multiple identities, encourages divided loyalties and weakens social cohesion. With the empirical evidence from my research on second generation Chinese youth, I argue that there is still a long way to go for second generation racialized minorities to be accepted as equal partners by the dominant White group in a multicultural society. Historically, Chinese immigrants, despite their contribution to Canada's nation building were subjugated through institutionalized and systemic racism reflected in laws and government policies. The identity label of "Chinese" has never been a neutral ethnic term but associated with various racial stereotypes, viewed as inferior, undesirable, inassimilable and dangerous to Western civilization. My research indicates that "race," to be exact, "racialization," is still an important concept and research topic in the contemporary multicultural society (Cui, in press). As Omi and Winant (1993) point out:

The main task facing racial theory today, in fact, is no longer to problematize a seemingly "natural" or "common sense" concept of race – although that effort has not been entirely completed by any means. Rather our central work is to focus attention on the *continuing significance and changing meaning of race*. It is to argue against the recent discovery of the illusory nature of race; against the supposed contemporary transcendence of race; against the widely reported death of the concept of race; and against the replacement of the category of race by other, supposedly more objective categories like ethnicity, nationality, or class. (p. 3)

Contemporary forms of racism are more implicit and invisible. They may be manifested in the teasing against racialized and ethnic minorities, ignorance at teacher-parent meetings, or a laugh, a slipped-in comment or a joke. It may also be manifested in negative comments regarding the foods Chinese youth bring to school, or in Chinese youth being picked on by teachers in English or Phys-Ed class. It may also be manifested in the media discourse in terms of who should be restricted from accessing post-secondary opportunities, and what is a normal university life. These experiences affect how Chinese-Canadian youth perceive themselves in relation to the dominant White group and their sense of belonging to Canada. As M3 revealed: "For me, the main factor [that affects his identification] is prejudice and discrimination that really gives me the idea that no, you are not Canadian, you are Chinese with Canadian citizenship." Obviously, the multiculturalism as an integration policy that only offers symbolic recognition of different cultures is far from adequate to deal with racial and ethnic relations in an increasingly diverse society. Despite the focus shift of multiculturalism policy, from addressing racism during the 1980s to the fostering of national unity since the 1990s, the task of anti-racism has yet to be completed. Research with Chinese Canadian youth shows that these two foci of multiculturalism policy, although distinct, do not contradict each other but rather are closely interrelated, in the sense that without dealing with the problem of racism, unity and social cohesion cannot be really achieved. Further, multiculturalism within a bilingual framework is more assimilation-oriented rather than a segregating force. Despite multiculturalism's official encouraging of ethnic language and cultural maintenance, in reality, the linguistic and cultural assimilation force is so strong that it is less likely for Chinese immigrant descendants to maintain their ethnic language and culture in the private sphere. In this sense, what affects Chinese youth's sense of belonging to Canada is not their ethnic heritage, symbolically encouraged by multiculturalism policy, but the racism which exists in their everyday lives. The lessons from second generation racialized minorities, particularly in terms of the racial discrimination they experienced in Canadian society will have significant implications for policy makers and researchers to rethink multiculturalism as an integration policy.

REFERENCES

Abu-Laban, Y. (2002). Liberalism, multiculturalism and the problem of essentialism. *Citizenship Studies, 6*(4), 459-482.

Ali, M. (2008). Second generation youth in Toronto: Are we all multicultural? *Canadian Issues, Spring 2007,* 87-89.

Apple, M. (2004). *Ideology and curriculum* (3rd ed.). New York: RoutledgeFalmer.

Bannerji, H. (2000). *The dark side of the nation: Essays on multiculturalism, nationalism and gender.* Toronto: Canadian Scholars' Press.

Byers, M., & Tastsoglou, E. (2008). Negotiating ethnocultural identity: The experiences of Greek and Jewish youth in Halifax. *Canadian Ethnic Studies, 40*(2), 5-33.

Cui, D. (in press). Capital, distinction and racialized habitus: Immigrant youth in the fields of Canadian schools. *Journal of Youth Studies.*

Cui, D., & Kelly, J. (2013). "Too Asian?" or the invisible citizen on the other side of the nation? *The Journal of International Migration and Integration, 14*(1), 157-174.

Day, R. J. F. (2000). *Multiculturalism and the history of Canadian diversity.* Toronto: University of Toronto Press.

Findlay, S., & Köhler, N. (2010, November 22). "Too Asian." *Maclean's, 123*(45), 76-81. Retrieved from http://www2.macleans.ca/2010/11/10/too-asian/

Fraser, N. (2000). Rethinking recognition. *New Left Review, 3,* 107-120.

Garcea, J., Kirova, A., & Wong, L. (2008). Introduction: Multiculturalism discourses in Canada. *Canadian Ethnic Studies, 40*(1), 1-10.

Garcea, J. (2008). Postulations on the fragmentary effects of multiculturalism in Canada. *Canadian Ethnic Studies, 40*(1), 142-160.

Henry, F., Tator, C., Mattis, W., & Rees, T. (2006). *The color of democracy: Racism in Canadian society* (3rd ed.). Toronto: Thomson Nelson.

Jantzen, L. (2008). Who is the second generation? A description of their ethnic origins and visible minority composition by age. *Canadian Diversity, 6*(2), 7-12.

Jedwab, J. (2008). The rise of the unmeltable Canadians? Ethnic and national belonging in Canada's second generation. *Canadian Diversity, 6*(2), 25-34.

Jurva, K., & Jaya, P. S. (2008). Ethnic identity among second generation Finnish immigrant youth in Canada: Some voices and perspectives. *Canadian Ethnic Studies, 40*(2), 109-128.

Kelly, J. (1998). *Under the gaze: Learning to be black in white society.* Halifax: Fernwood Publishing.

Kobayashi, A. (2008). A research and policy agenda for second generation Canadians: introduction. *Canadian diversity, 6*(2), 3-6.

Li, P. S. (1998). *The Chinese in Canada* (2nd ed.). Toronto, Oxford & New York: Oxford University Press.

Li, P. S. (1999). The multicultural debate. In P. S. Li (Ed.), *Race and ethnic relations in Canada* (2nd ed., pp. 148-177). Oxford: Oxford University Press.

Li, P. S. (2003). *Destination Canada: Immigration debates and issues.* Don Mills: Oxford University Press.

Louie, V. (2006). Growing up ethnic in transnational worlds: Identities among second-generation Chinese and Dominicans. *Identities: Global Studies in Culture and Power, 13*(3), 363-394.

McLaren, P. (2003). Critical pedagogy: A look at the major concepts. In A. Darder, M. Baltodano, & R. D. Torres (Eds.), *The critical pedagogy reader* (pp. 69-96). New York: RoutledgeFalmer.

Omi, M., & Winant, H. (1993). On the theoretical concept of race. In C. McCarthy & W. Crichlow (Eds.), *Race, identity and representation in education* (pp. 3-10). New York: Routledge.

Pfzelzer, J. (2007). *Driven Out: The forgotten war against Chinese Americans.* Berkeley, CA: University of California Press.

Portes, A., & Rumbaut, R. G. (2001). *Legacies: The story of the immigrant second generation.* Berkeley, CA: University of California Press.

Reitz, J. (2012). The distinctiveness of Canadian immigration experience. *Patterns of Prejudice, 46*(5), 518-538.

Reitz, J., & Somerville, K. (2004). Institutional change and emerging cohorts of the "new" immigrant second generation: Implications for the integration of racial minorities in Canada. *Journal of International Migration and Integration, 5*(4), 385-415.

Statistics Canada, 2011. Immigration and ethnocultural diversity in Canada, national household survey, 2011. Ottawa: Statistics Canada. Available from: http://www12.statcan.gc.ca/nhs-enm/2011/as-sa/99-010-x/99-010-x2011001-eng.cfm (accessed 16 March 2012).

Taylor, C. (1992). The politics of recognition. In A. Gutman (Ed.), *Multiculturalism and the politics of recognition* (pp. 25-73). Princeton, NJ: Princeton University Press.

Wilkinson, L. (2008). Visualizing Canada, identity and sense of belonging among second generation youth in Winnipeg. *Canadian Diversity, 6*(2), 84-86.

Wong, L. (2008). Multiculturalism and ethnic pluralism in sociology: An analysis of the fragmentation position discourse. *Canadian Ethnic Studies, 40*(1), 12-32.

Wotherspoon, T. (2009). *The sociology of education in Canada* (3rd ed.). Oxford: Oxford University Press.

Dan Cui
Werklund School of Education
University of Calgary

CARL E. JAMES AND SELOM CHAPMAN-NYAHO[1]

13. "AND HE WAS DANCING LIKE NO TOMORROW"

Police and Youth "Getting to Know" Each Other

INTRODUCTION

One of the highlights of the Youth in Policing Initiative (YIPI), a summer program with the Toronto Police Services, is the opportunity for participants – most of them Black and Brown youth of Caribbean and South Asian origin – to be part of the police officers' float in the Scotiabank Toronto Caribbean Carnival parade. This carnival, formerly known and still commonly referred to as Caribana, is a week-long series of celebratory events pertaining to Canada's Caribbean community which culminate on the first Saturday of August with a large parade of floats with costumed revellers and accompanying music. Caribana is one of Canada's largest summer festivals and a signature example of Canada's admired multiculturalism. As such, Caribana, like other cultural events, is used to showcase "creative encounters" among Caribbean-Canadian "culture group" members and institutions like the police. Two of the Caribbean Canadian participants told us of their initial hesitation to participate in the festival alongside police officers, but their trepidation seemed to have dissipated when they arrived at the event and a supervising officer told them: "You have to dance. That's a requirement." One young woman recalled the behaviour of one officer in particular, saying: "And there was this one officer and he was dancing like no tomorrow. He was so funny." This moment is illustrative of a program whose purpose, in the Canadian tradition of multiculturalism, was used to build bridges between the police and racialized youth from disadvantaged neighbourhoods, and have them, through cultural encounters, get to know each other, thereby dispelling unhelpful preconceived notions of each other.

The Youth in Policing Initiative (YIPI) is a program designed to give youth from Toronto's priority neighbourhoods[2] summer employment working in various police divisions. In addition to addressing antagonistic attitudes, dispelling stereotypes of each other, and countering the often contentious relationship between marginalized youth and police, it is thought that the program would provide these youth with social and educational opportunities and direction that they might otherwise not have had because of the disadvantaged socioeconomic neighbourhoods in which they reside. Indeed, in many ways, YIPI provides youth valuable summer employment opportunities and experiences, and along with the police affords occasions to "get to know" each other, thereby helping to reduce the social distance between police and youth – particularly in a context structured to

S. Guo & L. Wong (eds.), Revisiting Multiculturalism in Canada, 221–236.

facilitate mutually respectful exchanges. But to what extent does this program – grounded in multicultural assumptions that the solution to misinformation, hostility and conflict is interactions and exchanges – affect the attitudes, opinions, and most importantly, the practices of the youth and police participants?

In what follows, we explore this question with reference to research we conducted with participants in the 2010 program. In the research, we conducted individual and focus group interviews with police officers, supervisors, and youth, and administered surveys at both the beginning and end of the program. As participant observers, we observed all stages of the YIPI process: recruitment, applications, job interviews, employment, and graduation.[3] The rationale behind our methodological approach was that the interviews and focus groups would allow us to recognize not only the extent to which the youth's attitudes towards the police changed, but to also note the nature of that change. We wanted to know, from their experiences, how much their attitudes changed and how the very way they conceptualized and talked about police and policing changed. This experience allowed us to gain a comprehensive picture of how the program was administered and its impact on the youth and police participants. This chapter introduces a critical reflection on our original research.

We begin with a discussion of how programs designed for "at-risk" youth are caught up in racialized assumptions and anxieties. "Youth at risk" are positioned as in need of extraordinary attention and guidance, especially from professionals and "responsible adults." Their geographic location serves as proxy for racialized anxieties resulting from the disruptive potential of marginalized youth. We go on to discuss how the YIPI summer employment program, based on a need to guide, govern, and scrutinize young people from priority areas, and in the process operated, not only as a means of surveillance, but to protect and advance the material, moral, and psychological interests of the police. As such, YIPI, which set out to meet the social and economic needs of "at-risk youth" and build positive police-youth relations, is more likely to entrench and privilege the institutional interests of policing than the needs and interest of the youth and their communities.

THEORETICAL CONSIDERATIONS

According to Critical Race Theory, racialization is a perspective that "recognizes the complexity of racial dynamics" in contemporary society by exposing and deconstructing "seemingly 'colorblind' or 'race neutral' policies and practices which entrench the disparate treatment of non-White persons" (Stovall, 2008, pp. 244-245) – something that is "central to the way people of color are ordered and constrained" (Trevino, Harris, & Wallace, 2011, p. 7). Racialization also draws attention to the process by which ideas about race – an admittedly socially constructed category – and racism achieve a certain "normality" in North American society (Trevino et al., 2011, p. 9). The "permanent and pervasive nature of racism" is something Charles (2011) claims is exacerbated by the "chorus of denial" about racial elements in supposedly egalitarian societies (p. 63).

By "bringing race discourse to the forefront of informed discussions on civil society" (Trevino et al., 2011, p. 8), racialization provides insight into how well-intentioned attempts to intervene in the lives of marginalized youth may actually produce and sustain racial subordination. Constraint and subordination often typify programs involving educational support, guidance, and mentorship, which James (2012) asserted are frequently advocated to combat marginalization. He claimed that often the application of these interventions become so routine that they end up concealing the structural nature of inequality, instead locating disadvantage in the cultural and social practices of racialized youth (p. 4).

As such, these interventions constitute a form of governance, which Fox and Ward (2008) defined as "the guidance or control of an activity, in order to meet a specified objective" (p. 521). They outlined three broad perspectives of governance within sociology: interest-based accounts in which governance is thought to be shaped by influential groups with materially-based interests; value-based approaches, which assess the extent to which politics and the state are reflective of institutionalized values and culture; and governmentality, "a 'micro' approach that examines the 'mentalities' of government and the impact of governance on the subject-positions of those who are governed" (pp. 521-522). Scholars working within this third perspective generally concern themselves with the relationships between power, knowledge, and subjectivity. Focusing on the "conduct of conduct," governance scholars consider how power constructs and shapes "systems of knowledge" that influence people's behaviour and their understanding of "how to live a 'moral life'" (p. 524). According to Garland (1999), this framework attends to not only the forms of rule authorities put in place to control specific populations, but also the ways in which these populations internalize specific beliefs and practices. It is, in essence, a set of techniques by which state authorities act *through* rather than *on* the designated individuals and communities to render them governable (pp. 15, 21). Rather than relying on overt methods of control, governance works to subtly align the attitudes and beliefs of targeted populations with the material and social requirements of the governing institution.

In their article "Governing the Young," Ericson and Haggerty (1999) discussed how discourses of being "at-risk" are used to extend interventions beyond strictly traditional notions of policing. The police become one among many institutions – including, and especially, schools – that classify and manage youth through indirect methods of classification and intervention. Youth, particularly racialized and marginalized youth, are subjected to a variety of discourses and persuasions aimed at understanding and subsequently improving their lives and future opportunities. Raby (2002) wrote that, "Except perhaps for childhood, adolescence is one of the times of life that is most over determined" (p. 431); and later she pointed out that, "Young people's selves are constituted through techniques that foster self-governance" (2005, p. 74). Ideally, this self-governance leads to youth embracing, "a certain *kind* of self, one that is restrained, docile, and firmly located within hierarchy, property relations, equality, gender, and age" (Raby, 2005, p. 75). Through discourses of risk, youth are governed by linking notions of rights and opportunity to questions of conduct, restraint, and respect for authority.

223

Kelly (2000) wrote that "the crisis of youth-at-risk is a key marker in debates about youth" (p. 463) and that identifying youth as "at-risk" and subsequently mobilizing around this designation regulate and recode "institutionally structured relations of class, gender, ethnicity, (dis)ability and geography" (p. 469). This manufactured crisis serves to make youth and their parents themselves responsible for their situation and, at the same time, justifies invasive surveillance of risk-designated populations. Youth programs, such as YIPI, engage in this type of work to the extent that they stress individual responsibility and proper conduct as prerequisites to accessing opportunities which are considered necessary to improving the life chances, or potential success, of marginalized youth.

As a program, YIPI claims to provide an opportunity to youth that will also work in the interests of the police in ways that help to not only improve relations between police and marginalized youth but also promote the Toronto Police Service as a potential career option – an "employer of choice." This can be considered interest-convergence, a concept that, first articulated by Derrick Bell (1980), proposes that measures promoting racial progress are only accommodated to the degree that they also support elite white interests. Referring to the situation of Blacks, Bell stated: "The interest of blacks in achieving racial equality will be accommodated only when it converges with the interest of whites" (p. 523). The 1954 U.S. Supreme Court decision that prohibited state-sponsored school segregation (Brown vs. The Board of Education, 1954) served as a reference for Bell who argued that:

> the Court's long-held position on [issues of segregation] cannot be understood without some consideration of the decision's value to whites, not simply those concerned about the immorality of racial inequality, but also those whites in policymaking positions able to see the economic and political advances at home and abroad that would follow abandonment of segregation. (p. 524)

According to Bell, for many whites, the principle of racial equality was sufficient motivation to support school desegregation, but that, by itself, was insufficient to bring about reform.

In this context, programs that promise movement towards inclusivity or equality are structured in ways that are least threatening to elite interests. As such, while people may agree to measures providing opportunity to those deemed less fortunate, few are willing to engage in action which may result in a loss of status or privilege for themselves (Bell, 1980, p. 522). In his contribution to the conception of interest-convergence, Jackson (2011) contended that the factors that work as incentives for people to engage in progressive action operate on the basis of at least four disaggregated interests: material, emotional, psychological, and moral (pp. 439-442). While Material Interests involve actions that result in tangible economic benefits, Emotional and Moral Interests are more subtle and contribute to individuals feeling a sense of wellbeing and moral triumph over their actions as they use their privileged position to help others (p. 441). Finally, Psychological Interests refer to the assurance gained when practices and outcomes reaffirm individuals' fundamental worldviews. Essentially, Interest-convergence considers how those in privileged positions tend to be supportive of change that often benefits them, but at the very least, does not threaten or challenge their social and economic status. As Milner (2008) claimed:

> The point is that people in power are sometimes, in theory, supportive of policies and practices that do not oppress and discriminate against others as long as they – those in power – do not have to alter their own ways and systems, statuses, and privileges of experiencing life. (p. 334)

Canadian multiculturalism's policies, programs and practices are appropriate references here, in that they do more to maintain the status quo pertaining to dominant-subordinate ethno-racial stratification than to bring about cultural democracy. Essentially, the multicultural discourse which is premised on tolerance, personal encounters through cultural exchanges, and freedom of ethnic cultural expression as a means to facilitate integration (as opposed to assimilation) and achieve productive participation in the society, have been unable to avert or surmount the institutional and societal racism and discriminatory practices that account for poor police-youth and police-community relations (James, 2010; Perry, 2011). Indeed, state multiculturalism, as Perry (2011) proffers, is based on an ideology that promotes an idealized notion of cultural interaction to achieve tolerance and respect and to counter discriminatory attitudes and practices, but it does little to address persistent economic and institutional inequalities. In fact, Haque (2012) argues that the formulation of Canada's multicultural framework was intended to marginalize Aboriginals and other "cultural groups" by forswearing racialized exclusions in a way that preserved "white-settler hegemony" (p. 239).

Programs and measures, such as YIPI, that are designed to mutually benefit youth and police, are not necessarily without merit. But taking into account racialization, governance, and the interest-convergence principle in Canada's multicultural context allow us to critically examine how these types of programs can be, often inadvertently, structured to ensure that the interests of the powerful are protected and promoted. The claim that the Youth in Policing Initiative is able to benefit both youth and police because they mutually gain greater understanding and appreciation of each other, obfuscates the fact that the unequal power dynamic between the two results in the youth being more likely to adopt, embrace, and promote the interests of the police.

THE YOUTH IN POLICING INITIATIVE AND ITS GENESIS

The Youth in Policing Initiative (YIPI), established in 2006, is a program funded in partnership with the Ministry of Children and Youth Services, the Toronto Police Services Board, and the Toronto Police Service. Every summer, YIPI hires up to 150 youth to work in police divisions across the city. The program begins with a paid week-long orientation session designed to introduce youth to the Toronto Police Services and for them to hear the expectations of the program.

After the orientation week, the participants are placed in one of 45 different divisions where they work 35 hours a week for six weeks of the summer. Participants are paid slightly above minimum wage.

YIPI was initially conceived as a response to the social and employment needs of marginalized youth who reside in Toronto's priority areas, and was occasioned, in part, by the concerns of 2005 – the so-called "summer of the gun" – when some 52 homicides involving guns occurred in Toronto. The establishment of YIPI also coincided with a number of reports on the social and economic conditions of youth which precipitated youth violence in Toronto.

The reports *Poverty by Postal Code* (United Way, 2004) and *Strong Neighbourhoods: A Call to Action* (United Way, 2003) identified an increasing concentration of poverty in specific Toronto neighbourhoods, noting that this situation, in part, was a product of public investment in services and facilities that were not keeping pace with the demographic shifts that were occurring in the city. Calling for a place-based approach to services, both reports suggested that government agencies, ministries, and departments needed to invest in strategies aimed at strengthening what they identified as "priority" areas of the city. In their report on school safety following a shooting inside a Toronto school in one of these "priority areas," Falconer, MacKinnon, and Edwards (2008) stressed that the focus on discipline and zero tolerance was failing to decrease concerns of violence in schools and communities. The *Road to Health* report, commissioned by the Toronto District School Board, indicated that "hope needs to be restored through programs and initiatives that create prospects for success for youth who are currently on the outside looking in" (p. 6).

And following their "review of the roots of youth violence" in Toronto for the Ontario provincial government, McMurtry and Curling (2008) called for a move towards strengthening neighbourhoods and community agencies and an engagement of youth by providing them with hope and opportunities through positive and constructive community initiatives. The report indicated that while Ontario is a relatively safe province, there was an increasing concentration of violence and hopelessness found among youth who are often from racialized minority backgrounds and reside in disadvantaged communities (p. 102). Commissioners McMurtry and Curling emphasized that these trends were most evident in neighbourhoods characterized by higher concentrations of poverty, structural manifestations of racism, family breakdown, and the lack of both adequate transportation and public space for gathering and recreation (p. 141). In this regard, they asserted that "limited resources must be put where they will have the biggest impact on the roots of violence involving youth" (p. 144). In this context, YIPI is a program that seeks to enhance the relationship between marginalized youth and the police and, by extension, police and these priority-designated communities.

RACIALIZATION, GEOGRAPHY, AND "RISK"

As stated earlier, the youth accepted into YIPI were all required to reside in priority or marginalized neighbourhoods. One of the key criteria for determining "priority" was the disproportionately large concentrations of immigrants and racialized minorities in these neighbourhoods. In what Wacquant (2008) described as the, "moral panic about the 'ghettoization' of postcolonial immigrants in their urban periphery" (p. 200), marginalized youth become the targets of special attention, singled out for interventions designed to serve "at risk" youth. The selection criterion for YIPI reflects these anxieties. While two-thirds of the participating youth were born in Canada, the majority were born to immigrant parents and over 93% were non-white, with the largest proportion (almost half) identifying themselves as Black. While the perception was that these were "at-risk" youth based on where they lived, in reality, according to their interviews, few of these young people experienced significant problems at school. And none of them had a history of trouble with law enforcement. This has to do with the fact that to participate in the program, the youth could not have a police record or outstanding criminal charges. Nevertheless, despite the actual behaviour of these youth, their geographic location in priority areas positioned them as "at risk," and therefore in need of intervention.

Indeed, a number of police officers, even as they questioned the youth's participation in the program, admitted that the young people assigned to them were not, according to one officer, "problem kids." "These are good kids," claimed another. One officer agreed that in the priority neighbourhoods, you would more likely find, "parents who are struggling," but added that you will, "get that a lot in other neighbourhoods as well." But other members of the service who seemed more invested in YIPI would readily employ the language of "at risk" youth in their assessments of the youth. They emphasized the notion that while the youth may not seem "bad," without programs like this, their environment and lack of opportunity might lead them down a wrong path.

One supervisor commented, "You never know what would happen," adding:

> People get to where they are based on their surroundings. If we can take someone from these priority neighbourhoods and be a positive influence on their life and they in turn can go out and influence someone and turn them from going down the path of destruction, we can accomplish a lot and I think we have done that. You never know what would happen.

Another supervisor concurred, claiming that it was the program that was responsible for the youth's good behaviour because of the healthy positive environment provided to them. In other words, the youth were seen as pre-disposed to risk, hence the need to provide them with the right environment that would help to mitigate deviant behaviour:

> Given the opportunity, these kids are making the best of it and people are confusing it with [whether they are good or bad kids]. And it's not. Give a

227

kid an opportunity, encourage them, give them a healthy, positive environment and then you see what happens.

This supervisor claimed that with youth, "There's a level of being influenced by your peers that we try to facilitate."

Insofar as these youth's place of residence positioned them as being at risk, and hence, as Kelly (2000) would say, posing "dangerous possibilities," then they were in need of "increased surveillance of, and intervention into, [their] lives by regulatory authorities" (p. 463). Therefore their very presence has them in need of intervention, for they are "at risk" of being deviant. "Risk" is transferred from geographic location, or neighbourhoods, to the bodies of the youth who inhabit these areas. And once established, these risks must be effectively managed.

YOUTH GOVERNANCE

One of the guiding assumptions behind YIPI is that youth from priority neighbourhoods and police hold negative stereotypes of each other. The expectation is that bringing them together in a program that allows them to "get to know" each other will help dispel these attitudes, thereby improving police-youth and police-community relationships. There would be a mutual exchange. In practice, however, while we observed a significant change in the attitudes of the youth towards police, this change was not mirrored by changing police attitudes. In essence, the youth came to like the police more, while the officers we interviewed demonstrated more ambivalent and unchanging attitudes towards the youth. In fact, the attitudes of the youth who participated in YIPI were effectively brought in line with those of the policing institution.

While the youths' opinions varied and ranged from those who had an outright dislike for the police, to those who claimed they had never paid much attention to the policing of their neighbourhood, one consistent theme voiced by most of the youth was that they had very little direct contact with police officers or knowledge of policing before participating in YIPI. The participants spoke most frequently of being intimidated by police and how they were initially nervous about working with the police. As one female participant put it, "I was scared of the police, I was." And another, claiming to be scared about going to work in a police station, commented, "I thought they were going to be like strict, kind of like: 'This is what we're going to do, this is the way we're going to do it, be quiet.'" One male participant added, "I thought they'd be all like don't talk to me," and another male added, "I thought the police were going to be really tough people."

That participants had very little contact with police and even fewer encounters with individual police officers prior to their participation in YIPI seemingly contributed to the distance they kept from police. By the end of the six-week YIPI program, however, the participants who had spoken of being intimidated by the police all claimed that their experience had greatly changed their perceptions. One youth said emphatically, "I personally love everybody here!" Almost every youth we spoke with made some kind of comment about coming to the realization that the police were normal, or even nice, people. They remarked, "When I go to my station they're all nice, they like to play around. They're just normal people." Another agreed, saying, "They're really down to earth – very personable and stuff." A male participant said, "Now I know police are regular people." And a female participant added, "Now I see how they are; it's like they're human just like us. They're doing a job just like everybody else."

The original reluctance many of the youth felt surrounding police officers and policing at the beginning of the summer was replaced by wholesale endorsements of police officers. In large part, this was accomplished by officers going out of their way to make the youth feel comfortable. The youth seemed to separate the individual personalities of the officers from their role as representatives of the police. The preponderance of comments about police being "normal" or "just like us" powerfully counteracted any negative assessments the youth had based on the history and representation of policing in their neighbourhoods and among their friends. Their perceptions were changed in a way that was both subtle and effective.

The officers' sense of humour was something that the YIPI participants really seemed to appreciate. A few of them told lengthy stories about funny things officers said or did. The influence of the interpersonal relationships the youth believed they had formed with police officers was also noted in their journals. One participant wrote after orientation week, "Listening to other police officers' experiences really showed me that police officers were as real as us, and that opened my eyes to see that officers are human beings too." Another commented that after spending a day with two officers and going to lunch with them, "They are no longer 'just police officers' but they are my friends." And another participant concluded her journal entry with the observation that, "police officers are human beings, who have opinions and feelings just like everyone else.... I am amazed to see how kind-hearted and dedicated each and every worker is."

While these reactions may seem almost trivial, the enthusiasm with which the participants talked about their changing perceptions was profound. These interactions had an effect on all of the participants with whom we spoke. Perhaps the most remarkable aspect of the youths' changing attitudes was that they were the result of what would seem to be the rather benign actions of their police supervisors. As well as the humour of the officers that was frequently cited, the YIPI participants frequently gave examples of being taken to lunch or coffee, or having an officer they did not know speak to them in the elevator as having a significant impact on their feelings towards the police. There was a sense of awe that these people, in powerful positions, were paying attention to, and in some cases, helping them.

Many of the police officers also recognized and mentioned the significance of including the youth in fun or interesting activities. One officer expressed surprise at her youths' enthusiasm, claiming "I was surprised at the end when they said this was the best job ever because I had given them such tedious tasks. I thought they were going to hate it, but they enjoyed themselves." Others talked of taking the youth to meetings or different events. Officers were often willing to provide job references for former YIPI participants and this was something that was highly valued by the youth. The interpersonal aspect of the program was the issue that most profoundly affected the youth's perceptions of and attitudes towards the police. The most striking statement came from the male participant who had previously stated that he thought police officers were "assholes." When asked how much his perception of the police had changed, he said it had completely altered his views "because now, when I see a cop car, I don't look to see who's in it, I look to see who's driving it."

The youth who now looked to see who is driving the cop car has effectively switched allegiances. He no longer saw the police as an institution; rather, he viewed police officers as individual people to whom he could easily relate. But of course, police officers operate within an institution and their work, priorities, and outlooks are guided by that institutional cultural ethos. Rather than a mutual exchange, the officers' positive assessments of the program were largely dependent on the extent to which they believed the youths' attitudes towards police had changed. As Garland (1999) noted, the central goal of governance through governmentality is to "align the actors' objectives with those of the authorities; to make them active partners" (p. 20). This is YIPI's outstanding achievement. Through the classification of these youth as "at-risk" and the subsequent intervention and opportunities provided to them, the policing organization effectively created a group of allies within the neighbourhoods where police-community and police-youth relations are deemed most problematic. The admiration the youths developed for individual police officers was quickly and easily translated into an increased acceptance of and endorsement of policing. One participant commented that she realized: "Police have every bit of interest in saving our communities from various harm." Another one captured what seemed to be the general sentiment when she claimed: "I have to admit that I really have been quite oblivious to what the police actually do."

This style of governance – indirectly aligning the attitudes and beliefs of youth to those of the institution – is not something that is explicitly pursued. In fact, it is more effective due to its subtle and indirect nature. Youth are exposed to police officers on an interpersonal level where individual officer's personalities are allowed to "win them over," but they are also brought into the institution and exposed to policing outside of its enforcement capacity. Field trips to the mounted unit, the marine unit, the canine unit, and the Emergency Task Force were extremely popular with the youth because they exposed them to the more exciting aspects of policing, but in a way that was divorced from their actual enforcement function. The youth were also often included in the community relations aspects of policing. Throughout the program, the affability of police officers was linked to very select aspects of policing that resulted in an image of not just police officers, but the job itself, as friendly, helpful, and just.

The youth talked of how this program helped to dispel negative stereotypes of the police. A male participant said: "The media portrays the police as aggressive as this bad type of police and being here dispels everything." Another jumped in when someone brought up people's complaints about police not being involved in the community:

See how she said that? At my division they have all these BBQs and everybody's there [meaning police] but barely anybody ever shows up. On Saturday we had one where they brought the horses and stuff and the old police cars and everything and about 50 people showed up .... People just don't want to show up.

Accordingly, as one young woman explained, it is through YIPI that they have become aware of efforts by the police to reach out to the community. As she said:

[YIPI] opens up people's minds to what the police do. Because you might think the police are only out there to get you and doing negative things. But once you work here you see more about what they do. You know how people always say police stop you randomly; they always have no reason for stopping you? They [police] explain why they stop you – they might get a call or something and you might fit that description. They're just there to help you.

Instead of a more balanced view of the tensions between police and communities, many of the youth become ardent defenders of the actions of the police that others tend to criticize.

The youth's realization about the benevolent nature of policing come about as a result of what Jay (2003) called a "hidden curriculum of hegemony" (p. 6). Through the program, youth were socialized into the value system of the police organization through techniques designed to foster self-governance and restraint (see Raby, 2005). In this process, as Sukarieh and Tannock (2008) pointed out with reference to poor and working-class youth, their values and behaviours are "moulded and remoulded to fit functionally within industrial and post-industrial capitalist society by the enormous and complex structures and practices of schools, juvenile courts, youth organizations, psychological counselling and psychiatric treatment" (p. 304). Furthermore, such institutionally sponsored youth and summer employment programs, like YIPI, are enticing techniques to pacify disillusioned youth and condition them into a culture of "responsibilisation and entrepreneurship" (p. 309). The changing attitudes of the youth and their enthusiastic endorsements of not only police officers but police practices after participating in the program, was not an outcome that was nefariously designed, but it worked well to advance the institutional interests of the police.

YIPI AND INTEREST CONVERGENCE

In addition to exposing youth to police and thereby enhancing police-youth relationships, YIPI also seeks to promote the Toronto Police Service as a potential career choice for these marginalized youth, and eventually to have them act as ambassadors for the police in their communities. This might be considered an effective means of interest-convergence in that the program provided these marginalized youth with a valuable work experience, opportunities to make money, and connections with individuals and an institution that can benefit them in their future employment. At the same time, the police were able to boost their organizational image and encourage potential future recruits. The expectation is that through the employment process, both police and youth would develop greater mutual understanding and respect.

Indeed, YIPI did serve the interests of the youth who participated in the program. Most indicated that they chose to apply to the program either to gain meaningful work experience (i.e., a summer job) or because they had an interest in a career in policing that they wanted to explore. Having heard about the program from friends, family members, teachers, guidance counsellors, and school resource officers, participants believed working with the police for the summer was a good chance to gain and develop the skills and connections that would help their future career goals. While at the beginning of the summer, the money they would make was most frequently mentioned as what would be most beneficial to them, by the end of their summer employment, participants mentioned that the increased knowledge about police work and the job skills they gained throughout their employment were, in fact, more significant.

In one focus group, when participants were asked how many were now considering a career in policing, five of the eight youth raised their hands. A female participant who did not raise her hand mentioned that she had always wanted to be a social worker. To this one of the male participants immediately responded: "You can do that with the police." Even those who had other career aspirations began to see policing as an option. A male participant stated:

> Honestly, this is another career option for me but it's my second option. I want to be a psychologist and take either social work or teaching because I like listening to people and helping them with their problems.

But more significantly, it was the work-specific aspects of their experience on which they elaborated most. Participants expressed that, even though most of the work that they performed in their various placements was administrative-help, they gained a great deal of appreciation for the skills and experiences they were able to obtain. They believed that the skills they acquired would help them in the future. One female participant, for example, spoke of how she spent most of her time filing papers. Rather than viewing this negatively, she saw it as positive because, "It teaches you how to be well organized." Another one spoke about the work she did researching organizations and inviting their members to a police conference on diversity. She saw it as teaching her to be resourceful. Yet another called the administrative work useful because: "I can take the skills I've learned and then any office I go to I know what to do. It's easy for me." A number of participants spoke of learning to use Microsoft Excel. While these were all benefits cited by the participants and thus represent how their interests were served, it is useful to note the extent to which they also correspond to the subtle ways in which their learning, skill development, and knowledge were regulated by the police.

The police gained much from their interactions with the youth without having to sacrifice any of their interests, practices, or outlooks on the nature of police relations with youth and communities. Their role was affirmed and justified by the changing attitudes of the youth. Furthermore, materially and morally, much of the benefits accrued to the police were not only through the relatively cheap labour the YIPI youth provided, but by the ambassadorial role the youth took on. This could be seen in the reflections of the youth and officers and at the 2011 official launch. A senior police officer asked rhetorically during one interview, "Is it a good program?" and answered, indicating, "It's an excellent program, because it's giving those 150 kids that opportunity to go out there and do something." That YIPI presented a chance for both individual officers and the police service as a whole to celebrate their efforts to reach out to marginalized youth, and, in turn, change attitudes of the youth towards police, evinced much satisfaction.

The primary benefit of YIPI to the police, however, was that the enthusiasm and increased knowledge about policing the youth gained, effectively positioned the youth to be ambassadors for the police. Through winning the support and allegiance of the youth who participated in the program, the police service effectively recruited allies to enhance and promote their image within the communities where relationships with police were most problematic. For instance, with her new awareness and positive viewpoint of the police, a female participant said: "I told my friend make sure you sign up next year because it's really good." Another reflected that he was able to use the knowledge he gained to inform his friend about how to become a police officer:

> I was able to fill in one of my friends with the requirements of becoming a police officer. I told him about the training and the college he will have to attend. I was also able to assure some people that the police as a whole are not bad people. They are regular people like everyone else and they shouldn't judge all police by the actions of just a few.

While working in the interest of the police service, this capacity to "teach" their friends about policing also benefited some youth in that they acquired additional social capital upon which they could call when interacting with friends, family members, businesses, other institutions, and society as a whole. While many of the youth were guarded about who they told about participating in the program – citing the negative opinions of police for their discomfort with widely advertising their summer job – they spoke of their parents' pride and their friends envy over their stimulating and respectable summer experience.

The increased knowledge they had gained over the summer, as well as the personal relationships they had formed, positioned them as ambassadors for the Toronto Police Service. While they still perceived other youth in their community to have largely negative views of the police, they enthusiastically provided other friends and family members with information about YIPI and policing in general. All of this, the police were able to accomplish without having to adjust or change any of their own practices or assumptions.

CONCLUSION

The YIPI program emerged from an urban social context in which government and law enforcement officials sought to address, if not pre-empt, social problems specifically crime and violence – resulting from the poverty and social isolation that were to be found in Toronto's under-serviced priority-identified neighbourhoods. As youth in these neighbourhoods are considered to be "at-risk," authorities sought to develop programs based on racialized assumptions about possible social problems and risk. In many cases, the focus on Toronto's priority neighbourhoods means that resulting programs are unwittingly premised on preconceived notions or stereotypes about the youth's need for intensive intervention based on geography and race. Increasingly, these interventions operate in subtle ways to regulate youth into what are deemed appropriate values and beliefs including respect for authority. The consequence of these approaches, with their focus on conduct and behaviour, is that they promote and achieve the kind of reforms that never questions structural and systemic inequalities.

Clearly, the participating youth considered YIPI to have offered them valuable experiences that contributed to them having more positive attitudes towards police. That it provided them opportunities to "get to know" the police, and purportedly inspired them to actively pursue their goals and ambitions, are indeed benefits. But, while affording the youth material resources, as well as social and educational opportunities, the structure and organization of the program simultaneously worked to entrench and privilege the institutional interests of police. It could have been otherwise, if only YIPI operated within a context of institutional commitment to honesty, integrity and sincerity in tackling structural inequity that underlie the problems of the youth and their communities. In the absence of this commitment, the question of why police-youth and police-community relations in these priority areas were in need of improvement in the first place remains unaddressed.

NOTES

[1] An earlier version of this chapter appeared in the *Canadian Ethnic Studies Journal*, 2011/2012, 43-44(3-1) with the title, "'We Expect Much of You": Enlisting Youth in the Policing of Marginalized Communities', and under the authorship of Selom Chapman-Nyaho, Carl E. James, and Dani Kwan-Lafond. As such this chapter has been written in collaboration with Dani.

[2] The reports *Poverty by Postal Code* and *Strong Neighbourhoods: A Call to Action* identified an increasing concentration of poverty in specific Toronto neighbourhoods, noting that this situation, in part, was a product of public investment in services and facilities that were not keeping pace with these demographic shifts taking part in the city (United Way, 2003, 2004). Calling for a placed-based approach to services, both reports suggested that government agencies, ministries, and departments need to invest in strategies aimed at strengthening what they identified as thirteen "priority" areas of the city. YIPI participants are all drawn from these neighbourhoods, but the program also obtained permission to include an additional neighbourhood based on the notion that because that area is home to Canada's largest social housing project, it would contain many youth who could be classified as "at-risk."

[3] In addition to our participation in the program's activities, we held two focus groups with 16 YIPI participants and interviewed 15 Toronto Police Service employees (police and civilians) assigned to supervise the youth. The youth were selected based on their availability and the Toronto Police Services employees were drawn from a list of all of the employees who had direct supervisory roles for the youth and who agreed to be interviewed. We administered surveys at the beginning and again just before the conclusion of the program to note any change in the youths' attitudes towards the police. We also conducted an analysis of the journal entries all of the youth were required to keep throughout their employment.

REFERENCES

Bell, D. (1980). Brown v. board of education and the interest-convergence dilemma. *Harvard Law Review, 93*(3), 518-533.

Charles, H. (2011). Toward a critical race theory of education. *Contemporary Justice Review, 11*(1), 63-65.

Ericson, R. V., & Haggerty, K. D. (1999). Governing the young. In R. Smandych (Ed.), *Governable places: Readings on governmentality and crime control* (pp. 163-190). Hampshire: Ashgate Publishing Ltd.

Falconer, J. N., MacKinnon, L., & Edwards, P. (2008). *The road to health: A final report on school safety*. Toronto: Toronto District School Board.

Fox, N. J., & Ward, K. J. (2008). What governs governance, and how does it evolve? The sociology of governance-in-action. *British Journal of Sociology, 59*(3), 519-538.

Garland, D. (1999). "Governmentality" and the problem of crime. In R. Smandych (Ed.), *Governable places: Readings on governmentality and crime control* (pp. 15-43). Hampshire: Ashgate Publishing Ltd.

Haque, E. (2012). *Multiculturalism within a bilingual framework: Language, race, and belonging in Canada*. Toronto: University of Toronto Press.

Jackson, T. A. (2011). Which interests are served by the principle of interest convergence? Whiteness, collective trauma, and the case for anti-racism. *Race Ethnicity and Education, 14*(4), 435-459.

James, C. E. (2010). *Seeing ourselves: Exploring race, ethnicity and culture* (4th ed.). Toronto: Thompson Educational Publishing, Inc.

James, C. (2012). Students "at risk": Stereotypes and the schooling of black boys. *Urban Education, 47*(2), 464-494.

Jay, M. (2003). Critical race theory, multicultural education, and the hidden curriculum of hegemony. *Multicultural Perspectives, 5*(4), 3-9.

Kelly, P. (2000). The dangerousness of youth-at-risk: The possibilities of surveillance and intervention in uncertain times. *Journal of Adolescence, 23*(4), 463-476.

McMurtry, R., & Curling, A. (2008). *The review of the roots of youth violence*. Toronto: Government of Ontario.

Milner, H. R. (2008). Critical race theory and interest convergence as analytic tools in teacher education policies and practices. *Journal of Teacher Education, 59*(4), 332-346.

Perry, B. (2011). *Diversity, crime, and justice in Canada*. Don Mills, Ontario: Oxford University Press.

Raby, R. (2002). A tangle of discourses: Girls negotiating adolescence. *Journal of Youth Studies, 5*(4), 425-448.

Raby, R. (2005). Polite, well-dressed and on time: Secondary school conduct codes and the production of docile citizens. *The Canadian Review of Sociology and Anthropology, 42*(1), 71-91.

Smandych, R. (1999). Introduction: The Place of Governance Studies in Law and Criminology. In R. Smandych (Ed.), *Governable places: Readings on governmentality and crime control* (pp. 1-14). Hampshire: Ashgate Publishing Ltd.

Stovall, D. (2008). Forging community in race and class: Critical race theory and the quest for social justice in education. *Race, Ethnicity and Education, 9*(3), 243-259.

Sukarieh, M., & Tannock, S. (2008). In the best interests of youth or neoliberalism? The World Bank & the New Global Youth Empowerment Project. *Journal of Youth Studies, 11*(3), 301-312.

Toronto Police Service. (2011). YIPIs on the TPS frontlines. Retrieved from http://www.torontopolice.on.ca/modules.php?op=modload&name=News&file=article&sid=5496&mode=thread&order=0&thold=0

Trevino, A.J., Harris, M.A., & Wallace, D. (2011). What's so critical about critical race theory. *Contemporary Justice* Review, *11*(1), 7-10.

United Way. (2003). *Strong neighbourhoods: A call to action*. Toronto: City of Toronto and United Way of Greater Toronto.

United Way. (2004). *Poverty by postal code: The geography of neighbourhood poverty 1981-2001.* Toronto: United Way of Greater Toronto and The Canadian Council on Social Development.

Vaughan, B. (2000). The Government of Youth: Disorder *and* Dependence? *Social and Legal Studies,* 9(3), 347-366.

Wacquant, L. (2008). *Urban outcasts: A comparative sociology of advanced marginality.* Cambridge: Polity Press.

Youth in Policing Initiative. (2008). *Youth in policing initiative: Final report.* Toronto, ON: Toronto Police Service.

Carl James
Faculty of Education
York University

Selom Chapman-Nyaho
Department of Sociology
York University

SECTION IV

MULTICULTURAL EDUCATION

ANNA KIROVA

14. CRITICAL AND EMERGING DISCOURSES IN MULTICULTURAL EDUCATION LITERATURE[1]

An (Updated) Review

INTRODUCTION

Multicultural education in Canada was conceived as a response to cultural pluralism in society. Canadian educational policies, research, and practices, as well as the critique of these practices have followed a singular development path. Educational institutions are seen as having the obligation to provide continuity and content to the ongoing dialogue about the nature of multiculturalism and the management of diversity, and educational reforms are often identified as initiatives needed for the integration of immigrants into majority-language institutions (Kymlicka, 2001). A large scale OECD (2006) study established that a critical factor in Canada's comparative advantage in educating immigrant students is the presence of specific policies to address issues of cultural and linguistic diversity in the school population that emerged under the rubric of multiculturalism (Kymlicka, 2009).

In the past several decades, however, concern has increased among the general public, researchers, and practitioners that schools are poorly equipped to cope with increased diversity and that instead of playing a role in facilitating equity and belonging, they may have become locations that foster isolation and replicate racialized forms of injustice (Wideen & Barnard, 1999). The challenges faced by Black youth in the 1997 racial incidents in Cole Harbour School District High School that resulted in two external reviews (1997 and 2001) and more than 70 recommendations (Chan, 2007), and the fact that the second-generation immigrant youth (e.g., Filipino-Canadian youth) still experience a sense of dislocation and restrictions on belonging enforced by daily racism in the Canadian system (Pratt, 2002), indicate that multiculturalism is unable to provide protection from the sense of exclusion. The problem is rooted, in part, in the fact that "race relations are not always an explicit goal of multicultural education or multicultural policies" (Chan, 2007, p. 142).

The expectation that multicultural education policies and practices will result in equal participation of all students in education and thus allow for equal participation in the public and economic spheres has been challenged by the fact that visible-minority students' dropout rates exceed those of the Canadian-born (Derwing, DeCorby, Ichikawa, & Jamieson, 1999; Watt & Roessingh, 2001) and that some racial groups are overrepresented in the criminal system (Ngo, Rossiter,

S. Guo & L. Wong (eds.), Revisiting Multiculturalism in Canada, 239–254.

& Stewart, 2013). A number of studies (Gee & Prus, 2000; Kazemipur & Halli, 2000; Li, 1998) show that "non-White origin creates a penalty for visible minorities in the labour market" (Li, 1998, p. 126). The findings of these studies indicate that the idea of liberal multiculturalism has not been achieved if measured by household income and, as a result, racialized groups are more highly represented among the poor than are White Canadians (Galabuzi, 2005).

The purpose of this chapter is threefold. First, to examine the critical discourses in the academic literature on multicultural education pointing to the major conceptual flaws in multicultural education theory that have led to practices that have achieved effects opposite to the intent of the Canadian Multiculturalism Act. Second, to identify some of the suggestions being made in the context of the post-multiculturalism discourse defined as alternatives to multiculturalism on how to address these flaws in multicultural education theory and practice. And third, to discuss some implications of the key findings of the review for multicultural education.

A BRIEF HISTORICAL OVERVIEW OF MULTICULTURAL EDUCATION IN CANADA

The emergence of multicultural education in the Canadian educational system is influenced by the implementation of the 1971 federal Multicultural Policy statements (James, 2003; James & Shadd, 2001), the 1982 Canadian Charter of Rights and Freedoms, and the 1988 Canadian Multiculturalism Act. Multiculturalism policy has evolved from "celebrating differences" in the 1970s to "managing diversity" in the 1980s, to "constructive engagement" in the 1990s, largely in response to specific pressures and issues of the day (Kunz & Sykes, 2007, p. 6). Dwindling support for multiculturalism in the 1990s rebounded following the 1995 Québec referendum, when only a slim majority voted against separation, and as the goals of multicultural policy increasingly shifted to fostering a sense of shared citizenship through "constructive engagement" and the removal of barriers to full economic and civic participation. A focus on "inclusive citizenship" characterized multiculturalism policy in the first decade of the 21st century due, in part, to the attacks on the World Trade Centre in New York on September 11, 2001, and advances in global and instantaneous communications, and concerns about the possibility divisive effects of multiculturalism amidst increasing global tensions (Kunz & Sykes, 2007). From its inception, multicultural education has been linked to the goals of the original federal multiculturalism policy which promotes ethnocultural retention, fosters appreciation of the cultural heritages of others, and assumes increased intergroup harmony (Lund, 2003).

A major problem of the implementation of Canadian multicultural education is that "the Multiculturalism clause [of the federal Multicultural Policy] for education is vague" and that the "lack of federal control over education, and provincial legislation in general, has limited federal ability to influence education in this direction to any meaningful degree" (Ghosh & Abdi, 2004, p. 45). Because education is a provincial responsibility, multiculturalism, as a federal policy, is interpreted differently by the provincial educational authorities and is translated into varying forms of educational policies. Currently, five provinces have officially accepted multiculturalism in education, with Saskatchewan being the first to implement this policy in 1974 followed by Ontario in 1977 and Quebec with its own intercultural education perspective. Other provinces in Canada, such as Alberta in 1984, Manitoba in 1992, and British Columbia in 1993, have followed suit with Multiculturalism Acts or combined acts and policies that include human rights and citizenship. Since 1995, some of these acts have been revised, repealed, or reduced in composition and statue (Chan, 2007).

Despite the differences among multicultural educational policies across Canada, a synthesis of the components of multicultural education identifies three specific goals: "(1) equivalency in achievement; (2) more positive intergroup attitudes; and (3) developing pride in heritage" (Kehoe & Mansfield, 1997, p. 3). These goals are to be achieved using a number of strategies including, but not limited to, teaching English as a second language while encouraging retention of heritage languages; removing ethnocentric bias from the curriculum; providing information about other cultures, which follows the criteria of teaching about similarities, institutionalizing in-school cultural celebrations as well as those of the Anglo-Celtic majority; and acquainting all students with their own and other cultures through the exchange of literature, art, dance, food, clothing, folk rhymes, religion, and so forth.

The Report on the State of the Art of Multicultural Education in Canada led by Keith A. McLeod (1993) from 1992 to 1996 identifies the following major tasks in the field of education: (a) to develop a more inclusive conceptualization, and (b) to improve curriculum and pedagogy. The report stresses that the current climate has reopened the debate on multiculturalism and Canadian identity (Elliston, 1997). From a Canadian perspective, the future of multiculturalism, as McCreath (1997) suggests, needs to be seen in the context of the question of "whether there is a future for Canada" (p. 24). More recently Ghosh and Abdi (2004) concluded that multicultural and intercultural education programs only theoretically give access for all ethnocultural groups and that these programs have not resulted in equal participation in the educational or economic spheres. Thus they claim, "Canadians cannot afford to ignore the implications of a failed multicultural policy, and now face a challenge of redefining meaning in the quest for peace and collective prosperity" (p. 139).

CRITICISMS OF MULTICULTURAL EDUCATION

The ability of multicultural education to become a vehicle for achieving justice, liberty, and equality that pervade the social, economic, and political life of society (Giroux, 2001) has been challenged since its inception.

The first criticisms of multicultural education come from anti-racist theorists who are typically seen as holding opposing views to those of multiculturalists (e.g., Dei, 1996; Tator & Henry, 1991). They stress that multicultural education ignores racial differences and racial discrimination and fails to challenge the organizational structures of institutions as a basis for this discrimination. The debate between the two views on the focus of multicultural education is described by some as harmful because it diverts educators' attention away from making practical curriculum changes. Others call for a closer examination of similarities of the goals of race relations and multiculturalism articulated in the context of historical racialization and the political and social elements of schooling (Chan, 2007).

The gap between theory and practice is also identified as a major weakness of multicultural education by critical pedagogy theorists (Brown & Kysilka, 1994; May, 1994; Wilhelm, 1994). In their review of multicultural education research from 1990 to 2001, Grant, Elsbree and Fondrie (2004) confirm an earlier description of the field as "troubled" (p. 185) traced to "conceptual confusion, research epistemological bias, funding, [and] research acceptance in the academy" (p. 200). Kincheloe and Steinberg (1997) describe the field as involving conservative, liberal, pluralist, left-essentialist, and critical multiculturalism, and McLaren (1997) adds to the list critical/resistance and revolutionary multiculturalism.

Divisions and communalities between the three theoretical perspectives reviewed in this chapter— antiracism, critical theory, and critical race theory are outlined in the following sections.

Emphasizing Exoticized, Knowable (Other) Cultures Solidifies the Boundaries between Majority and Minority Cultures

As noted above, multicultural education in Canada is premised partly on the idea of the importance of preserving heritage. Critics point out that this emphasis results in "reductive striving for cultural simplicity and knowability" (Walcott, 1997, p. 122). The need for learners to "study 'foreign' cultures, participate in multicultural days or go on field trips to 'cultural communities' and community centres" (Pon, 2000, p. 284) is viewed by multicultural educators as a remedy for the racism and ethnic hostilities that stem from people's lack of familiarity with other cultures (Gosine, 2002).

Teaching students about the similarities and differences of many cultures is encouraged. Activities tend to focus on cultural celebrations and thus remain at the superficial level of food, dance, and music represented in the "*piñata* curriculum or the *snowshoe* curriculum" (Hoffman, 1996, p. 550).

Critics (Stables, 2005) argue that increased knowledge of other groups might, in fact, enhance the feeling of difference, may not necessarily lead to critical examination of the dominant culture, and thus not only does not encourage dialogue among groups about how to work through differences but also leads to folklorization. In some instances, the work done in the name of multicultural education can exoticize and marginalize some groups through its own kind of myth-making as in the case of the "Asiatic Canadians" who, by the very label "model minority" have been denied equal opportunities because they have been portrayed as having reached "the pinnacle of success and were thereby fully incorporated into the fabric of society" (Pak, 2009, p. 47). In others, as Flecha

(1999) shows, the emphasis on the concept of difference can also be used, as in the case of the Neo-Nazis in Europe, for the development of hate programs.

Another outcome of the emphasis by multicultural education on cultural heritage, critics argue, is that the concept of culture is simplified and reified to fit multicultural discourses that support visions of personal, ethnic, or national cultural identity that are fixed, essentialized, stereotyped, and normalized (Bateson, 1994; Perry, 1992; Turner,1993). However, "the tendency to view non-Western cultures as stable, tradition-bound, timeless entities shifts us dangerously back toward viewing others as beings who are profoundly and inherently different from ourselves" (Perry, 1992, p. 52). Treating cultures as discrete units strengthens the boundaries between majority and minority cultures in which difference is created in relation to the "norm." Therefore, non-White, non-Western "citizens" cannot be part of the nation-building project because the nation is constituted by their exclusion (Mitchell, 2001).

Critics in Canadian education academic literature trace the above outcome of multiculturalism back to Trudeau's (1971) pluralistic notion of the Canadian "mosaic" that is still "the favored metaphor of Canadian education administrators and policy makers when seeking to underline the pluralistic nature of their national culture and society" (Carrington & Bonnett, 1997, p. 412). However, in the mosaic metaphor, and in other popular representations of diversity such as quilts, salads, tapestries, and so forth that purport to recognize difference, the unity of cultures is a given. "Difference is thereby diluted or made to support overarching frameworks of shared values or world view firmly enshrined in that privileged existential space called '*culture*'" (emphasis in original, Hoffman, 1996, p. 550).

By Renaming the Difference from Racial to Cultural, White Dominance is Reproduced

Although "multiculturalism policy officially recognized cultural, ethnic, and racial diversity as categories of consideration, rather than categories of separation or exclusion" (Chan, 2007, p. 137), overemphasis on culture had ideological ramifications as it shifted the naming of difference from racial to cultural. For example, in the three multiculturalism policy objectives in which education is implied, there is no reference to race or racial groups:

- The government will assist members of all cultural groups to overcome cultural barriers to full participation in Canadian society.
- The government will promote creative encounters and interchange among all Canadian cultural groups in the interest of national unity.
- The government will continue to assist immigrants to acquire at least one of Canada's official languages in order to become full participants in Canadian society. (Canada, House of Commons, 1971, p. 8545)

This, critics point out, represents a shift in the epistemic site of racism. Willinsky (1999), for example, suggests that "renaming the difference" (p. 95) obscures the important social processes that shape education, and thus "fails to make clear the

KIROVA

relationship between racial and cultural difference" (p. 97). It also results in changing the common code for racial difference in Canada, which is currently *cultural difference* (emphasis in original, Schick & St. Denis, 2005): a quality that racial minority children, especially Aboriginal children, are said to have and that is given as the reason for any lack of school success. Rejection of the biological definition of race and consequent cultural conceptions of race, "indicates a shift in the strategies of racism from overt to covert forms" (Ghosh & Abdi, 2004, p. 58). The shift from racial to cultural difference is viewed as serving the "ideology of racelessness," which is consistent with a "national mythology that Canada is not a racist country" (Backhouse, 1999, p. 14). Multiculturalism, therefore, "has failed to question the norm of whiteness and the domination of white culture by making it invisible. By remaining concealed, and removing the dominant group from race and/or ethnicity, the focus on difference is depoliticized" (Ghosh & Abdi, 2004, p. 34), and asymmetrical relations of power are maintained.

Multiculturalism's View of the Self/Culture Relationship Reiterates the Cultural Hegemony Associated with Eurocentrism

The essentialized views of culture assumed in multicultural education lead to understanding self/cultural identity and self-esteem as fundamentally the same in all cultures and ethnic groups (Hoffman, 1996). This view is found both in Taylor's (1994) and in Kymlicka's (1995) conceptualizations of self as a property of human nature animated by those human qualities assumed to be universal. In multicultural education theory and practice, it is assumed that "there is a one-to-one relationship between self and culture characterized by a clear, fixed, commitment to a particular cultural or ethnic identity" (Hoffman, 1996, p. 557). The argument goes further to suggest that the ownership formulation of identity as something one has (i.e., "All students have an ethnic identity" or "every student has a culture") represents the relationship between person and culture as one of possession, which reflects notions of property rights and makes ethnicity compatible with the dominant economic structure of society. This argument is supported by Appiah's (1997) assertion that most of the social identities that make up our diverse society do not actually have independent cultures that need to be represented in school curricula. He maintains that what are frequently coded as cultural identities are, in fact, social identities that cannot be understood as independent cultures. Thus by being told that everyone should have a clear ethnic or cultural identity, minority children are not only forced to choose their identity, but also to "live within separate spheres defined by the common culture of their race, religion, or ethnicity" (p. 34).

Related to the self/culture property assumptions are identity politics as a response to minority cultures' demands for political and cultural recognition that are articulated with the supposition of the authenticity of minority identity assumed to be an already formed or pre-given stable identity constructed in relation to Whiteness. When "recognition" is understood and practiced as a form of tolerance, it masks or even reiterates the cultural hierarchization associated with Eurocentrism (Cornell & Murphy, 2002).

Multiculturalism's Culturalist Ideology Reinforces Existing Inequalities

Critical theorists (e. g., May, 1994; McCarthy, 1994; McLaren, 1995) and critical race educational theorists (e.g., Bennet, 2001) challenge multicultural education for its obsessive concern with culture, which they claim masks political and socioeconomic conditions that contribute to real inequity in contemporary plural societies, thereby making multiculturalism a safe way of sidestepping the important issue. This in turn leaves the status quo intact. Culturalist orientation can serve only to reinforce the dominant Western ideology that supports existing inequalities. Thus critical theorists assert that multicultural education locates discrimination in individuals' lack of sensitivity and knowledge and assumes that it can be changed by efforts to reduce prejudice, promote cultural awareness and knowledge, and achieve equal accessibility.

In contrast, antiracist education challenges systemic racism, which consists of the policies and practices of organizations that directly or indirectly operate to sustain the advantages of people of certain "social races" (Henry et al., 2009. Antiracist is defined as an "action-oriented strategy for institutional, systemic change to address racism and the interlocking systems of social oppression" (Dei, 1996, p. 25). However, as Willinsky (1999) points out, although "the move from multicultural to anti-racist education is a promising step in pursuit of how collectives are constructed," what remains is "the history of the learned investment in the significance of the differences and divides among humankind" (p. 393).

Multicultural Education is Assimilationist in Creating National Citizenship and Identity

In reviewing the role of the school in revealing national Canadian culture and identity, Diakiw (1997) indicates that the discussion is fraught with dangers, because Trudeau proclaimed in 1971 in the House of Commons, "while we have two official languages, we have no official culture, no one culture is more official than another." Ever since "one enduring feature of Canadian identity is its indefinability" (Derwing & Munro, 2007 p. 99). In defence of multiculturalism, Diakiw (1997) however, stresses that this proclamation has "contributed to a backlash manifested in the Reform Party, Quebec Separatism, and a fundamentalist resurgence across Canada" (p. 27).

Critical theorists pointed out that "multiculturalism posits a serious threat to the school's traditional task of defending and transmitting an authentic national history, a uniform standard of cultural literacy, and singular national identity" (Giroux, 1992 as cited in Diakiw, 1997, p. 27). They argue that multicultural education theory creates problems, contradictions, and dilemmas for members of minority groups living in a liberal democracy. In particular, it has created difficulties for people who find it difficult to reconcile some of the cultural norms and values of two communities and thus has contributed to self-alienation and consequent problems with citizenship and national identity.

Similarly, the promotion of a homogeneous vision of Canada, regardless of the diversity of its citizens, is identified by Strong-Boag (2002) as a sign of Canada's inability to address the shortcomings of citizenship education based on universal citizenship. In her view, women, Native people, and working-class people have suffered exclusion from this kind of citizenship education that has resulted in even greater inequalities for these groups.

The primary challenge to existing models of citizenship education in Canada is identified by Hébert and Wilkinson (2002) as the need to respect differences while identifying and nurturing commonalities. Thus although acknowledging that certain individuals and groups experience limited sociopolitical participation in liberal democracies, Hébert and Wilkinson suggest that social cohesion is both a desirable goal and a nebulous concept that may never be fully resolved because societies and human beings are always in a state of flux.

EMERGENT POST-MULTICULTURALISM DISCOURSE ON MULTICULTURAL EDUCATION

The review of the emerging post-multiculturalism discourse in the academic education literature offered theoretical suggestions about rearticulating the main concepts of multicultural education in order to reflect their complexity and to create an education system that is inclusive of all students.

In his 2009 review of the current state of multiculturalism in Canada, Kymlicka concludes that "what has dominated the debate in Canada in the 2006–8 period is the spectre of backlash and retreat from multiculturalism" (p. 22). He points that as a member of an international community in which the perception that multiculturalism has "failed" and that it is time to "pull back" from multiculturalism that has been taken "too far" is widespread, Canada is not an exception. "Post-multiculturalism" that is viewed by Gregg (2006) as "avoiding the 'excesses' of multiculturalism without reverting to the sort of harsh assimilationism that we see in many European countries" (in Kymlicka, 2009, p. 25) is one of the ways in which Canada can deal with the greater segregation, greater stereotyping and prejudice, as well as greater polarization that Gregg, along with others, blamed on multiculturalism. Quebec's recent "reasonable accommodation" debate stirred by media's reports on "excessive" accommodation of minorities led to the first major political party in many years in Canada (i.e., the Action Democratique du Quebec) to run on an anti-immigrant and anti-multiculturalism platform (Kymlicka, 2009, p. 28). Although after the Bouchard-Taylor Report (2008) that demonstrated that the initial media reports were inaccurate and there was no need for dramatic revision to the existing policy of accommodation, the debate itself can be seen (as Kymlicka did) as an instance in which "long-term critics of multiculturalism have jumped on the European anti-multiculturalist wagon, and have hoped to ride it into Canada" (p. 29). However, Kymlicka acknowledges that "the debate about the future of multiculturalism as a concept or model and whether inherited ideas of multiculturalism need to be replaced with new "post-multicultural" approaches in an era of "hyper-diversity" (p. 36) is an emerging research theme on Canadian multiculturalism.

The term "super-diversity" is coined by Vertovec (2007) and attempts to capture the interplay of multiple factors that contribute to the complex nature of contemporary, migration-driven diversity. These include, among others, not only the multiplicity of immigrants' countries of origin but also the fact that there are, within groups, differences and "distinctions in ethnicity, religious affiliations and practices, regional and local identities, kinship, clan and tribal affiliation, political parties and movements and other criteria of collective belonging" (Vertovec, 2010, p. 87). Thus, the emerging post-multiculturalism discourse indicates that some significant shifts in understanding and articulating central concepts such as culture; power; and cultural, national, and civic identity can no longer be based on narrow definitions of ethnicity or country of origin. Such tendencies are observed worldwide. As "corrective measures" (Vertovec, 2010, p. 90), "post-multicultural" policies aim to foster community cohesion – a stronger national identity. In Canada, in the latest annual report on the implementation and direction of the Act, identity is defined as belonging and attachment to Canada rather than to any particular subgroup in the country (Abu-Laban & Gabriel, 2002; Nugent, 2006).

The following section outlines trends in post-multiculturalism discourse in the English-language academic education literature.

The Shift in Understanding Culture and Cultural Difference

To address one of the main criticisms of multiculturalism and multicultural education – simplification of culture, human culture is now understood as "both historical ('backward-looking') and dynamic ('forward-looking')" (Shi-Xu, 2001, p. 283). Culture is also seen as being able to "re- and trans-form itself" (p. 283). From this point of view, the purpose of multicultural education now is "to create possibilities in confronting the views in which we see the world" (Ghosh & Abdi, 2004, p. 31), and thus it represents a site of struggle.

Building on Bhabha's (1994) notion of the third space, Ghosh and Abdi (2004) suggest developing broader horizons where we negotiate new ideas and vocabularies to enable us to make comparisons partly through transforming our own standards. The fusion of cultures in the third space does not mean difference-blindness or homogenization; rather, it emphasizes identity because individuals see the world from their own perspectives and have multiple identities, some of which may be contradictory. Therefore, validating cultural, social, and gender differences and developing individual identities should be the focus of multicultural education.

The Shift in Understanding Cultural and Ethnic Identities

Gosine's (2002) review of conceptions of racial identity construction identified a theoretical shift in education-related scholarship. That is, rather than treating these concepts as fixed, discrete, and easily represented entities (Fordham & Ogbu,

247

1992), they are now viewed as hybrid and contradictory concepts continually produced and reproduced in relation to shifting constellations of knowledge (e.g., racializing discourses) and power in the larger society (James, 1996; Yon, 2000). However, overemphasizing hybridity and the associated blurring of ethnoracial boundaries can also result in playing down the bitter tensions that arise in conflicts between marginalized and dominant groups, thereby misrepresenting the nature of Canadian racism (Loomba, 1998).

Helfenbein (2003) argues that schools, in general, must change in order to prepare young people for the new work order and that multicultural education in particular "needs to address the changing nature of identity in a globalized technologically connected world" (p. 14). Articulating the novel life conditions, subjectivities, and identities of youth; cultivating new multiple literacies as a response to new technologies and the challenges of globalization and multiculturalism; and proposing a radical reconstruction and democratization of education to counter the trend toward the imposition of a neoliberal business model on education are the three major tasks of the new critical pedagogy according to Kellner (2003). He emphasizes, however, that reconstruction of education should not fulfil the agenda of capital and high-tech industries, but should "radically democratize education in order to advance Deweyan and Freirean conceptions of the development of individuality, the promotion of citizenship and community, and the strengthening of democratic participation in all modes of life" (p. 62).

The Shift in Understanding Citizenship, Civic, and National Identity

Critical theorists such as Giroux (1991), Dryzek (1996), and Kincheloe (2001) emphasize that "democratic citizenship needs to be 'multidimensional... often unconventional' and often should be waged 'against the state, and apart from the state'" (Dryzek, 1996, p. 36). Critical reconstructionists too tend to advocate "types of civic knowledge that unmask and derail official and state-sponsored 'fairy tales'" (Abowitz & Harmish, 2006, p. 673). They also advocate for a critical civic curriculum that will foster civic identity by embracing the values and skills of questioning, rethinking, and confronting when necessary powerful democratic institutions, including the government and state-sponsored schooling (Giroux, 2003) when they are not working on behalf of all citizens. This process of learning the actual workings of political life instead of mere facts about it would lead to the development of public agency (Boyte, 1994).

Hébert and Wilkinson (2002) call for the development of a conceptual framework for analyzing citizenship that will "be modified and enriched as necessary to enclose all unforeseen aspects of citizenship," that will allow us to "grasp the overall meaning of citizenship," and whose "full development is achieved when saturation is reached" (p. 233).

Ghosh and Abdi (2004) suggest that a "syncretic national identity" (p. 88) can be achieved in Canada if the notion of critical pedagogy is extended beyond minority groups, and promoting democratic values is combined with school, classroom, and curriculum reorganization, and a revisioning of teacher-student,

student-student, and home-school relationships. This, in turn, can lead to a change in the *we-they* configuration and the construction of an inclusive *us*. They point to the need for the emergence of a new kind of citizenship that allows "the expression of the multiple identities that we possess" (p. 87). Ghosh and Abdi suggest that political culture and citizenship in postmodern democracies "involve the interconnection between the national and the global, such as the citizen of any one country and citizens of the world in a transnational interdependency" (p. 88). Therefore, in the post-multiculturalism discourse, "belonging, loyalty and sense of attachment are not parts of a zero-sum game based on a single place. That is, it is not automatically true that the more transnational individuals are the less integrated they are, or the less integrated they are the stronger their transnational patterns of association" (Vertovec, 2010, p. 90). But what does this change mean for the education theory and practice?

IMPLICATIONS FOR (POST)MULTICULTURAL EDUCATION

Given the continued heated debate in the English-language academic education literature about which theoretical perspective of multicultural education is best equipped to lead the field in the future, it seems appropriate to heed to Ladson-Billings' (2004) suggestion that "Current ideas about the term multicultural must give way to new expressions of human and social diversity ... [We] must reconceptualize views of difference that are often forced to operate in old social schemes" (p. 50). Vertovec (2010) suggested how this might be accomplished: "In order to avoid the conventional trap of addressing newcomers just in terms of some presumably fixed ethnic identity, an awareness of the new super-diversity suggests that policy-makers and practitioners should take account of new immigrants' plurality of affiliations (recognizing multiple identities, only some of which concern ethnicity)" (p. 94).

As the review presented here shows, when binaries are overemphasized, complex phenomena are simplified, leaving no room for individual variations and nuances of experience and often reproducing the status quo. Current multicultural education practices in Canada based on ethno-racial distinctions (i.e., curricula essentializing knowledge about Other cultures and celebrating them) have not contributed to the elimination of racism or the unequal treatment of minority, non-White students. Neither have they led to a critical examination of the dominant White, middle-class, Eurocentric culture.

However, the review also shows that the complexity of the issues identified as problematic in multicultural theory makes it difficult to formulate a unified multicultural education mission that speaks to the multiplicity of identities, fluidity of culture, negotiation of power in the cultural space, and the new politics of difference based on universal dignity and equality. It is even more difficult to organize and implement such a mission, especially in the absence of a federal multicultural education policy. Therefore, education ministries across the provinces need to take it upon themselves to re-examine how better to integrate disparate and marginalized voices into the privileged domain and to reinvest in employment equity such that the presence and concerns of minorities are introduced into the classroom by closing the visible-minority gap. In other words, a commitment to ensuring that non-Christian, non-White, non-native English- or French-speaking teachers are well represented in the public school system is critical for providing nodal points of immediate cross-cultural and multi-ethnic identification for students outside the so-called Canadian majority. In this process, opportunity to develop stronger consultative partnerships between communities and educational ministries should not be overlooked as an effective and cost-efficient means of infusing alternative epistemologies into curricula.

Recent examples of postmulicultural education praxis (Wilgus, 2013) demonstrate that post-multiculturalism does not mean returning to assimilation and that despite the strong rhetoric about cohesion, national identity and dominant cultural values, diversity not only can be, but also already is institutionally embedded. By participating in "experimental pedagogies," student teachers interrogate, disaggregate and understand the forces and historical processes that have contributed to the identities they have formulated for themselves. Such praxis has potential to position students to "self-consciously and forthrightly decide if these identities are ones that they, in full self-awareness, wish to continue to embrace, or if these identities are in need of revisions and reconstruction" (p. 192).

Now when the "M-word" seems to evoke criticisms from both the political Right and Left and there is a worldwide call to rethink multiculturalism, post-multiculturalism seems to provide an answer: "post-multiculturalism policies and discourses seek to have it both ways: a strong common identity and values coupled with the recognition of cultural differences (alongside differences based on gender, sexuality, age and disability)" (Vertovec, 2010, p. 91). In the Canadian context, where multiculturalism is still part of the national identity (Kymlicka, 2009), it needs to be conceived of as a global societal project of which institutionalized education is only one component. Heterogeneity of the student body is a fact that education as an institution must address in order to participate in the reevaluation, rearticulation, and renegotiation of the meaning of national unity in the democratic state.

NOTE

¹ An earlier version of this chapter was published in *Canadian Ethnic Studies, 40*(1), 2008.

REFERENCES

Abowitz, K. K., & Harnish, J. (2006). Contemporary discourses of citizenship. *Review of Educational Research, 76*(4), 653-690.

Abu-Laban, Y., & Gabriel, C. (2008). *Selling diversity: Immigration, multiculturalism, employment equity, and globalization.* North York, ON: University of Toronto Press.

Appiah, K. A. (1997). What is African art? *The New York Review of Books, XLIV* 7(15), 30-36.

Backhouse, C. (1999). *Colour-coded: A legal history of racism in Canada, 1900-1950.* Toronto, ON: Osgoode Society for Canadian Legal History, University of Toronto Press.

Bateson, M. C. (1994). *Peripheral visions: Learning along the way*. New York, NY: HarperCollins Publishers.

Bennett, C. (2001). Genres of research in multicultural education. *Rev. Educ. Res., 71*(2), 171-217.

Bhabha, H. K. (1994). *The location of culture*. London. New York, NY: Routledge.

Boyte, H. (1994). Review of civitas: A framework for civic education. *Teachers College Record, 3*(95), 414-418.

Bouchard, G., & Taylor, C. (2008). Building the future: A time for reconciliation. Consultation Commission on Accommodation Practices Related to Cultural Differences. Retrieved from http://collections.banq.qc.ca/ark:/52327/bs1565996

Brown, S. C., & Kysilka, M. L. (1994). In search of multicultural and global education in real classrooms. *Journal of Curriculum and Supervision, 9*(3), 313-316.

Canada, House of Commons. (1971). Debates (October, Pierre Trudeau), p. 8545.

Carrington, B., & Bonnett, A. (1997). The other Canadian 'mosaic'-'race' equity education in Ontario and British Columbia. *Comparative Education, 3*, 411. doi:10.2307/3099499

Chan, A. S. (2007). Race-based policies in Canada: Education and social context. In R. Joshee & L. Johnson (Eds.), *Multicultural education policies in Canada and the United States* (pp. 131-145). Vancouver, Canada: UBC Press.

Cornell, D., & Murphy, S. (2002). Anti-racism, multiculturalism, and the ethics of identification. *Philosophy & Social Criticism, 28*(4), 419-449.

Dei, G. J. S. (1996). *Anti-racism education: Theory and practice*. Halifax, N.S.: Fernwood Publishing.

Derwing, T. M., DeCorby, E., Ichikawa, J., & Jamieson, K. (1999). Some factors that affect the success of ESL high school students. *Canadian Modern Language Review, 55*, 532-547.

Derwing, T. M., & Munro, M. J. (2007). Canadian policies on immigrant language education. In R. Joshee & L. Johnson (Eds.), *Multicultural education policies in Canada and the United States* (pp. 93-106). Vancouver, Canada: UBC Press.

Diakiw, J. (1997). *The school's role in revealing the commonplaces of our national culture and identity: A multicultural perspective*. Ottawa, ON: Canadian Association of Second Language Teachers.

Dryzek, J. S. (1996). *Democracy in capitalist times: Ideals, limits, and struggles*. New York, NY: Oxford University Press.

Elliston, I. (1997). Reforming education for diversity. *The state of the art national study, report #4*. Toronto, ON: University of Toronto.

Flecha, R. (1999). Modern and postmodern racism in Europe: Dialogic approach and anti-racist pedagogies. *Harvard Education Review, 69*(2), 150-1171.

Fordham, S., & Ogbu, J. U. (1995). Black students school success: Coping with the burden of acting White. In J. J. Macionis & N. V. Benokraitis (Eds.), *Seeing ourselves: Classic, contemporary, and cross-cultural readings in sociology* (3rd ed., pp. 287-303). Englewood Cliffs, NJ: Prentice Hall.

Galabuzi, G. (2005). Factors affecting the social economic status of Canadian immigrants in the new millenium. *Canadian Issues*, Spring, 53-57.

Gee, E., & Prus, S. (2000). Income inequality in Canada: A racial divide. In W. E. Kalbach & M. A. Kalbach (Eds.), *Perspectives on ethnicity in Canada: A reader* (pp. 238-256). Toronto, ON, Canada: Harcourt Canada.

Ghosh, R., & Abdi, A. A. (2004). *Education and the politics of difference: Canadian perspectives*. Toronto, ON: Canadian Scholars' Press Inc.

Giroux, H. A. (1991). Beyond the ethics of flag waving: Schooling and citizenship for a critical democracy. *The Clearing House, 64*(5), 305-308. doi:10.2307/30188623

Giroux, H. A.(1992). Curriculum, multiculturalism and the politics of identity. *National Association of Secondary School Principals Bulletin, 76*(548), 1-11.

Giroux, H. A. (2001). *Public spaces, private lives: Beyond the culture of cynicism*. Lanham, MD: Rowman & Littlefield Publishers.

Giroux, S. S. (2003). Reconstructing the future: Du Bois, racial pedagogy and the post-civil rights era. *Social Identities, 9*(4), 563-598. doi:10.1080/1350463032000174678

Gosine, K. (2002). Essentialism versus complexity: Conceptions of racial identity construction in educational scholarship. *Canadian Journal of Education, 27*(1), 81-100.

Grant, C., Elsbree, A. R., & Fondrie, S. (2004). A decade of research the changing terrain of multicultural education research. In J. A. Banks & C. A. M. Banks (Eds.), *Handbook of research on multicultural education* (pp. 184-207). San Francisco, CA: Jossey-Bass.

Gregg, A. (2006, March). Identity crisis. Multiculturalism a twentieth-century dream becomes a twentieth-first century conundrum. *The Walrus Magazine, 3*(2). Retrieved from http://allangregg.com/identity-crisis/

Hébert, Y., & Wilksinson, L. (2002). The citizenship debates: Conceptual, policy, experiential and educational issues. In Y. Hébert (Ed.), *Citizenship in transformation in Canada* (pp. 112-134). Toronto, ON: University of Toronto.

Helfenbein, R.J. (2003). Troubling multiculturalism: The new work order, anti anti-essentialism, and a cultural studies approach to education. *Multicultural Perspectives, 5*(4), 10-16.

Henry, F., Rees, T., & Tator, C. (2009). *The colour of democracy: Racism in Canadian society* (4th ed.). Toronto, ON: Nelson Education.

Hoffman, D. M. (1996). Culture and self in multicultural education: Reflections on discourse, text, and practice (English). *American Educational Research Journal, 33*(3), 545-569.

James, C. E. (1996). Race, culture and identity. In C. E. James (Ed.), *Perspectives on racism and human services sector: A case of change* (pp. 15-35). Toronto, ON: University of Toronto.

James, C. (2000). *Experiencing difference*. Halifax, NS: Fernwood Pub.

James, C. (2003). *Seeing ourselves: Exploring ethnicity, race and culture* (3rd ed.) Toronto, ON: Thompson Educational.

James, C., & Shadd, A. L. (2001). *Talking about identity: Encounters in race, ethnicity, and language*. Toronto, ON: Between The Lines.

Kazemipur, A., & Halli, S. S. (2000). *The new poverty in Canada: Ethnic groups and ghetto neighbourhoods*. Toronto, ON: Thompson Educational Publishers.

Kehoe, J., & Mansfeld, E. (1997). *The limitations of multicultural education and anti-racist education*. Ottawa, ON: Canadian Association of Second Language Teachers.

Kellner, D. (2003). Toward a critical theory of education. *Democracy & Nature, 9*(1), 51-64.

Kincheloe, J. L. (2001). *Getting beyond the facts: Teaching social studies/social sciences in the twenty-first century* (2nd ed.). New York, NY: P. Lang.

Kincheloe, J. L., & Steinberg, S. R. (1997). *Changing multiculturalism*. Philadelphia, PA: Open University Press.

Kunz, J. L., & Sykes, S. (2007). *From mosaic to harmony [electronic resource]: Multicultural Canada in the 21st century: Results of regional roundtables*. Ottawa, ON: Policy Research Initiative.

Kymlicka, W. (1995). *Multicultural citizenship: A liberal theory of minority rights*. New York, NY: Clarendon Press.

Kymlicka, W. (2001) *Politics in the vernacular: Nationalism, multiculturalism, and citizenship*. Oxford: Oxford University Press. doi:10.1093/0199240981.001.0001

Kymlicka, W. (2008). Research themes on Canadian multiculturalism. *Canadian Journal of Social Research, 2*(1), 35-50.

Kymlicka, W. (2009). The current state of multiculturalism in Canada. *Canadian Journal of Social Research, 2*(1), 15-34.

Ladson-Billings, G. (2004). New directions in multicultural education: Complexities, boundaries, and critical race theory. In J. A. Banks & C. A. M. Banks (Eds.), *Handbook of research on multicultural education* (pp. 50-65). San Francisco, CA: Jossey-Bass.

Li, P. (1998). The market value and social value of race. In V. Satzewicch (Ed.), *Racism and social inequity in Canada* (pp. 115-130). Toronto, ON: Thompson Educational.

Loomba, A. (1998). *Colonialism-postcolonialism*. London/New York, NY: Routledge.

Lund, D. E. (2003). Educating for social justice: Making sense of multicultural and antiracist theory and practice with Canadian teacher activists. *Intercultural Education, 14*(1), 3.

May, S. (1994). *Making multicultural education work.* Clevedon, England/Philadelphia, PA: Multilingual Matter.

McCarthy, C. (1994). Multicultural discourses and curriculum reform: A critical perspective. *Educational Theory, 44*(1), 81-98.

McCreath, P. L. (1997). *Multiculturalism: Failed or untried concept. In state of the art – National study.* Retrieved from http://caslt.org?research/multicult.htm

McLaren, P. (1995). *Critical pedagogy and predatory culture: Oppositional politics in a postmodern age.* New York, NY: Routledge.

McLaren, P. (1997). *Revolutionary multiculturalism: Pedagogies of dissent for the new millenium.* Boulder, CO: Westview Press.

McLeod, K. A. (1993). Introduction: Multicultural education. In K. A. McLeod (Ed.), *Multicultural education: The state of the art national study: Report #1.* Toronto, ON: Faculty of Education, University of Toronto.

Mitchell, K. (2001). Education for democratic citizenship: Transnationalism, multiculturalism, and the limits of liberalism. *Harvard Education Review, 71*(1), 51-78.

Ngo, H. V., Rossiter, M. J., & Stewart, C. (2013). Understanding risk and protective factors associated with criminal involvement in a multicultural society. *International Journal of Child. Youth & Family Studies, 4*(1), 54-71.

Nugent, A. (2006). Demography, national myths, and political origins: Perceiving official multiculturalism in Quebec. *Canadian Ethnic Studies Journal, 38*(3), 21-36.

Organisation for Economic Co-operation and Development. (2006). *Where immigrant students succeed: A comparative review of performance and engagement in PISA 2003* Paris, and Washington, D.C.

Pak, Y. (2009). We are already multicultural: Why policy and leadership matter. In L. Johnson & R. Joshee (Eds.), *Multicultural education policies in Canada and the United States* (pp. 42-50). Vancouver, BC, Canada. UBC Press.

Perry, R. J. (1992). Why do multiculturalists ignore anthropologists? *Chronicle of Higher Education, 38*(26), 52-52.

Pon, G. (2000). Beamers, cells, malls and cantopop: Thinking through the geographies of Chineseness. In C. E. James (Ed.), *Experiencing difference* (pp. 222-234). Halifax, NS: Fernwood Publishing.

Pratt, G. (2002). *Between homes: Displacement and belonging for second generation Filipino-Canadian youth* (No. RIIM WP 02-13). Vancouver, BC: Vancouver Centre of Excellence: Research on Immigration and Integration in the Metropolis.

Schick, C., & St. Denis, V. (2005). Troubling national discourses in anti-racist curricular planning. *Canadian Journal of Education, 28*(3), 295-317.

Shi-Xu. (2001). Critical pedagogy and intercultural communication: Creating discourses of diversity, equality, common goals and rational-moral motivation. *Journal of Intercultural Studies, 22*(3), 279-293.

Stables, A. (2005). Multiculturalism and moral education: Individual positioning, dialogue and cultural practice. *Journal of Moral Education, 34*(2), 185-197.

Strong-Boag, V. (2002). Who counts? Late nineteenth- and early twentieth-century struggles about gender, race, and class in Canada. In Y. Hébert (Ed.), *Citizenship in transformation in Canada* (pp. 37–56). Toronto, ON: University of Toronto.

Tator, C., & Henry, F. (1991). *Multicultural education: Translating policy into practice.* Ottawa, ON: Multiculturalism and Citizenship Canada.

Taylor, C. (1994). The Politics of recognition. In Gutman A. (Ed.), *Multiculturalism: Examining the politics of recognition.* (pp. 25-75). Princeton, NJ: Princeton University Press.

Turner, T. (1993). Anthropology and multiculturalism: What is anthropology that multiculturalism should be mindful of? *Cultural Anthropology, 8*(4), 411-429.

Vertovec, S. (2007). Super-diversity and its implications. *Ethnic and Racial Studies, 30*(6), 1024-1054. doi: 10.1080/01419870701599465

Vertovec, S. (2010). Towards post-multiculturalism? Changing communities, conditions and contexts of diversity. *International Social Science Journal, 61*(199), 83-95. doi: 10.1111/j.1468-2451.2010.01749.x

Walcott, R. (1997). *Black like who? Writing Black Canada.* Toronto, ON: Insomniac Press.

Watt, D., & Roessingh, H. (2001). The dynamics of ESL dropout: Plus ça change. *Canadian Modern Language Review, 58*(2), 203-222.

Wideen, M., & Barnard, K. A. (1999). *Impacts of immigration on education in British Columbia: An analysis of efforts to implement policies of multiculturalism in schools.* (No. RIIM WP 99-02). Vancouver, BC, Canada: Vancouver Centre of Excellence: Research on Immigration and Integration in the Metropolis.

Wilgus, G. (2013). Postmuticulturalism: Cultivating alternative cannons, a critical vernacular, and student-generated understandings of the 'lived-situatedness. In G. Wilgus & M. Blumenreich (Eds.), *Knowledge, pedagogy, and postmulticulturalism: Shifting the locus of learning in urban teacher education* (pp. 177-194). New York, NY: Palgrave Macmillan.

Wilhelm, R. (1994). Exploring the practice-rhetoric gap: Current curriculum for African-American history month in some Texas elementary schools. *Journal of Curriculum and Supervision, 9*(2), 217-223.

Willinsky, J. (1999). Curriculum, after culture, race, nation. *Discourse: Studies in the Cultural Politics of Education, 20*(1), 89-103.

Yon, D. A. (2000). *Elusive culture: Schooling, race, and identity in global times.* Albany, NY: State University of New York Press.

Zine, J. (2003). Dealing with September 12th: The challenge of anti-islamophobia education. *Orbit, 33*(3), 39-41.

Anna Kirova
Department of Elementary Education
University of Alberta

YAN GUO

15. MULTICULTURALISM AND MINORITY RELIGION IN PUBLIC SCHOOLS

Perspectives of Immigrant Parents

INTRODUCTION

Immigration is now the main source of Canada's population growth. According to the 2011 Census, almost 20.6% of the population was born outside Canada (Statistics Canada, 2013). One way in which these newcomers differ from earlier immigrants is that many have brought non-Western faith traditions from Africa, Asia, and the Middle East. Between the years 2001 and 2011 specifically, about 7.2% of Canada's population reported affiliations with one of Islam, Buddhism, Sikhism, or Hinduism, up from 4.9% a decade earlier, as recorded in the 2001 Census (Statistics Canada, 2013). It is estimated that by the year 2017, more than 10% of Canadians will be non-Christians (Statistics Canada, 2005). This demographic change has profound implications for Canadian public school systems. Canada promotes many ways of recognizing diversity, but it seems to have an aversion on the word "religion." The Canadian Charter of Rights and Freedoms enshrines the right to practice one's own religion and this move is a form of accommodating the needs of religious minorities within a multicultural society. On the other hand, public education in Canada follows a fundamentalist Christian curriculum and its calendar fits the needs of Christians (Karmani & Pennycook, 2005; Spinner-Halev, 2000). The Eurocentric nature of public schools means that religious minority parents need to constantly negotiate parameters for their children's involvement in school curricula and activities (Zine, 2001). The negotiation is challenging for Muslim immigrant parents as Islam is often portrayed as an inherently violent religion and Muslims as threatening the peace and security of Western nations (McDonough & Hoodfar, 2005), particularly after the September 11th event. Little attention has been paid to how religious minority parents negotiate their religious practices within public schools. This study examines how Muslim immigrant parents struggled to negotiate the continuity of their Islamic practices and to counteract their marginality, often connected with other sites of oppression such as race and gender, in public education.

S. Guo & L. Wong (eds.), Revisiting Multiculturalism in Canada, 255–270.
© *2015 Sense Publishers. All rights reserved.*

THOERETICAL FRAMEWORKS AND PRIOR RESEARRCH

Critical Multiculturalism

Critical multiculturalism sheds light on the parents' struggles that follow. Multiculturalism has a plurality of meanings and definitions. According to Kincheloe and Steinberg (1997), there are five prevailing philosophical positions that inform multicultural policies and practices: conservative, liberal, pluralist, radical and critical. The conservative approach presumes the superiority of Eurocentric values and beliefs and Christianity, devalues immigrants' native cultures and religions, and places uneven expectations on immigrants to conform over time to the norms, values, and religious traditions of the receiving society (Li, 2003). The liberal position acknowledges diversity, but has a low level of tolerance of non-Christian faiths. It superficially focuses on the neutrality of secularism, a separation of church and state. In reality such separation does not exist in Canada as we see the residual influence of Christianity in the national anthem, statutory holidays, currency, architecture, textbooks and so on (Biles & Ibrahim, 2005). An alternative form of liberal multiculturalism is pluralist multiculturalism, which sees differences in cultures and religions. However, the cultural and religious differences are often trivialized, exoticized, and essentialized as ends in themselves (Kincheloe & Steinberg, 1997). Multicultural discussions and practices often involve othering of non-Christians, with lists of how "they are" different from "us." Such conservative and liberal approaches to multiculturalism erase systemic racism and power inequities by perpetuating superiority and promoting the superficial rhetoric of equality, diversity, and political correctness. Radical multiculturalism stresses respect for cultural differences in values and socio-cultural practices. Radical educators must evaluate how schools deal with differences in personal, social and pedagogical interactions that influence the way teachers and students define themselves and each other (Ghosh, 2002; Sleeter & Grant, 1987). Critical multiculturalism extends the examination of the relations between dominant power structures within the school as well as the large society. Critical multiculturalism makes explicit those hidden or masked structures, discourses, and relations of inequity that discriminate against one group and enhance the privileges of another. It calls for a critical examination of liberal secular discourses and policies, often used to maintain the status quo of the dominant group and to deny minority group rights, as we see most obviously in the French government's prohibition of expressions of religious affiliation in public schools. Critical multiculturalism will be employed to analyze the narratives about how Muslim immigrant parents struggled for religious diversity in public education.

Multiculturalism in Canada and the United States

In 1971, Canada became the first country in the world to declare multiculturalism as official state policy. Official multiculturalism was introduced largely as a political exercise for bolstering national unity. Multiculturalism arose in the aftermath of the Report of the Royal Commission on Bilingualism and Biculturalism in 1969, a possible means of neutralizing Canada's French-English rift (Fleras & Elliott, 2002). Various ethnic groups, especially the Ukrainians and the Germans, had argued vigorously that their language and culture were as vital as Quebec's to Canadian nation building. The liberal government struck a compromise with the ethnic groups and arrived at a policy of multiculturalism within a bilingual framework. The commitment to multiculturalism was not only enshrined in legislation (the 1988 Canadian Multiculturalism Act), but in fact constitutionalized in section 27 of the Charter of Rights and Freedoms in 1982. In the past forty years, Canada's multiculturalism has been praised and adopted internationally. At the same time Canada's multiculturalism has been criticized for it "endorsed diversity in principle without actually changing any fundamental way how power and resources were distributed" (Fleras & Elliott, 2002, p. 56). In that sense, Canada adopts conservative and liberal approaches to multiculturalism by endorsing consensus, conformity, and accommodation.

In the United States, multiculturalism is not clearly established in policy at the federal level. Americans have long considered assimilation or the melting pot approach as key to society building. The melting pot implied that each individual immigrant, and each group of immigrants, assimilated into American society at their own pace. Unlike the official multiculturalism as accommodation between French-speaking and English speaking groups in Canada, the emergence of multiculturalism in education was incorporation of African Americans into society in the United States. The foundations of multicultural education began in the 1960s with calls for the improvement of education among African Americans, also known as the Black Civil Rights Movement (Banks, 2004). As part of the movement, there was a call for educational reform by incorporating curriculum and material that accurately reflected the cultural backgrounds, needs, and goals of African Americans. Subsequently, other ethnic groups also called for similar reforms. More critical approaches to multicultural education developed in the 1980s and 1990s (Giroux, 1994; McLaren, 1994; Nieto & Bode, 2008; Sleeter & Grant, 1987). Critical multiculturalism challenges dominant power structures, resists white hegemony, and empowers minorities. Unlike Canada's multiculturalism which is state-sanctioned and aims to transform the mainstream without questioning power structures, American multiculturalism is outside the state and aims to empower minorities by challenging the superiority and neutrality of mainstream values and by transforming the state (Fleras & Elliott, 2002).

Despite the official rhetoric of Canada being a multicultural mosaic and the United States being a melting pot, extensive survey data showed surprisingly little difference between the basic attitudes of the white citizens of these two North American nations toward immigrants of colour. A majority of both Canadians (70%) and Americans (76%) believed that new immigrants should adapt to their new country's way of life (Innovative Research Group, 2005). In the United States and Canada one of the most influential meta-narratives in effect today is a presumed "clash" between the western and the Islamic civilizations. The recent backlash against multiculturalism in North America is directly linked to the perceived threat of Muslim immigrants. One consequence of this rising perception has been a growing intolerance for religious difference. At the heart of the multiculturalism debate, Muslim immigrant parent voices are not always heard or solicited, yet parents may be very concerned about the appropriateness of education in public schools in Canada.

Fear of Diversity and Difference as Deficit

Over the years, research has repeatedly revealed that many teachers are not well prepared to work effectively with immigrant parents (Guo, 2006; Malatest & Associates, 2003; Turner, 2007). In their daily encounters with cultural diversity, many teachers still confront many challenges. One of the challenges is the fear of diversity (Palmer, 1998), the fear of Muslims, particularly after the September 11th event (McDonough & Hoodfar, 2005), partially resulting from a lack of knowledge and readiness to approach cultural and religious diversity. The current curriculum and teaching practice in K-12 education, characterized by Eurocentric perspectives, standards and values, do not reflect the knowledge and experiences of our culturally and religiously diverse student and parent population. Another challenge is the "difference as deficit" perspective (Dei, 1996). Rather than seeing difference and diversity as an opportunity to enhance learning by using the diverse strengths, experiences, knowledge, perspectives of students and parents from various cultural groups, the "difference as deficit" model sees diversity ignored, minimized, or as an obstacle to the learning process (Cummins, 2003; Dei, 1996). For example, the unique way that immigrant parents engage in their children's education is often ignored by teachers and school administrators (Jones, 2003; Ramirez, 2003).

Rethinking Immigrant Parent Involvement

The conventional North American model for parental involvement in education involves forms of parent participation in school-based activities and events. This model intends to promote equal opportunity, but in practice has many failings (Dehli, 1994; Guo, 2006; Guo & Mohan, 2008; McLaren & Dyck, 2004). Barriers such as class and race play a role in parent-school interaction. These include educators' cultural biases, and generally low expectations of immigrant parents (Jones, 2003; Ramirez, 2003). As Cline and Necochea (2001) observed of the involvement of Latino parents in the Lampoc United School District in California,

> only parental involvement that is supportive of school policies and instructional practices are welcome here ... parents whose culture, ethnicity, SES, and language background differ drastically from the white middle-class norms are usually kept at a distance, for their views, values, and behaviors seem 'foreign' and strange to traditional school personnel. (p. 23)

Probing further, Lareau (2003) found that middle class white and black parents were more strategic in intervening in their children's schools than were black working class parents. Lareau also found that both middle- and working-class black parents were continually concerned with schools' racial discrimination. Perceived racial discrimination may have been a form of acquiescence among parents who were not strategic. In this regard, it is worth noting that North American models of parent involvement have tended to focus more on middle-class than working-class values and concerns and on experiences more relevant to parents of Anglo-Celtic descent than to those from non-English-speaking backgrounds. When immigrant parents do not conform to the dominant culture in their receiving country, schooling may end up undermining and subordinating parents' educative and child-rearing practices (Bernhard, Freire, Pacini-Ketchabaw, & Villanueva, 1998).

Immigrant Parent Knowledge

The knowledge that immigrants hold about their children is often unrecognized by teachers and school administrators (Jones, 2003). These forms of non-recognition of immigrant parents can be attributed to misconceptions of difference, and lack of knowledge about different cultures (Guo, 2009; Honneth, 1995). A deficit model of difference leads to the belief that difference is equal to deficiency, that the knowledge of others, particularly those from developing countries, is incompatible, inferior, and hence, invalid (Abdi, 2007; Dei, 1996). If school staff members hold these attitudes, even tacitly, they may fail to recognize and make use of the knowledge of immigrant parents.

The extent to which parent knowledge is gained and used may be modelled as "transcultural knowledge construction," whereby individuals in immigrant societies of the new world change themselves by integrating diverse cultural life-ways into dynamic new ones. The resulting blended forms lead either to, opposition and discrimination, or to cultural creativity and the integration of new knowledge within academic and societal positionings (Hoerder, Hébert, & Schmitt, 2006). For example, in her study of Chinese immigrants in Toronto, Liu (2007) reported Chinese parents adapted to the Canadian way of educating children by integrating new knowledge gained from interactions with Canadian schools.

Knowledge is power; knowledge is socially constructed, culturally mediated, and historically situated (McLaren, 2003). At the heart of the nature of knowledge as social relations is a notion of culture as a dynamic entity, as a way of using social, cultural, physical, spiritual, economic, and symbolic resources to make one's way in the world. Mobilizing such knowledge systematically in the classroom by teachers and administrators would promote insightful connections between curricular goals and immigrant students' experiences in countries of origin, in transition, and in residence in the local community, in turn making sense of transcultural flows and attachments to locality (Appadurai, 1996; Hannerz, 1992).

In addition to socially mediated forms of knowledge, immigrant parents' personal knowledge can play an important role in school relations. Personal knowledge refers to wisdom that comes with embodied meaning (Polanyi, 1958). Parent personal knowledge is knowledge gained from lived experience in all aspects of life – at work, at play, with family and friends, and so on. It has temporal dimensions in that it resides in "the person's past experience, in the person's present mind and body, and in the person's future plans and actions" (Connelly & Clandinin, 1988, p. 25). Parent knowledge includes that drawn from their own educational backgrounds, their professional and personal experiences of interacting with schools in their countries of origin as well as their current understanding of the host country's education system, their own struggles as immigrant parents, and their future aspirations for their children (Pushor, 2008). Therefore, it is important to address issues such as who counts as knower, what knowledge counts, and how knower and knowledge interact in contexts (Hébert, Guo, & Pellerin, 2008).

METHODOLOGY

Context and Participants

Calgary, Alberta, Canada, was purposefully selected as its research sites for this case study because Calgary as a city is the largest recipient of immigrants and English as a Second Language (ESL) students in Alberta, making it the fourth largest destination city for immigrants in Canada after Toronto, Vancouver, and Montreal (Statistics Canada, 2013). There are three school systems in Calgary: public, Catholic, and private. Both public and Catholic schools are funded by the provincial government. The Calgary Board of Education, the public school system, enrolls over 26,305 coded K-12 ESL students in 2013 – about 25% of the total student population. The public board has no official policy on religious accommodation, but has policy on physical education clothing (Calgary Board of Education, 2005). The school board leaves the decision of religious accommodation to school principals, who are expected to respond to the wishes of students and parents.

38 parents were recruited through the Coalition for Equal Access to Education in Calgary, Alberta, a local umbrella organization of community agencies, groups and individuals, concerned with the current state of ESL instruction in the K-12 public education system and its consequences. This chapter reports the experiences of 13 Muslim parents who arrived in the city from Algeria, Bangladesh, India, Pakistan, Somalia, and Suriname. Three of these parents held master's degrees, nine had bachelor of degrees, and one had a high school diploma in their countries of origin, where their occupations varied from university instructors, teachers, engineers, social workers, principals, to managers. In contrast, they became community liaison workers, cashiers, production workers, and unemployed after their arrival in Canada, representing a downward mobility. Some parents volunteered in Canadian schools, participated in school councils, worked as lunch supervisors or teacher assistants. Some had experiences of observations of teachers working with their children.

Data Collection

Semi-structured interviews were conducted with parents individually to gain an understanding of what the participants thought teachers should know about their children. Open-ended questions were used to elicit rich descriptive accounts of the experiences the parents had with their children's teachers and schools. Parents were also invited to share what they believed that teachers needed to know about their children, their community, and their culture, religion, and values, in order to be more effective in teaching their children. With participants' requests, the interviews took place in parent participants' homes, in the researcher's office, or in the public library. Each interview lasted from 60 to 90 minutes.

Data Analysis

An inductive analysis strategy was applied to the interview data (McMillan & Schumacher, 2001), throughout the study as the data are collected and processed. This was accomplished by searching for domains that emerge from the data rather than being imposed on data prior to collection. Domains are large cultural categories that contain smaller categories and subcategories and whose relationships are linked by a semantic relationship (Spradley, 1980). Demographic information such as level of education, cultural background, and religious background was used to further examine the emerging categories and domains. All findings were further analyzed in terms of the theoretical framework in this article and further relevant concepts so as to generate insightful findings and to develop a new theoretical model for future application, action and research. These findings were not intended to generalize the experience of all religious immigrant parents in Canada since Canadian Muslims do not constitute a monolithic bloc, but rather to provide insights into the complex religious issues that were salient for these particular participants.

FINDINGS

The thirteen Muslim parents whose perspectives are considered in this study stated that one of the reasons they chose to immigrate to Canada had been their attraction to its official policies on multiculturalism. Understanding, as one of these parents observed, that religious freedom is enshrined in Canada's Charter of Rights and Freedoms, the parents had expected the accommodation of religious practices in schools. They requested recognition of religious symbolic clothing, exemptions from certain classes, and accommodation of prayer in public schools.

Religious Symbolic Clothing

One of the issues that Muslim immigrant parents faced was the negotiation of the religious expressions of minority groups in schools. This included allowing Muslim girls to wear a headscarf. The participants explained that Muslim girls and women wearing the headscarf were merely exercising their right to practice their religion, but this practice was not widely accepted by the Canadian society. Sana (all participants are referred to by pseudonyms) commented:

> I think it is a basic rule from our religion. When a woman goes out in public, she will be covering her hair. If I want to cover my head, I should be accepted. Right now I think there are about more than sixty percent people who don't accept that. (Sana, Pakistan)

Manibha, mother of 17-year-old daughter, reflected on how her daughter was perceived by her peers when she wore a headscarf in physical activities in school:

> She (her daughter) is involved in all kinds of activities. She plays football, soccer, volleyball, mountain climbing, everything. They (her daughter's peers) comment why you wear this, you might get hurt. (Manibha, Bangladesh)

For Manibha's daughter, wearing a headscarf did not prohibit her from participating in all kinds of physical activities. Her peers perceived that wearing a headscarf would pose a risk to her safety in the sports. Other participants stated the belief that wearing a headscarf can be harmful was unfounded. Hassan said:

> If they have some studies to claim that this is harmful, that these girls get hurt when they play soccer because of the headscarf, it is good. They don't have a single incidence to prove that. This is more political prejudice than the fact. (Hassan, Pakistan)

Hassan referred to a controversy about an 11-year-old girl who was banned from a soccer tournament by a Quebec referee because she wore a headscarf. The referee applied the rules of the soccer federation, insisting the ban can protect children from being strangled. Hassan argued that this ban, based on misconceptions rather than evidences, was "political prejudice."

The "political prejudice" informed the way Muslim parents were perceived and treated in school. Sarita explained how some teachers initially reacted toward her:

> I wear a headscarf when I go to parent-teacher conferences. The majority of the people, I have noticed, their initial impression about me would be I am a dumb person because I wear that. (Sarita, India)

Sarita's statement revealed how she perceived the attitudes of some teachers toward her. She was considered as "dumb" because of the teacher's misconception about the headscarf. In fact, Sarita received all her education in English and obtained a Master of Science in India before she immigrated to Canada. She spoke fluent English, volunteered in school activities, and participated in the school council. Sarita responded: "They (the teachers) thought I am oppressed. I am not oppressed at home." As a single mother, she raised two children by herself and encouraged her daughter to pursue a law career.

Sometimes the perceptions of Muslim parents' religious dresses informed the way their children were perceived and treated in school. Baljeet recalled an incident about how her son was perceived by the school counselor:

> My younger son was close to finish his junior high and he had 94% average. We went to a school open house and talked to a counselor. The counselor should ask what options you were looking or what your grade was. She didn't ask. She just said 'we have great options in our school. You can become a cook. We have a very wonderful chef program.' I didn't say anything. But my son said, 'but I don't want to become a cook. I am not interested in chef.' But she said, 'they make good money.' He said 'no, I am looking for math, doing more advanced courses.' 'Oh, in that case, you need at least 85% of math.' he said 'yes, in math, I have 97.' And then she said 'oh, yes, we have scholarship.' She changed, but she assumed. Maybe I was wearing a headscarf. Though there was a change, but still I could see that was the assumption. (Baljeet, India)

Exemptions from Certain Classes

Twelve out of the thirteen Muslim parents believed that Muslim girls should be segregated from the opposite sex, so girls are not allowed to wear swimming suits or dance with boys. Aneeka, mother of a 15-year-old daughter said:

> In our religion we believe in gender segregation. The man is not supposed to see the beauty of women. I did go and talk to the teacher at the beginning of the school year that my daughter does not swim and dance with boys. (Aneeka, Pakistan)

Aneeka requested her children to exempt from swimming and dancing classes. Sana, mother of a 12-year-old daughter expressed her disappointment that some teachers were not sensitive to her religious needs and did not allow exemptions:

> I went to the school and told her teacher we don't allow her to participate in the swimming classes. The teacher was annoyed. She didn't understand and made a big deal: 'This is physical education class. She has to be part of it.'

Donika went beyond exemptions by suggesting that schools need to rethink the requirement for swim wear:

> This kid was crying because she was not allowed to wear the swimming suit. The teacher in fact forced her to wear the swimming suit. The only thing that this teacher had in her mind is that you can only swim in the swimming suit. That's not true, a real mistake. (Donika, Suriname)

Donika stressed the importance for educators to be open to different perspectives and realize that there are many different ways of doing the same thing. She suggested that schools should allow Muslim girls to wear full body suits instead of swim suits.

GUO

Not all the participants were dismayed. Some participants expressed their satisfactions that their children's schools have made accommodation to their religious practices:

> The teacher understood that they (Muslim girls) can swim, wearing full clothes, and there should be no men with them. The teacher would close the door and they have a separate swimming time for the girls. She respects our religion. I was very satisfied. (Manibha, Bangladesh)

While some parents did not permit their daughters to participate in swimming classes, Noreen, mother of 10-year-old and 16-year-old daughters had no objection to her daughters swimming with boys: "My younger daughter is a good swimmer. She already had swimming lessons when she was back at home and her instructor was a man, so I have no problem." Noreen considered herself more liberal than other parents.

With regard to sex education, the participants expressed different views. Aneeka expressed her fear that sex education would expose her daughter to pre-marital sex, which violates her religious beliefs: "We just take one partner and that is after marriage. It has to be spiritually blessed, legal and religious. We don't believe in sex before marriage, so they (girls) don't need to take sex education." Aneeka believed that sex education should leave to the parents. Sana had a different perspective:

> Why don't they just have the girls in one room to teach them? It is good to know because my daughter is twelve and she has to know about the stuff (sex education). They can have boys in another room because most of girls do not feel comfortable in the same group with the boys. My daughter told me the boys made fun of her. (Sana, Pakistan)

Sana did not object to sex education if it was offered to girls separate from boys. Unlike Aneeka, Noreen allowed her daughters to participate in sex education classes because she believed that "in a couple of years even my younger daughter will have changes in her body. It is better that she knows this happens and what the effect will be."

Accommodation of Prayer

The Muslim parents in the study believed that Muslim students should be allowed to pray during school hours because Islam requires them to pray five times daily. Hassan proposed that "if they (Muslim students) have to do it in school, I think they should be allowed, especially in the winter there are one or two prayers which occur during the school time." Nim and Hassan expressed their satisfactions that their children's schools have made accommodation to their religious practices:

> We have Friday prayer. The school set up a room for the Muslim kids and they pray there. I'm so happy this has been done. (Nim, Pakistan)

For Muslim, Friday is our holy day. I wrote a letter to my son's school and asked him to take off on Friday afternoon so that he can perform his prayer in the mosque. The principal gave his permission. (Hassan, Pakistan)

Moreover, Hassan stated that Muslim students should not be penalized for taking Friday afternoon off and tests should not be administered on Friday afternoon.

On the contrary, Manibha expressed feeling frustrated by some schools' unwillingness to accommodate her religious practices:

A friend of mine told the principal that her daughter has to pray. 'Could you just give her five minutes in any corner of the room?' The principal told her, 'I'm sorry. I can't do that. I don't want to make the school into a mosque.'

One parent commented this kind of unwillingness was targeted toward Muslim:

I think as far as I know, no other religion than Islam prays five times a day … in many religions, they pray in the morning or maybe in the evening, or maybe on the weekend. For example, Jews are on Saturdays, Christians have Sundays, so most of religions are not praying during the day. (Hassan, Pakistan)

Religious Discrimination

Many participants reported that despite the promotion of multiculturalism in Canadian schools, their children continued to be the victims of demeaning treatments by some students motivated by ignorance and stereotypes. The participants learned different strategies to help their children. When her son was called "Osama bin Laden" by one of his peers in Grade 5, Aneeka advised her son to ignore such racist comments:

My child told me somebody called him Osama bin Laden. I asked him, 'are you?' 'No, Mom.' 'Don't worry. You know you are not anything like that. You are a good Muslim boy. You believe in peace. You are not a terrorist. Don't let them make fun of you. (Aneeka, Pakistan)

Aneeka stated how stereotypes and misconceptions about Muslim immigrants sometimes create low self-esteem among Muslim immigrant children and stress the importance of building her son's confidence. She helped her son to overcome adversity, teasing and stereotypes from classmates by cultivating the child's spiritual (Muslim) identity. Aneeka turned to her spiritual resources to develop her son's confidence at home.

DISCUSSION AND IMPLICATIONS

Given that Statistics Canada predicts that the number of Canadians belonging to minority religious communities will grow to approximately 10% of the population by 2017, public schools that promote multiculturalism can no longer afford to ignore questions of religious pluralism and barriers to religious freedom (Seljak,

Schmidt, Stewart, & Bramadat, 2008). Muslim parents in the study requested the recognition of immigrant communities, especially those with a different religion in public education. These requests include the acceptance of religious symbolic clothing, exemptions from certain classes, and accommodation of prayer in public schools. These requests call for going beyond conservative and liberal multiculturalism by challenging the normality of secularism and Christian curricula of public schools with the recognition of the religious diversity (Karmani & Pennycook, 2005; Spinner-Halev, 2000). The Canadian Charter of Rights and Freedoms (1982) and the Canadian Multiculturalism Act (1988) recognize that all individuals have the right to freedom of religion. Recognition of minority group special rights, particularly their religious-based exemptions and accommodation become crucial for a multicultural Canada (Levy, 1997).

The participants' requests in this study can create tensions by pitting conflicting interests against each other. On the one hand, educators believe that they have a responsibility to maintain safe learning environments that may require them to impose reasonable limits on how students dress and maintain a non-religious environment in public schools (Russo & Hee, 2008). On the other hand, for many participants, the right to wear religious attire in public schools is associated with the right to practice and observe their religion. Religious freedom is a fundamental right (Russo & Hee, 2008; Syed, 2008). Public schools are obliged to accept religious symbols such as permitting Muslim girls to wear a headscarf given the fact this freedom of religious expression does not constitute a real risk to personal safety or learning environments (Barnett, 2008; Levy, 1997). It is also important for educators to challenge their assumptions about Muslim women wearing a headscarf. The example about how a teacher perceived Sarita, a parent to be "dumb" because Sarita wore her headscarf when she went to the parent-teacher conference revealed the teacher's misconceptions about the Muslim headdress. The misconceptions also affect how their children were perceived and treated in the case of Baljeet. These assumptions were largely based on stereotypes "reminiscent of the long-gone colonial era" (Rezai-Rashti, 1994, p. 37). In this case, Sarita, Baljeet, and her son received messages of unintelligence because these women were wearing a headscarf. The headscarf became a marker of incompetence. On the contrary, Sarita, with a Master of Science in English in India, actively participated in her children's education in Canadian schools. Her participation challenges the global frameworks that depict Muslim women as submissive figures being in need of emancipation (Syed, 2008).

Muslim parents in the study requested to exempt their children from certain classes such as dancing and swimming in public schools. Zine (2001) explained the reason why Muslim children are not allowed to dance is that "physical contact between males and females is allowed only among close family members ... Social distance within the Islamic tradition is therefore also gendered and situations of casual physical contact between males and females violate Islamic moral codes" (p. 407). For some Muslim parents, looking at members of the opposite sex in 'immodest dress' is against their beliefs (Spinner-Halev, 2000). Religious continuity within Canadian schools is important for some Muslim parents. For teachers, dancing and swimming are part of school curricula and students are required to participate in these classes for their physical and social development. Where the rule in swimming class is that everyone must wear swimming suits or in gym class shorts and T-shirts, religious students should be exempt from the class, or be put in an alternative class (Levy, 1997; Spinner-Halev, 2000). The clothing requirement should also be rethought and students should be allowed to wear full body suits.

Parents in the study held differing positions on sex education: some objected to it, some accepted it as long as it was offered separate from boys, and some fully supported it. Parents should be allowed to exempt their children from sex education classes if they so desire. These courses often "discuss sex graphically and teach students how to have sex without getting pregnant" (Spinner-Halev, 2000). Since dating and premarital sex are strictly forbidden in Islam (Zine, 2001), there is no reason to insist that their children attend sex education. At the same time, parents should be aware that it is almost impossible to protect their children from sexual images in the media given the wide access to the internet and TV.

Some Muslim parents in the study requested accommodation of prayer in public schools. Some public schools in Calgary provided classrooms or gym rooms for prayer while other schools rejected parents' requests. According to the Calgary Board of Education policy, the principal can authorize student-initiated prayer (Calgary Board of Education, 2005). However, one principal stated that "I don't want to make the school into a mosque." This statement reveals the principal's duty to maintain a secular school environment. It also reveals that the principal fails to recognize that religion is an essential part of education for some students and fails to accommodate religious difference. Zine (2000) recounts a similar story of an Arabic Canadian who, as a member of a Muslim students' association, tried to secure a room for prayer in his public school. The principal adamantly refused, stating "this is not a place for religion, it's a place for education" (p. 303). Neither of these principals has reflected deeply on Christian privilege in public schools. They fail to recognize that Christian privilege is maintained by "institutional policies, curricular priorities, mandatory dress codes, mandatory attendance, and even the food available in school cafeterias" (Blumenfeld, 2006, p. 204). These principals are blind to the religious marginalization that Canadian Sihks, Muslims, Hindus, Buddhists, and Jewish people, as well as aboriginal peoples, suffer under structures defined first by Christianity and later by Canadian-style secularism (Seljak, 2012). Their approaches therefore remain ethnocentric.

In response to the recognition of the religious diversity, public schools are required to inform administrators and teachers about the religious practices of their students. Religious discrimination derives in part from religious illiteracy. This illiteracy has meant that teachers (the majority of who are at least nominally Christian) often fail to discuss or even understand the religions dimensions of policy challenges (Sumyu Neufeld, personal communication, January 6, 2010). Religious illiteracy can be addressed with mandatory education on world religions as subjects for respectful study but not indoctrination for all pre-service teachers, elementary and secondary students (Bouchard & Taylor, 2008; Bramadat &

Selijak, 2005). Religion is an important part of a well-rounded academic education. Learning about it will help teachers and students overcome their fear and support social interaction between immigrant and non-immigrant students (Spinner-Halev, 2000).

It is important for educators to provide institutionalized means for the explicit recognition and representation of oppressed groups. Part of these means include modifications of school curricula, dress codes, provision of prayer rooms for Muslim students (Kanu, 2008), and also state funding for privately established Muslims schools in the same way that Catholic schools are funded, which are necessary to reflect contemporary and religiously pluralistic realities.

REFERENCES

Abdi, A. (2007). Global multiculturalism: Africa and the recasting of the philosophical and epistemological plateaus. *Diaspora, Indigenous and Minority Education, 1*(4), 1-14.

Appadurai, A. (1996). *Modernity at large: Cultural dimensions of modernity.* London and Minneapolis: University of Minnesota Press.

Banks, J. A. (2004). Multicultural education: Historical development, dimensions, and practice. In J. A. Banks & C. A. M. Banks (Eds.), *Handbook of research on multicultural education* (pp. 3-29). San Francisco: Jossey-Bass.

Barnett, L. (2008). Freedom of religion and religious symbols in the public sphere. Retrieved from http://www.parl.gc.ca/information/library/PRBpubs/prb0441-e.htm

Bernhard, J.K., Freire, M., Pacini-Ketchabaw, V., & Villanueva, V. (1998). A Latin-American parents' group participates in their children schooling: Parent involvement reconsidered. *Canadian Ethnic Studies, 30*(3), 77-99.

Biles, J., & Ibrahim, H. (2005). Religion and public policy: Immigration, citizenship, and multiculturalism-Guess who's coming to dinner? In P. Bramadat & D. Seljak (Eds.), *Religion and ethnicity in Canada* (pp. 154-177). Toronto: Pearson.

Blumenfeld, W. J. (2006). Christian privilege and the promotion of "secular" and not-so "secular" mainline Christianity in public schooling and in the larger society. *Equity & Excellence in Education, 39*(3), 195-210.

Bouchard, G., & Taylor, C. (2008). Building the future: A time for reconciliation. Retrieved from http://www.accommodements.qc.ca/documentation/rapports/rapport-final-abrege-en.pdf

Bramadat, P., & Seljak, D. (2005). (Eds.). *Religion and ethnicity in Canada.* Toronto: Pearson.

Calgary Board of Education. (2005). The role of religion in the Calgary Board of Education. Policy adopted September 2005. Retrieved from http://www.cbe.ab.ca/Policies/policies/AR3067.pdf

Canadian Charter of Rights and Freedoms. (1982). Retrieved from http://www.efc.ca/pages/law/charter/charter.text.html

Canadian Multiculturalism Act. (1988). Retrieved from http://laws.justice.gc.ca/PDF/Statute/C/C-18.7.pdf

Cline, Z., & Necochea, J. (2001). ¡Basta Ya! Latino parents fighting entrenched racism. *Bilingual Research Journal, 25*(1-2), 1-26.

Connelly, F.M., & Clandinin, D.J. (1988). *Teachers as curriculum planners: Narratives of experience.* New York, NY: Teachers College Press.

Cummins, J. (2003). Challenging the construction of difference as deficit: Where are identity, intellect, imagination, and power in the new regime of truth? In P. P. Trifonas (Ed.), *Pedagogy of difference: Rethinking education for social change* (pp. 41-60). New York: RoutledgeFalmer.

Dehli, K. (1994). *Parent activism and school reform in Toronto.* Toronto: Department of Sociology in Education, Ontario Institute for Studies in Education.

Dei, G. (1996). *Anti-racism education: Theory and practice.* Halifax: Fernwood Publishing.

Fleras, A., & Elliott, J.L. (2002). *Engaging diversity: Multiculturalism in Canada* (2nd ed.). Toronto, ON: Nelson Thomson Learning.

Ghosh, R. (2002). *Redefining multicultural education* (2nd ed.). Toronto, ON: Harcourt Brace.

Giroux, H. E. (1994). Insurgent multiculturalism as the promise of pedagogy. In D.T. Goldberg (Ed.), *Multiculturalism: A critical reader* (pp. 325-343). Oxford, UK: Blackwell Publishers.

Guo, S. (2009). Difference, deficiency, and devaluation: Tracing the roots of non/recognition of foreign credentials for immigrant professionals in Canada. *Canadian Journal for the Study of Adult Education, 22*(1), 37-52.

Guo, Y. (2006). "Why didn't they show up?": Rethinking ESL parent involvement in K-12 education. *TESL Canada Journal, 24*(1), 80-95.

Guo, Y., & Mohan, B. (2008). ESL parents and teachers: Towards dialogue? *Language and Education, 22*(1), 17-33.

Hannerz, U. (1992). *Flows, boundaries and hybrids: Keywords in transcultural anthropology.* Working Paper Series, WPTC-2K-02 (A. Rogers, Ed.), Transnational Communities Programme, Oxford University. Retrieved from www.transcomm.ox.ac.uk/working%20papers/hannerz.pdf

Hébert, Y., Guo, Y., & Pellerin, M. (2008). New horizons for research on bilingualism and plurilingualism: A focus on languages of immigration in Canada. *Encounters on Education, 9* (Fall), 57-74.

Hoerder, D., Hébert, Y., & Schmitt, I. (Eds.). (2006). *Negotiating transcultural lives: Belongings and social capital among youth in comparative perspectives.* Toronto: University of Toronto Press.

Honneth, A. (1995). *The struggle for recognition: The moral grammar of social conflicts.* Boston, MA: MIT Press.

Innovative Research Group. (2005). *Illusion that Canada's multicultural mosaic and the United States is a melting pot.* Retrieved from http://www.dominion.ca/americanmyths/2005_multiculturalism.pdf

Jones, T.G. (2003). Contributions of Hispanic parents' perspectives to teacher preparation. *The School Community Journal, 13*(2), 73-96.

Kanu, Y. (2008). Educational needs and barriers for African refugee students in Manitoba. *Canadian Journal of Education, 31*(4), 915-940.

Karmani, S., & Pennycook, A. (2005). Islam, English, and 9/11. *Journal of Language, Identity & Education, 4*(2), 157-172.

Kincheloe, J.L., & Steinberg, S.R. (1997). *Changing multiculturalism.* Buckingham, UK: Open University.

Lareau, A. (2003). *Unequal childhoods: Class, race, and family life.* Berkeley, CA: University of California Press.

Levy, J.T. (1997). Classifying cultural rights. In I. Shapiro & W. Kymlicka (Eds.), *Ethnicity and group rights* (pp. 22-66). New York, NY: New York University Press.

Li, P. (2003). *Destination Canada: Immigration debates and issues.* Don Mills, ON: Oxford University.

Liu, L. (2007). Unveiling the invisible learning from unpaid household work: Chinese immigrants' perspective. *The Canadian Journal for the Study of Adult Education, 20*(2), 25-40.

Malatest, R. A., & Associates Ltd. (2003). *Efficacy of Alberta teacher preparation programs and beginning teachers' professional development opportunities, 2002 survey report.* Unpublished manuscript. Edmonton, AB: Alberta Learning.

McDonough, S., & Hoodfar, H. (2005). Muslims in Canada: From ethnic groups to religious community. In P. Bramadat & D. Seljak (Eds.), *Religion and ethnicity in Canada* (pp. 133-153). Toronto: Pearson Education Canada Inc.

McLaren, P. (1994). White terror and oppositional agency: Towards a critical multiculturalism. In D. T. Goldberg (Ed.), *Multiculturalism: A critical reader* (pp. 45-74). Oxford, UK: Blackwell Publishers.

McLaren, P. (2003). *Life in schools: An introduction to critical pedagogy in the foundations of education.* Boston, MA: Pearson Education.

McLaren, A.T., & Dyck, I. (2004). Mothering, human capital, and the "ideal immigrant." *Women's Studies International Forum, 27,* 41-53.

McMillan, J., & Schumacher, S. (2001). *Research in education: A conceptual introduction* (5th ed.). New York: Longman.

Nieto, S., & Bode, P. (2008). *Affirming diversity: The sociopolitical context of multicultural education* (5th ed.). New York: Allyn & Bacon.

Palmer, P. (1998). *The courage to teach: Exploring the inner landscape of a teacher's life.* San Francisco, CA: Jossey-Bass.

Polanyi, M. (1958). *Personal knowledge: Towards a post-critical philosophy.* Chicago, IL: University of Chicago Press.

Pushor, D. (2008, March). *Parent knowledge: Acknowledging parents.* Paper presented at the Annual Meeting of the American Educational Research Association, New York, NY.

Ramirez, A.Y. (2003). Dismay and disappointment: Parental involvement of Latino immigrant parents. *The Urban Review, 35*(2), 93-110.

Rezai-Rashti, G. (1994). Islamic identity and racism. *Orbit, 25*(2), 37-38.

Russo, C.J., & Hee, T. F. (2008). The right of students to wear religious garb in public schools: A comparative analysis of the United States and Malaysia. *Education Law Journal, 18*(1), 1-19.

Seljak, D. (2012). Protecting religious freedom in a multicultural Canada. *Canadian Diversity, 9*(3), 8-11.

Seljak, D., Schmidt, A., Stewart, A., & Bramadat, P. (2008). Secularization and the separation of church and state in Canada. *Canadian Diversity, 6*(1), 6-24.

Sleeter, C. E., & Grant, C. A. (1987). An analysis of multicultural education in the United States. *Harvard Educational Review, 57*(4), 421-444.

Spinner-Halev, J. (2000). Extending diversity: Religion in public and private education. In W. Kymlicka & W. Norman (Eds.), *Citizenship in diverse society* (pp. 68-95). Oxford: Oxford University Press.

Spradley, J. (1980). *Participant observation.* New York: Holt, Rinehart & Winston.

Statistics Canada. (2005). *Population projections of visible minority groups, Canada, provinces and regions 2001-2017.* Ottawa: Statistics Canada.

Statistics Canada. (2013). *Immigration and ethnocultural diversity.* Retrieved on December 11, 2013, from http://www12.statcan.gc.ca/nhs-enm/2011/as-sa/99-010-x/99-010-x2011001-eng.pdf

Syed, K.T. (2008). Misconceptions about human rights and women's rights in Islam. *Interchange, 39*(2), 245-257.

Turner, J. D (2007). Beyond cultural awareness: Prospective teachers' visions of culturally responsive literacy teaching. *Action in Teacher Education, 29*(3), 12-24.

Zine, J. (2000). Redefining resistance: Towards an Islamic subculture in schools. *Race, Ethnicity and Education, 3*(3), 293-316.

Zine, J. (2001). Muslim youth in Canadian schools: Education and the politics of religious identity. *Anthropology and Education Quarterly, 32*(4), 399-423.

Yan Guo
Werklund School of Education
University of Calgary

JOHANNE JEAN-PIERRE AND FERNANDO NUNES

16. FROM INTEGRATION TO EMPOWERMENT

*Multicultural Education in the Board of Education of the City of Toronto,
from 1960 to 1975*

INTRODUCTION

While much has been written about the link between the Canadian *Policy of
Multiculturalism* on this nation's national policies and attitudes, the impact which
this legislation has had over the work of local governing bodies has less often been
examined. One example is the influence which Multiculturalism has wielded over
the policies and practices of regional school boards. While Multiculturalism is a
nation-wide policy, directing mainly the work of the Federal Government, the
responsibility for education in Canada is charged to provincial authorities, with
local school boards often having a great deal of freedom in choosing priorities and
orientations. Thus, while the idea and practices of multicultural education can often
be regarded as a natural outcome of the federal Policy of Multiculturalism, a much
more difficult endeavour is actually tracing the effect of this legislation on the
decisions of local school councils.

In this regard, we propose that the influence of the Policy of Multiculturalism on
the practices of local schools can be explored through a historical-comparative
approach. By comparing the written records of the meetings of school boards prior
to, and following, the initiation of this Policy, we can illustrate, in an indirect
fashion, its influence on regional-level educational choices.

Following from this, the present chapter will present a case study of the
diversity-related decisions of the *Board of Education for the City of Toronto* prior
to, and after, the announcement and implementation of Multiculturalism. This was
accomplished through an examination of the *Minutes of the Board of Education for
the City of Toronto* between 1960 and 1975, which were made available through
the *Toronto District School Board Sesquicentennial Museum and Archives*. As we
will see reflected in these *Minutes*, the diversity-related decisions of the Board
indicated a paradigm shift in the Board's approach to diversity, moving from the
promotion of an *integrationist* approach throughout the 1960's, towards an
empowerment model of multicultural education, following 1972 and the
implementation of the Policy of Multiculturalism. As we will also show, the
involvement of ethnic community-based organizations, during this time,
contributed significantly to this shift.

This chapter will firstly present a brief review of the definition of multicultural
education and its three currents. Secondly, it will detail the diversity-related

S. Guo & L. Wong (eds.), Revisiting Multiculturalism in Canada, 271–288.

practices and comments, related in these minutes prior to, and following, the adoption of the federal Policy of Multiculturalism, accompanied by an analysis of the rationale behind the Board's decisions. The final section will discuss the implications of these results. Through this case study, we illustrate how policies that are adopted at the Federal level can have direct impacts on the philosophies and practices at local levels of policy and administration.

THE POLICY OF MULTICULTURALISM

The federal policy of Multiculturalism, which was adopted in 1971, following the *Royal Commission on Bilingualism and Biculturalism* of 1963, was formally affirmed in 1988 through the adoption of the Canadian Multiculturalism Act (Canadian Multiculturalism Act, 1988). This landmark legislation marked the world's first nationally-sanctioned, official Multiculturalism Policy and represented for the Canadian government a mark of leadership in relation to other countries.

Yet, as a number of scholars have illustrated, the focus of multiculturalism has shifted several times (Fleras & Elliott, 2002; Hyman, Meinhard, & Shields, 2011). The original intent of the Multiculturalism Policy was to support the maintenance of the languages and cultures of Canada's ethnic minorities, as well as to actively promote these within mainstream society. However, over the years, criticism has surfaced suggesting that multiculturalism both "balkanizes" ethnic groups as well as fails to address the discrimination which many new immigrants experience (Bissoondath, 1994; Garcea, 2008), or unequal relations of power (Ghosh, 2011). Such critiques have been acknowledged in the reports of public consultations, such as the *Citizen's Forum on Canada's Future* (Spicer, 1991), which stated that Canadians valued diversity, but that the federal government should not spend public money to support the language and culture of its immigrant minorities.

As a consequence of these concerns, the priorities of the Multiculturalism Policy have shifted over the decades to a focus on promoting the integration of newcomers, the reduction of racism and seeking equity for all citizens. The budget for implementing multiculturalism has also been slashed from a high of $30 million in the 1980's, to $10 million in 2001 and $15 million in 2011 (Citizenship and Immigration Canada, 2012; Isajiw 1999, p. 247).

The actual implementation of multiculturalism varies according to different social-historical and political contexts (Banting & Kymlicka, 2010). Kymlicka (2010) contends that the preconditions for the successful lasting implementation of multicultural policies in a country require regional security and a wide support for human rights. The trajectories of multiculturalism also differ greatly per country as illustrated by Winter's comparison of Germany, the Netherlands, and Canada. Winter (2010) suggests that national trajectories of multiculturalism are influenced by: (1) whether or not a country is defined with ethno-racial terms, (2) whether or not there is a conflict between two historical groups and (3) whether or not pluralist arrangements are important.

MULTICULTURAL EDUCATION

Education is one domain in which multicultural societies may innovate with school-based multicultural practices and initiatives. Thus, the idea of multicultural education arose as a way to respond to the plurality of Canadian society, within the nation's classrooms. Swartz (1992) offers a comprehensive definition of multicultural education:

> ... an education that uses methodologies and instructional materials which promote equity of information and high standards of academic scholarship in an environment that respects the potential of each student. An education that is multicultural conforms to the highest standards of educational practice: the use of well-researched content that is accurate and up-to-date; the presentation of diverse indigenous accounts and perspectives that encourage critical thinking; the avoidance of dated terminologies, stereotypes, and demeaning, distorted characterizations; the use of intellectually challenging materials presented in an environment of free and open discussion. In short, multicultural education is a restatement of sound educational pedagogy and practice that requires the collective representation of all cultures and groups as significant to the production of knowledge. (Swartz, 1992, p. 34)

In this fashion, multicultural education is regarded as highly beneficial, in facilitating the retention of cultural heritage, fostering interethnic harmony, and equalizing academic achievement.

Yet, several typologies and discussions of multicultural educational models exist in the literature (Fleras & Elliott, 2002; Guo & Jamal, 2007; Tator & Henry, 1991). For the purposes of this analysis, we have used Fleras and Elliott's (2002) typology, which proposes three models of multicultural education: the *enrichment model*, the *enlightenment model* and the *empowerment model*.

The *enrichment model* of multicultural education aims to expose all students to a variety of cultures, through the addition of multicultural elements to the curriculum, such as: the planning of special days for multicultural awareness, the challenging of stereotypes, cross-cultural communication and intercultural sensitivity awareness (Fleras & Elliott 2002, p. 336). Fleras and Elliott (2002) suggest that this form of multicultural education is non-threatening, but carries the danger of over-romanticizing minorities by studying culture out of its cultural and temporal contexts.

Many critiques of multicultural education are particularly directed at the *enrichment model*. These scholars contend that, when multicultural education involves the retention of cultural heritage, it infers that culture is fixed, rigid and stereotyped (Dalley & Begley, 2008; Mohan, 2007). Others have criticized multicultural education for ignoring racial differences and racial discrimination (Dei, Mazzuca, McIsaac, & Zine, 1997; Tator & Henry, 1991) and have called for the inclusion of anti-racist and anti-supremacist pedagogies (Schick & St. Denis, 2005).

In contrast to the *enrichment model*, the *enlightenment model* proposes a transformative approach focusing on social justice, designed to change students' attitudes about diversity and leading these to recognize hierarchical and unequal relationships of power (Fleras & Elliott, 2002, p. 336). For example, dark chapters of our history can be examined to encourage students to reflect on inequality and seek ways to transform these relationships.

The third typology, the *empowerment model,* focuses predominantly on the needs of minority students. Whereas the first two models address the needs of all students to become aware of diversity or to seek to transform unequal relationships, the *empowerment model* is based on the premises that the school system is failing these students and that what is required, is a school-context that capitalizes on their strengths and learning styles, in order to achieve academic achievement (Fleras & Elliott, 2002). In practice, this means creating culturally safe spaces for minority students, which may include separate schools such as Africentric schools. From a critical race perspective, the *empowerment model* of multicultural education is believed to facilitate equity and equal access to education, especially for marginalized groups (Dei et al., 1997).

Like in the case of Multiculturalism, multicultural education in Canada has been critiqued for its promotion of the belief in a colour-blind, or raceless, society (Schick & St. Denis, 2005) and for its inability to reduce racism (Kirova, 2008). Nugent (2006) further remarks that in discussions about multicultural education, there has been a shift from an emphasis on difference to an emphasis on integration.

We can clearly see this shift reflected in the French Canadian literature on intercultural education, a fourth model of multicultural education. *Intercultural education* aims to foster inclusion and social cohesion and attempts to avoid the social fragmentation of essentialized groups (Dalley & Begley, 2008). French Canadian academics suggest that *intercultural education* facilitates the conciliation of similarities and differences through dialogue and provides the potential for the negotiation of a common culture (Dalley & Begley, 2008). However, this literature neglects to highlight that an equal access to language, in this case French, is essential in order for intercultural education to take place. Dalley and Begley (2008) conclude that if there is no equal access to language, social inequalities can hinder the efforts for social cohesion.

The particular model that local school authorities choose to implement is often influenced by the wider social policies of governments and social institutions. This chapter will illustrate this by showcasing the evolution of multicultural education initiatives at the *Board of Education for the City of Toronto* between 1960 and 1975 and, in this way, tracing the influence of the federal policy of Multiculturalism on the decisions of this Board. In addition, it will also assess any preferences with respect to models of multicultural education.

METHODOLOGY

This study applied a historical-comparative analysis to the *Minutes of the Board of Education for the City of Toronto*, between 1960 and 1975, through the ideal-types methodology as discussed by Burke (2005). This analysis was conducted in order to investigate how the Board's decisions regarding issues of diversity evolved before and after the federal policy of Multiculturalism. The analysis included a categorization of the practices that relate to diversity, in relation to "ideal-types," as defined by Weber (1978, pp. 20-21). The four ideal-types that were selected as models in this study were the pre-mentioned *enrichment model, enlightenment model, empowerment model* and *intercultural model* of multicultural education (Fleras & Elliott, 2002).

Before an administrative amalgamation in 1998, the greater metropolitan area of the City of Toronto was home to independent and separate Boards for the former cities including: *York, East York, North York, Scarborough, Etobicoke,* and the *City of Toronto.* This study examines documents of one of these former cities' Boards, *The Board of Education for the City of Toronto*, whose mandate was to serve what is today, the central and downtown area of the current city of Toronto.

Our sampling method examined index pages that contained the words: "New Canadians," "English and citizenship classes," "English as a second language," "bicultural/bilingual" and "multicultural," from the *Minutes of the Board of Education for the City of Toronto* between 1960 and 1975. These minutes contain decisions from all the meetings held by trustees, all the motions that were amended, adopted or rejected, along with sub-committee and special committee reports and recommendations.

RESULTS

In the sixties, the Board offered New Canadian classes, English as a second language (ESL) and heritage language classes to promote integration. As Thomas A. Wardle, a trustee, mentioned it in his address on the 7th of January 1960, the curriculum of the Board was inspired by the educational systems of specific countries:

> Education in Toronto has a long and noble tradition. Following the pattern set by the Province, we have drawn from educational systems in the British Isles, Europe and the United States. However, it is most important that we should examine and evaluate carefully educational programmes from whatever source they come. (The Board, 1960, p. 1)

Besides having a curriculum that was influenced mainly by Europe and the United States of America, there were initiatives targeting the needs of "New Canadians." When trustees referred to "New Canadians," they meant immigrants or newcomers. Therefore, for the purpose of this chapter, we will use the same expression.

There were two main types of programs that were intended to serve New Canadians: New Canadian Adult programs, that were meant to help adults to learn English during evening, day and summer classes and, starting in 1962, ESL programs for New Canadian pupils. These programs evolved not with the objective of promoting any model of multicultural education, but to promote integration.

New Canadian Classes

In the sixties, there were several motions for the opening of 4 week programs, opening classes, evening classes, day classes and summer classes for New Canadian adults and pupils due to high demand and the success of these programs (The Board, 1960, p. 300; 1961, pp. 47, 105, 118; 1962, p. 194; 1963, pp. 236, 328, 467; 1964, pp. 234, 353, 528; 1965, p. 302; 1966, pp. 8, 26, 100; 1967, pp. 25, 57, 301). Many initiatives were discussed to facilitate the participation of parents with children by offering pre-kinderkarten or nursery services, especially to encourage the attendance of mothers with children (The Board, 1968, pp. 315, 493, 586, 615, 733; 1969, pp. 33, 522). In order to improve these programs, in 1967, a motion was proposed to ask the Director of Education to consider the possibility of enabling "New Canadians to obtain upgrading in subjects required obtaining entrance to apprenticeship training programmes" (The Board, 1967, p. 57).

New advertisement strategies were sought and there were discussions in relation to how the Board could prepare notices in different languages for parents. The discussion surrounding the purpose of these programmes reveals how important it was to assist New Canadians in their integration and promote programs targeted to newcomers:

> ... the Board's Attendance Department has conducted a number of evening programmes in the schools for various ethnic groups which were in the nature of entertainments and were called *Greek Nights, Italian Night*, etc., and similar programmes are planned for the future. The programmes are intended to help the immigrant adjust to the community in which he lives and to broaden his understanding of Canadian society. The programmes already held were very successful and they are an ideal way in which to advertise the Board's educational programmes for immigrants, for example, classes for New Canadian mothers. (The Board, 1969, p. 523)

The increasing need of funding for New Canadian classes led to a decision in March 1970 to send a delegation from the Board to the Federal Department of Immigration in Ottawa, to request financial assistance for these programmes with their exact costs (The Board, 1970, pp. 217, 367, 739). It was even recommended that the Board request that part of the funding transferred by the Federal Government to provinces to promote bilingualism should support New Canadian programs (The Board, 1970, p. 898).

Although the Board lacked resources, it continued to expand New Canadian programs. In August 1971, the New Canadian Committee appointed a new Chairman to co-ordinate all New Canadian programmes. As previously mentioned,

New Canadian classes as well as ESL classes, sought to foster integration into Canadian society.

English as a Second Language (ESL)

In 1962, ESL classes for pupils, sometimes referred to as English and citizenship classes, were introduced (The Board, 1962, p. 78; 1963, p. 117; 1964, pp. 164, 197, 374; 1965, pp. 184, 303, 581; 1966, pp. 8, 116, 124). In 1965, ESL programs came under much scrutiny and a motion was carried in order to examine many aspects of these programs. The motion moved that the Director of Education be requested to submit to the Management Committee a detailed research report on such items as: the number and language grouping of children in Board schools who were learning English as a second language; their age and gender; the schools and districts involved; the percentage of a school's population who were ESL; the percentage of each grouping to the total population; the incidence of dropouts, in relation to English-speaking pupils (The Board, 1965, p. 42). In addition, it also asked for information on: the methods of teaching; the type of ESL teacher; how these were selected, trained and supervised and by whom; and who co-ordinated the programme. Finally, it sought to know about: the roles of libraries and other departments; contacts and knowledge of similar programs in other cities; and other pertinent information.

The desire to look at the incidence of dropout rates in groups of students who required ESL indicated an emerging interest in equity. In 1965, the Board approved the opening of a reception school, exclusively for non-English-speaking New Canadian students, aged twelve years and older, and this was a pilot project to assist students with cultural challenges (The Board, 1965, pp. 184, 356).

What is worth mentioning, is the increasing attention paid by the trustees to the then-recent scientific knowledge that had been accumulated in the field of English as second language at the *National Council of Teachers of English* and at universities such as *Laval, Columbia, Hunter College, Buffalo* and *London*. As a result of the emergence of this new expertise, trustees believed that teachers involved in programmes for New Canadians should attend professional development workshops and complete extensive training (The Board, 1965, p. 557; 1966, pp. 93, 136, 273, 276). An explanation of this increased attention to ESL can be found in a 1966 report from the special committee. In this report, trustees discussed the great number of pupils in the schools who spoke little English and the anticipated prospective large number of pupils who would not speak English at all for the following school year (The Board, 1966, p. 175).

As a result of the diversification of the student body, initiatives were adopted in May 1966 to print two issues of the Board's newsletter and forms in other languages than English and to allocate additional classes and resources (The Board, 1966, pp. 272-273).

In 1965, *Main Street School* was opened for exclusively ESL programs. As a result of this new school's specific mandate, innovation was encouraged with new teaching methodologies and extensive teacher's training. Two years later, the

Board approved a recommendation from the New Canadian Special Committee to establish regional reception centres for New Canadian pupils where the teaching techniques developed at *Main Street School* could be put into practice (The Board, 1967, p. 471). The Board also approved the recommendation that the Board's Research Department begin a full-scale research project involving New Canadians in order to compare the methods applied at the *Main Street School* to other programmes (The Board, 1967, p. 471). *Main Street School* exemplified how an alternative school could successfully develop an expertise that facilitated the learning experiences of a specific student population.

Overall, during the sixties, resources for New Canadian programs and ESL programs kept increasing, with more teachers, lay assistants, classrooms rentals, furniture and equipment allocated. Nevertheless, in 1968, trustees had to examine assertions raised in a newspaper article that the Board was not allocating enough resources to meet the needs of New Canadians (The Board, 1968, p. 63). Two years later, in 1970, following the reception of a letter from Mr. Elio Costa, the New Canadian Committee also examined allegations about the overrepresentation of New Canadian children in vocational schools, two-year terminal schools and low achievement groups. In relation to these allegations, the committee discussed the role that the Board should play in representing the history and culture of New Canadian groups in the school system in collaboration with representatives of various ethnic groups (The Board, 1970, p. 208). It was suggested that instead of informal buffets, general meetings should be held to assess the situation thoroughly with different ethnic groups' representatives (The Board, 1970, pp. 738, 899). This indicates that a concern for equity and for the representation of all ethnic groups in the school pre-existed the federal policy of Multiculturalism.

In sum, the overall practices and policies of the Board in the sixties were aimed at integration and did not correspond to any of the four ideal-types of multicultural education. A lack of equity, a lack of immigrants' cultural heritage representation in the school and the non-mastery of English were understood as hindering the full integration of New Canadian parents and students. Therefore, the emerging interest in equity and representation cannot be interpreted as an adoption of any model of multicultural education.

Heritage Languages

Before the rise of discussions about equity and ethnic representation in the school, the idea of communicating with New Canadian parents in their own languages was considered in 1967 (The Board, 1967, p. 212). In 1970, there were discussions about the need to improve the first contact that immigrants had with the school system. It was acknowledged that immigrants experienced difficulties due to language barriers and the lack of information on educational opportunities available during the summer for their children (The Board, 1970, pp. 469, 738). In June 1967, for the first time, a motion was adopted to consider strategies through which New Canadians would be able to retain their native languages. The Board applied to the Department of Education to have permission to excuse students from the French programme in Grades 5-10 in order to study their own heritage language (The Board, 1967, p. 393). This permission was eventually granted by the Department of Education the same year (The Board, 1967, p. 438). In 1968, some members of the staff were also delegated to attend the Convention of the Association of Teachers of English to Speakers of Other Languages in March 1968 at San Antonio, Texas (The Board, 1968, p. 100). Furthermore, in 1971, it became more apparent that community-based organizations wanted to cooperate with the Board. For example, members of the Italian community brought forward the following proposition:

> Mr. R. V. Marino, Executive Director of the Italian Community Education Centre (COSTI), has submitted a proposed plan involving COSTI, O.I.S.E., and the Toronto Board of Education, in a project for recently arrived Italian children at the grade 4 to 6 level. The project is expected to fulfil the purposes of evaluating the merits of teaching in Italian in preparation for the students' entrance into an English instruction setting, and to develop a process for involving Italian parents in the educational partnership. It is felt that an educational partnership involving the teacher, the Italian child and his parents is of primary importance in encouraging and facilitating integration of the total family into Canadian society. (The Board, 1971, p. 855)

Here again, we see that the goal of these initiatives was the integration of immigrants' families in Canadian society. ESL programs for parents and children, the promotion of heritage language, the discussion about the representation of different cultures and equity issues could be considered multicultural practices. Yet, the integrationist objective of these initiatives, as well as the absence of other essential practices for the implementation of multicultural education, such as curriculum revisions and new hiring practices, indicate that the rationale behind these initiatives had nothing to do with multicultural education. None of the four ideal types of multicultural education can apply to what was being done before 1971. Nevertheless, we can see that the Board was already aware of the merits of some multicultural initiatives, such as developing ESL programs, the promotion of heritage language, acknowledging the relevance of partnership with different New Canadian community-based organizations, discussing equity issues and attempting to use different strategies to communicate with New Canadian parents who do not speak English. After 1971, the multicultural practices already in place remained, but there was a shift in paradigm from a focus on integration to multicultural education. This shift was indicated by a change in semantics in relation to diversity issues, an increase in formal partnerships with ethnic community-based organizations and the implementation of bicultural/bilingual pilot projects.

From the New Canadian Committee to the Multi-Cultural Program Work Group

New Canadian programs and ESL programs continued to grow while discussions regarding funding of New Canadian programs became more frequent (The Board, 1972, pp. 113, 155, 313; 1973, pp. 192, 308, 564, 565, 839; 1974, p. 355).

The influence of the federal policy of Multiculturalism is explicit when we observe the change in the language that is used for diversity. In fact, the word "multicultural" was used for the first time in the index of the 1974 *Board of Education for the City of Toronto Minutes* paralleling the disappearance of the expression New Canadian. The goals of the *Work Group on Multi-cultural Programs* were slightly different from those of the previous committee, since the focus would be to investigate and explore the philosophy and programs of the multi-cultural population, to analyse the Board's practices for multi-cultural programs and to make recommendations (The Board, 1974, p. 418). Thus, this change of name also signals a change of paradigm from that of integration to multicultural education.

> Programs for New Canadians were originally set up with the distinct intention of enabling students and later parents to become as fluent in English as possible in order that they might adapt more quickly to what is viewed as, "the Canadian way of life." As these programs developed and as the population of Canada, and particularly the centre core of the city changed, two new thrusts became apparent. First, there was a strong desire on the part of the immigrant population to preserve much of their own cultural heritage, in particular their language. Second, there was a recognition that Canada was a multi-cultural nation and that considerable strength could be derived from preserving aspects of different cultures including the maintenance of their own languages. (The Board, 1974, p. 419)

Increasing Partnerships with Community-Based Organizations

Community-based organizations continued to present collaborative projects to the school Board. For example, the *Federation of Italian Canadian Associations and Clubs* in collaboration with the *Department of Citizenship of the Provincial Government* initiated a project to promote the interest of Italian parents in the school system (The Board, 1972, p. 184). In 1973, the idea of evaluating immigrant students in their first language in order to better measure their potential and abilities was raised to avoid systematically placing these students in vocational schools (The Board, 1973, p. 230). There were also discussions about co-operating with immigrant groups who felt that the Board did not really understand their problems (The Board, 1973, p. 230). For example, a pilot project was considered for Italian-speaking children at the Junior Kindergarten level in Italian (The Board, 1972, p. 114). In 1974, there were other decisions in relation to heritage language such as: the extension of Italian language programs at *Harbord* and *Bloor Collegiate Institutes*, the introduction of a new Italian program at *Monarch Park Secondary School*, the implementation of a Portuguese language program at *Harbord Collegiate Institute* and a Ukrainian language program at *Bloor Collegiate Institute* (The Board, 1974, p. 35). The Research Department was also invited to assist the Board in developing a survey to examine the demand for ethnic languages in secondary schools, in order to create additional language programs

(The Board, 1974, p. 35). It is also in 1974 and 1975 that French schools and French programs were developed for Francophones since, at the time, French school Boards did not yet exist (The Board, 1975, p. 413).

In May 1974, a report was presented summarizing survey results about third language requests and the measures to be taken to respond to these needs. The third languages were Italian, Portuguese, Ukrainian, Lithuanian, Polish, Greek, Chinese, Spanish, French and Hebrew (The Board, 1974, p. 399). In addition, there was a proposal to examine the needs of the growing Spanish speaking population (The Board, 1974, p. 775). Yet, besides the change in semantics and the increased attention given to heritage language programs, the most important change that indicated a paradigm shift towards multicultural education after 1971 was the presence of increasing consideration for bicultural and bilingual programs.

Bicultural and Bilingual Programs

In February 1972, trustees discussed a brief sent by the English Department of *King Edward Public School* entitled "Bilingual Education in the Portuguese Community." This brief proposed the hiring of a full-time qualified Portuguese teacher for all students who wish to receive instruction in Portuguese starting with grades 7 and 8 (The Board, 1972, p. 113). The bicultural programs for Portuguese students had several objectives:

(a) To provide an effective bridge to instruction in English for newly arrived Portuguese students as a means of avoiding progressive academic retardation and damage to the student's self-image induced by the rejection of his language and culture.

(b) To maintain and further develop the student's Portuguese language facility and to enhance his appreciation and pride in the Portuguese culture.

(c) To close the gap between values of the school and the values of the home so that the student is not put in the position of rejecting one in favour of the other.

(d) To provide a vehicle by which the Portuguese parents can become more fully involved in the educational partnership. (The Board, 1972, pp. 114-115)

This list of objectives indicates a shift from the goal of integration to a greater concern towards the needs of New Canadian students, such as fostering the student's self-image and pride in cultural heritage. These objectives correspond to the *empowerment* model ideal-type of multicultural education. Trustees wished to bring coherence between the home and the school and hoped to encourage parents' involvement. It was discussed that the Board would ask permission to the Minister of Education to implement experimental courses in languages other than English and French, since *The Schools Administration Act* was not specific in this matter. However, in May 1972, the committee reported that: "the Minister was not receptive to the idea of implementing at the public school level, experimental courses in languages other than English and French" (The Board, 1972, p. 314).

Nevertheless, the Board continued to move forward by studying proposals for other bicultural pilot projects, which were coherent with an *empowerment model* ideal-type of multicultural education. A Chinese-Canadian Bicultural/Bilingual Immersion Program at *Ogden and Orde Street Public Schools* was proposed contingent on the approval of the Toronto Board of Education and the Provincial Ministry of Education (The Board, 1973, pp. 535, 569). The New Canadian Committee also proposed the creation of a Greco-Canadian Bicultural/Bilingual Programs at *Jackman Avenue Public School* and *Frankland Public School* as proposed by the *Greek Parents' Associations* where Greek parents would collaborate with schools (The Board, 1973, p. 566). The enrolment of children in all these bilingual/bicultural programs would be voluntary and no parent would be coerced to adhere to these programs.

In 1973, there was another illustration of a clear shift towards multicultural education in a letter by the New Canadian Committee, detailing the benefits of a Chinese-Canadian Bicultural/Bilingual programs. This rationale argues that the Chinese child could experience cultural alienation due to the institutional messages and the repression of its own cultural heritage. This letter also argues the necessity of creating a school environment, which is compatible, and not competing, with the family's:

> While the young alien may be the subject of positive supportive efforts of the staff, the negative message imbedded in the cultural character of the environment itself is formidable and overwhelming. Even the very attention which teachers, lay assistants and social workers display for the purpose of assisting his transfer from one cultural world to another carries its own negative message. Regardless of the softness, patience and subtlety of the coercion, the message of the intent is always the same: The student's cultural heritage and, by extension, his very personality has little integrity and less worth; therefore, he must school himself to conform the new life order in the cause of recapturing recognition, greater worth and a healthier image. The schooling implies the displacement and eventual dissolution of an original heritage. School, for that given student, is not a growth environment, but a transition medium. (The Board, 1973, p. 744)

It was also believed that these bilingual/bicultural programs were beneficial since they were: "Building upon what a child has already learned because that learning forms a positive and stable plateau for future growth is a strategy which hardly needs more than mention here, (The Board, 1973, p. 746)." The letter also highlighted the active involvement of communities in the design of the programs, the structure of daily life in the school, the role of certificated teachers, the focus on culture and not language, the endorsement of these alternative programs by minorities and the fact that those who committed to these programs still valued the general principle of acculturation into Canadian society (The Board, 1974, p. 136).

In February 1974, the minutes mention that the Minister of Education requested detailed information about the final proposals for Greek and Chinese bicultural programs (The Board, 1974, p. 120). In October 1974, it was communicated that the Minister of Education had provided temporary approval to the Chino-Canadian Bicultural/Bilingual Immersion Program for Orde Street and Ogden Public Schools (The Board, 1974, p. 745). The approval for the Greco-Canadian Bicultural/ Bilingual Immersion Program in Jackman Avenue and Frankland Public School also followed as a pilot project (The Board, 1975, pp. 226, 412). The *Comitao Scolastico Italiano* submitted a proposal for an Italo-Canadian Bicultural/Bilingual immersion program while the only available bilingual/bicultural programs were the Chinese and Greek programs (The Board, 1975, p. 290).

In the minutes, it seems clear that the continuing involvement and perseverance of community-based partners were essential for the program's maintenance. In fact, the Greek and Chinese proposals were initiated prior to 1973 and it took two years of procedures for the program to start. This illustrates the long delays that community-based organizations experienced from the time a proposal was made to the time a project materialized.

The Board followed the progress of the *Board of Education for the City of New York* in the development of bilingual programs and a visit to New York was considered beneficial to the Board to learn from their policies and practices (The Board, 1974, pp. 735, 845).

The goals and the rationale behind bilingual/bicultural programs, which appeared after 1971, correspond clearly to the *empowerment model* ideal-type of multicultural education with an emphasis on ethnic minority students' strengths to promote academic success. Nevertheless, the cohabitation of diverse cultures was challenging, as illustrated in 1974 when the Board considered the establishment of programs to forestall conflicts and tensions between established Torontonians and ethnic, religious and racial minority groups (The Board, 1974, p. 744).

DISCUSSION AND CONCLUSION

As we have seen in this chapter, the policy of the Board changed from one of integration to an *empowerment model* ideal-type of multicultural education paralleling the adoption of Multiculturalism. While New Canadian classes, ESL classes and heritage language programs were believed to facilitate integration in the sixties, a change in semantics, partnerships with community-based organizations and the promotion of bicultural/bilingual pilot projects indicate that there was a shift towards the *empowerment model* ideal-type of multicultural education.

Prior to 1971, much effort and energy were directed to the development of effective ESL programs. Funding was allocated to teachers' training, a school was opened exclusively for ESL classes and attention was paid to new teaching strategies. Finally, at the end of the 1960s, before the declaration of the federal policy of Multiculturalism, there were discussions about equity issues and heritage language retention to promote integration. The Board's interest in language and cultural retention was not due to any belief in the inherent value of these cultures; rather, it was a consequence of the general belief that not addressing these issues could jeopardize the integration of newcomers.

One could consider that the practices promoting integration of the sixties in this school Board were equivalent to an insistence on assimilation and James and Wood (2005) suggest that assimilation is still the dominant paradigm in most school Boards across the country. However, there is a clear shift after 1972 towards an *empowerment model* of multicultural education in the *Board of Education for the City of Toronto*. The *New Canadian Committee* that was pursuing the integration of newcomers became the *Multi-Cultural Program Work Group* pursuing the implementation of the best practices to serve a diverse student body. There were increasing discussions with community-based organizations to expand heritage language programs and better cooperate with parents from different ethnic backgrounds. Bicultural/bilingual pilot projects were also conceived in collaboration with community-based organizations to promote academic success built on students' strengths and abilities.

The shift towards an *empowerment model* ideal-type can be considered a disconnect from the orientation of the federal policy of Multiculturalism. In the early years of the Multiculturalism policy, the promotion of heritage retention and the celebration of differences were emphasized (Fleras & Elliott, 2002). Thus, a coherent ideal-type of multicultural education for this time period could have been the *enrichment model*. One could in fact expect that in parallel with the federal policy, the school Board would have emphasized the *enrichment model* with heritage language programs, multicultural days and a celebration of diversity, but this was not the case.

Thus, how may we explain that the paradigm shift tilted towards the *empowerment model* ideal-type of multicultural education? Firstly, the requests and active involvement of ethnic community-based organizations can partially explain the paradigm shift of the school Board towards the *empowerment model*. These groups kept bringing forward requests for better services to respond to the needs of their children and they asserted leadership by proposing collaborative innovative projects.

The dominance of the *empowerment model* in the early seventies illustrates how agency, especially from community-based organizations or grassroots movements, can actually influence institutional debates. These ethnic community-based organizations were already participating in the Board's meetings in the sixties, but we suggest that the federal policy of Multiculturalism facilitated the funding and implementation of initiatives such as the bicultural/bilingual pilot projects, by legitimizing both the ethnic community organizations, as well as their objectives. In fact, at least one recent report has recognized the importance of ethnic organizations in creating bonding social capital and has called for the Multiculturalism Program to further support these groups (Hyman, Meinhard, & Shields, 2011).

A second explanation for the presence of the *empowerment model* instead of the *enrichment model* lies partially in the social and political historical context that encouraged social change at the time: with the rise of the New Left, decolonization in third world countries, social movements such as the African-American civil rights movements, the anti-war movements or the American Indian movement. Kymlicka (2010) contends that the revolution of human rights that followed the horrors of the Second World War contributed to the emergence of decolonization movements at the end of the forties, to the African-American civil rights movement in the fifties and finally, to the rise of multiculturalism and minority rights in the late sixties. This movement towards minority rights thus found its expression in multicultural education, through the *empowerment model*. In fact, one could even argue that the embrace of the *empowerment model* by the Board, the development of the federal policy of Multiculturalism, as well as the community based organizations' objectives, were all influenced by this specific historical context.

Finally, the federal policy of Multiculturalism in and of itself influenced the paradigm shift because it changed the way trustees discussed, understood and envisioned Canadian diversity. This is demonstrated by the change of semantics at the Board: For example, the change of name from the *New Canadian Committee* to the *Multi-Cultural Program Work Group*. Ultimately, the fact to which such evidence points is the apparent sensitivity and responsiveness of seemingly independent and unconnected policy and procedures, each administered at different levels of government, but being influenced both by social movements, as well as by the decisions of other levels of government.

There are limitations to the use of ideal-type models to analyze historical events, movements and policies in social research. Firstly, ideal-types can sometimes ignore change and oversimplify reality (Burke 2005, p. 30). Indeed, one could argue that an alternative typology could be used or that one model of multicultural education overlaps another. Secondly, it is acknowledged that these archival documents provide only the perspectives of trustees and Board personnel and do not necessarily provide evidence for the thoughts and experiences of students, teachers, parents, leaders of community-based organizations, as well as the general population of Toronto. We also acknowledge that we do not know how teachers and principals received and implemented new multicultural practices. Since schools are loosely coupled institutions, teachers and principals have great freedom in the extent to which they apply new policies (Davies & Guppy 2010, p. 204). Nevertheless, these minutes provide us with insight about the decision-making process and the changing perceptions of trustees regarding diversity in education. Finally, what happened in this Board was not necessarily representative of what was happening in other school Boards in the rest of the country. Despite these limitations, these documents illustrate how a relationship existed between a national federal policy and the decisions and programs that actually evolved in local communities and structures.

This analysis stops in 1975, very early after the adoption of the federal policy of Multiculturalism. Consequently, further research is necessary to understand the evolution of bicultural/bilingual programs, heritage language programs and English as a second language programs. There is also a need to uncover how the complex relationships between community-based organizations, the school Board, the Ministry of Education and the federal policy of Multiculturalism evolved over time. Future research projects could examine how paradigm shifts in diversity-related policies actually take place in school Boards in different contexts using a historical-comparative methodology. In sum, the mission and goals of a federal policy may differ or parallel those adopted by provincial ministries and local structures.

ACKNOWLEDGEMENTS

We thank Greg McKinnon, manager and archivist, and Marie Passerino from the *Toronto District School Board Sesquicentennial Museum and Archives*.

REFERENCES

Banting, K., & Kymlicka, W. (2010). Canadian multiculturalism: Global anxieties and local debates. *British Journal of Canadian Studies, 23*(1), 43-72.

Bissoondath, N. (1994). *Selling illusions: The cult of multiculturalism in Canada.* Toronto: Penguin Canada.

The Board of Education for the City of Toronto. (1960). The Board of Education for the City of Toronto Minutes. Toronto.

The Board of Education for the City of Toronto. (1961). The Board of Education for the City of Toronto Minutes. Toronto.

The Board of Education for the City of Toronto. (1962). The Board of Education for the City of Toronto Minutes. Toronto.

The Board of Education for the City of Toronto. (1963). The Board of Education for the City of Toronto Minutes. Toronto.

The Board of Education for the City of Toronto. (1964). The Board of Education for the City of Toronto Minutes. Toronto.

The Board of Education for the City of Toronto. (1965). The Board of Education for the City of Toronto Minutes. Toronto.

The Board of Education for the City of Toronto. (1966). The Board of Education for the City of Toronto Minutes. Toronto.

The Board of Education for the City of Toronto. (1967). The Board of Education for the City of Toronto Minutes. Toronto.

The Board of Education for the City of Toronto. (1968). The Board of Education for the City of Toronto Minutes. Toronto.

The Board of Education for the City of Toronto. (1969). The Board of Education for the City of Toronto Minutes. Toronto.

The Board of Education for the City of Toronto. (1970). The Board of Education for the City of Toronto Minutes. Toronto.

The Board of Education for the City of Toronto. (1971). The Board of Education for the City of Toronto Minutes. Toronto.

The Board of Education for the City of Toronto. (1972). The Board of Education for the City of Toronto Minutes. Toronto.

The Board of Education for the City of Toronto. (1973). The Board of Education for the City of Toronto Minutes. Toronto.

The Board of Education for the City of Toronto. (1974). The Board of Education for the City of Toronto Minutes. Toronto.

The Board of Education for the City of Toronto. (1975). The Board of Education for the City of Toronto Minutes. Toronto.

Breton, R. (1998). Ethnicity and race in social organization: Recent development in Canadian society. In R. Helms-Hayes & C. James (Eds.), *The vertical mosaic revisited* (pp. 60-115). Toronto: University of Toronto Press.

Burke, P. (2005). *History and social theory* (2ⁿᵈ ed.). New York: Cornell University Press.

Canadian Multiculturalism Act. (1988). Department of Justice Canada.

Dalley, P., & Michael, B. (2008). Fragmentation sociale et cohésion sociale en éducation au Canada. *Canadian Ethnic Studies/Études Ethniques au Canada, 40*(1), 125-139.

Davies, S., & Neil, G. (2010). *The schooled society: An introduction to the sociology of education*. Don Mills: Oxford University Press.

Dei, G. J. S., Mazzuca, J., McIsaac, E., & Zine, J. (1997). *Reconstructing 'drop-out': A critical ethnography of the dynamics of black students' disengagement from school*. Toronto: University of Toronto Press.

Citizenship and Immigration Canada. (2014). Evaluation of the Multiculturalism Program. *Citizenship and Immigration Canada* Retrieved from http://www.cic.gc.ca/english/resources/evaluation/multi/section1.asp

Fleras, A., & Elliott, J. L. (2002). *Unequal relations: An introduction to race and ethnic dynamics in Canada* (4ᵗʰ ed.). Toronto: Prentice Hall.

Garcea, J. (2008). Postulations on the fragmentary effects of multiculturalism in Canada. *Canadian Ethnic Studies/Études Ethniques au Canada, 40*(1), 141-160.

Ghosh, R. (2011). The liberating potential of multiculturalism in Canada: Ideals and realities. *Canadian Issues/Thèmes Canadiens*, Spring, 3-8.

Guo, S. & Jamal, Z. (2007). Nurturing cultural diversity in higher education: A critical review of selected models. *Canadian Journal of Higher Education, 37*(3), 27-49.

Hyman, I., Meinhard, A., & Shields, J. (2011). *The role of multiculturalism policy in addressing social inclusion processes in Canada*. Toronto: Centre for Voluntary Sector Studies and Canadian Multicultural Education Foundation.

Isajiw, W. (1999). *Understanding diversity: Ethnicity and race in the Canadian context*. Toronto: Thompson Educational Publishing.

James, C., & Wood M. (2005). Multicultural education in Canada: Opportunities, limitations and contradictions. In C. E. James (Ed.) *Possibilities & limitations: Multicultural policies and programs in Canada* (pp. 97-103). Halifax: Fernwood Publishing.

Kirova, A. (2008). Critical and emerging discourses in multicultural education literature: A review. *Canadian Ethnic Studies/Études Ethniques au Canada, 40*(1), 101-124.

Kymlicka, W. (2010). The rise and fall of multiculturalism? New debates on inclusion and accommodation in diverse societies. *International Social Science Journal, 61*(199), 97-112.

Mohan, E. (2007). Challenging multiculturalism: is it right for everyone? *Journal of Cases in Educational Leadership, 10*(1), 7-13.

Nugent, A. (2006). Demography, national myths, and political origins: perceiving official multiculturalism in Quebec. *Canadian Ethnic Studies/Études Ethniques au Canada, 38*(3), 21-36.

Schick, C., & St. Denis, V. (2005). The troubling national discourses in anti-racist curricular planning. *Canadian Journal of Education, 28*(3), 295-317.

Spicer, K. (1991). *Citizens' forum on Canada's future: Report to the people and Government of Canada*. Ottawa: Minister of Supply and Services Canada.

Swartz, E. (1992). Multicultural education: From a compensatory to a scholarly foundation. In C. A. Grant (Ed.), *Research and multicultural education: from the margin to the mainstream* (pp. 31-43). London: The Falmer Press.

Tator, C., & Henry, F. (1991). *Multicultural education: Translating policy into practice*. Ottawa: Multiculturalism and Citizenship Canada.

Weber, M. (1978). *Economy and society*. Berkeley, CA: University of California Press.

Winter, E. (2010). Trajectories of multiculturalism in Germany, the Netherlands and Canada: In search of common patterns. *Government and Opposition. 45*(2), 166-186.

Johanne Jean-Pierre
Department of Sociology
McMaster University

Fernando Nunes
Child and Youth Study
Mount Saint Vincent University

MARIUSZ GALCZYNSKI, VILELMINI TSAGKARAKI AND
RATNA GHOSH

17. FURTHER UNPACKING MULTICULTURALISM IN THE CLASSROOM

Continuing to Explore the Politics of Difference through Current Events

INTRODUCTION

In McGill University's Faculty of Education, *Multicultural Education* is a required course in the degree programs of all students pursuing teacher certification, regardless of the subject areas or grade levels in which they plan to specialize – much as it is at other institutions within Québec and in the rest of Canada. Yet in the authors' experiences teaching this course, we have witnessed that the most challenging aspect of multicultural education is helping preservice teachers to gain understanding of how the legislative policy of multiculturalism might be applied to their every day teaching practice. Although the scope of multiculturalism has expanded considerably since its conception decades ago, it remains indistinctly conceptualized in the minds of many Canadian teachers (and Canadians in general). But if our teachers have a diffident relationship with multiculturalism, how can we expect them to integrate its ideology into their pedagogy and convey its principles to their students? To be sure, bridging the divide between policy and practice is the fundamental objective of multicultural education, and so in our teaching practices we have developed various methods and materials to scaffold students' understanding of multiculturalism as it relates to the classroom, the school, and every other level of the educational system.

In this chapter, we explore how discussing current events in the classroom can be an effective strategy for getting students to begin "unpacking" the complexities of multiculturalism. In doing so, we draw upon our experience organizing an interactive workshop for the 2nd Joint Annual Conference of the Association for Canadian Studies and the Canadian Ethnic Studies Association, which took place in Ottawa in the fall of 2011 and had as its theme, "Revisiting 40 Years of Multicultural Policy in Canada." For our workshop, which attracted university course instructors, schoolteachers, graduate students, and other education practitioners as participants, we selected six brief news articles describing events that had taken place in Canada or the United States within the past year. These media events were chosen because they exposed issues of *difference*, in the sense that each one highlighted the stories of individuals who did not represent the societal norm in terms of factors such as race, gender, class, sexual orientation, (dis)ability, or religion. The workshop was structured in three parts: first, we asked

S. Guo & L. Wong (eds.), Revisiting Multiculturalism in Canada, 289–308.

participants to conceptualize multiculturalism in clear terms; second, we introduced the concept of privilege and discussed how societal norms created interlocking hierarchies (McIntosh, 1990) that often serve as barriers to educational opportunity; and third, we challenged the participants to come up with ideas for lesson plans that incorporated the news media as well as curricular objectives.

The purpose of our workshop was to encourage participants to understand how multiculturalism can (and should) infuse the curriculum, all while engaging students through the discussion of happenings in their world. This chapter, then, continues that dialogue. While the theoretical framework of this chapter is preserved from our earlier article published in a special edition of *Canadian Ethnic Studies* (Galczynski, Tsagkaraki, & Ghosh, 2012), all of the media reports included previously have been replaced with more recent news stories – thus adhering to the authors' commitment to drawing on "current" events, as well as illustrating the regularity with which news media is founded upon multicultural themes. As in our previous work, this chapter deconstructs six Canadian- and American-based news stories, allowing us to continue exploring the politics of difference and to further unpack the concept of multiculturalism within the classroom.

MULTICULTURALISM AND EDUCATION

Although Canada's official policy on multiculturalism was introduced into legislation over thirty years ago with the Canadian Charter of Rights and Freedoms (1982), and further delineated through the Canadian Multiculturalism Act (1988), neither the terms *education* nor *school* appear in either document. These legislative acts, like Trudeau's announcement of "multiculturalism within a bilingual framework" (1971) a decade earlier, were not aimed specifically at education reform. Rather, they were general directives meant to address the social reality of 1970s Canada – of increased immigration and changing demographics, of new complexities in race relations, and of heightened tensions between francophones and anglophones (Dewing, 2006; Ghosh & Abdi, 2012). In response to the development of French nationalism in Quebec, coupled with the assertive demands of minority ethnocultural groups (Anderson & Frideres, 1981), multicultural policy represented the state's commitment not only to the recognition of its citizens' diversity, but also to their equitable participation in society. What made Canadian multicultural policy so unique is that it went beyond legislation to become *constitutionalized* within the very definition of nationhood (Kymlicka, 2003). Yet the pronouncement of cultural equality would not be enough to guarantee equal access to power (Gérin-Lajoie, 2011), and such a goal certainly would not be possible without the conduit of education. Indeed, if Canada's policy of multiculturalism was to "be interpreted in a manner consistent with the preservation and enhancement of the multicultural heritage of Canadians" (Canadian Charter of Rights and Freedoms, 1982), how could this be done successfully without the active involvement of all actors within the education system?

In order to transpose the spirit of multiculturalism from policy into pedagogy, provincial ministries of education would need to revise curriculum, schools would need to offer professional development for in-service teachers, teacher education programs would need to be reorganized in order to adequately prepare preservice teachers, and, in classrooms, students would need to be guided to think more critically about Canadian history and their national identity. While these developments have taken place over the past four decades, at varying levels of success, the rich discourse on multiculturalism has given light to the existence of a gap between theory and practice. Indeed, educational programs based on the official definitions of multiculturalism have often been inadequate in addressing the fundamental problems we encounter in schools due to cultural differences and their social connotations (Ghosh & Galczynski, 2014). Often, multicultural education has been limited to isolated lessons in prejudice reduction or separate units about cultural artifacts and ethnic holidays (Nieto, 2003). But such approaches are not enough to make multicultural education happen in a manner that permeates the school's philosophy on all levels: its organization, its curriculum, its pedagogy, and its physical space. Thus the concept of multicultural education has not only needed to be pioneered, but also to be redefined.

Making educational actors, practice, and content more culturally-sensitive has been an integral part of the country's educational agenda since the enactment of multicultural policy (Ng, Staton, & Scane, 1995). Although initially the main focus of multicultural education was on students who are racially and ethnically different from the dominant group, a later and more radical version of multiculturalism underlines the need to address all cultural differences, be it in values, behaviours, ways of learning, or sociocultural practices (McLaren, 1998; Macedo, 1999; Torres, 1998). Following this radical path, Ghosh and Galczynski (2014) propose a redefined version of multicultural education that goes beyond students' ethnicity and race to recognize a range of human differences, all of which have political and pedagogical ramifications inside and outside of the classroom. In doing so, the "many cultures" encompassed by "multiculturalism" have become inseparable from the very elements of culture, including gender, class, religion, sexual orientation, and other political factors, which incontrovertibly shape human identity.

Understanding multiculturalism in its broadly inclusive, redefined form is not possible without "unpacking" the concept of privilege. Informed by a feminist perspective, Peggy McIntosh (1990) explored how men "work from a base of unacknowledged privilege" (p. 6), meaning that society is structured in a way that assumes the male perspective as the default and thus men, as the historically dominant gender, unconsciously and disproportionally benefit from their positionality in the social order. But the more McIntosh considered how women are put at a disadvantage because of their subordinate position, she began to understand that analogous power structures exist in terms of skin colour. Her seminal article, "White Privilege and Male Privilege" (1990), points out that although we can agree that minority groups in our society are disadvantaged in certain ways, it is much more problematic for us to admit to the inverse of this idea: that representatives of majority groups must therefore be *over*-privileged.

To make the redefined concept of multiculturalism accessible to students, teachers must strive to weave its focus on the politics of difference into the curriculum and into their teaching practice. This process, suffice to say, is not easy, as it simultaneously involves: (1) engaging the attention of students, so that they may find the subject matter personally relevant and be encouraged to construct their own interpretations of morals and citizenship; (2) broaching controversial issues, about which students may be initially reluctant to share their perspectives and opinions; (3) facilitating meaningful dialogue, by thoughtfully conceiving guided talking points and discussion questions in order to help empower students in articulating their points of view to the teacher and to one another; (4) promoting critical thinking, by encouraging students to be reflective and questioning of the world around them; and (5) making connections to the "bigger picture," by framing local events within societal and global perspectives.

USING CURRENT EVENTS TO UNPACK MULTICULTURALISM IN THE CLASSROOM

Rooted in the principles of multiculturalism, one possible approach that teachers can take to unpack the concept of privilege is through the discussion of current events with their students. This is because empowerment begins by asking questions that arise out of the everyday living conditions of people, and by refusing to accept answers and explanations as true without investigation (Freire, 1970). As such, "the school is an ideal place for young people to learn collectively how to make an impact on social institutions" (Grant & Sleeter, 2009, p. 261). When students develop the habit of questioning and thinking critically about their immediate environment, their beliefs, and their identity, the foundation is laid for them to become conscious and participating citizens. The teacher who is keen to discuss current events in his or her classroom, then, can capitalize on the opportunity to pique students' interests by bringing up news that they may have already heard about through television, internet, and social media, or simply through discussions with family and friends. The professional expertise and experience of the teacher as a pedagogue, however, is necessary to steer such discussion in a productive direction, one that enables students to develop greater empathy for those whom society labels as "different."

Although schools generally avoid engaging students in discussion about controversial issues, we believe that analyzing events that take place in the students' school, community, city, and country will help them become aware that discrimination and inequity in power are not distant, disconnected theoretical concepts; rather, they are part of the reality that occurs everyday in students' own lives and is present in many facets of the social spectrum. When students begin to feel more comfortable with these issues, the teacher can gradually redirect the discussion back to the lives of the students themselves (Pang, 2001). This will make the lesson more interesting to the students, as they often cannot make the connection between the relevance of what they are taught in school with what is happening in their own lives and communities. Discussion of current events serves as a supplement to textbooks and curriculum, which are filled with omissions, half-truths, and selective interpretations.

In the article which preceded this chapter (Galczynski et al., 2012), we deconstructed the six news events included in our workshop. As a follow-up, the next section of this chapter unpacks six, more recent media reports, each of which emphasizes an analogous multicultural theme. Like our original article, this chapter proposes a line of questioning that presents discussion points, which cascade from story-specific to societal (global) to personal (local) in scope, that can be adapted for any grade level. While the questions themselves may need to be reworded depending on the age of students, we have intended them to model how the teacher can guide the discussion towards exposing underlying issues of difference. This updated chapter not only illustrates how frequently the politics of difference are at play in (often controversial) North American news media, but it also symbolizes, in essence, our commitment to kick-starting discussion of current events in school classrooms. We would note, moreover, that the process of finding recent and relevant news stories for inclusion in this chapter was considerably effortless – as it would be for any teacher committed to unpacking multiculturalism in his or her classroom – and that our primary challenge was in limiting our search results to just one media story per multicultural theme.

Unpacking Race: U.S. Patent Office Cancels NFL Team's "Redskins" Trademark

Although nearly a quarter of a century has passed since McIntosh's (1990) initial dissection of white privilege, there is still a need to unpack the political ramifications of race in our society. Canadians can often comfortably articulate their national identity as "multicultural," implying a sort of harmony in terms of race relations, as their daily interactions bring them into contact with individuals from diverse racial and ethnic backgrounds and conflict does not appear to occur. Yet while we may contend that we rarely, if ever, witness racist acts personally, we have less difficulty acknowledging that attitudes of prejudice do exist within our society and that discriminatory acts do occur. This incongruity between our personal experiences and our collective consciousness restricts our recognition of racism only to direct encounters and expressions of prejudice, or "individual acts of meanness"; the "invisible system" that confers privilege to the dominant (white) racial group continues to be imperceptible (McIntosh, 1990). It is possible to bridge this divide, however, in the way that we take up discussion of current events in our classrooms – by emphasizing how white privilege allows the dominant group to separate itself from the liability for individual racist acts, to begin to comprehend "why we are justly seen as oppressive, even when we don't see ourselves that way" (McIntosh, 1990, p. 149).

As part of our workshop activity, we referred to a 2011 incident in which business school students at the Université de Montréal donned blackface as part of Olympics-themed orientation events (Galczynski et al., 2012). For this chapter, we have opted to deconstruct an American-based current event: the cancellation of the Washington Redskins franchise trademark by the United States Patent and Trademark Office (USPTO). Both events involve the intersection of race and sport, and they exemplify how judgments of whether or not racism has occurred are passed down by dominant racial groups. Such media stories reinforce the politicization of race as difference, and thus offer us an invitation to unpack the concept of white privilege in our classrooms.

In June 2014, news outlets began reporting that the USPTO had cancelled protection of the Washington, D.C.-based National Football League (NFL) team's "Redskins" trademark. Despite counterarguments that *Redskins* holds a distinct meaning as the name of a sports team and honors the achievements of both that team specifically and Native peoples more generally, the USPTO concluded in its 99-page decision that the franchise name was culturally derogatory – as evidenced by significant criticisms from leading Indigenous groups, widespread eschewal of the term among newspaper and media outlets, and nearly universal reference to the term's negative connotations within English-language dictionaries (Handy, 2014). Although various scholars, civil rights leaders, athletes, and journalists had been protesting the Redskins name on grounds of ethnic stereotyping since the 1980s, mainstream awareness of the controversy surrounding the franchise's use of Native-inspired mascots and symbols was notably buoyed by U.S. President Barack Obama's support for a name change just a few months prior to the USPTO's decision (Vargas & Shin, 2013).

Whereas the USPTO decision did not actually demand that the Washington NFL franchise discontinue its use of the Redskins nickname, it did withhold federal protection for anyone using the trademark. As such, the impact of the decision sets a precedent for challenging other team names that may be considered disparaging to Native peoples or to other groups. This extends beyond professional sports to the education system, where schools have also come under fire for controversial team names and mascots. For instance, over forty schools in Massachusetts use Native-themed images or names for their sports teams (McGovern, 2014). In Washington state, the USPTO decision already prompted one high school to change the name of its teams from the Redskins to the Redhawks (Strauss, 2014).

At the same time, it is important to note that some scholars and activists have challenged the labeling of discrimination against Native peoples as a race issue, insisting that such acts should be recognized as distinct from those committed against other cultural groups. Indeed, the complexities of how we interpret and recount the struggles of Aboriginal peoples continue to be questioned and explored (Forbes, 1993; Reynolds, 1996; Saunt, 2005). In viewing this news story through the lens of multiculturalism, therefore, we would need to raise some critical questions about how the politics of difference came into play in the debate over the Washington Redskins team name:

– Which other American- and Canadian-based sports teams make reference to Indigenous peoples? Do such teams make use of mascots, logos, or nicknames that might be considered derogatory? By whom?

- How often is there debate over the use of team mascots, logos, or nicknames that draw on the imagery of dominant group culture? Are there instances where minority groups have invoked such imagery to honor the cultural identities or historical contributions of individuals representing majority groups? Why has there not been a history of such practices in non-white societies?
- How often is the opportunity to stereotype reserved only for the dominant racial group? Is the ability to invoke stereotypical portrayals of others a privilege in itself?
- How is race represented in your school environment? In your textbooks? In the media? Do these depictions clash with how you identify yourself?

Unpacking Gender: Labrador School Sends Home Over Two Dozen Students for Dress Code Violations

As with race, each passing decade has brought with it a shift towards greater gender equity in Canada; but this is not to say that privileges for women have become equivalent to those of men, the dominant group. From the time they are identified as female, girls are attributed certain "feminine" characteristics that position them to feel inferior and to grow up to expect and do less, all of which reinforces the hierarchical gender order that confers greater power and resources on men (Berkowitz, Manohar, & Tinkler, 2010).

In our workshop, we discussed how the realization of the imbalance in male and female privileges convinced one Canadian couple to conceal the sex of their baby, in hopes that their child's exploration of gender identity would be unaffected by external influences (Galczynski et al., 2012). For this chapter, we draw on recent controversy surrounding dress codes in Canadian and American schools, again for the purpose of confronting the inequitable distribution of privilege between boys and girls. In both examples, we are provided the opportunity to unpack multiculturalism in terms of gender and how it affects students during their childhood development, defining how they make sense of themselves as well as how they perceive the opposite sex.

When a bout of unseasonably warm weather affected Labrador in May 2014, school officials at Mehinek High School in Labrador City went from class to class in search of dress code violations. As a result, 28 students were sent home that day – 26 girls, most of whom were admonished for having visible bra straps, and 2 boys, who had worn sleeveless shirts. Although the school's dress code was ostensibly intended to be gender-neutral, certain female students recounted that teachers explained its purpose was to prevent teenage boys (and male teachers) from being distracted by girls' bare shoulders and other exposed body parts; they confirmed that even some boys were offended by a presentation at the beginning of the school year during which the dress code was outlined, suggesting boys' limitations in enacting self-control. District Director of Education Darrin Pike denied the dress code's intent to avoid distracting male students and explained that "there's nothing wrong with having standards and expectations, it's balancing those with individual rights and freedoms" (Hopper, 2014).

Similar cases of students' dissent over gendered dress code policies in other Canadian provinces (Nova Scotia, Ontario, Quebec) and in the United States (California, Illinois, New Jersey, Virginia) also garnered significant media attention; a group of New Jersey students even launched a social media campaign utilizing the Twitter hashtag *#IAmNotADistraction* (Cunnane, 2014). As *The Globe and Mail* columnist Elizabeth Renzetti (2014) argued, "It should not be a crime for a girl to be in possession of a girl's body...It's been 85 years since five Alberta women brought about the landmark ruling that women are 'persons' under the law, and now we're in danger of sliding from 'persons' to 'parts.'" Hence, from a multicultural perspective, deconstruction of this particular case in Newfoundland and Labrador gives rise to the following discussion questions:

— What kinds of factors should teachers and school administrators consider when enforcing school policies such as dress codes? Under what circumstances can we justify removing students from class or from school as a consequence of breaking the rules?
— To what extent are gendered behavioral expectations embedded in school rules? Is it possible for rules and policies to be considered gender-neutral if they affect different genders disproportionally?
— How have historical trends influenced our perceptions of "traditional" gender roles and "appropriate" behaviour? Whose traditions are they? Are these gender roles and expectations consistent from one culture to another?
— What limitations do you see for yourself in terms of your own gender? What advantages do you see? Do you think you have experienced more advantages or encountered more limitations?
— How is gender represented in your school environment? In your textbooks? In the media? Do these depictions clash with how you identify yourself?

Unpacking Sexual Orientation: Kentucky School Implements Non-discriminatory Bathroom Policy

If schools strive to be gender-neutral in their policymaking, they must consider how societal pressure for individuals to adhere to traditional gender roles extends to the expression of their sexuality. Teachers must be especially aware, therefore, that students who identify as lesbian, gay, bisexual, or transgender face the tremendous obstacle of a society that privileges individuals who belong to the dominant heterosexual norm and often antagonizes those who do not. In our workshop, for example, we shared the story of a 14-year-old boy who committed suicide as a result of aggressive bullying over his sexual orientation (Galczynski et al., 2012). The context of teen bullying prominently underscores the concept of privilege, as youth who struggle to identify with the heterosexual norm face having their sexuality contested or ridiculed by their peers. Even tacit disapproval from those in the dominant group can cause individuals to question their self-worth and potential to achieve. Nevertheless, teachers may be hesitant to broach the topic of sexual orientation with students. Grant and Sleeter (2009) explain that this is because "as a society we remain perplexed about how to deal with homophobia, even though we know that the gay, lesbian, transgender, and bisexual population make up a significant portion of our society" (p. 260).

In this section, we begin to unpack multiculturalism in relation to sexual orientation by deconstructing news reports of one American school's efforts to implement a non-discriminatory bathroom policy. This news story is a particularly good example for dissection in the classroom because it somewhat conflates gender and sexual orientation, inviting teachers to help their students distinguish between the two concepts. For instance, the popular blog *BuzzFeed* categorized its media report (Merevick, 2014) under the LGBT section – an acronym which itself groups together sexuality (lesbian, gay, bisexual) with gender identity (transgender).

While gender identity and sexual orientation are related, they are independent constructs. Transgender identity refers to how individuals identify their own gender, not their sexuality. Yet despite this distinction, transgendered people have historically found inclusivity among gay, lesbian, and bisexual communities. From a legal standpoint, moreover, protections in consideration of sexual orientation are entwined with gender rights; this is because cases of discrimination are typically founded upon failure to conform to conventional gender norms (Flynn, 2001). This helps to explain how school leaders at J. M. Atherton High School in Louisville, Kentucky, conceptualized their new non-discrimination policy, which barred discrimination in regards to both gender identity and sexual orientation, as well as to age and race.

In the spring of 2014, the school formally approved the non-discrimination policy. Media outlets picked up the story as controversy erupted over one (male-to-female) transgender student's access to the girls' bathroom and locker room. Some parents and students complained that the policy violated other students' privacy rights. Atherton Principal Thomas Aberli noted that "the loudest opposition came from those outside of the school community...such as a lawyer from a Christian anti-LGBT organization, Alliance Defending Freedom" (Merevick, 2014). Nevertheless, within a few weeks the new policy had withstood its critics' formal appeal. In response, the school board upheld that "forcing transgender students to use a separate bathroom means forcing them to 'out' themselves in a way that violates their own privacy rights" (Kenning, 2014). Assistant Principal Dianna Kurtz added that despite some people's discomfort with the policy, the alternative would have been discrimination: "By not implementing the policy we would be saying 'you are too different for us to accommodate you'" (McKay, 2014). Earlier that year, similar rationale was expressed by the U.S. Department of Education in expanding Title IX guidance for schools to secure protections for transgender students, who are especially at-risk as the targets of bullying behaviour and sexual assault. Questions that could be asked in the classroom may include:

- Why are homosexuality and transgender identity perceived as such threatening differences to warrant bullying?
- How are moral values integrated into societal perceptions of human sexuality and gender identity? Which societal parameters influence our perception of the norm in terms of sexual orientation?

- What privileges are granted to youth that identify themselves as heterosexual versus those that identify with alternative sexualities? What privileges are granted to youth that identify themselves as either male or female versus those that identify as transgender?
- Do you find that all individuals in your environment are free to express their own sexuality and gender identity? Why or why not?
- How is sexual orientation represented in your textbooks? In the media? Do these depictions clash with how you identify yourself?

Unpacking (Dis)ability: U.S. Supreme Court Ruling Green Lights Ratification of U.N. Disability Treaty

As is the case with underprivileged groups in terms of race, gender, and sexual orientation, the recognition of those with physical or mental disabilities as different propagates stereotyping and discrimination. Because such individuals' differences are measured against a vaguely defined norm, one that is "able," the term *disability* labels them as deficient. Some scholars posit that the "importance of physical [and mental] difference lies solely in discriminatory social reaction to or ignorance of the effects of that difference" (Koch, 2001), which reminds us that individuals with disabilities must deal not only with the limitations of their conditions, but also the impositions of societal barriers.

In schools, students with physical or mental disabilities are at-risk as targets of bullying or sexual crimes – like others who fail to identify with dominant group norms. In our workshop, we included a news story about an 11-year-old Ontario boy diagnosed with muscular dystrophy who committed suicide after being physically attacked by classmate (Galczynski et al., 2012). For this chapter, we draw on American media reports detailing recent developments in the process of obtaining federal ratification of the United Nations' Convention on the Rights of Persons with Disabilities (CRPD) (UN General Assembly, 2007).

In recognition of the estimated one billion people worldwide living with a disability, 159 countries joined together in 2009 to craft the CRPD. The CRPD is a human rights treaty intended to safeguard the rights and recognize the inherent dignity of persons with disabilities. In certain parts of the world, people with disabilities have been perceived as sexually immature or inactive, consequently denied appropriate gynecologic and obstetrical care, and sometimes even forcibly sterilized (Frisk, 2013). Thus, the Treaty's articles delineate, among many other social rights, the right to political and cultural participation, the right to sport and recreation, the right to accessible information and communication technology (ICT), and the right to live independently and be included in the community.

Despite being modeled on the Americans with Disabilities Act (ADA) of 1990, the CRPD has not been ratified by the United States; in contrast, 147 countries (including Canada) have formally ratified the CRPD as of June 2014 (UN Treaty Collection, 2014). In December 2012, the U.S. Senate failed to ratify the CRPD, mainly because Republicans hesitated in regards to the Treaty's referral to sexual and reproductive health and because parental groups expressed concern over speculative limits on the homeschooling of disabled children (Frisk, 2013). While discussion of ratifying the CRPD stalled for the next two years, the U.S. Supreme Court decision on *Bond v. United States* in June 2014 served to reignite calls for action. Media outlets interpreted the court decision, which reaffirmed balance of federal powers in regards to international treaties, as a green light to proceed with CRPD ratification. Susan L. Parish, Nancy Lurie Marks Professor of Disability Policy at Brandeis University, sagely explains why the American government's ratification of the CPRD is crucial:

> Even 24 years after [passage of the ADA], thousands of US students with disabilities still spend most of their day in segregated classrooms, out of sight and mind of their nondisabled peers. Employment rates for men and women with disabilities remain woefully low. A paltry 21 percent of working-age adults with disabilities are employed full time ... People with disabilities and their families are the poorest group in the US, and they often live with hardship and deprivation, including food insecurity, housing instability, and unmet medical needs ... The ADA has not made full inclusion a reality for many Americans with disabilities. The baton should be passed to the UN Convention, which ... will require the federal government to assertively promote disability rights. (Parish, 2014)

Without doubt, news reports on the progress towards the United States' ratification of the CRPD can serve as an invitation to discuss with students the notion of (dis)ability, as well as to consider the daily effects of living with a physical or mental limitation. The kinds of questions that can help students to unpack multiculturalism through the lens of (dis)ability should prompt them to consider how people with disabilities perceive themselves, how others project the label of disability onto them, and how the politics of difference position "disabled" people in relation to their "able" counterparts.

- What are the connotations of labeling someone as "handicapped" or "disabled"? How has the popularity of using such labels changed over time?
- How do you think these labels affect the perceptions that people with special needs have of themselves and also others' perceptions of them?
- Does the perception of the norm in society contribute to the marginalization of people with physical or mental impairments? Why or why not?
- What coping mechanisms would you suggest if you had a friend or classmate who perceived his or her difference as an insurmountable problem?
- How is (dis)ability represented in your school environment? In your textbooks? In the media? Do these depictions clash with how you identify yourself?

Unpacking Religion: Proposed Quebec Charter of Values Delimits Display of Religious Symbols

Of course, the politics of difference do not only operate in terms of physically-apparent components of an individual's identity. The development of Canada as a nation has certainly been entrenched in the religious morals, values, and ideals of

Christianity, the dominant faith of Canadian society. We need not look much further than the leadership of the country to note that every prime minister to date has had affiliation with a branch of Christianity (Campbell, 2006). Then again, while the Canadian Constitution does allude to God (Canadian Charter of Rights and Freedoms, 1982), the Canada 2011 National Household Survey revealed that approximately one-quarter (23.9%) of Canadians do not identify with any religion at all (Statistics Canada, 2013). While the inclusion of non-Christian religions has varied from province to province, particularly in regards to funding practices of faith-based schools, religious accommodation in schools has even been challenged for being too accommodating – perhaps to the extent of compromising the rights of non-religious persons. In our workshop, we focused on such a case: Toronto's Valley Park Middle School, whose predominantly Muslim students were permitted to congregate in the cafeteria for weekly communal prayer services (Galczynski et al., 2012). For this chapter, on the other hand, we have chosen to deconstruct the inflammatory secularism of Quebec's proposed Charter of Values.

In early 2013, Quebec's governing political party introduced legislation (Bill 14) to make amendments to its French language charter. This would have removed certain exemptions that allowed English education in special cases, required large workplaces to operate in French for all business purposes, and empowered language inspectors to seize anything deemed to be in offence of the language charter. By May of that year, after a highly publicized incident informally called "Pastagate," in which an inspector of the *Office québécois de la langue française* (Quebec Board of the French Language) warned the owner of an Italian restaurant against using non-French words on his menu, the focus on Bill 14 was largely abandoned in favor of a push for an even more controversial piece of legislation: Bill 60, or the Quebec Charter of Values (Ghosh & Galczynski, 2014). This new Charter would amend Quebec's existing Charter of Human Rights and Freedoms by asserting Quebec's secular values and establishing a commitment to neutrality of religion on the part of all state personnel.

Quebec's proposed new Charter of Values would be operationalized by implementing limits on the wearing of conspicuous religious symbols by provincial employees and by making it mandatory to have one's face uncovered as a stipulation for providing or receiving governmental services. Spearheaded by Minister Bernard Drainville, the Charter explicitly outlined that civil servants such as teachers, police officers, doctors, and nurses would no longer be allowed to wear hijabs, turbans, burqas, kippas, or large crosses when working. As it would directly affect all levels of education, the Charter notably earned condemnation from Quebec's human rights commission, the English Montreal School Board, and all of Quebec's universities (Authier, 2014).

Supporters of the Charter cited its restrictions as a step towards greater gender equity, but critics quashed such claims as faux-feminist. "The wording [of the Charter] suggests that certain religious symbols – the Islamic veil, for instance – speak to the wearer's inherent disregard for gender equality ... This co-opting of liberal values essentially confuses the concept of secularism. There is little difference between a Muslim imposing Muslim dress on a non-Muslim, and an atheist demanding all Muslim women go bareheaded" (Flanigan, 2014). Even key members of the Catholic Church, which was responsible for Quebec's historic secularization during the Quiet Revolution of the 1960s, spoke out publicly against the proposed Charter. As Monsignor Pierre-Andre Pournier of the Assembly of Quebec Catholic Bishops warned, "While it may be true that the state is secular, society is pluralist. ... People are free to believe or not believe ... no official religion, but no official atheism, either" (Flanigan, 2014).

With the Charter as a primary focus of its platform – reflecting its sovereignist agenda – the party in power, Parti Québécois, called an election in early 2014 in an attempt to increase representation in the National Assembly. Because of its resounding defeat in the polls, an indication of weakening support for the separatist movement, the proposed legislation was not passed. With election of Liberal Philippe Couillard, Federal Liberal Leader Justin Trudeau inferred that "Quebecers rejected the 'politics of division' embodied by the Charter ... [deciding] that it's unacceptable that someone can be forced to pick between his or her religion and his or her job" (Janus, 2014).

News media concerning debate over the proposed Charter of Values in Quebec can serve as a platform for promoting healthy debate among students in regards to how religion has affected and continues to affect Canadian life. In awareness of a multicultural Canada, students can be guided to consider the spaces created for religious and non-religious people within Canadian society:

- Do you think that the Quebec Charter of Values was inclusive in its commitment to secularism? Why or why not?
- Are individuals from certain religious backgrounds more welcome to express their beliefs than others? Do you think that there is space for non-religious students to express their perspectives?
  What makes certain religious traditions seem more unusual than others? How are labels like "devout" or "extremist" used to describe religious people?
- Do you feel that your school has allowed you to freely express your religious identity? Why or why not?
- How is religion represented in your textbooks? In the media? Do these depictions clash with how you identify yourself?

Unpacking Class: Expanding Charter Rights to Include Affordable Housing and Environmental Protections

Like religion, class is another invisible yet important component of identity. Education is often heralded as the gateway towards socioeconomic mobility, but such a correlation is overly simplistic if it ignores the reality of inequity both within the education system and outside of it. For our workshop, we included a media report that exposed universities' prioritization of admissions for full-pay students, or who those did not need financial aid and would pay non-discounted tuition (Galczynski et al., 2012). In this chapter, we highlight positive strides being made by the federal and provincial governments in Canada to guarantee essential protections to people from lower socioeconomic backgrounds.

In 2011, four homeless and formerly homeless Torontonians (including a then 19-year old single mother and a 48-year-old cancer patient) backed by the Centre for Equality Rights in Accommodation (CERA) filed an application against the Attorney Generals of Canada and of Ontario in *Tanudjaja et al. v. Attorney General (Canada) et al.*, alleging that two of their Canadian Charter rights had been violated: the right to life, liberty, and security of the person (section 7) and the right to equality before and under law and equal protection and benefit of law (section 15). They reasoned that the government's failure to operationalize a national housing strategy, as dictated by Bill C-304 (Secure, Adequate, Accessible, and Affordable Housing Act, 2011), created and maintained conditions leading to inadequate housing and subsequent homelessness. They further alleged that "homelessness reduces life expectancy, causes single mothers to lose custody of their children, and forces victims of domestic violence to return to abusive spouses" (Makin, 2010). Considering the reality that as many as 300,000 Canadians are homeless, and that Aboriginal Canadians and recent immigrants are disproportionally affected by inadequate housing (Monsebraaten, 2010), the case set a historic precedent because the claimants demanded the government's fulfillment of positive obligations (institution of rights); heretofore, Charter violations had only been acknowledged inversely, in the context of negative action (denial of rights) (Ali, 2014). Although the application was initially dismissed without a full hearing, the case was appealed and gained additional support from a coalition of social welfare groups. In April 2014, news broke that the Ontario Human Rights Commission had been granted leave to intervene.

Around the same time, a draft environmental bill of rights was proposed in Eastern Canada by a collaborative of agencies and individuals representing academic, governmental, and non-governmental sectors (New Brunswick Environmental Network, 2014). Acknowledging that exposure to environmental hazards can cause life-long health impacts, the New Brunswick Children's Environmental Health Collaborative selected Canadian children's entertainer Raffi Cavoukian as its spokesperson and called on the New Brunswick government to recognize the particular vulnerability of children. The proposed bill would go beyond the Canadian Charter and even the United Nations' Convention on the Rights of the Child (U.N. Human Rights, 1989) to explicitly identify the harms of environmental hazards as they affect children into adulthood and throughout their lives. If adopted by the provincial government, the bill would obligate New Brunswick to prevent children's exposure to contaminants in the air, soil, and water, whether outdoors or indoors. Even though the bill does not explicitly claim to tackle socioeconomic inequity, a plethora of research has demonstrated that low income households are most likely to be affected by environmental hazards (Adler & Newman, 2002; Buzzeli, 2008; Buzzeli et al., 2006; Harter, 2004; Institute of Medicine, 1999). Thus, the demand for governmental protection, like that in the *Tanudjaja* case, can be interpreted as a class issue from a multicultural perspective.

Media reports on the draft environmental bill of rights extended an invitation to the public to offer input during the summer of 2014, so that it could be formally presented to the provincial government in the fall (Campbell, 2014). A Canadian

Environmental Bill of Rights (Bill C-469) had been presented before Parliament in 2009 but never passed. At the same time, "it represented a possible milepost on the road to constitutional recognition of the right to a healthy environment and could have spurred the enactment of similar laws at the provincial level" (Boyd, 2012, p. 61). Although limited environmental rights have been set forth in legislation in Quebec, Ontario, the Yukon, the Northwest Territories, and Nunavut, these laws focus more on procedural rights rather than substantive entitlements to a clean and healthy environment.

These news stories about expanding Charter rights can be used to get students thinking about how socioeconomic status can significantly affect one's future educational and professional opportunities. Even without having to identify themselves (and their families) as belonging to a particular class, students can be trained to recognize the hierarchy of class structure. Once they become "aware of class dynamics ... this can be extended to lessons about oppression and class differences in the neighborhood, the community, and the wider society (Grant & Sleeter, 2009, p. 274).

- How do socioeconomic factors influence where and how we live? To what extent can people exert choice over where they live? Why do so many Canadians live under less than ideal circumstances?
- How can you tell if someone is rich or poor? What leads people to become either rich or poor?
- What kinds of things do you need to be successful in life? How many of these things cost money? Is it easy for every family to buy these things?
- How much power do you think that people have to determine their own socio-economic status? Do you think that this changes much from generation to generation?
- How is class represented in your school environment? In your textbooks? In the media? Do these depictions clash with how you identify yourself?

CONCLUSION

In this chapter, we have explored how the effects of privilege are manifested on many levels in our everyday lives. Working with an expanded definition of culture – and, consequently, a broadly inclusive interpretation of multiculturalism – we have emphasized that societal differences such as gender, sexual orientation, (dis)ability, religion, and class, in addition to race and ethnicity, must be at the center of education. And, if education is to help students develop positive identities and make them critical and democratic citizens, we argue that it is the school's (and teacher's) responsibility to "unpack" privilege in order to raise students' awareness of the politics of difference. We suggest doing this through the infusion of current events into classroom content, which may yield discussions that lead students to think critically and become more aware of how their identities are shaped by interactions with others.

As a reminder, the discussion questions provided in the previous sections are indicative of the line of questioning that can be utilized in the classroom. The teacher will need to think about issues of difference, power, and privilege raised in the current events he or she decides to focus on — and then cultivate discussions with students in a manner appropriate for the their level of maturity. Even so, current events can be incorporated by the multicultural teacher in a myriad of ways — as an introduction to the day's lesson or as a compelling supplement to conventional language, mathematical, or historical content. In fact, these were precisely the kinds of suggestions made by our workshop participants when we asked them to brainstorm lesson ideas in the final part of our workshop at the ACS/CESA Conference in 2011. Their suggestions for using current events to unpack multiculturalism in social studies, language arts, mathematics, performing arts, and physical education classrooms are detailed in our earlier article (Galczynski et al., 2012).

Drawing on the media reports highlighted in this chapter, we can brainstorm similar ideas for infusing current events and multicultural themes into the curriculum. In drama classes, teachers can encourage their students to unpack concepts of race and ethnicity by drawing on the controversy surrounding the Washington Redskins' trademark cancellation in introducing a playwriting assignment that prompts students to parallel themes of cultural appropriation through allegory. In physical education classes, teachers can invoke the school dress code protests in Labrador as an invitation to disseminate how influences of fashion version function dictate the styles of male and female uniforms in various sports. For language arts teachers, news reports of Atherton High School's new non-discriminatory bathroom policy can inspire creative writing activities in which students revise traditional fables or stories to be more inclusive, allowing for the development of characters who represent a fuller spectrum of sexuality and gender identity. Meanwhile, in science classrooms, lessons on genetics, genotype-phenotype distinction, and sexual reproduction can incorporate people with disabilities as examples – in order to broaden students' understanding of how much (or how little) effect physical or mental limitations have on people's life trajectories; here, teachers can tie in media reports of debate over ratification of the UN Convention on the Rights of Persons with Disabilities. News stories about Quebec's proposed Charter of Values, on the other hand, might be taken up in art classrooms, where teachers can explore graphic design elements such as shape, line, and symmetry by tracing the historical development of religious symbols. Math teachers, too, can bookend lessons on finance with class discussions on expanding Charter rights to include affordable housing: students can participate in role-play scenarios where resources are distributed unequally and they must consider how best to complete certain tasks, buy certain goods, and spend money proportionally in relation to their means.

All of the above classroom ideas not only model how curriculum can be infused with multiculturalism, but they also stress the interdisciplinary of multicultural concepts. For instance, the context of a physical education classroom might seem more suitable for discussion of how sports teams can commodify the imagery of another culture. But in sharing an example of how the topic might be broached in a drama classroom, we hope to convey how any teacher can infuse his or her subject-specific pedagogy with multicultural ideology. We also posit that students may engage with the politics of difference more effectively if multiculturalism is woven throughout the curriculum less conspicuously, allowing them to make sense of the interlocking hierarchies of privilege in a deeper and more meaningful way. Creativity is required on the part of the teacher, but the possibilities are endless in making use of current events to enrich curricular topics being studied.

By employing teaching methods such as those outlined in this chapter, bolstered by challenging and engaging lines of questioning (Grant & Sleeter, 2009), teachers make the concept of multiculturalism more accessible and meaningful for students. Through the scaffolding process, they become transformative educators (Gay, 2000; Giroux, 1988) who go beyond the prescribed curriculum and accustom their students to think critically about their lives, their schools, and their communities. In doing so, they promote the ideology of multiculturalism in a manner that supersedes the policy's legislative roots with a more utilitarian and inclusive version of the concept – to the effect of reaffirming multiculturalism as an intrinsic component of Canadian identity (Kymlicka, 2003). Hence, we believe that, through the framework of a redefined multicultural education (Ghosh & Galczynski, 2014), Canadian society can begin moving beyond simply "managing difference to a point where difference becomes an intrinsic component of the 'norm'" (p. 23), in fulfillment of the intentions of its national multicultural policy.

REFERENCES

Adler, N. E., & Newman, K. (2002). Socioeconomic disparities in health: Pathways and policies. *Health Affairs, 21*(2), 60-76.

Ali, S. (2014, May 19). Does the right to housing belong in Canada's Charter of Rights and Freedoms? *rabble.ca*. Retrieved from: http://rabble.ca/columnists/2014/05/does-right-to-housing-belong-canadas-charter-rights-and-freedoms

Anderson, A., & Frideres, J. (1981). *Ethnicity in Canada: Theoretical perspectives*. Toronto, ON: Butterworths.

Authier, P. (2014, January 23). Concordia University defends its stance against charter at hearings. *Montreal Gazette*. Retrieved from: www.montrealgazette.com/news/Concordia+University+defends+stance+against+charter+hearings/9423606/story.html

Berkowitz, D., Manohar, N. N., & Tinkler, J. E. (2010). Walk like a man, talk like a woman: Teaching the social construction of gender. *Teaching Sociology, 38*(2), 132-143.

Boyd, D. R. (2012). *The right to a healthy environment: Revitalizing Canada's constitution*. Vancouver: UBC Press.

Buzzeli, M. (2008). *Environmental justice in Canada: It matters where you live*. Ottawa, ON: Canadian Policy Research Networks.

Buzzeli, M., Su, J., Le, N., & Bache, T. (2006). Health hazards and socio-economic status: A neighbourhood cohort approach, Vancouver, 1976–2001. *The Canadian Geographer, 50*(3), 376–391.

Campbell, A. (2014, June 17). Proposed bill of rights would protect children's environmental health. *CTV Atlantic*. Retrieved from: http://atlantic.ctvnews.ca/proposed-bill-of-rights-would-protect-children-s-environmental-health-1.1873596

Campbell, C. (2006, February 20). The Church of Stephen Harper. *Maclean's*.

Canadian Charter of Rights and Freedoms, s. 2, Part I of the Constitution Act. (1982).

Canadian Multiculturalism Act, R.S.C., 1985, c. 24 (4th Supp.). (1988).

Cunnane, S. (2014, June 18). "Don't objectify us" say girls in rebellion against restrictive dress codes. *TES Connect*. Retrieved from: http://news.tes.co.uk/b/todays-news-tomorrows-lesson/2014/06/19/39-don-39-t-objectify-us-39-say-girls-in-rebellion-against-restrictive-dress-codes.aspx

Dewing, M., & Leman, M. (2006). *Canadian multiculturalism*. Ottawa: Library of Parliament.

Flanigan, J. (2014, January 23). The dangerous logic of Quebec's "Charter of Values." *The Atlantic*. Retrieved from: http://www.theatlantic.com/international/archive/2014/01/the-dangerous-logic-of-quebecs-charter-of-values/283272/

Flynn, T. (2001). "Transforming" the debate: Why we need to include transgender rights in the struggles for sex and sexual orientation equality. *Columbia Law Review, 101*(2), 393-420.

Forbes, J. D. (1993). *Africans and Native Americans: The language of race and the evolution of red-black peoples* (2nd ed.). Champaign, IL: University of Illinois Press.

Foucault, M. (1977). *Discipline and punish: The birth of the prison*. New York: Pantheon Books.

Freire, P. (1970). *Pedagogy of the oppressed*. New York: Herder & Herder.

Frisk, B. (2013, November 5). Why the U.S. must lead on disabilities treaty. *Reuters*. Retrieved from: http://blogs.reuters.com/great-debate/2013/11/05/why-the-u-s-must-lead-on-disabilities-treaty/

Galczynski, M., Tsagkaraki, V., & Ghosh, R. (2012). Unpacking multiculturalism in the classroom: Using current events to explore the politics of difference. *Canadian Ethnic Studies, 43-44*(3-1), 145-164.

Gay, G. (2000). *Culturally responsive teaching: Theory, research, and practice*. New York: Teachers College Press.

Gérin-Lajoie, D. (2011). Multicultural education: Nothing more than folklore? *Canadian Issues*, Spring, 24–27.

Ghosh, R., & Abdi, A. A. (2012). *Education and the politics of difference: Canadian perspectives* (2nd ed.). Toronto: Canadian Scholar's Press.

Ghosh, R., & Galczynski, M. (2014). *Redefining multicultural education: Inclusion and the right to be different* (3rd ed.). Toronto: Canadian Scholars' Press.

Giroux, H. A. (1988). *Teachers as intellectuals: Toward a critical pedagogy of learning*. Granby, MA: Bergin & Garvey.

Grant, C. A., & Sleeter, C. E. (2009). *Turning on learning: Five approaches for multicultural teaching plans for race, class, gender and disability* (5th ed.). Hoboken, NJ: Wiley.

Handy, B. (2014, June 25). The complex and hidden story behind the Washington Redskins trademark decision. *Vanity Fair*. Retrieved from: http://www.vanityfair.com/online/daily/2014/06/story-behind-washington-redskins-name

Harter, J. (2004). Environmental justice for whom? Class, new social movements, and the environment: A case study of Greenpeace Canada, 1971-2000. *Labour / Le Travail, 54*(2), 83-119.

Hopper, T. (2014, May 29). Labrador school sends dozens of students home for exposing their shoulders and knees. *National Post*. Retrieved from: http://news.nationalpost.com/2014/05/29/labrador-school-sends-dozens-of-students-home-for-exposing-their-shoulders-and-knees/?_federated=1

Institute of Medicine. (1999). *Toward environmental justice: Research, education, and health policy needs*. Washington, DC: The National Academies Press.

Janus, A. (2014, April 8). Couillard promises "most transparent government" in Quebec history. *CTV News*. Retrieved from: http://www.ctvnews.ca/canada/couillard-promises-most-transparent-government-in-quebec-history-1.1765991

Kenning, C. (2014, May 15). Ky. school OKs transgender non-discrimination policy. *USA Today*. Retrieved from: http://www.usatoday.com/story/news/nation/2014/05/15/ky-school-transgender-controversy-discrimination-policy/9158619/

Koch, T. (2001). Disability and difference: Balancing social and physical constructions. *Journal of Medical Ethics, 27*(6), 370-376.

Kymlicka, W. (2003). Canadian multiculturalism in historical and comparative perspective: Is Canada unique? *Constitutional Forum, 13*(1), 1-8.

Macedo, D. & Bartolome. L. (1999). *Dancing with bigotry: Beyond the politics of tolerance.* New York: St. Martin's Press.

Makin, K. (2010, May 27). Fighting for the right to a roof over your head. *The Globe and Mail.* Retrieved from: http://socialrightscura.ca/documents/globe-article.pdf

McGovern, B. (2014, June 19). Redskins decision may threaten 40+ Bay State high schools with Indian-themed mascots. *Boston Herald.* Retrieved from: http://bostonherald.com/news_opinion/local_coverage/2014/06/redskins_decision_may_threaten_40_bay_state_high_schools_with

McIntosh, P. (1990). White privilege and male privilege: A personal account of coming to see correspondences through work in women's studies. In M. S. Kimmel, & A. L. Ferber (Eds.), *Privilege: A reader* (p. 147-160). Boulder, CO: Westview Press.

McKay, M. (2014, July 9). Transgender restroom policy stands after appeal. *The Courier-Journal.* Retrieved from: http://www.courier-journal.com/story/news/education/2014/07/08/atherton-will-hear-transgender-policy-appeal-tonight/12364185/

McLaren, P. (1998). *Life in schools: An introduction to critical pedagogy in the foundations of education* (3rd ed.). New York: Longman.

Merevick, T. (2014, June 16). This Kentucky high school just set the bar for protecting transgender students. *BuzzFeed.* Retrieved from: http://www.buzzfeed.com/tonymerevick/this-kentucky-high-school-just-set-the-bar-for-protecting-tr

Monsebraaten, L. (2010, May 27). Toronto homeless launch charter challenge. *Toronto Star.* Retrieved from:
http://www.thestar.com/news/gta/2010/05/27/toronto_homeless_launch_charter_challenge.html

New Brunswick Environmental Network. (2014). *A bill of rights to protect children's health from environmental hazards.* Retrieved from: http://www.nben.ca/en/collaborative-action/collaboratives/childrens-environmental-health-collaborative-effort/bill-of-rights

Ng, R., Staton, P. A., & Scane, J.. (1995). *Anti-racism, feminism, and critical approaches to education (Critical studies in education and culture series).* Toronto: OISE Press.

Nieto, S. (2003). School reform and student learning: A multicultural perspective. In J. Banks & C. A. McGee Banks (Eds.), *Multicultural education: Issues and perspectives* (p. 381-397). New York: Wiley.

Pang, V. O. (2001). *Multicultural education: A caring-centered approach to reflective approach.* Boston, MA: McGraw-Hill.

Parish, S. L. (2014, June 26). Is ratifying the U.N. convention on the rights of people with disabilities necessary for the U.S.? *Zeh Lezeh (For One Another).* Retrieved from: http://zehlezeh.wordpress.com/2014/06/26/is-ratifying-the-u-n-convention-on-the-rights-of-people-with-disabilities-necessary-for-the-u-s/

Renzetti, E. (2014, June 23). Girls are more than the sum of their parts. *The Globe and Mail.* Retrieved from: http://www.theglobeandmail.com/globe-debate/girls-are-more-than-the-sum-of-their-parts/article19286515/

Reynolds, H. (1996). *Aboriginal sovereignty: Reflections on race, state, and nation.* Crows Nest, NSW: Allen & Unwin.

Saunt, C. (2005). *Black, White, and Indian: Race and the unmaking of an American family.* Oxford: Oxford University Press.

Secure, Adequate, Accessible and Affordable Housing Act, Bill C-304, House of Commons of Canada. (2011).

Statistics Canada. (2013). 2011 National household survey, Catalogue no. 99-010-X2011037. Retrieved from: http://www.statcan.gc.ca/daily-quotidien/130508/dq130508b-eng.htm?HPA

Strauss, V. (2014, June 19). From Redskins to Redhawks: Why one Washington high school changed team name after 88 years. *Washington Post.* Retrieved from: http://www.washingtonpost.com/blogs/answer-sheet/wp/2014/06/19/from-redskins-to-redhawks-why-one-washington-high-school-changed-team-name-after-88-years/

Torres, C. A. (1998). *Democracy, education, and multiculturalism: Dilemmas of citizenship in a global world.* Oxford: Rowman & Littlefield Publishers.

Trudeau, P. E. (1971, October). *Multiculturalism*. Speech presented at the House of Commons, Ottawa, Canada. Retrieved from: http://www.canadahistory.com/sections/documents/Primeministers/trudeau/docs-onmulticulturalism.htm

U.N. General Assembly. (2007). *Convention on the rights of persons with disabilities*. Document A/RES/61/106. Retrieved from: http://www.un.org/disabilities/convention/conventionfull.shtml

U.N. Human Rights. (1989). *Convention on the rights of the child*. Office of the High Commissioner for Human Rights. Retrieved from: http://www.ohchr.org/en/professionalinterest/pages/crc.aspx

U.N. Treaty Collection. (2014, June). *Chapter IV. human rights. Convention on the rights of persons with disabilities*. Retrieved from: https://treaties.un.org/Pages/ViewDetails.aspx?src=TREATY&mtdsg_no=IV-15&chapter=4&lang=en

Vargas, T., & Shin, A. (2013, October 5). President Obama says, "I'd think about changing" name of Washington Redskins. *Washington Post*. Retrieved from: http://www.washingtonpost.com/local/president-obama-says-id-think-about-changing-name-of-washington-redskins/2013/10/05/e170b914-2b70-11e3-8ade-a1f23cda135e_story.html

Mariusz Galczynski
Department of Integrated Studies in Education
McGill University

Vilelmini Tsagkaraki
Department of History and Classical Studies
McGill University

Ratna Ghosh
Department of Integrated Studies in Education
McGill University

SECTION V

FUTURE OF MULTICULTURALISM

AUGIE FLERAS

18. BEYOND MULTICULTURALISM

Managing Complex Diversities in a Postmulticultural Canada

INTRODUCTION: UNSETTLING DIVERSITY GOVERNANCE

To say we live in provocative and perplexing times is (to borrow a phrase) a cliché of understated proportions. The movement of people and diversification of mobility on an unprecedented global scale elevates the management of complex diversities into one of the more critical challenges of the 21st century (Castles & Miller, 2009; Spoonley & Tolley, 2012; Rodriguez-Garcia, 2012). The border-bleeding dynamics of transmigration and transnationalism are unsettling conventional notions of governance pertaining to national identity and society unity. Orthodox patterns of belongings and identities are increasingly contested in a diasporic world of both crossings and connections yet also stricter citizenship protocols and ramped-up border surveillance (Fleras, 2011; Geislerova, 2007). The growing popularity of cosmopolitanism in advancing a global governance principle is no less disruptive to the society-building project (Kymlicka & Walker, 2012). Its humanistic commitment to universal social justice and a global citizenship adds yet another layer of complexity to an already complex world (Brown, 2014; Fleras, 2014b). The interplay of these dynamics raises a raft of governance dilemmas related to: (a) the relevance of place-based governance model in a transmigrant and diasporic world of 'here,' 'there,' and 'everywhere'; (b) the possibility of living together in a spatialized multiculturalism when people's notions of identity and belonging may be uncoupled (deterritorialized) from place; (c) the establishment of a national framework that encompasses civic participation and meaningful belonging against the backdrop of splintered loyalties, multiple identities, and fragmented affiliations; and (d) the creation of a relatively new discursive framework for managing complex and diversifying diversities at local, national, and global levels (Neerup, 2012; Putnam, 2007). That policy responses to these governance puzzles are slow to materialize is consequential: Ulrich Beck (2011, p. 53) writes of the dangers that await those foolish enough to pour new diversity wine into old governance skins:

> … [O]ver the last decades the cultural, social, and political landscapes of diversity are changing radically, but we still use old maps to orient ourselves. In other words, my main thesis is: *we do not even have the language through which contemporary superdiversity in the world can be described, conceptualized, understood, explained, and researched.* (Italics in original)

S. Guo & L. Wong (eds.), Revisiting Multiculturalism in Canada, 311–334.

The politics of managing a complex diversity and diverse complexities — simultaneously fluid and non-linear as well as contested and politicized — is proving a formidable governance challenge (Garcea, Kirova, & Wong 2008; Kraus, 2011). The seemingly ceaseless movement of people accentuates global anxieties over a 'coming anarchy' in disrupting long established national markers of identity and belonging, unity and security (Bourbeau, 2011). The politics of diasporic transmigration are known to: (a) blur a defense of territorial boundaries, (b) encourage cross-border movements of migrants in search of safety or success, (c) undermine regimes of multicultural governance, (d) transform public space into a contested site, (e) coax identities away from a strict national focus, and (f) complicate the search for political forms that balance a respect for diversities without reneging on a sense of community, consensus, and commitment (Ang, 2010; Birt, 2007). Not unexpectedly, national jurisdictions in the post 9/11 era are looking to discipline both the complexities of diversity/the diversity of complexities by tightening up conditions for naturalization; introducing tougher criteria as precondition for integration and citizenship (Winter, 2014); imposing more restrictions over unwanted immigration flows through robust border enforcement and multi/bi/lateral agreements related to deterrence and deportation; and increasingly promoting the idea of nation-states as a community of value and values rather than a disparate collection of migrants and minorities (Anderson, 2013; Fleras, 2014b).

These emergent yet clashing dynamics raise additional questions about the relevance of an official multiculturalism as a territorially-bounded diversity governance within the seemingly opposed contexts of an inhospitable national yet the uninhabitable transnational (Ang, 2010; Karim, 2007; Vertovec & Wessendorf, 2004). The 'globalization of migration' (Castles & Miller, 2009) is thought to have expanded the number of countries concurrently affected by the volume, range, scope, and complexities of global mobility patterns (but see Czaika & de Haas, 2014), in the process exerting pressure for re-conceptualizing the governance of managing complex diversities (Wessendorf, 2014). Consider the following as points of contestation in a Canada that many regard as the world's quintessential model for managing diversity and integrating newcomers (Christiano, 2013; Jedwab, 2014; Papillon, 2012): To what extent can an official multiculturalism and its related conceptual constructs (e.g., 'inclusion') provide an optimal governance for managing complex diversities in a diversifying Canada (also Mansouri & de B'beri, 2014)? Is an inclusive multiculturalism capable of differently accommodating the more fluid and fragmented dynamic of diversities-within-diversities? How relevant is a bounded and managed multiculturalism as a national governance framework (physically circumscribed, culturally specific, and spatially exclusive national identity) in a relatively unbounded and unmanaged world of transmigratory movements, translocal linkages, hyperdiverse identities, cosmopolitan yearnings, and deterritorialized belongings (Carruthers, 2013; Walton-Roberts, 2011)? Why even bother to invoke a place-based ('spatialized') multiculturalism as governance model for managing complex diversities when migrant notions of identity and belonging become delinked from conventional points of reference (Mawani, 2008)?

Responses to these questions are critical in sorting out the politics of managing complex diversities without the complexities getting in the way of diversity management (Kraus, 2011). Then, as now, the managerial challenge revolves around the society-building project of forging a 'unity in/from/with/through diversity' (Jenson & Papillon, 2001). Or to rephrase the diversity challenge along governance lines: *How to transform a disparate array of migrants and minorities into a cohesive community ('nation') of citizens, with a corresponding sense of commitment and conviction, consensus and communication?* Only the details of this society-building challenge evolve over time, with multicultural models giving way to postmulticultural governance platforms that bolster the prospect of managing increasingly complex and diverse societies (RECODE Conference Notes, 2013; also Mor Barak, 2014). Too much of what passes for contemporary multiculturalism as diversity management governance is grounded in the metaphorical equivalent of a 'multi cul de sac' multiculturalism (see Rohinton Mistry, 1995), including concomitant notions of fixed and homogenous mosaic of ethnocultures within the territorially bounded framework of a modern nation-state (Beck, 2011). But the hyperdiverse dynamics of a diversifying world cannot be easily pigeon-holed into such a governance straitjacket. Societies such as Canada are no longer simply diverse societies. Rather they are diversifyingly complex and complexly diverse because of demographics, mobility movements, attachments, and socioeconomic profile, and this emergent hyperdiversity exerts pressure for a new interpretive lens to frame what is going on (Latham, 2008). A new postmulticultural governance model is proposed that builds on, yet goes beyond, an inclusive multiculturalism, while securing an inclusivity framework for accommodating different ways of accommodating this diversified diversity.

To date, most signs point to a failure of imagination to imagine a new theoretical tool kit to unthink and rethink some of the most basic governance concepts such as multiculturalism for managing a complexity of diversities (Blommaert, 2012; Duit & Galaz, 2008; Li & Juffermans, 2011; Vertovec, 2012). The hyperdiversities associated with multidimensional shifts in migration and migrants creates a range of challenges for service providers in customizing programs and targeting them more accurately for the needs of different groups and intra-group diversities (Meissner & Vertovec, 2015; Phillimore, 2015; Jimenez, Fields, & Schacter, 2015). But an emergent postmulticulturalism project anchored in the principle of multiversality may secure an escape from this governance gridlock. A multiversal-based postmulticulturalism not only constitutes a new discourse and imaginary for managing complex diversities. It also possesses the potential to address the diverse complexities of new (trans)migrants and (hyper)minorities by acknowledging the reality of their cultural comings and goings, yet simultaneously recognizing their translocal identities and belongings beyond fixed boundaries and permanent locales (Carruthers, 2013). Reference to postmulticulturalism as multiculturalism 2.0 governance provides an innovative vantage point for engaging the lived realities of diverse diversities and their multiple modes of coexistence, belonging and identity (Berns-McGown, 2013; Blommaert, 2012; Collett & Petrovic, 2014; Vertovec, 2013; Wessendorf, 2014).

This chapter argues that the challenge of managing complex diversities within diversifying contexts puts pressure on a postmulticultural governance model that positively transcends an inclusive multiculturalism by embracing the principle of multiversal inclusivity as grounds for differential accommodation. However progressive for its time, a managed multiculturalism is no longer positioned to differently accommodate the different ways of accommodating complex diversities. A postmulticulturalism model of governance is proposed instead as an interpretive lensfor capturing the creative tension between the universal (a 'multicultural inclusion') and the particular (a 'multiversal inclusivity'). The chapter begins by examining three models of diversity governance for managing diversities, namely, monoculturalism, multiculturalism, and postmulticulturalism. It continues by drawing on the concept of a postmulticulturalism as a proposed governance model for engaging complex diversities in a 'postnational' society. The chapter concludes by discussing the possibility and promise of a 'post-Canada' for putting into practice the postmulticultural dynamic of living together with/in/through a diversity-of-diversities.

CONCEPTUALIZING GOVERNANCE MODELS FOR MANAGING DIVERSITY

Reference to governance has progressed from relatively obscurity to obligatory slogan in less than a decade. Despite its popularity at conceptual and practical levels, the concept is prone to uncertainties over definition and characteristics (Fleras, 2009). For our purposes, governance can be defined as a *framework of rules that establishes a principled relationship between ruler and ruled, alongside a corresponding distribution of power and authority in addition to an exchange of rights and obligations.* With governance, a principled framework is created for addressing how authority is divided; power is distributed; policies are formulated; valued resources are allocated in a given jurisdiction; priorities and agendas are set; decisions are made and enforced; accountability and accountability are rendered; implementation is secured; services are delivered; and rules of the political game are played out to prevent conflict and promote cohesion (Fukuyama, 2013; Turton et al., 2007; also see Fox & Ward, 2008). Three governance models can be discerned for managing diversities: monocultural, multicultural, and postmulticultural.

Monoculturalism as Exclusionary Governance

A commitment to monocultural governance embodies a Westphalian model of society building. 19th century nationalist ideologies conflated the notion of a nation with a sovereign state in striving for unity through uniformity by rejecting public affirmation of diversity as contrary to successful governance (Coleman, 2011). This Wesphalian commitment to monocultural governance and national homogeneity as the first modernity was organized along the lines of a centrist state that embraced an essentialized and uncontested concept of national unity and societal identity (Ben-Eliezer, 2008; Smith, 2013). The mono-national state possessed and was possessed by a dominant national group who manipulated its hegemonic powers to control and contain. Those who didn't belong to the dominant national group endured the lash of annihilation or expulsion, discrimination or assimilation (Kymlicka, 2004/07). The consequences of this monoculturalism governance persist into the present as Parekh (2005, pp. 8-9) writes:

> [C]ontemporary multicultural societies have emerged against the backdrop of several centuries of the culturally homogenising nation-state ... Since the state required cultural and social homogenization as a necessary basis [for a new kind of societal unity], it has for centuries sought to mould the wider society in that direction. Thanks to this, we have become so accustomed to equating unity with homogeneity, and equality with uniformity, that unlike many of our premodern counterparts we feel morally and emotionally disoriented by, and do not quite know how to accommodate, the political demands of a deep and defiant diversity.

Multiculturalism as Inclusion Governance

Monoculturalism as an exclusionary governance was eventually discredited for a variety of reasons (Fleras, 2011). A multicultural governance model evolved that challenged exclusive notions of belonging and identity, especially those that relegated minorities and migrants to second class status. The inclusion principles of universal personhood and the practices of active citizenship prevailed instead whose governance pattern (a) remained ostensibly neutral and impartial when engaging its constituent individuals and communities; (b) promulgated the principle that the state belongs to all its citizens not just a single national group; (c) embraced the rights of all migrants and minorities to full and equal participation without forfeiting a right to identity and equality; and (d) ensured all citizens have the same institutional access as the dominant group (Berns-McGown, 2007/08; Foster, 2014; Kymlicka, 2004/07). To be sure, articulating a multicultural framework for managing diversity was one thing; putting these principles into practice has proven quite another. Bhikhu Parekh captures a sense of the obstacles and contradictions that confront multiculturalism, albeit within a different context:

> Multicultural societies throw up problems that have no parallel in history. They need to find ways of reconciling the legitimate demands of unity and diversity, achieving political unity without cultural uniformity, being inclusive without being assimilationist, cultivating among their citizens a commonsense of belonging while respecting their legitimate cultural differences and cherishing plural cultural identities without weakening the shared and precious identity of shared citizenship. This is a formidable political task and no multicultural society so far has succeeded. (Parekh, 2005, p. 343)

315

Introduction of a multicultural governance was premised on an integration promise (Berry, 2014). Members from diverse ethnocultural groups would coexist with each other through a process of national integration – a kind of unity within diversity framework paralleled at the global level by the United Nations where each nation-state member possesses a separate seat at the table to maintain its distinctiveness yet everyone must abide by common rules (Ang, 2011, p. 28). A mosaic metaphor informed the logic behind this 'multi-cul-de-sac model of multiculturalism, with its attendant notion that (a) the whole is greater than the sum of the parts; (b) every person was affiliated with a cultural tradition, either by birth or by choice; (c) promotion of group-specific rights to protect and enhance ethnocultures; and (d) adherence to the tolerance principle of agreeing to disagree in advancing a cooperative coexistence. Diversity was tolerated and respected; nevertheless, acceptance came with 'strings' attached, that is, central authorities defined what counts as differences, what differences count. Admittedly, fears of extremism or separation/isolation in the post 9/11 era tightened the reins of a laissez-faire multiculturalism prompting, instead, a call for a neo-assimilationist governance to discipline diversity and its management. The growing securitization of society alongside the militarization of borders also reinforced the salience of a bounded and managed multiculturalism for fostering social cohesion and loyal citizenship (Ang, 2010).

Canada's official multiculturalism as national governance provides the quintessential model for managing diversity (Jedwab, 2014; Rodriguez-Garcia, 2012). It's widely touted as the most successful paradigm for diversity management based on the seemingly counterintuitive governance principle that confidence in one's identity facilitates integration and cohesion provided, of course, an overarching framework is in place (Berry, 2014; Heath, 2014). Shifts in emphasis, notwithstanding – ranging in focus from ethnicity to equity to civic to integrative (Fleras, 2012) – an official multiculturalism has never wavered from its central mission as a political project to construct *an inclusive Canada by integrating migrants and minorities into the existing system.* Three governance objectives prevail: (1) to foster migrant integration and minority involvement; (2) to promote an inclusive Canada by accommodating diversity; and (3) to advance a Canada-building without losing control of the agenda or disrupting the status quo (Haque, 2012). Canada's multicultural model of diversity management endorses an inclusionary commitment to an integrated and socially cohesive society, primarily by fostering intercultural/interfaith understanding through dialogue and interaction; promoting shared values and civic pride in Canadian history and society; encouraging a climate of acceptance for diversity; respecting core democratic values and common citizenship; supporting the creation of institutions responsive to the needs of Canada's diverse population; advancing equal opportunities for all Canadians through removal of discriminatory barriers while empowering individuals to regulate the pace and scope of their adjustment to Canada (Biles, 2014; Hansen, 2014; Jedwab, 2014). As might be expected of any state program in defence of dominant ideology ('hegemony'), a managed multiculturalism extols neither power-sharing nor disruptions to the prevailing distribution of power or privilege (Fleras, 2014a). The focus of a 'seeing-like-a-state' multiculturalism as a centrally planned social engineering project is quietly hegemonic: to impose order on those aspects of society in need of regulation and control by simplifying complex phenomena under singular solutions (see Scott, 1998).

Canada's state-sponsored multiculturalism secures a principled platform for managing diversity (Jedwab, 2014). It's primarily aimed at constructing an inclusive Canadian governance of many ("multi") cultures through removal of discriminatory/prejudicial barriers to ensure full interaction and equal participation for all Canadians (Fleras, 2014b). An inclusive multiculturalism model focuses on ensuring no one is excluded from the existing societal framework for reasons beyond their control. It acknowledges the right of newcomers to become Canadian on their own terms if they comply with the law of the land, respect people's individual rights, subscribe to core constitutional values such as gender equality, and use their ethnicity as a basis for belonging and identifying with Canada. Of course, no one is suggesting a commitment to inclusion as governance principle is beyond politics. To the contrary, a commitment to integrate newcomers by respecting differences, reflecting diversity, and creating more responsive institutions reinforces the logic of state multiculturalism as a political act to achieve political goals (related to national unity and identity) in a politically expedient manner (Peter, 1978; also Clarke, 2009). But a static and categorical multicultural inclusion will no longer suffice under increasingly diverse and deterritorialized conditions. In a globalized world of 235 million people living outside their homeland and where technology transforms borders into paper-thin membranes, people are questioning the concept of multicultural inclusion (Adams, Macklin, & Omidvar 2014). So too are those politicized diversities who insist their differences must be taken seriously, in large part by claiming the right to ensure differences are made safe from society as well as safe for society, while exercising control over defining what differences count, what counts as difference.

However progressive for its time, a multicultural governance model for managing complex diversities is losing its saliency. The globalizing processes whose transmigatory dynamics threaten to decouple multicultural governances from a place-based model of inclusion have seen to that (Ferguson & Mansbach, 2012). Such a restriction raises the prickly question of whether a bounded multiculturalism can cope the realities and challenges of an increasingly unbounded (or 'trans-bounded') Canada in a freewheeling yet networked global world of transcendental ties, transmigratory movements, transnational connections, and diasporic identities (Walton-Roberts, 2011)? More complex responses are required to address the challenges of accommodating different ways of accommodating a diversification of diversities.These tensions and paradoxes can be collapsed into an all-encompassing conundrum: *In a globalizing and postnational world of transmigration and hyperdiversity, does it still make sense to talk about multiculturalism and inclusion as place-based governance models when migrant notions of identity and belonging traverse a single location to connect inter-spatially?* Put somewhat differently, what is the point of talking about the migration-integration nexus from the vantage point of territorialized multiculturalism when notions of identity and belonging are fractured along multiple lines rather than collapsed into a single national space? A profoundly unsettling response looms large when hyperdiversity dynamics challenge the principle of multicultural inclusion as governance in a postmulticultural world of complex diversities and diverse complexities?

Postmulticulturalism Governance

There is no consensus regarding the meaning of postmulticulturalism (Gozdecka, Dorota, Ercan, & Kmak, 2014; Pakulski, 2014). Part of the problem is whether the prefix 'post' refers to a retreat from or rejection of the past; a hybridic synthesis of competing perspectives (past + present); or sequential advance that moves beyond the past – from pre to post – without necessarily abdicating it. No less problematic is the prospect of determining whether the prefix refers to something that already happened, is already happening, or should be happening if people had their way (Sanchez-Ruiz, n.d.). Many including Joppke (2004) and Prior (2009) allude to postmulticulturalism as a ground-breaking shift from European multicultural discourses (whose endorsement of multiple loyalties and splintered identities is problematic and divisive) to those involving the language of civic integration, citizenship, and social cohesion (also Fleras, 1994). Others such as Vertovec (2010) frame postmulticulturalism as a hybrid agenda that fuses the agendas of the left (respecting diversity yet reducing social inequality) with the right's ambitions for national unity, shared values, and collective identity. Still others are doubtful it even exists or needs to exist; for example, Kymlicka (2010, p. 99) writes disapprovingly of postmulticulturalism as a so-called advance over a multicultural past that never existed except as caricature:

> According to post-multiculturalists, it is the gradual recognition of these flaws that explains the retreat from multiculturalism and the search for a new post-multicultural models of citizenship that emphasize the priority of political participation and economic opportunities over the symbolic politics of cultural recognition, the priority of human rights and individual freedom over respect for cultural traditions, the priority of building inclusive common national identities over the recognition of ancestral cultural identities, and the priority of cultural change and cultural mixing over the reification of cultural differences.

Finally, postmulticulturalism has been framed as a constructive engagement with the past by building on it and moving positively beyond a universalistic (one-size-fits-all) multiculturalism model (Latham, 2007/08; Pinder, 2010). The post in postmulturalism is thus wielded in the sense of 'engaging constructively with' multiculturalism rather than employed as a 'qualitative break' with the past (Maaka & Fleras, 2005). David Ley (2005, p. 15) writes to this effect:

... [A] post-multiculturalism is not a rejection of multiculturalism as much as it is a recognition that renewed energies are needed to create a global understanding of diversity across multiple contexts and locales that can be an asset, and not simply a set of problems in need of better judgement.

The postmulticultural challenge revolves around creating a diversity governance framework that engages complex forms of identity and belonging at both individual and group levels against a backdrop of a societal framework of social inclusion, full participation, and democratic rights. It achieves this goal by acknowledging the shift from managing-the-mosaic model of multiculturalism to a kaleidoscope model for engaging those complex diversities that are fluid, contested, multidimensional, and consistent with the intersecting and overlapping realities of a postmodern world of change, uncertainty, unpredictability and contradiction (Fleras, 2014b). A commitment to postmulticulturalism does it differently than the static and managed framework of mosaic multiculturalism (also Vertovec, 2010). An official multiculturalism is limited because it continues to be foundationally grounded within the constitutional order of a monocultural state. Such a monoculturality is antithetical to diversity by virtue of imposing its definition of what counts as diversity, and what diversities count. It's also commensurate with white Eurocentricity as the unmarked norm and systemic standard by which others are judged (Pinder, 2010). In attempting to unite diversities under the banner of a common Canadian identity, multiculturalism tends to paper over differences, while reinforcing a kind of hierarchy that locates a Eurocentric whiteness at the centre while marginalizing migrants/minorities (Latham, 2007/08). Or alternatively, a state multiculturalism may accentuate differences, albeit for controlling purposes of divide and rule. The end result is the ascent of rigid identity politics managed by the state in which diverse yet aggrieved groups proclaim their specialness or victimhood by setting themselves apart from others (Hrushetska, 2013).

A world of proliferating diversity and intragroup diversities, notwithstanding, governments continue to employ governance models that seem out of sync. The seemingly simple diversities of the past have given way to social, political, and cultural cleavages that overlap and compete for recognition; are imbricated with distributive demand; and hinge on the metaphor of simultaneity as exemplified by multiple embeddedness, axis of differentiation, and intersectionality (Glick-Schiller & Caglar, 2013; RECODE 2013). Or they resort to disciplining diversity and its management to reclaim order and centralized control. Kenan Malik (3 June 2012) writes of the schism between diversity as a lived experience vs multiculturalism as a political program for managing diversity in his Milton K Wong Lecture "What is Wrong with Multiculturalism":

As a political process, however, multiculturalism means something very different. It prescribes a set of policies, the aim of which is to manage and institutionalize diversity by putting people into ethnic and cultural boxes, defining individual needs and rights by virtue of the boxes into which people are put, and using these boxes to shape public policy. It is a case, not for open borders and minds, but for policing of borders, whether physical, cultural, or imaginative.

By contrast, a postmulticultural governance seeks to delegitimize the barriers to hyper-diverse ways of being and becoming ('superdiversity'). Such an inclusivity commitment renders it compatible with a wide range of transmigrant belongings and transnational identities within and beyond borders once denied or silenced by the discourses of modernity (McKenzie, 2013). The logic behind post-multiculturalism governance recognizes the reality of differences-within-differences. It also acknowledges a corresponding necessity to find ways of accommodating different ways of accommodating increasingly complex and diverse differences. That alone exerts pressure for new postmulticultural governance models for managing ('engaging') those diversities that transcend the limitations of a multiculturalism paradigm. A multiversal perspective may secure a fitting answer to the question of 'what's a postmulticulturalism for in a postnational world of complex diversities.'

Multiversal Inclusivity as Postmulticultural Governance

What is multiversality and how does it reflect, reinforce, and advance a postmulticultural model of complex diversity governance (Catanzano, 2009; Hanlon, 2014)? According to the Robert Latham (2007/08), the word multiverse conveys the idea of multiple social universes, with a corresponding set of diverse perspectives, tacitly assumed premises, and lived realities. Differences in a multiverse don't just exist in one universe; more to the point, they prevail within and across many overlapping and intersecting multi-universes, resulting in a proliferation of *fissions, fissures and fusions. Fissions* within migrant and minority communities are increasingly compounded by those intersecting axes of differentiation, distinction, and demands related to legal status, religion, gender age, nationality, class, and so on (Vertovec, 2007; also Vertovec & Wessendorf, 2004). *Fissures* within migrant and minority communities reflect social cleavages, both temporary and permanent, due to internal politics, conflicting agendas, and variable socioeconomic statuses. Cue *fusions:* Canada's urban centres are outgrowing both the traditional model of multiculturalism and the language once used to describe ethnocultural diversity (Habacan, 2007; Sandercock, 2003, 2006). Thanks in part to Canada's vibrant immigration program, Canadian cities now exhibit the dynamics of hybridity, concludes Daniel Hiebert, a co-director of Vancouver's Metropolis Project (Globe and Mail, 2011), namely, a robust *fusion* of cultures, religions, homeland linkages, and sexual orientations as people renegotiate their multiple differences in/with/through everyday experiences (Wessendorf, 2014). Unlike the 'multi cul de sacism' of a mosaic multi-culturalism model that shackles people around their ethnicity and ancestry (regardless of their importance to a person's identity), a multiversal model acknowledges ethnicity as but one component of a multidimensional identity (Ang, 2011; Hollinger, 2006). Yes, ethnicity may inform their complex and dynamic identity across multiple cultural spaces. Yet for those Canadians whose ethnicity is not all consuming as a dominant category of differentiation, it should neither define who they are nor should it box them into an ethnic multi-cul-de-sac (Malik, 2012; Wong, 2007). This passage is instructive of an emerging immigrant experience that neither severs ties with the home country nor passively assimilates into the host country preferring, instead, to thrive in the positives of such ambivalence.

My Name is Sophie and I am Canadian. And what does that mean? According to Canadian census, it means: I am third generation Canadian on my mother's side and second generation Canadian on my father's side. My maternal grandparents are Canadian and British. My paternal grandparents are Senegalese. My aunts and uncles come from Canada, Thailand, Senegal, and the Ivory Coast. I am Muslim by birth, my father is Muslim, and my mother is Roman Catholic. Our family celebrates Aid El-Fitr and Eid Al-Adha, as well as, Christmas and Easter. I have multiple citizenships: British, Canadian, and Senegalese. I attend French primary and secondary schools and then went to university in English and French. At home I speak English with my mother and French with my father. I don't remember which language I learned first … At the moment … I divide my time living between Abbotsford and Dubai, while working for three companies headquartered in Hong Kong, South Africa, and Guatemala. My taxes are paid on the amount of time I spend in each of my residences. (Gaye, 2011)

In short, Canada is much more than a multicultural social formation. Its multiculturality is also aligned along the cross-cutting and overlapping lines of multiracial, multiclass, multigendered, multisexual, multilingual, multireligious, multigenerational, multihistorical, and multicitizenshipsn that compete for recognition, legitimacy, and accommodation (Latham, 2008, 2009). This tectonic shift in complex coexistence reflects a dizzying range of differences and entitlements, not only between identifiable groups and communities, but also *within* groups and *across* spaces and borders. The mosaic concept of bounded ethnic entities as basis for diversity/migrant governance is being usurped by the rearticulation of identity and belonging along fluid and hybridic lines within a changing and connected world. The interplay of transmigration (transnationalism) with hyperdiversities may subvert the salience of multiculturalism as a diversity governance model, particularly when immigrant notions of identity and affiliation are increasingly dislodged from territorial place (Satzewich & Wong, 2006; Wong, 2007/08). For example, trans-immigrants participate simultaneously across different spheres of life in both host and home countries. They identify with multiple identities across national borders as they settle into their new homeland; they construct diasporic communities that offer solidarity, support, information, and identity; and they participate across multiple universes ('multiverses') without necessarily dissolving attachment to the territorially defined sentiments of the host country (Pieterse, 2006). Faisal Bhabha (2009, p. 48) speaks to the prospect of living in what amounts to the multiversality of an increasingly complex and diversifying postmulticultural Canada:

> Controversies surrounding multiculturalism are neither unique to Canada nor new. However, the recent prominence, and growing hyper-consciousness of culture in the public realm, reveals the profound underlying social cleavages of our modern, multi-ethnic society. Members of minority cultures are increasingly demanding not only equality and non-discrimination when integrating into the dominant culture but also that their collective identity be made a matter of public importance and accommodation. Claims can be complex and confusing; distinctions between groups and individuals are often muddled. For instance, during the now infamous sharia controversy in Ontario, the most acute debate raged between different factions of the same minority community [namely "devout" Muslims vs "silent majority" of moderate Muslims, insertion, mine].

The principle of inclusivity strikes at the core of multiversality as postmulticultural governance (Table 1).[1] In contrast to the concept of inclusion based on the multicultural principle of not *excluding* anyone because of their differences by fitting them into the existing system, inclusivity as principle promotes an accommodation model for transforming institutions to ensure that everyone is *included* precisely because of their differences, therebye adjusting the system to make it fit new realities. Instead of simply adding to something that already exists, inclusivity promotes the prospect of breaking with the past by changing the culture, structure, environment, and social-organizational life (Dei, 2010). The focus is on changing the system (not just individuals) to accommodate the specific challenges of an internally diverse and fractious demographic (Battaini-Dragoni, 2008; Berns-McGown, 2013). Reference to inclusivity proposes a difference model that questions existing arrangements, posits a relational and multiversal view of culture, and frames diversities within contexts of power and inequality (Glasser, Awad, & Kim, 2009). Access to services is rooted in the principle of rights and relations rather than needs or cultural differences; as a result, the focus is on mainstreaming equitable provisions rather than perfunctory add-ons such as minority hires or sensitivity sessions. A commitment to inclusivity proposes the creation of a new game with a different set of rules for belonging *in* (not just to) society. It exerts pressure for doing things differently, that is, by contesting and changing the rules that refer to the conventions instead of simply tweaking the conventions that inform the rules. The conclusion is inescapable as Pinder (2010) reminds us (albeit in an American context): to move beyond multiculturalism toward postmulticulturalism, the monocultural state must first transition into a truly multicultural state that embraces the creation, complexity, and diversity of new cultural expressions.

Table 1. Inclusion vs inclusivity as inclusive governance models for managing diversity.

Inclusion/Inclusive Models	Inclusivity Models
• People must fit into existing system • One way process of incorporation • Diversities – challenge or problem • We/they mentality • Make society safe from, safe for, differences • Culture blind: One size fits all accommodation • Everyone treated the same (equal treatment) • Minority hires + sensitivity training = create the right change • Modify: Change conventions that refer to rules ("adding to what already exists" • Society as given and potentially neutral + level playing field • Top down approach to decision making ("we know what's best") • Modernist bias (managing the mosaic) • Modern Nation-state • Multicultural Discourse	• System changes to accommodate diversity • Two way process of mutual accommodation • Diversities = asset • Us/our mindset • Make differences safe from, safe for, society • Culture conscious: Differential accommodation, i.e., accommodating differences-within-differences • A diversity of differences taken into account when needed • Structural changes through removal of discriminatory barriers. • Transform: Change rules that inform conventions ("breaking with existing order and starting fresh") • Society as socially constructed and ideologically loaded (a racialized playing field) • Bottom up decision making ('listen & learn' dialogue) • Postmodernist bias (engaging the kaleidoscope) • Postnational society • Postmulticultural Discourse

TOWARDS A POSTMULTICULTURALISM GOVERNANCE IN A POSTNATIONAL CONTEXT

The world at present is an untidy and unruly place. Societies are no longer the ordered jurisdications of centralized planning and social engineering that many imagined them to be or what they themselves aspired to (see James Scott, *Seeing Like the State*, 1999). To the contrary, they are complex and contested domains of identities, perspectives, and sites of actions, including multiple universes within universes (multiverse) that cross borders and collapse notions of time and space into a kind of timeless immediacy (Latham, 2008). Nation-states confront the challenge of maintaining their integrity, unity, and identity in the face of increasingly disruptive dynamics related to internal pressures ('hyperdiversity') and external dynamics ('transmigration') (Ang, 2010). Not surprisingly, the governance of managing diversity is fundamentally different at present than in the past because of the level of complexities at play. Systems and relations – once separate – are now interconnected and interdependent because of digital technologies, in the process making them more complex by definition, while making it more difficult to manage the unpredictable, the surprising, and the unexpected (Sargut & McGrath, 2011). Yet governance models have not kept pace with the transformation, resulting in some trepidation over a pending postmulticulturalism turn:

> [Nation states] are de facto diverse in ways that can no longer be contained within the neat model of unity in diversity. After many generations of immigration history, migrants and their descendants are no longer containable within a fixed and internally homogeneous category of 'ethnic community,' as tended to be assumed in the formative years of a state-sponsored multiculturalism. Witness the second, third, and fourth generations, whose ethnic identities are increasingly fluid, hybridized and Westernized. Nor has there been a smooth process of integration of migrants into the national community, not because multiculturalism encouraged them to lead parallel lives, but because differences between people(s) – racial, cultural, religious – are very resistant to erasure: processes of inclusion and exclusion, the differentiation of the self and other, and the drawing of dividing lines between us and them are an enduring feature of the human way of life. (Ang, 2011, p. 29)

A postnational commitment reflects the postmulticultural principle of doing it differently. An era of politicized difference and multiversal differences challenges the founding assumptions and foundational principles of a monocultural constitutional order (Maaka & Fleras, 2005). The emergence and growing awareness of a proliferating differences-within-differences as the basis for complex diversity governance also demonstrates the futility of defending the legitimacy of monocultural goals related to clarity, coherence, centralized authority, commonality, and consensus. The lofty position of a monocultural nation-state as the privileged unit of sovereign identity and agency, including references to a bounded entity with territorial integrity and historical continuity, no longer reigns uncontested as the exclusive governance space for fostering security and community, identity and belonging. It is being challenged instead by rampant internal fragmentation, instability and contestation, and potentially porous borders. A centralized and fixed mono-uniformity is displaced by a more fluid sense of impermanence, fragmentation, and mutability, thus reflecting a radically skeptical world where everything is relative and contested because nothing is absolute and definitive (Dustin, 2007). Traditional criteria are contested as grounds for defining a nation-state such as the goal of matching a bureaucratized territory (state) with that of culture, identity, a peoples, and history (nation). A postnational society embraces a plurality of identities and ethnicities within the context of a national community; as a result, belonging to society is not contingent on belonging to a specific (and usually dominant) ethnocultural group (Wilton, 2009).

What is meant by moving positively beyond multiculturalism? Instead of a rejection or retreat from multiculturalism, postmulticulturalism should be framed as building on yet transcending an inclusive governance model. A multicultural approach to normalizing diversity may have once symbolized a positive step forward in (a) integrating historically marginalized migrants and newcomers as equals into the existing framework; (b) promoting the concept of respecting differences as a basis for good governance; (c) encouraging full and equal participation to foster social cohesion; (d) acknowledging the importance of accommodative institutions to ensure no one was excluded for reasons beyond their control; e) securing the tolerance principle of agreeing to disagree in advancing a cooperative coexistence; and (f) coping with the demands of a specific historic period – namely, equality, respect, inclusion, integration, and unity – in hopes of superimposing a shared 'we' morality to displace an 'us' versus 'them' mentality (Hrushetska 2013). But responses under a one-size-fits-all multiculturalism are now holding it back from addressing new governance challenges, largely because of the generality of the commitments to which they owe their existence (Hollinger 2006). It's time to move on to the next phase – postmulticulturalism – given how the limitations of a managed multiculturalism are increasingly transparent in attending to the challenges and complexities of a multiversal world of hyperdiversities and transmigration (Heath, 2014; Kymlicka, 2014; Tunis, 2010). A newer 'post-ethnic' governance model 2.0 is required that (a) recognizes the realities of shifting group boundaries, (b) acknowledges new cultural hybrids and combination, and (c) endorses multiple identities and hybridic affiliations at odds with conventional notions of identity politics, group rights, deterministic communities of descent, essentializing cultures, and fixed identities (Hollinger 2006). A commitment to postmulticulturalism as a principled governance is better suited to address the realities of those whose commitments and connections are trans-national; who reject the prospect of being boxed into a homogeneous and essentialized ethnic category preferring, instead, to visualize identity as a cultural web to be negotiated and navigated (Habacan 2012); who are the lookout for arrangements that can differently accommodate the accommodation of diverse diversities; who insist their differences be framed *as assets* to nurture rather than deficits to control; and who expect to engaged as valued contributors rather than managed as social problems.

To be sure, neither the liberal universalism of an inclusive multiculturalism nor the 'multiversal inclusivity' of postmulticultural particularism should be framed as mutually exclusive principles for managing diversity – complex or otherwise. They should be positioned instead as starting points for re-negotiating a new (post)multiculturalism 2.0 governance model that embraces a diversity of diversities across a range of inclusivity channels (Latour & Balint, 2013). In other words, as Pinder (2010) reminds us (albeit in an American context): to move beyond multiculturalism toward postmulticulturalism, the monocultural state must first transition into a truly multicultural state that embraces the complexity and diversity of new cultural expressions. A commitment to postmulticulturalism is less a rejection of multiculturalism 1.0 but more of a recognition that a renewed governance model better engages the complex diversities and diverse complexities of the 21st century.

In brief, postnationality challenges the rules upon which convention is based rather than simply modifying the conventions (or practices) that refer to the rules (Angus, 2002). A new governance game is proposed, along with a different set of rules of engagement for belonging, identity, and loyalty. Two playful inversions capture the distinction between national/multicultural model for managing diversity versus a postnational/postmulticultural model[2] (Table 2) as site for engaging complex diversities and diverse complexities: (1) a modern society embarks on a project to *make society safe from diversities yet safe diversity* – primarily by monopolizing the right to define what counts as diversity, and what diversities count. By contrast a postmulticultural/postnational society is more inclined to invert this postulate by ensuring that *diversities are made safe from society yet ensure they are safe for society;* (2) a modern society begins with a model of the good society, then incorporates differences accordingly (the principle of 'diversity-in-society'). In opposition, a postmodern/postnational society begins

Table 2. Models of diversity governance in Canada.

	Model A Pre-Multicultural Governance. 1867-1960s	Model B Multiculturalism Governance. 1970s-2010s	Model C Postmulticulturalism Governance (into the future)
Diversity Management Model	Monoculturalism	Mosaic Multiculturalism	Multiversal Multiculturalism
Logic behind Diversity Management Models	Exclusion	Inclusion principle rooted in liberal universalism.	Inclusivity principle rooted in ethnic particularlism
Immigration Model	Restrictive	National (or European)	Trans-migration/ Transnationalism
Model of Society	Pre-modern/Mononational	Modern/National	Postmodern/Postnational
Model of Canada	A White, British, Christian colony	A Multicultural Nation-state	PostCanada: A Postmulticultural Notion-state

with primacy of diversity as inherently valued, then constructs the good society around the prioritizing of diverse diversities (the principle of 'society-in-diversity') (Sandercock, 2003).

RE-IMAGINING A POSTCANADA

Canada is a camel of a country, an ungaingly, confounding confederation of disparate regions that somehow have combined to form one of the most successful countries in the world. It is a blessed oddity, "an historical accident," in the appreciative words of former Prime Minister Pierre Elliott Trudeau, who also characterized Canada as a "country built against any common geographic, historic, or cultural sense." (Solomon, 2014, p. FP11)

This chapter has argued that Canada's official multiculturalism as a governance model for managing complex diversities is experiencing an identity crisis of confidence. This crisis of legitimacy is animated by perceptions of official multiculturalism as a bad idea unfolding according to plan or, alternatively, a marvel of social engineering in danger of corruption by misguided ideologues. Perceived flaws within multiculturalism embody a wide spectrum of criticism, including (1) the right/conseratives who argue multiculturalism is divisive and/or fosters extremism (2) the left/radicals who critique multiculturalism as an illusion of inclusion that glosses over social inequalities and power relations, and (3) those in between who believe it mistakenly frames cultures as static, essentializing, and deterministic (Fleras, 2014a; Vertovec, 2010). The legitimacy crisis also stems from developments largely beyond the control of multiculturalism such as patterns of transmigration and transnationalism owing to the unprecedented and diverse movement of people on a global scale (Fleras, 2014b), in addition to a proliferating hyperdiversity in major urban regions whose kaleidoscopic complexities have outgrown the conventional language of mosaic metaphors to describe the new complexities (Habacan, 2007).

Multicultural governance models for managing complex diversities rarely resonate with meaning or relevance. National governments are no longer equipped to address complex global issues and multiple identities associated with transmigration and the hyperdiversities of multiversal world. International migration poses a governance challenge in confronting the concept of the nation-state with respect to borders, organization, identity, services, and 'belongingness' (Consterdine, 2013). The interplay of unsettled boundaries, transnational loyalties, and multiple identities has proven consequential in deconstructing the monocultural ideal of a unitary nation-state. Society is ensnared in a pincer between the proverbial rock and a hard place. It can neither uphold the rigidities of a fixed national identity for fear of looking inflexible in a world of fluidity. Nor can it afford a no-holds-barred commitment to diversity without dismantling borders or eroding sovereignty. Canada appears to be weathering the pending legitimacy crisis for balancing global forces with those of national interests and minority rights. The juggling act tends to be wobbly at times; nonetheless, this ongoing project in Canada-building should be commended because of the enormity of the challenges.

Unlike the more complete (or civilizational) societies of Europe (Castles & Miller, 2009; Nussbaum, 2012), Canada *represents* an idea and a set of ideals ('a notion') rather than a peoples with a history, language, and culture ('a nation'). But it is precisely this fundamental ambiguity of a nation as a notion that underscores the logic of a postCanada. "Canada is not a real country," as Quebec Premier Lucien Bouchard once taunted English-speaking Canadians, but a collection of shreds and patches, with no *raison d'etre* (historical or cultural) to claim nationality or peoplehood (see also Christiano, 2013, p. 4). Outside of Quebec, Canadians share little of the organic categories of history, language, culture, or ethnicity generally associated with nationality (Florby, Shackleton, & Suhonen, 2009). They appear to have little in common – no shared ancestry or genetic pool, no origin myths, and few common rituals – except a commitment to ideals from rule of law to public institutions such as universal healthcare (Fleras, 2012). Or rephrased, Canada is not so much a mosaic of culturally distinct tiles, notwithstanding its popularity as a metaphor. More aptly, it's a complex matrix of wiggly lines and contested angles responding to the demands of multiple identities and competing sovereignties.

This assessment of Canada as all "lines" and "angles" may not flatter. Yet the persistence of these very vulnerabilities may yield a host of possibilities for crafting a Canada in the vanguard of managing complex diversities. Canada may be poised on the brink of becoming the world's first postnational society, even if nobody can agree on exactly what this means or what it's worth (Florby et al., 2009).[3] A postCanada appears to excel in the art of managing the politics of managing complex diversities without splintering apart in the process. Instead of a definitive centre that categorically defines, defuses and controls, a postCanada is constructed around a society-building process that not only accommodates difference at the level of belonging, identity, recognition, and entitlements, but also condone the principle of accommodating different ways of accommodating these difference. Reference to Canada as a nation with a shared history, geography, or ethnicity ("nation") is displaced by 'notion' of postCanada as an ongoing socially constructed and perpetually contested convention, created and evolving, relative to a particular time and place, and subject to reformative change. With postnationality, in other words, weaknesses become society-building strengths; conversely, assets may prove to be liabilities when contexts undergo transformative changes. In truth, nobody really knows what a postmulticulturalism governance would look like; after all, Canada is currently in the midst of paradigm shift between a mosaic multiculturalism model that has lost its lustre and a multiversal multiculturalism 2.0 that has yet to attract sufficient political traction. But in moving beyond a managed multiculturalism in a postCanada, the postmulticultural politics of engaging complex diversities along multiversal lines may prove a 21st century game-changer.

NOTES

[1] To be sure, inclusion and inclusivity constitute ideal typical models for managing diversity. In a world that is contextual rather than categorical, no society fits into one or the other; rather societies consist of inconsistent mixtures ('hybrids') of both governances. Moreover, it would be a mistake to simply declare an inclusivity model to be superior to an inclusion model. In the same way that an inclusion multiculturalism must precede an inclusivity-based multiversal multiculturalism 2.0, so too is an inclusion model a necessary precondition for inclusivity principles to come into play. Or alternatively, one could argue that, to ensure both equality and differences by balancing unity with hyperdiversity, both models are critical in managing complex diversities.

[2] Table 2 demonstrates the possibility of three (ideal-typical) diversity governance models. They may be viewed in a chronological sequence or concurrently (albeit inconsistently) within any given context, although each encapsulates fundamentally different assumptions and approaches for managing migrant diversity (Siemiatycki, 2012; Spoonley & Tolley, 2012). A premulticultural ('monocultural') society (Model A) is built on the premise that good governance is impossible without removing differences. Groups of people (races) are fundamentally different and their differences can be aligned along ascending lines of inferiority and superiority, then discarded or suppressed accordingly as tainted or as threat. A modern multicultural society (Model B) is constructed on the basis that good governance is tolerant of differences in the private domain while ensuring a relatively neutral public domain that is free of diversity entanglements. The principle of liberal universalism prevails so that everyone is basically the same; no one deserves special treatment; everyone is equal before the law; and a one size fits all intervention applies since differences are perceived as superficial or unimportant as well as static, fixed, and deterministic. To be sure, special measures may be enacted when the situation demands it, but they come with strings attached (i.e., temporary and needs based rather than racial) and is aimed at fitting individuals into the existing system. A postmodern and postmulticultural society (Model C) reflects the principle that good governance is impossible without taking differences seriously, in large part by taking these differences into account as a framework for living together, decision making, and reward allocation. A commitment to multiversal-inspired postmulticulturalism also acknowledges the reality of diversities-within-diversities as grounds for good governance, while conceding the importance of differential accommodation, that is, the inclusivity principle of accommodating different ways of accommodating differences.

[3] For some, reference to Canada as a postnationality is a misnomer. It mistakenly downplays its history, makes few demands on Canadians, allows its citizens to construct identities and belongings wherever they like, and dismisses notions of national unity and common purpose as out of date and disadvantaging in a global world (Griffiths, 2009). For others, Canada represents a prototype of postnational society, its inhabitants are seen as cosmopolitan citizens of the world (rather than people of a single nation with a distinctive civic tradition) connected by common humanity and their shared cultural differences (Baird, 2009). Still others frame postnationality as a condition involving the greater ease of movement across borders, resulting in peoples' identities and allegiances spanning the parameters of national boundaries (Sanchez-Ruiz, n.d.).

REFERENCES

Adams, M., Macklin, A., & Omidvar, R. (2014, May 21). Citizenship act will create two classes of Canadians. *Toronto Globe and Mail.*

Anderson, B. (2013). *Us & them? The dangerous politics of immigration control.* New York: Oxford University Press.

Ang, I. (2010, March). *Between the National and the Transnational: Multiculturalism in a globalising world.* Keynote address at the Biennial Malaysian Studies Conference. Penang.

Ang, I. (2011). Ethnicities and our precarious future. *Ethnicities, 11*(1), 27-31.

Angus, I. (2002). Cultural plurality and democracy. *International Journal of Canadian Studies, 25,* 69-86.

Baird, D. (2009, May). The Walrus reader: Eight essential spring books. *The Walrus, 11*(6), 232.

Battaini-Dragoni, G. (2008). *Living together as equals in dignity: White paper on intercultural dialogue.* Strasbourg: Council of Europe.

Beck, U. (2011). Multiculturalism or cosmpolitanism: How can we describe and understand the diversity of the world? *Social Sciences in China, 32*(4), 52-58.

Ben-Eliezer, U. (2008). Multicultural society and everyday cultural racism: Second generation of Ethiopian Jews in Israel's 'Crisis of Modernization.' *Ethnic and Racial Studies, 31*(5), 935-961.

Berns-McGown, R. (2007/08). Redefining "diaspora": The challenge of connection and inclusion. *International Journal, 63*(1), 3-21.

Berns-McGown, R. (2013). "I am Canadian": Challenging stereotypes about young Somali-Canadians. *IRPP (Institute for Research on Public Policy), 48,* 1-29.

Berry, J. (2014). Multiculturalism: Psychological perspectives. In J. Jedwab (Ed.), *The multiculturalism question. Debating identity in 21st-century Canada* (pp. 225-240). Queen's Policy Studies Series. School of Policy Studies, Queen's University. McGill-Queen's University Press: Montreal & Kingston.

Bhabha, F. (2009). Between exclusion and assimilation. Experimentalizing Multiculturalism. *McGill Law Journal, 54,* 45-67.

Biles, J. (2014). The Government of Canada's multiculturalism program: Key to Canada's inclusion reflex. In J. Jedwab (Ed.), *The multiculturalism question. Debating identity in 21st-century Canada* (pp. 11-52). Queen's Policy Studies Series. School of Policy Studies, Queen's University. McGill-Queen's University Press: Montreal & Kingston.

Birt, Y. (2007). Multiculturalism and the discontents of globalisation. Retrieved from http://www.opendemocracy.net

Blommaert, J. (2012). *Chronicles of complexity: Ethnography, superdiversity, and linguistic landscapes.* Tilburg Papers in Culture Studies. No 29. Tilburg University.

Bourbeau, P. (2011). *The securitization of migration: A study of movement and order.* New York: Routledge.

Brown, W. (2014). *Walled states, waning sovereignty.* Cambridge, MA: MIT Press.

Carruthers, A. (2013). National multiculturalism, transnational identities. *Journal of Intercultural Studies, 34*(2), 214-228.

Catanzano, A. (2009). *Multiversal.* New York: Fordham University Press

Castles, S., & Miller, M. (2009). *The age of migration* (4th ed.). New York: Guildford Press.

Christiano, K. J. (2013). European principles and Canadian practices: Developing secular contexts for religious diversity. RECODE Working Paper Series no 15. Retrieved from http://www.recode.fi/publications

Clarke, G. E. (2009). Multiculturalism and its (usual) discontents. *Canada Watch,* Fall, 24-25.

Coleman, D. (2011). Imposing subcitizenship. In A. Fleischmann, N. van Styvendale, & C. Maccaroll (Eds.), *Narratives of citizenship: Indigenous and diasporic peoples unsettle the nation-state* (pp. 177-188). Edmonton, Alberta: University of Alberta Press.

Collett, E., & Petrovic, M. (2014). *The future of immigrant integration in Europe: Mainstreaming approaches for inclusion.* Brussels: Migration Policy Institute for Public Policy Research.

Consterdine, E. (2013). *One step forward, two steps back: Evaluating the institutions of British immigration policymaking.* London: Institute for Public Policy Research.

Czaika, M., & de Haas, H. (2014). The globalization of migration: Has the world become more 'migratory'? *International Migration Review, 48*(2), 283-323.

Dei, G. J. S. (2010). Black focused schools: A call for re-visioning. *Education Canada, 46*(3), 27-31. Retrieved from www.cea-ace.ca

Duit, A., & Galaz, V. (2008). Governance and complexity – Emerging issues for governance theory. *Governance, 21*(3), 311-335.

Dustin, D. (2007). *The McDonaldization of social work.* Aldershot UK: Ashgate.

Ferguson, Y. H., & Mansbach, R. (2012). *Globalization: The return of borders to a borderless world?* New York: Routledge.

Fleras, A. (1994). Media and minorities in a post-multicultural society. In J. Berry, & J. Laponce (Eds.), *Overview and appraisal in ethnicity and culture in Canada* (pp. 267-292). Toronto: University of Toronto Press.

Fleras, A. (2009). *The politics of multiculturalism: Cross national perspectives in multicultural governance.* New York: Palgrave Macmillan

Fleras, A. (2011). *Forty years of multiculturalism.* Paper presented to the 40 Years of Multiculturalism Conference, Ottawa, September 25.

Fleras, A. (2012). *Unequal relations. The politics of race, ethnic, and aboriginal relations in Canada* (7th ed). Toronto: Pearson.

Fleras, A. (2014a). *Racisms in a multicultural Canada.* Waterloo ON: Wilfrid Laurier Press.

Fleras, A. (2014b). *Immigration Canada.* Vancouver: UBC Press.

Florby, G., Shackleton, M., & Suhonen K. (Eds.) (2009). *Canada: Images of a post/national society.* New York: Peter Lang Publishing.

Foster, C. (2014). *Genuine multiculturalism. The tragedy and comedy of diversity.* Montreal/Kingston: McGill-Queen's University Press.

Fox, N. J., & Ward, K. J. (2008). What governs governance, and how does it evolve? The sociology of governance-in-action. *British Journal of Sociology, 59*(3), 519-538.

Fukuyama, F. (2013). What is governance? *Governance, 26*(3), 347-368.

Garcea, J., Kirova, A., & Wong, L. (2008). Introduction: Multiculturalism discourses in Canada. *Canadian Ethnic Studies, 40*(1), 1-10.

Gaye, N. (2011). Super diversity in Canada. *Policy horizons Canada.* Retrieved from http://www.horizons.gc.ca/sites/default/files/Publication-alt-format/0072_pag_superdiversity_e.pdf

Geislerova, M. (2007). The role of diasporas in foreign policy: The case of Canada. *CEJISS 1*(2), 90-108.

Glasser, T. L., Isabel A., & John W. K. (2009). The claims of multiculturalism and the journalists' promise of diversity. *Journal of Communication 59*, 57-78.

Glick-Schiller, N., & Caglar, A. (2013). Locating migrant pathways of economic placement: Thinking beyond the ethnic lens. *Ethnicities, 13*(4), 494-514.

Globe and Mail. (2011, March 12). Super-diversity.

Gozdecka, D. A., Selen, A. E., & Magdalena, K. (2014). From multiculturalism to post-multiculturalism: Trends and paradoxes. *Journal of Sociology, 50*(1), 51-64.

Griffiths, R. (2009). *Who we are: A citizen's manifesto.* Vancouver: Douglas & McIntyre

Habacan, A. E. (2007). *Beyond the mosaic: Canada's multiculturalism 2.0.* Paper presented to the Annual Summer Conference, The Stranger Next Door: Making Diversity Work, August 9-12. Orillia ON: Couchiching Institute on Public Affairs.

Habacan, A. E. (2012). A renewal of multiculturalism. *Culture West*, Winter, 13-19.

Hanlon, M. (2014). The concept there is not just a universe, but a multiverse, has come into the scientific mainstream. *The Telegraph*, April 22 (printed in the National).

Hansen, R. (2014). Assimilation by stealth: Why Canada's multicultural policy is really a repackaged integration policy. In J. Jedwab (Ed.), *The multiculturalism question. Debating identity in 21st-century Canada* (pp. 73-88). Queen's Policy Studies Series. School of Policy Studies, Queen's University. McGill-Queen's University Press: Montreal & Kingston.

Haque, E. (2012). *Multiculturalism within a bilingual framework: Language, race, and belonging in Canada.* Toronto: University of Toronto Press.

Heath, J. (2014, March 24). Misunderstanding Canadian multiculturalism. *Global Brief.* Retrieved from: http://globalbrief.ca/blog/2014/03/24/misunderstanding-canadian-multiculturalism/

Hollinger, D. A. (2006). *Postethnic America: Beyond multiculturalism.* New York: Basic Books.

Hrushetska, M. (2013). Beyond multiculturalism. *Al Jazeera.* Retrieved from http://www.aljazeera.com

Jedwab, Jack (2014). Debating multiculturalism in 21st century Canada. In J. Jedwab (Ed.), *The multiculturalism question* (pp. 1-29). Queen's Policy Studies Series. School of Policy Studies, Queen's University. McGill-Queen's University Press: Montreal & Kingston.

Jenson, J., & Papillon, M. (2001). *The Canadian diversity model: A repertoire in search of a framework.* CPRN Discussion Paper F/19. November.

Jimenez, T. R., Fields, C. D., & Schacter, A. (2015). How ethnoraciality matters: Looking inside ethnoracial 'groups.' *Social Currents, 2*(2), 107-115.

Joppke, C. (2004). The retreat of multiculturalism in the liberal state: Theory and policy *British Journal of Sociology, 55*(2), 273-357.

Karim, K. (2007). Nation and diaspora: Rethinking multiculturalism in a transnational context. *International Journal of Media & Cultural Politics, 2*(3), 267-282.

Kraus, P. (2011). The politics of complex diversity: A European perspective. *Ethnicities, 12*(1), 3-25.

Kymlicka, W. (2004/07). *The global diffusion of multiculturalism: Trends, causes, and consequences.* Paper originally delivered to the International Conference on Leadership, Education, and Multiculturalism in the Armed Forces, La Paz, Bolivia (2004), Reprinted in S. Tierney (Ed.), *Accommodating cultural diversity* (pp. 17-34). Aldershot, UK: Ashgate; also In R. Panossian et al. (Eds.) (2007), *Governing diversity* (pp. 11-18). EDG Kingston.

Kymlicka, W. (2010). The rise and fall of multiculturalism? New debates on inclusion and accommodation in diverse societies. *International Social Science Journal, 61*(199), 97-122.

Kymlicka, W. (2014). *The essentialist critique of multiculturalism: Theories, policies, ethos.* EUI Working Paper RSCAS 2014/59. Budapest: European University Institute.

Kymlicka, W., & Walker, K. (Eds.) (2012). *Rooted cosmopolitanism.* Vancouver, BC: UBC Press.

Latham, R. (2007/08). What are we? From a multicultural to a multiversal Canada. *International Journal, 63*(1), 23-42.

Latham, R. (2008). *Canadian society is not just multicultural: It is multiversal* ResearchSnapShot, York University, Toronto.

Latham, R. (2009). After multiculturalism: Canada and its multiversal future. *Canada Watch,* Fall, 28-30.

Latour, S. G. de and Balint, P. (2013). The fair terms of integration: Liberal multiculturalism reconsidered. In P. Balint & S. Latour (Eds.), *Liberal multiculturalism and the fair terms of integration* (pp. 1-16). New York: Palgrave.

Ley, D. (2005). *Post-multiculturalism?* Working Paper No. 05-17. Vancouver: Centre of Excellence for Research on Immigration and Diversity.

Li , J., & Jufferman, K. (2011). *Multilingual Europe 2.0: Dutch-Chinese youth identities in an era of superdiversity.* Working Papers in Urban Language & Literacies. Paper no 71.

Maaka, R., & Fleras, A. (2005). *The politics of indigeneity.* Dunedin NZ: University of Otago Press.

Malik, K. (2012, May 21). *Conflicting credos but the same vision of the world.* Paper presented at the Criticise This: Rethinking the Question of Difference Seminar, Ulcinj, Montenegro. Retrieved from http://kenanmalik.wordpress.com

Malik, K. (2012, June 2). *What is wrong with multiculturalism? A European perspective.* Milton K. Wong Lecture. Vancouver: University of British Columbia.

Mansouri, F., & de B'beri, B. E. (2014). *Global perspectives on the politics of multiculturalism in the 21st century: A case study analysis.* New York: Routledge.

Mawani, A. (2008). *Transnationalism: A modern day challenge to Canadian multiculturalism.* Paper presented to the Annual Meeting of the International Communication Association, Montreal, Canada, 22 May. Retrieved from http://www.allacademic.com

McKenzie, H. (2013). Decolonial aesthetics. *Fuse Magazine, 36*(4), 8.

Meissner, F., & Vertovec, S. (2015). Comparing super-diversity. *Ethnic and Racial Studies, 38*(4), 541-555.

Mistry, Rohinton. (1995). *A fine balance.* Toronto: McClelland and Stewart.

Mor Barak, M. E. (2014). *Managing diversity: Toward a globally inclusive workplace* (3rd ed.). Los Angeles, CA: Sage.

Neerup, Stine (2012). Social Cohesion and Ethnic Diversity in Australia. In E. Tolley & P. Spoonley, (Eds.), *Diverse nations, diverse responses: Approaches to social cohesion in immigrant societies* (pp. 59-80). Queen's Policy Studies Series. Kingston: School of Policy Studies, Queen's University.

Nussbaum, M. C. (2012). *Philosophical interventions and reviews: 1986-2011*. New York: Oxford University Press

Pakulski, J. (2014). Confusions about multiculturalism. *Journal of Sociology, 50*(1), 23-36.

Papillon, M. (2012). Social cohesion, citizenship, and diversity in Canada. In E. Tolley & P. Spoonley (Eds.), *Diverse nations, diverse responses: Approaches to social cohesion in immigrant societies* (pp. 15-34). Queen's Policy Studies Series. Kingston: School of Policy Studies, Queen's University.

Parekh, B. (2005). *Rethinking multiculturalism: Cultural diversity and political theory* (2nd ed.). New York: Palgrave Macmillan.

Peter, K. (1978). Multi-cultural politics, money, and the conduct of the Canadian ethnic studies association. *Bulletin of the Canadian Ethnic Studies Association, 5*(1), 2-3.

Phillimore, J. (2015). Delivering maternity services in an era of superdiversity: The challenges of novelty and newness. *Ethnic and Racial Studies, 38*(4), 568-582.

Pieterse, J. N. (2006). *Global multiculturalism, flexible acculturation*. Paper presented at various conferences in North America and Europe.

Pinder, S. O. (2010). *The politics of race and ethnicity in the United States*. New York: Palgrave Macmillan.

Prior, D. (2009). Disciplining the multicultural community: Ethnic diversity and the governance of anti-social behaviour. *Social Policy and Society, 9*(1), 133-143.

Putnam, R. D. (2007). E pluribus unum: Diversity and community in the twenty-first century. *Scandinavian Political Studies, 30*(2), 137-174.

RECODE Conference Notes. (2013, September 12-13). European-Canadian research meeting: Responding to complex diversity in Europe and Canada – Future research directions. Montreal, Canada.

Rodriguez-Garcia, D. (2012). Managing immigration and diversity in the new age of migration. A transatlantic dialogue. In D. Rodríguez-García (Ed.), *Managing immigration and diversity in Canada* (pp. 1-60). Montreal/Kingston: McGill-Queen's University Press.

Rohinton, M. (1995). *A fine balance*. Toronto: McClelland and Stewart.

Sanchez-Ruiz, Enrique E. (n.d.). Identities in transition in North America: Paradoxes of the "post-national" condition. Retrieved from www.er.uqam.ca

Sandercock, L. (2003). *Cosmopolis 11: Mongrel cities in the 21st century*. London: Continuum.

Sandercock, L. (2006). Rethinking multiculturalism for the 21st century. Working Paper No. 03-14. *Research on immigration and integration in the metropolis*. Vancouver: Vancouver Centre of Excellence.

Sargut, G., & McGrath, R. G. (2011). Learning to live with complexity. *Harvard Business Review, 89*(9), 68-76.

Satzewich, V. & Wong, L. (Eds.) (2006). *Transnational identities and practices in Canada*. Vancouver, British Columbia: UBC Press.

Scott, James C. (1998). *Seeing like a state*. Institution for Social and Policy Studies: Yale University.

Siemiatycki, M. (2012). The place of immigrants: Citizenship, settlement, and socio-cultural integration in Canada. In D. Rodríguez-García, (Ed.), *Managing immigration and diversity in Canada* (pp 223-248). Montreal/Kingston: McGill-Queen's University Press.

Smith, A. (2013). The land and its people: Reflections on an artistic identification in an age of nations and nationalism. *Nations and Nationalism, 19*(1), 87-106.

Solomon, L. (2014, March 21). Canada needs Quebec. *Financial Post*.

Spoonley, P., & Tolley E. (Eds.). (2012). *Diverse nations, diverse responses: Approaches to social cohesion in immigrant societies*. Queen's Policy Studies Series. Kingston: School of Policy Studies, Queen's University.

Tunis, D. (2010). *Fostering an integrated society*. Talk delivered to the University of Western Ontario. London ON, 19 October.

333

Turton, A. R., Hattingh H. J., Maree G. A., Roux D. J, Classen M., & Stydom W. F. (Eds.). (2007). *Governance as a trialogue: Government-society-science in transition.* Berlin/Heidelberg/New York: Springer.

Vertovec, S. (2007). Super-diversity and its implications. *Ethnic and Racial Studies, 30*(6), 1024-1054.

Vertovec, S. (2010). Toward post-multiculturalism? Changing communities, conditions, and contexts of diversity. *International Social Science Journal, 61*(199), 83-95.

Vertovec, S. (2012). "Diversity" and the social imaginary. *European Journal of Sociology, 53*(3), 287-312.

Vertovec, S. (2013, December). Reading super-diversity. *MPI-MMG.* Retrieved from http://www.mmg.mpg.de

Vertovec. S., & Wessendorf, S. (2004). *Migration and cultural, religious, and linguistic diversity in Europe: An overview of issues and trends.* Oxford: COMPAS, University of Oxford.

Walton-Roberts, M. (2011). Multiculturalism already unbound. In M. Chazan, L. Helps, A. Stanley, & S. Thakkar (Eds.), *Home and native land: Unsettling multiculturalism in Canada* (pp. 102-122). Toronto: Between the Lines.

Wessendorf, S. (2014). *Researching social relations in super-diverse neighbourhoods: Mapping the field.* IRiS Working Paper Series No 2. University of Birmingham.

Wilton, S. (2009). Immigration policy and literature: Contradictions of a "post-national" state. In G. Florby, M. Shackleton, & K. Suhonen (Eds.), *Canada: Images of a post/national society* (pp. 25-37). New York: Peter Lang Publishing.

Winter, E. (2014, January 16). *Becoming Canadian: Making sense of recent changes to citizenship rules.* Institute for Research on Public Policy.

Wong, L. L. (2007/08). Transnationalism, active citizenship, and belonging in Canada. *International Journal, 63*(1), 79-100.

Augie Fleras
Sociology and Legal Studies
University of Waterloo

NOTES ON CONTRIBUTORS

John W. Berry (PhD, University of Edinburgh) is Professor Emeritus of Psychology at Queen's University, Canada, and Research Professor, National Research University Higher School of Economics, Moscow, Russia. He received Honorary Doctorates from the University of Athens, and Université de Geneve. He has published over 30 books in the areas of cross-cultural, intercultural, social and cognitive psychology with various colleagues. He is a Fellow of the Canadian Psychological Association, the Netherlands Institute for Advanced Study, the International Association for Cross-Cultural Psychology, and the International Academy for Intercultural Research. He received the Hebb Award for Contributions to Psychology as a Science, and the award for Contributions to the Advancement of International Psychology (from CPA), the Interamerican Psychology Prize (from SIP), and the Lifetime Contribution Award (from IAIR). His main research interests are in the role of culture in human development and in acculturation and intercultural relations, with an emphasis on applications to immigration, multiculturalism, educational and health policy.

Selom Chapman-Nyaho is a PhD candidate in Sociology at York University. His research interests include work on youth, risk and regulation, qualitative methods, and race. Currently he teaches courses in criminology and sociology at York University and Centennial College. He worked previously as a Restorative Justice caseworker in Halifax, Nova Scotia.

Dan Cui is an Eyes High Postdoctoral Fellow in the Werklund School of Education at the University of Calgary. Her research interests include immigrant youth, international students, immigration and integration, sociology of education, and social justice and equity in education. She is the author of "'Too Asian?' or the Invisible Citizen on the Other Side of the Nation?" (2013), and "Capital, Distinction, and Racialized Habitus: Immigrant Youth in the Educational Field" (in press).

Augie Fleras is an adjunct professor of sociology at the University of Waterloo. Received his PhD at Victoria University in Wellington on Maori-nonMaori relations and governance in Aotearoa New Zealand – a research interest that continues into present. Primary fields of study include Multiculturalism and Immigration; the Politics of Indigeneity; Media and Minorities, Social Inequality; Racisms in Canada. Most recent publications include: *Racisms in a Multicultural Canada* (WLU Press) and *Immigration Canada* (UBC Press).

Mariusz Galczynski earned his PhD in Educational Studies from the Department of Integrated Studies in Education (DISE) at McGill University. His research interests include multicultural education, teacher education and professionalization, large-scale cross-national studies, and assessment literacy. A former secondary school teacher in the United States, he now works as a lecturer at McGill and administrator of the Québec Ministry of Education's English Exam for Teacher Certification. Most recently, he joined Ratna Ghosh as co-author for the new edition of *Redefining Multicultural Education: Inclusion and the Right to Be Different* (2014).

Ratna Ghosh is James McGill Professor and William C. Macdonald Professor of Education at McGill University, where she was Dean of Education. She was featured in *Time* Magazine (Canadian Edition, October 13, 2003) in an article on "Canada's Best in Education." Her work in Multiculturalism has won her many awards and honours such as the Order of Canada, Order of Quebec, and Fellowship in the Royal Society of Canada. From 2011-2012, she served as President of the Comparative and International Education Society (CIES) of the US. She publishes regularly in books and journals, and her most recent works are *Redefining Multicultural Education: Inclusion and the Right to Be Different* (2014, co-authored with Mariusz Galczynski) and *Education and the Politics of Difference* (2013, co-authored with Ali Abdi).

Shibao Guo is Professor in the Werklund School of Education at the University of Calgary. He is specialized in citizenship and immigration, race and ethnic relations, adult and lifelong education, and comparative and international education. His research had been funded by a number of organizations, including the Social Sciences and Humanities Council of Canada (SSHRC), International Organization for Migration (IOM), and Education International. Dr. Guo has numerous publications, including books, journal articles, and book chapters. He is former president of Canadian Association for the Study of Adult Education (2009-2011). Currently he serves as president of Canadian Ethnic Studies Association. He is also a co-editor of *Canadian Ethnic Studies* and two Sense book series: *Transnational Migration and Education* and *Spotlight on China*.

Yan Guo is Associate Professor of Language and Diversity in the Werklund School of Education at the University of Calgary. Her research interests include critical perspectives in teaching English as an Additional Language (TEAL), immigrant parent engagement, intercultural communication, language and identity, and language policy. Her recent publications appeared in *Canadian Journal of Education, Language and Education, Intercultural Education, Canadian Ethnic Studies, and Journal of Contemporary Issues in Education*.

Carl E. James teaches in the Faculty of Education and in the graduate program in Sociology at York University, and is currently the Director of the York Centre for Education and Community. His research interests include educational and occupational access and equity for racialized youth. His most recent book is *Life at the Intersection: Community, Class and Schooling* (Fernwood Publishing, 2012).

Johanne Jean-Pierre is a Ph.D. candidate in the Department of Sociology at McMaster University. Her dissertation is a qualitative inquiry of young Franco-Ontarians and Anglo-Quebecers' identity processes, cultural boundaries and status. Her research interests include education, inequality, race, ethnicity, language, and culture.

Anna Kirova is professor of early childhood education in the Faculty of Education, University of Alberta. Her research focuses on the need for understanding culturally and linguistically diverse families with young children's experiences in school, and the possibility such an understanding offers for culturally sustaining pedagogy. She has published widely on issues of integration of visible and religious minority immigrants and refugees. Her international work in this area has resulted in the book, *Global Migration and Education: Schools, Children and Families.*

Will Kymlicka is the Canada Research Chair in Political Philosophy at Queen's University in Kingston, Canada, where he has taught since 1998. His research interests focus on issues of democracy and diversity, and in particular on models of citizenship and social justice within multicultural societies. He has published eight books and over 200 articles, which have been translated into 32 languages, and has received several awards, including the Queen Elizabeth II Diamond Jubilee Medal in 2012.

Ho Hon Leung received his doctoral degree in Sociology, McGill University, Canada. He is a professor of Department of Sociology of SUNY Oneonta. His research interests include ethnic relations, immigration, urban studies, and comparative aging. His most recent work is focused on a cross-cultural comparative project that examines cultural and heritage values of local time-honored restaurants that can stand test of time. Leung is the Chair of the Center for Social Science Research, and Academic Excellent Committee at his college. His publications appear in national and international journals and a good number of book chapter.

Rebecca Margolis is an associate professor in the University of Ottawa's Vered Jewish Canadian Studies Program. Her research on Yiddish culture in Canada has appeared in *Canadian Ethnic Studies, TTR, Nashim, Shofar*, and other journals. Her book, *Jewish Roots, Canadian Soil: Yiddish Culture in Montreal, 1905-1945*, was the recipient of the Helen and Stan Vine Canadian Jewish Book Award and the J.I Segal Award. Her current research focuses on Yiddish in Canada after the Holocaust.

Sourayan Mookerjea is a social and cultural theorist whose research addresses contradictions of globalization, migration, urbanization, subalternity, intermedia and class politics. He is Director of the Intermedia Research Studio, Department of

Sociology at the University of Alberta and also co-editor of *Canadian Cultural Studies: A Reader* (Duke University Press, 2009).

Fernando Nunes is an Assistant Professor in the Department of Child and Youth Study, Mount Saint Vincent University. His research and publications have focused on minority academic underachievement, at-risk youth, critical pedagogy, immigrant settlement and integration, with a focus on the Luso-Canadian community and Portuguese Diaspora. He has also acquired over 30 years of employment, consultancy and volunteer experience within the fields of education and social services, predominantly in Toronto's settlement sector.

Sandy (Xanthi) Petrinioti is Adjunct Professor, Saint Mary's University, and Professor Emerita, Panteion University, Athens. She was Co-Director of the Mediterranean Migration Observatory, 1998-2014. She is the author of five books and co-editor of four as well as numerous articles on migration to Greece the political economy of migration, women' employment and gendering of labour economics. She participated in commissioned research on immigrant integration and on government employees' attitudes to immigrants in Greece.

Evangelia Tastsoglou is Professor of Sociology at Saint Mary's University. She has published extensively from a feminist and intersectional perspective on women, gender and various aspects of migration, diasporas, settlement, integration and citizenship. Her recent books include: *Immigrant Women in Atlantic Canada. Challenges, Negotiations, Re-constructions* (Canadian Scholars' Press / Women's Press, 2011; co-edited) and *The Warmth of the Welcome: Is Atlantic Canada a Home Away from Home for Immigrants?* (UCBP, 2015, forthcoming; co-edited).

Kalyani Thurairajah is an Assistant Professor in the Department of Sociology at MacEwan University. Her research is focused on understanding how immigrants negotiate between their loyalties to their countries of settlement and countries of origin at times of conflict and tension. She is currently exploring how the different multiculturalism and immigration policies of countries of settlement may impact immigrant integration, thus altering both their loyalties and their political engagements in both the homeland and the country of settlement.

Vilelmini Tsagkaraki earned her PhD in Educational Studies from the Department of Integrated Studies in Education (DISE) at McGill University. In addition to her research focus on Greek history textbooks, her academic interests include theories on teaching history in multicultural contexts, historical thinking, racism and immigration, and comparative and international education. After working as a teacher in Greece, USA, and Canada, she is now a visiting instructor in Modern Greek Studies in McGill's Department of History and Classical Studies, as well as the administrative coordinator for the McGill Summer Studies in Greece program. She is the recipient of the Alexander S. Onassis Foundation Scholarship and the Wing Trust Fellowship.

Morton Weinfeld is Professor of Sociology at McGill University, where he holds the Chair in Canadian Ethnic Studies. He has published widely in the areas of ethnic and race relations in Canada, and in the field of Canadian Jewish Studies. In 2013 he was awarded the Marshall Sklare Prize by the Association for the Social Scientific Study of Jewry. Among his many publications is the volume *Ethnicity, Politics, and Public Policy*, co-edited with Harold Troper, and *Like Everyone Else but Different: The Paradoxical Success of Canadian Jews*.

Elke Winter is Associate Professor of Sociology at the University of Ottawa, and research director at the Centre for Interdisciplinary Research on Citizenship and Minorities (CIRCEM). She is the recipient of the Canadian Sociology Association's John Porter Best Book of the Year Award (for *Us, Them, and Others: Pluralism and National Identity in Diverse Societies* (University of Toronto Press, 2011) and a member of the Royal Society of Canada's College of New Scholars, Artists and Scientists. Prof. Winter's current research examines the boundaries of membership articulated in citizenship policy and practice, as well as the impact of national security and immigration policies on public representations of Muslim and Arab Canadians.

Lloyd Wong is an Associate Professor of Sociology at the University of Calgary. His research interests include multiculturalism, transnationalism, immigration and citizenship. Recent journal articles appear in *Journal of Immigrant and Refugee Studies, Canadian Public Policy, Journal of Chinese Overseas, and International Journal*. Recent book chapters appear in *Mobilities, Knowledge and Social Justice* (McGill-Queens Press), *Researching Amongst Elites: Challenges and Opportunities in Studying Up* (Ashgate), *Sport and Migration: Borders, Boundaries and Crossings* (Routledge), and *Race and Racism in 21ˢᵗ Century Canada* (Broadview).

INDEX

341